Family Factors and the Educational Success of Children

Edited by William Jeynes

Routledge
Taylor & Francis Group

LONDON AND NEW YORK

First published 2010 by Routledge
2 Park Square, Milton Park, Abingdon, Oxon, OX14 4RN

Simultaneously published in the USA and Canada
by Routledge
270 Madison Avenue, New York, NY 10016

Routledge is an imprint of the Taylor & Francis Group, an informa business

Typeset in Times by Value Chain, India
Printed and bound in Great Britain by MPG Books Group

British Library Cataloguing in Publication Data
A catalogue record for this book is available from the British Library

ISBN10: 0-7890-3761-0 (hbk)
ISBN10: 0-7890-3762-9 (pbk)
ISBN13: 978-0-7890-3761-9 (hbk)
ISBN13: 978-0-7890-3762-6 (pbk)

Contents

Acknowledgments   vii

1. Introduction: The Salience of Family Factors in Children's School
   Experiences
   William Jeynes   1

Summaries of the Effects of Parental Style and Parental Involvement

2. Parenting Styles: The impact on student achievement
   Lola Brown and *Shrinidhi Iyengar*   11

3. Families, their children's education, and the public school: An
   historical review
   Diana Hiatt-Michael   36

4. Father Involvement and Children's Early Learning: A Critical Review
   of Published Empirical Work from the Past 15 Years
   Jason Downer, Rodrigo Campos, Christine McWayne, and
   Tara Gartner   64

**Parental Involvement and the Academic Achievement of Hispanic
Students**

5. Community Literacy Resources and Home Literacy practices
   among Immigrant Latino Families
   Leslie Reese and *Claude Goldenberg*   106

6. Examining Familial-Based Academic Success Factors in Urban High
   School Students: The Case of Puerto Rican Female High Achievers
   René Antrop-González, William Vélez, and *Tomás Garrett*   137

7. Expectations, Aspirations, and Achievement among Latino
   Students of Immigrant Families
   Dick M. Carpenter II   161

Education & Religion as a means of improving family life

8. Family, denomination and the adolescent world view: an empirical
   enquiry among 13- to 15-year-old girls in England and Wales
   Leslie J. Francis   183

9. The Influence of Religion on Latino Education, Marriage,
   and Social Views in the United States
   Gastón Espinosa   203

Parental Involvement as a Means of Improving the Quality of Life

10. Increased Family Involvement in School Predicts Improved Child-
    Teacher Relationships and Feelings about School for Low-income
    Children
    Eric Dearing, *Holly Kreider*, and *Heather B. Weiss*   224

11. Effects Of Parental Involvement On Experiences of
    Discrimination And Bullying
    William H. Jeynes   253

Improving Parental Involvement & Building Partnerships

12. How Parents and Teachers View their School Communities
    Sam Redding   267

13. Altering the Curriculum of the Home: Learning Environments
    for Korean and U.S. Students
    Susan J. Paik   287

14. Caregiver Engagement in Religious Urban Elementary Schools
    Martin Scanlan   306

15. High School Family Centers: Transformative Spaces Linking
    Schools and Families in Support of Student Learning
    Karen L. Mapp, *Vivian R. Johnson*, *Carol Sills Strickland*, and
    Catherine Meza   336

16. Families Home Schooling in a Virtual Charter School System
    Carol Klein and *Mary Poplin*   367

    Index   395

Acknowledgments

I am very thankful to many individuals who played a large role in making this work possible. I want to thank numerous people in the academic world at Harvard University and the University of Chicago for helping me give birth to this project and in guiding me through the early stages of planning this book. I especially want to thank the late Bob Jewell for his encouragement. I want to thank several academics for their input into this project. These individuals include Wendy Naylor, Chris Ullman, and Dick Carpenter. I especially want to thank Suzanne Steinmetz for her diligent work and advice regarding this project. I also want to thank several dear friends whose encouragement with respect to this project touched me deeply. Among these friends are Wayne Ruhland, Jean Donohue, Rick Smith, Larry and Vada DeWerd, Joyce Decker, and Jessica Choi.

I am incredibly blessed to have been married for 23 years to my wife, Hyelee, whose support has been exemplary. Without her prayers and support, this work never could have been completed. I am blessed and honored to have three wonderful boys, whom I thank for their love and inspiration. The support of my wife and children gave me the encouragement I needed to rely on God's strength and providence to complete this project. I am very grateful for that encouragement and strength.

Introduction: The Salience of Family Factors in Children's School Experiences

William H. Jeynes

This collection of articles will focus on the factors that influence the relationship between the family and education. Over the last 40 years, social scientists have become increasing concerned with the relationship between family factors and student academic outcomes (Hetherington & Clingempeel, 1992). At first the concern with this association focused primarily on family structure (Hetherington, Stanley-Hagan, & Anderson, 1989). This initial orientation was understandable because during the 1963–1980 period the divorce rate surged for 17 consecutive years (Wirtz, 1977; Jeynes, 2007). During the mid- to late 1960s, other non-traditional family structures began to increase (Popenoe, 1994; Zill and Nord, 1994). Parental remarriage, never married single-parent families, cohabitation, and numerous other family structures rose during this period (Jeynes, 2000). The dramatic changes in family structure fostered a copious amount of new research on the influence of divorce, remarriage, and other family structure on the school outcomes of children (Jeynes, 2005).

The call for a huge increase in the amount of family research intensified with the release of the Coleman report in 1966. This report was quite sobering because it concluded that home factors, such as family structure, parental education level, and parent availability, exerted a greater impact on educational outcomes than did school factors. Suddenly, the academic community ostensibly comprehended a truth that the American public had recognized for centuries. That is, family

William H. Jeynes, PhD, is Professor in the Department of Education, California State University.

factors exerted a puissant impact on educational outcomes that school variables could not rival (Chamberlin, 1961; Gangel & Benson, 1983).

A pervasive body of research resulted from these developments that gave theorists, leaders, teachers, and lay people a greater understanding of the reasons why family structure had the impact that it did on student academic achievement. Naturally, various social scientists gave a plethora of reasons why family structure had the effect that it did (Hetherington & Jodl, 1994). Certain factors, however, regularly rose to the top of the list of explanations (Hetherington, Stanley-Hagan, & Anderson, 1989; Zill, 1994). Researchers propounded explanations that included various manifestations of psychological stress, reduced levels of parental involvement and access, emotional turmoil, depression, and reduced educational and economic resources (Hetherington & Clingempeel, 1992; Zill, 1994).

Because reduced parental involvement and access emerged as some of the most important reasons why family structure influenced achievement to the extent that it did helped initiate the discipline of parental involvement research (Jeynes, 2002; Wallerstein & Blakeslee, 1989). The fact that reduced parental engagement influenced achievement among children from single-parent and blended or reconstituted families made social scientists realize that insufficient parental involvement could also have a negative impact on achievement among children in intact families as well (Jeynes, 2007).

The study of parental involvement, as distinguished from the examination of family structure emerged during the 1980s. As interest in the study of parental involvement has grown, social scientists have especially displayed an interest in examining the effects of parental involvement on children of color (Epstein, 2001; Jeynes, 2003). This development emerged as a natural result of the nation's concern with the achievement gap between African American and Hispanic students on the one hand and white students on the other (Green, 2001; Simpson, 1981). Beginning in the 1960s, the achievement gap became probably the most central debate in education (Green, Blasik, Hartshorn, & Shatten-Jones, 2000; Roach, 2001). Part of the reason for the national interest in the achievement gap is because the nature of the gap not only exists by race, but also by socioeconomic status (Slavin & Madden, 2001). In other words, there exists an equally wide achievement gap between those of high and low socioeconomic status (Slavin & Madden, 2001). The main component of SES that appears to explain this gap is the educational component (Mullen, Goyette, & Soares, 2003). That is, students with parents of high educational achievement have a considerable advantage in school grades than their counterparts whose parents who do not have a strong educational background (Wojtkiewicz & Donato, 1995).

The results of various studies examining the effects of parental involvement on the educational outcomes of minority students indicate that the parental involvement is as strongly related with educational achievement for African American and Latino youth as it is for white youth (Georgiou, 1999; Hampton, Mumford, & Bond, 1998). Meta-analyses that were conducted over the last several years, in order to synthesize the existing research, that indicate that parental involvement and academic achievement among children of color are strongly related (Jeynes 2003, 2005, 2007). These results confirm the findings of other studies that have utilized a variety of analytical strategies that have included the use of nationwide data sets, programs a variety of school settings, and the examination of a full gamut of home environments (Georgiou, 1999; Hampton, Mumford, & Bond, 1998).

The findings that demonstrate a relationship between parental involvement and student outcomes for racial minority students have spurred a high level of research examining how to best utilize the use of parental engagement to maximize its educational advantage. Largely because of the salience of this issue, three of the studies included in this double issue are dedicated to examining parental minority students. These articles examine the relationship between family variables and educational outcomes, with a special emphasis of parental involvement in one form or another.

The collection opens with three review articles: one on parenting styles, another a historical review of children's education and the public school, and a final article on the effect of fathers' involvement on children's early learning. These provide excellent reviews of the state of parental involvement research from different perspectives. Lola Brown and Shrinidhi Iyengar review the literature on the effects of parental style on academic outcomes in their article entitled, "Parenting Styles: The impact on student achievement." Past studies of parental involvement (Jeynes, 2005, 2007) have cited parental style as one of the most salient elements of parental involvement. Brown and Iyengar examine parental style in five research domains that include parental control, gender and parenting style, parental education, perceptual differences, and ethnicity and diversity. The researchers found that parental style has an impact on educational outcomes in a number of ways.

The second review article is written by Diana Hiatt-Michael and is entitled, "Families, Their Children's Education, and the Public School: An Historical Review." In this article Dr. Hiatt-Michael examines the history of the practice of parental involvement from colonial times until the present era. She particularly focuses on the four forces she believes ultimately influence the kind and degree of parental involvement. They include the cultural beliefs of families, the social structure of the family, the state of the economy, and the political pressures in the country. In addition, Hiatt-Michael's article is especially penetrating in its analysis of the growing tension between parents and teachers. She points out that this friction is a direct consequence of many teachers' desire for parents to treat them as professionals, free from parental interference.

In the final article in this section, "Father Involvement and Children's Early Learning: A Critical Review of Published Empirical Work from the Past 15 Years," Downer, Campos, McWayne, and Gartner focus their attention on the importance of father involvement. They note that traditional social science research addresses parental involvement and mother involvement much more than the participation of fathers. The researchers not only point out this gap in the research, but also provide compelling evidence that father involvement plays a salient role in children's lives. Their survey of the research indicates that fathers may play certain unique roles in the lives of children that are difficult to replicate by others.

The second set of articles examines family factors as they relate to the educational achievement of Hispanic students. Leslie Reese and Claude Goldenberg conduct an intriguing study entitled, "Community Literacy Resources and Home Literacy Practices Among Immigrant Latino Families." Reese and Goldenberg address the importance of family and community involvement in maximizing literacy among Latino students. They examine 35 schools located in Texas and California in order to address the practices of family and community literacy. They also sample a wide range of language programs for English language learners to help ensure the generalizability of their results.

Reese and Goldenberg's study, "Community Literacy Resources and Home Literacy Practices Among Immigrant Latino Families," produced two prominent findings. The first was that, as expected, variables such as education, income, and ethnicity are associated with literacy rates. The second finding, and certainly the most intriguing of the two, found that there was no relationship between literacy resources in the community and literacy practices in the family. Family literacy practices refer to the fact that families maintain certain disciplines that encourage or discourage literacy apart from the resources in the community. This result supports the notion that a parental involvement policy that aids and supports families will probably have more of an influence than one that is focused primarily on increased funding.

René Antrop-González, William Veléz, and Tomás Garrett's qualitative study entitled, "Examining Famial-Based Academic Success Factors in Urban High School Students: The Case of Puerto Rican Female High Achievers," dispelled the notion that Puerto Rican students living in poverty cannot achieve at high academic levels. They found that religiosity, in particular, as well as maternal factors and caring teachers all played a role in increasing the achievement of these female Puerto Rican youth. These in-depth interviews revealed that the subjects in the study specifically credited their religious family and their own personal religious commitment, maternal factors, and caring teachers as a source of personal strength and as contributing to their scholastic success.

"Expectations, Aspirations, and Achievement among Latino Students of Immigrant Families" by Dick Carpenter II, beautifully complements the two studies on Hispanic students. Carpenter uses the Educational Longitudinal Study (2002) database. Carpenter found the neither parental expectations nor socioeconomic status was a good predictor of academic outcomes, once he controlled for various covariates. However, probably the most interesting aspect of Carpenter's study involves the covariates that he included and his conclusions regarding them. Two of these covariates are the number of parents in the home and parental attendance at educational events. Carpenter notes that his results therefore do not suggest that parental factors lack influence. Rather, he believes that it is likely "that parent expectations influence achievement indirectly" through other factors such as family structure and parental involvement.

Two articles examined the relationship between education and religion as a means for improving family lives and address that vital interrelationship of family, education, and religion. Leslie J. Francis is probably the most prolific academic writer in Europe on education and religion. Francis' article entitled, "Family denomination, and the adolescent Worldview: An Empirical Enquiry Among 13- to 15-Year Old Females in England and Wales" gives insight into the inextricably connected roles that family and denominational affiliation play in helping to shape the way that adolescent student view the world around them. Francis' study alerts the reader to the understanding that education is a multidimensional process that involves schools, the family, and religion. In addition, his article suggests that understanding the breadth of the educational process will help social scientists, parents, and others better understand the developmental process.

In Gastòn Espinosa's article entitled, "Latino Religion, Education, and Marriage in the United States," he examines a national data set to assess trends among the Latino population in the United States. What he finds is that the religious beliefs and educational experiences of Latinos are far more diverse than most Americans perceive and that this diversity clearly does not match the misconceptions that many people have of the Latino population. Moreover, Espinosa asserts that religion likely plays a considerably larger role in understanding marital and education patterns among Latinos than many social scientists currently assume.

Two papers examine how parental involvement can have ameliorative effects on the experiences of children that go well beyond the bounds of school outcomes. Eric Dearing, Holly Kreider and Heather B. Weiss in their article, "Increased Family Involvement in School Predicts Improved Child-Teacher Relationships and Feelings About School for Low-income Children," focus on the effects of family involvement in school on children's relationships with their teachers and children's feelings about school. Their study focuses on low-income students from kindergarten through the fifth grade. The findings of the study indicate that increases in family involvement are associated with improvements in students' relationship with teachers and improved attitudes towards school.

"Effects of Parental Involvement on Experiences of Discrimination and Bullying," by William H. Jeynes examined the effects of parental involvement in a unique study examining its effect on bullying and discrimination experienced by students. Jeynes found that those students who had parents who were highly involved in their education and possessed high expectations of them were less likely to be bullied and were somewhat less likely to be discriminated against. These results suggest that the impact of parental involvement may be much broader than previously recognized.

In the section "*Improving Parental Involvement & Building Partnerships,*" articles focus on ways to enhance the educational environment with parental involvement and partnerships with traditional and alternative academic settings. Sam Redding's article, "How Parents and Teachers View Their School Communities," examines the views of more than 11,000 parents and 1,500 teachers about their schools and their relationship with one another. He presents an intriguing set of findings comparing the responses of parents and teachers. Some of the highlights include the fact that parents and teachers rate schools higher in terms of efforts than results and rate the school higher in the centrality of academic purpose than they do in the school's ability to teach children respect for others. Parents also view their own involvement much more positively than teachers do. Redding's article also notes some differences by race, including the fact that African Americans are twice as likely to report that there are home visitations by the teachers than are white parents. In his conclusion, Redding does an excellent job of relating his findings to James Coleman's social capital theory.

In her article, "Altering the Curriculum of the Home: Learning Environments for Korean and U.S. Students," Susan Paik conducts a study in which she examines the parental practices of educational support in both Korean and American homes. She found that Korean children were much more likely to be enrolled in after school programs and spend more time on their homework. Paik attributes much of this gap to differences in the home environments of American and Korean children, although she recognizes that there are other factors as well. She asserts that, "education begins in the home." She notes that Korean children are much more likely to grow up in an intact family and are therefore much more likely to have parents who are available to give the kind of support that is necessary for academic success. On the other hand, she observes that American divorce rates have surged and most American children today will spend some time in a nontraditional family structure. Paik concludes, "Early intervention is essential for students at home and in the early school years." She asserts a variety of actions are necessary in order "to constructively change the curriculum of the home." To be sure, part of this involves changing American attitudes toward family cohesiveness and its effects on children, but also involves enhancing family-school partnerships and improving after-school programs.

Martin Scanlon examines how religious school leaders which serve "traditionally marginalized students" improve their school atmosphere by encouraging parental involvement. His article, "Caregiver Engagement in Religious Urban Elementary Schools" provides information on a very creative techniques employed by a Catholic urban elementary school in order to foster parental engagement. Scanlon's article will encourage readers to value the place of creativity and vision in reaching out to families.

In "High School Family Centers: Transformative Spaces. Linking Schools and Families in Support of Student Learning" Karen L. Mapp and her colleagues, Vivian R. Johnson, Carol Sills Strickland, and Catherine Meza examine the factors that best provide parents and students with a supportive learning community in which families realize that they are welcome participants. They examine eight family centers in order to identify successful principles that encourage parental involvement. Specifically, they develop a rubric that identifies three inputs that are key to producing desirable outputs. Perhaps the most intriguing results of this analysis indicate that certain more subtle aspects of parental involvement programs such as the degree of loving support and responsiveness appear to be more salient than applying particular techniques of eliciting family engagement in order to maximize parental involvement.

The final article in the group entitled, "Families Home Schooling in a Virtual Charter School System" is authored by Carol Klein and Mary Poplin. Poplin and Klein examine the extent to which virtual schools are sensitive to the needs of the families utilizing them. It focuses on the experiences of these families and seeks to uncover why it is that families pursue virtual schools as a means of education. The study examines the extent to which parental choice makes families feel more like partners the education of their children.

Taken together, this series of articles on the family and education contains vital information on the effects of various parental practices on student outcomes. Social scientists are rediscovering the primacy of the family as it relates to maximizing academic achievement and beneficial student behavior. These articles will no doubt help answer some questions, and create new ones. They will help resolve some debates and stir up others. Through this entire process, the relationship between family factors and academic outcomes will patently gain a greater place of import in the social sciences and in society as a whole.

REFERENCES

Chamberlin, G. J. (1961). *Parents and religion: A preface to Christian education.* Philadelphia: Westminster Press.

Coleman, J. S. (1966), *Equality of Educational Opportunity,* US Department of Health, Education, and Welfare, Office of Education/National Center for Education Statistics. Washington, DC.

Epstein, J. (2001). *School, family, and community partnerships.* Boulder: Westview Press.

Gangel, K. O., & Benson, W. S. (1983). *Christian education: Its history and philosophy.* Chicago: Moody.

Georgiou, S. N. (1999). Parental attributions as predictors of involvement and influences on child development. *British Journal of Educational Psychology, 69,* 409–429.

Green, S. R. (2001). Closing the achievement gap: Lessons learned and challenges ahead. *Teaching and Change, 8,* 215–224.

Green, L. R., Blasik, K., Hartshorn, K., & Shatten-Jones, E. (2000). Closing the achievement gap in science: A program to encourage minority and female students to participate and succeed. *ERS Spectrum, 18,* 3–13.

Hampton, F. M., Mumford, D. A., & Bond, L. (1998). Parental involvement in inner city schools: The project FAST extended family approach to success. *Urban Education, 33,* 410–427.

Hetherington, E. M., & Clingempeel, W. G. (1992). Coping with marital transitions: A family systems perspective. *Monographs of the Society for Research in Child Development, 57* (2/3), 1–242.

Hetherington, E. M., & Jodl, K. M. (1994). Stepfamilies as settings for child development. In A. Booth & J. Dunn (Eds.), *Stepfamilies: Who benefits? Who does not?* (pp. 55–79). Hillsdale, NJ: Erlbaum Associates.

Hetherington, E. M., Stanley-Hagan, M., & Anderson, E. R. (1989). Marital Transitions: A child's perspective. *American Psychologist, 44,* 303–312.

Jeynes, W. (2003). The effects of black and Hispanic twelfth graders living in intact families and being religious on their academic achievement. *Urban Education, 38,* 35–57.

Jeynes, W. (2005). A Meta-analysis of the relation of parental involvement to urban elementary school student achievement. *Urban Education, 49,* 237–269.

Jeynes, W. (2007). *American educational history: School, society & the common good.* Thousand Oaks, CA: Sage Publications.

Jeynes, W. H. (2002). *Divorce, family structure, & the academic success of children.* Binghamton, New York: Haworth Press.

Jeynes, W. H. (2000). Effects of several of the most common family structures on the academic achievement of children. *Marriage & Family Review, 30,* 73–97.

Mullen, A. L., Goyette, K. A., & Soares, J. A. (2003). Who goes to graduate school? Social and academic correlates of educational continuation after college. *Sociology of Education, 76,* 143–169.

Popenoe, D. (1994). The evolution of marriage and the problem of stepfamilies: A biosocial perspective. In A. Booth & J. Dunn (Eds.), *Stepfamilies: Who benefits? Who does not?* (pp. 55–79). Hillsdale, New Jersey: Erlbaum Associates.

Roach, R. (2001). In the academic and think-tank world, pondering achievement-gap remedies take center stage. *Black Issues in Higher Education, 18,* 26–27.

Simpson, C. (1981). Classroom organization and the gap between minority and non-minority student performance levels. *Educational Research Quarterly, 6,* 43–53.

Slavin, R. E., & Madden, N. A. (2001). Reducing the Gap: Education for all and the achievement of African American and Latino students. Paper presented at the Annual Conference of the American Educational Research Association in Seattle, Washington.

Wallerstein, J. S., & Blakeslee, S. (1989). *Second chances: Men, women, and children a decade after divorce.* New York: Ticknor and Fields.

Wirtz, W. (1977). *On further examination.* New York: College Entrance Examination Board.

Wojtkiewicz, R. A., & Donato, K. M. (1995). Hispanic educational attainment: The effects of family background and nativity. *Social Forces, 74,* 559–574.

Zill, N. (1994). Understanding why children in stepfamilies have more learning and behavior problems than children in nuclear families. In A. Booth & J. Dunn (Eds.), *Stepfamilies: Who benefits? Who does not?* (pp. 109–137). Hillsdale: Erlbaum.

Zill, N., & Nord, C. W. (1994). *Running in place.* Washington, DC: Child Trends.

Parenting Styles: The Impact on Student Achievement

Lola Brown
Shrinidhi Iyengar

ABSTRACT. Parenting style and its impact on student achievement in a multidimensional society continues to pose significant challenges to clinicians, researchers, educators, and parents alike. This literature review summarizes the research surrounding five domains: (1) parental control; (2) gender and parenting style; (3) parental education; (4) perceptual differences between parents and their children; and (5) ethnicity and diversity. Behavioral control and psychological control were found to be two inherent features of parental style that have a direct affect on student achievement. Adolescents' perceived level of independence when interacting with their parents also seemed to have

Lola Brown, PhD, is affiliated with Division of Counseling Psychology, Rossier School of Education, University of Southern California, Los Angeles, CA. Shrinidhi Iyengar, PhD, MFT, is affiliated with Department of Counseling, California State University, CA.

a direct relationship on their academic achievement. Research concerning children's progress in mathematics as related to parenting style and gender stereotype was also uncovered. Evidence was found to support the notion that parental education can have an indirect impact on children's academic achievement in various cultures. Implications for future research are identified including the need for applied research in learning communities factoring in variables for family structure, expectations, ethnicity, communication, and involvement.

INTRODUCTION

Individual influences of parents, teachers, and school environments are well documented in the educational and developmental literature (Barber, 1996; Baumrind, 1966, 1967, 1968, 1971, 1978; Dornbush, Ritter, Leiderman, Roberts, & Fraleigh, 1987; Steinberg, Lamborn, Dornbusch, & Darling, 1992). However, the research on the linkage between student achievement and parenting style has yet to be more clearly defined. The purpose of this article is to synthesize the literature surrounding the influence of parenting style on student achievement, with the goal to provide a multicultural perspective that has implications for researchers as well as clinicians. A preliminary review of the literature resulted in the information being categorized into the following five domains: (1) parental control; (2) gender and parenting style; (3) parental education; (4) perceptual differences between parents and their children; and (5) ethnicity and diversity.

Student achievement involves all aspects of learning including cognition, decision-making, and adjustment and has mediating factors that are confounding to students, parents, and educators alike. Parenting style significantly influences achievement and performance of children as described by both parents and children in clinical as well as school settings. Parents and educators often seek assistance in clinical settings for a minor with achievement concerns. As student achievement impacts the areas of learning, instruction, school environment, and family conditions, the impact of student achievement on society can be staggering when considering the ramifications for the next generation. Clinicians and educators face a daunting task in addressing families as they struggle with student achievement.

Student achievement has been consistently associated with positive identity constructs which include self-esteem, self-efficacy, and motivation (Bandura, 1997). The parenting style of addressing these concerns significantly influences self-efficacy, self-esteem, identity development, and identifying relevant constructs within parenting style clarifies the linkage with achievement. Parenting styles are frequently adapted from previous generations. There is growing evidence to establish the fact that the Western concept of neglectful versus permissive versus authoritarian versus authoritative styles does not correlate with the empirical observations of student achievement across cultures. According to Smetana (1995), parents in Western cultures see themselves as authoritative while their children tend to perceive them as being more permissive and authoritarian. Chao (1994) and Chao and Sue (1996) presented the notion of "guan" or "training" implemented by Chinese parents which is largely absent in Western style parenting. Chao (1994) explains that control, care, and concern are synonymous and the controlling parenting style does not easily translate to a Western concept of authoritarian style.

A meta-analysis examined the relationship between parental involvement and the academic achievement of urban elementary school children (Jeynes, 2005). Findings for academic achievement among urban students at the elementary level revealed a strong correlation with parental involvement; however, the meta-analysis did not distinguish between the dimensions of parenting style. The multifaceted nature of research on parenting style supports the need to understand its influence on student achievement. The information on parenting style also needs clarification. For example, some researchers have found that parents and their adolescents can differ in their perception of parenting style and that neither parenting style nor measures of parents' beliefs in training their children are associated with student self-reports of school achievement (McBride-Chang & Chang, 1998; Chao, 1994).

Parental Control

The control exerted by parents impacts the style of parenting. The research literature investigating the nature and effects of parental control of children and adolescents is broad and complex; therefore, it is important to provide some differentiation between behavioral control and psychological control. Behavioral control is thought to facilitate development by providing necessary supervision, whereas psychological control is seen as inhibiting development through an excess of control.

Behavioral control. Family influence on children's achievement is well established in the literature (e.g., Baumrind, 1978; Dornbusch, Ritter, Leiderman, Roberts, & Fraleigh, 1987; Steinberg, Lamborn, Darling, Mounts, & Dornbusch, 1994), and most researchers agree on the significant role of authoritative parenting style and active parental involvement in maximizing children's academic success across grades, gender, and ethnic groups.

Forty years ago Baumrind's seminal studies of the socialization of competence (1966, 1967) concluded that theory-derived parent classification that resulted in certain parental control would generate different behaviors in children. Her theory-derived parent classification resulted in the original parenting style prototype: authoritative, authoritarian, and permissive.

According to Baumrind (1966) the permissive parent behaves in a "nonpunitive, acceptant and affirmative manner toward the child's impulses, desires and actions" (1966, p. 889). There is an attempt by this parent to allow the child to regulate his/her own activities as much as possible and to avoid the exercise of control. The authoritarian parent "attempts to shape, control, and evaluate the behavior and attitudes of the child in accordance with a set standard of conduct" (1966, p. 890). The authoritarian parent values obedience and favors punitive, forceful measures to curb the child's self-will. This parent does not encourage verbal give and take, and believes that the child should accept the parent's word for what is right. The authoritative parent "encourages verbal give and take and shares with the child the reasoning behind the policy" (1966, p. 891). This parent enforces his/her own perspective as an adult, but recognizes the child's individual interests and special ways.

Subsequent research on the role of parents in children's academic performance relied on traditional parenting style paradigm that adopts the three prototypes of adult control; namely, permissive, authoritarian, authoritative. Baumrind's (1967, 1971) studies noted that preschool children reared by parents with differing parenting attitudes or styles, differed in their mastery of social competence. Her conclusions defended the position that authoritative control may effectively generate in the child, behavior which while well socialized is also willful and independent, whereas authoritarian control and permissive noncontrol may both deprive the child of the opportunity to engage in vigorous interaction with people.

Subsequent research also continued to increase the age range for which significance of parenting style applies (Dornbusch et al., 1987). Dornbusch and colleagues tested Baumrind's (1966, 1967) typology of authoritarian, permissive, and authoritative parenting styles in the context of adolescent school performance. Using a large and diverse sample of approximately 8,000 high school students, Dornbusch et al. (1987) found that both authoritarian and permissive parenting styles were negatively associated with grades, and authoritative parenting was positively associated with grades. However, authoritarian parenting tended to have a stronger association with grades than did the other two parenting styles, except among Hispanic males. This research supported the premise that children of authoritative parents have a higher academic performance than do children of either authoritarian or permissive parents.

Later, researchers split the permissive type into permissive-indulgent and permissive-indifferent (Baumrind, 1978; Maccoby & Martin, 1983) as a result of a two-dimensional (demandedness and responsiveness) typology of parenting patterns. This resulted in a scheme that established the four parenting styles that are commonly employed in today's research literature (e.g., Lamborn, Mounts, Steinberg, & Dornbusch, 1991; Steinberg et al., 1994): authoritative, authoritarian, indulgent, and neglectful.

The research of Lamborn et al. (1991) provided further support for Maccoby and Martin's (1983) framework which indicated the need to distinguish between two types of "permissive" families: those that are indulgent and those that are neglectful. Lamborn et al. (1991) classified the families into 1 of 4 groups (authoritative, authoritarian, indulgent, or neglectful) on the basis of the adolescents' ratings of these parents on two dimensions: acceptance/involvement and strictness/supervision. The adolescents were contrasted along four sets of outcomes: psychosocial development, school achievement, internalized distress and problem behaviors. Results indicated that adolescents who characterize their parents as authoritative score highest on measures of psychosocial competence and lowest on measures of psychological and behavioral dysfunction; the reverse is true for adolescents who describe their parents as neglectful. Adolescents whose parents are characterized as authoritarian score reasonably well on measures indexing obedience and conformity to the standards of adults but have relatively poorer self-conceptions than other adolescents. In contrast, adolescents from indulgent homes evidence a strong sense of self-confidence but report a higher frequency of substance abuse and school misconduct and are less engaged in school.

In another study using a sample of 120 older children and adolescents (aged 10–16), Steinberg et al. (1989), utilized the over-time relation of three components of authoritativeness: parental acceptance, psychological autonomy, and behavioral control, to test the hypothesis that authoritative parenting facilitates, rather than simply accompanies, school success. Steinberg and colleagues (1989) found that school success is mediated, in part, through the effects of authoritativeness on the development of a healthy sense of autonomy, and more specifically, a healthy psychological orientation toward work. Adolescents who described their parents as treating them warmly, democratically, and firmly were more likely than their peers to develop positive attitudes toward, and beliefs about their achievement, and as a consequence, they are more likely to do better in school.

Older adolescents approaching high school graduation who rated their parents as authoritative (or authoritative plus), authoritarian, midrange indulgent, and neglectful were studied by Slicker (1998). It was found that those adolescents experiencing the most favorable adjustments rated their parents as authoritative and authoritative plus. Not only was neglectful parenting consistently and significantly related to the most negative adjustments for older adolescents in all areas surveyed, but indulgent parenting was also related to the gamut of problem behavior.

Authoritative parenting is multifaceted; therefore, specific components of authoritativeness have also been studied. Steinberg and associates (1989, 1991, 1992) have suggested that in adolescence, three specific components of authoritativeness contribute to healthy psychological development and school success: parental acceptance or warmth, behavioral supervision and strictness, and psychological autonomy granting or democracy. According to Steinberg et al. (1989), positive impact of authoritative parenting on achievement is mediated at least, in part, through the effects of authoritativeness on the development of a healthy sense of autonomy, and more specifically, a healthy psychological orientation toward work.

In a one-year follow-up study to examine whether the observed differences in adolescent adjustment varied as a function of their parents' style (e.g., authoritative, authoritarian, indulgent, neglectful) and are maintained over time, Steinberg et al. (1994) found that adolescents from indulgent homes continued to display a psychological and behavioral profile that is mixed. The clearest evidence of the impact of parenting on adjustment during the high school years came from those who were neglectfully raised. These youth, already at a psychological and behavioral disadvantage at the time of first assessment, showed continued declines over the one-year period, with sharp drops in work orientation and school orientation, and increased delinquency and alcohol and drug use (Lamborn et al., 1991, p. 1062). The overall pattern suggests that youngsters that are neglectfully raised proceed on a downward and troublesome spiral characterized by academic disengagement and problem behavior.

Psychological control. Recent research has demonstrated the importance of distinguishing between parental, psychological, and behavioral control (Barber, 1996; Barber & Harman, 2002). Psychological control refers to control attempts that intrude into the psychological and emotional development of the child (e.g., thinking processes, self expression, emotions, and attachment to parents). Psychological control, including parental intrusiveness, guilt induction, and love withdrawal, interferes with the child's ability to become independent and to develop a healthy sense of self and personal identity.

The subject of mathematics served as a basis for examining psychological control in a study conducted by Aunola and Nurmi (2004). They found that a high level of psychological control exercised by mothers predicted slow progress in mathematics. They give three possible explanations for this finding. The first is that psychological control, defined as guilt-inducing and manipulative child rearing, combined with high affection leads to an enmeshment of parent–child communication. Psychological control that is not accompanied by high levels of affection may, in turn, be less enmeshing and therefore less harmful for child development. The second explanation is that a child-rearing pattern characterized by both a high level of affection and a high level of psychological control may communicate inconsistent and discrepant messages of maternal approval and love to a child (Barber, 1996; see also Baumrind, 1966). The third possible explanation for this major finding is that guilt-inducing mothers who simultaneously show high affection are themselves emotional and impulsive and may not be capable of providing cognitively oriented school-related advice and support, which may be particularly important for the development of math-related skills among children.

In a sample of 93 middle-class African–American early adolescents (Mean age 13.11) and their mothers, Smetana and Daddis (2002) examined the influence of parenting beliefs and practices over a two-year period. They found that more restrictive control (e.g., more rules and more unilateral decision-making by parents) was associated with both greater monitoring and more psychological control of early adolescent girls. In contrast, mothers of early adolescent boys who exerted more restrictive control reported using less psychological control.

In another study involving outcome of parental monitoring and psychological control, Dodge, Bates, and Criss (2001) found that early adolescents (especially girls) whose mothers used psychologically controlling strategies had higher levels of anxiety/depression and delinquent behaviors in middle childhood and adolescence.

Recently, Bronstein, Ginsburg, and Herrera (2005) found that greater external control (e.g., demands, directives, criticism, punishment, rewards, enticements) and lack of guidance by parents in the 5th-grade year were related to children's poorer academic achievement that year, which in turn predicted a more extrinsic motivational orientation in 7th grade. In contrast, greater parental autonomy-supporting behavior in the 5th-grade year was related to children's high academic achievement that year, which in turn predicted a more intrinsic motivational orientation in 7th grade.

Gender and Parenting Style

Gender roles in marriage differ as do the effects on student achievement as was indicated by Updegraff, McHale, and Crouter (1996) who explored the implications of parents' traditional versus egalitarian marital roles for girls' and boys' patterns of math and science achievement. Their findings revealed that girls from egalitarian families maintained a high level of achievement after the transition to the 7th grade, whereas girls from traditional families declined in math and science performance. There were important implications for academic achievement for girls growing up in egalitarian families with relatively more powerful mothers and more involved fathers. Parents with less traditional sex-role attitudes appeared to have important implications for their academic achievement. In families with boys, no significant patterns emerged.

Math performance has often been chosen to be an indicator of academic performance. Gadeyne, Ghesquiere, and Onghena (2004) studied the relations between parenting and child adjustment using data gathered for 352 children and their parents from kindergarten to 2nd grade. They reported that in the academic domain, low-supportive and high-controlling parenting practice was modestly related to poor subsequent math achievement and that externalizing and attention problem behavior was clearly predictive of high levels of control in mothers and low levels of support in fathers.

Early parenting factors have been found to be important for children's academic achievement. Englund, Luckner, Whaley, and Egelund (2004) studied 187 low-income children and their mothers from birth of the child through 3rd grade to determine whether the quality of assistance, parental involvement, and expectations had an effect on their academic achievement. They found that mothers' quality of instruction prior to school entry had significant direct effects on IQ and indirect effects on achievement in 1st and 3rd grades.

There may also be gender differences in the relationships of adolescents and their parents. Demo, Small and Savin-William (1987) found support for the proposition that adolescents and their parents have independent yet overlapping perceptions of the relationships and the individual perceptions of the relationship are consistently related to his or her self-esteem. Their findings indicate that the self-esteem of boys compared to that of girls is more strongly related to family relations. This suggests that adolescent boys may express and communicate their self-esteem in ways that prompt parents to respond (with support, control or communication) while girls provide fewer or more subtle expressions and thereby deny parents the potential cues they need for appropriate responses.

There is continued evidence to support the fact that when parents bridge the gap between home and school, children experience benefits in their psychological functioning as well as achievement (e.g., Englund et al., 2004; Steinberg, Lamborn, Dornbush, & Darling, 1995). The research of Pomeranz, Wang, and Ng (2005) found that on days children have homework, mothers' negative affect is elevated but mothers' positive affect is not dampened. Mother's negative affect is further intensified on days mothers provide assistance. Mothers' maintenance of positive affect in the homework context appears to offset the undermining effects of mothers' negative affect as well as of children's helplessness. Thus, if parents are to get involved in children's homework, a key goal is to keep the interaction fun and loving, despite the irritation and annoyance parents may experience.

Further evidence to support different effects of gender on parenting style were given by Jacobs (1991) and Jacobs and Eccles (1992). In the first study Jacobs (1991) reported that parents who held traditional gender stereotypes favoring boys in mathematics expressed less confidence in their children's math abilities if they had daughters and more confidence if they had sons, regardless of their children's actual abilities and performance levels. In the second study, Jacobs and Eccles (1992) reported that mothers' perceptions of their children mediated the interaction of child's gender and mothers' gender stereotype of children's self-perceptions. Thus, when mothers held stereotypic beliefs and had children of the gender not favored by the stereotype (girls, in the case of mathematics) they held less favorable perception of their children's abilities to succeed in such domains even after controlling for ability.

On the basis of data from 355 students (mean age 10.6) and their mothers, Noack (2004) found that maternal behavior predicted the value that students attribute to education. Thus, if preadolescents experience their mothers to be involved in activities that are somehow linked to education, they seem to get the impression that their mothers also appreciate education.

In another study concerning parental beliefs about adolescents' abilities, Bleeker and Jacobs (2004) found that mothers' beliefs about their adolescents' abilities in math and science are shaped by gender stereotypes and are related to the development of their adolescent children's self-perceptions of math ability. Furthermore, mothers' early beliefs are related to older adolescents' feelings of math–science career self-efficacy and ultimately to whether young adults pursue careers in certain areas of math and science. The findings of these studies, Bleeker and Jacobs (2004); Jacobs (1991); and Jacobs and Eccles (1992), clearly indicated the importance of parental beliefs in adolescents' later educational and career choices.

Finally, parent differential of self has an impact on family functioning and student achievement, and is thought to be most critical to healthy individual development and family functioning (Kerr & Bowen, 1988; Titelman, 1998). Differentiation of self is defined as the capacity of a system and its members to manage emotional reactivity, act thoughtfully under stress, and allow for both intimacy and autonomy in relationship. Support for parent differentiation of self and child competence was reported by Skowron (2005) who found that those mothers who were better at modulating emotion and capable of both intimacy and autonomy had children who demonstrated higher verbal and math achievement scores and were less aggressive.

Parental Education

The literature on achievement consistently has shown that parent education is important in predicting children's success in the educational system. Parent education can influence children's education via different routes: (1) through the transmission of cognitive competencies, (2) through increased opportunities, and (3) through the transmission of parental beliefs and attitudes concerning the value and utility of education. Parents' views on school and education which are observed by children may affect children's views either directly or through such indirect processes as parents' engagement in cultural or educational activities (e.g. Noach, 2004).

In several studies representing a wide range of cultural diversity, Alnabhan, Al-Zegoul, and Harwell (2001); Cherian (2001); Davis-Kean (2005); Hill, Castellino, Lansford, Nowlin, Dodge, Bates, and Pettit (2004); Hortcsu (1995); Jackson (2003); Livaditus, Zaphiriadis, Samakouri; Tellidou, Tzavaras, and Xenitidis (2003); Tavani and Losh (2003); parents' own behavior as well as joint family activities have been shown to influence children's academic motivation and behavior. Using a sample of 868 children ranging from 8 to 12 years of age (49% non-Hispanic European American and 47% African–American), Davis-Kean (2005) found that for both groups, parents' education influenced child achievement indirectly through its impact on the parents' achievement beliefs and stimulating home behaviors. However, for the African–American sample, in addition to parental education, educational expectations and positive parent–child interactions were directly related to children's achievement.

Using a longitudinal model, Hill et al. (2004) examined parent academic involvement, behavioral problems, achievement, and aspirations in a sample of 463 adolescents from 7th through 11th grades, Hill et al. found that among the higher parental education group, parent academic involvement was related to fewer behavioral problems, which in turn were related to achievement and then aspirations. For the lower parental education group, parent academic involvement was related to aspirations but not to behavior or achievement. Across ethnicity, parent academic involvement was more strongly related to achievement for African–Americans than for European Americans. Of interest is the finding that for the families with higher parental education levels, 7th-grade parent academic involvement was not directly related to achievement or aspirations even though it was associated with fewer school behavior problems at 8th grade. These fewer behavior problems in the 8th grade were related to higher 9th grade achievement and 11th grade aspirations.

Mothers' employment appeared to have an effect on their children's math scores according to Jackson (2003) who investigated the child development outcomes in early school years among African–American welfare recipients and their young children. This study found that children whose mothers had some (even inconsistent) employment were more likely to have higher math scores that those whose mothers are consistently unemployed. The results of Jackson's (2003) study also indicated that mothers' higher educational attainment, being a female child, and small family size were associated with higher reading scores. This research clearly supports the need for early interventions for "at-risk" children.

Parental education levels may not always directly affect their children's performance; however, it does tend to play a strong indirect role in how the children are raised. According to Georgiou (1999), parents with high education degrees are typically more involved in their children's academic careers, thereby placing more emphasis on academics than those parents with lower education degrees and less involvement in their children's education. Tavani and Losh (2003) found that parental education was an important variable in predicting high school students' academic success. The results resembled prior studies (Riggio, Watering, & Throdmorton, 1993; Robbins, Lese, & Herrick, 1993; Zea, Jamama, & Bianchi, 1995).

There is also much evidence to support the premise that parental education plays an important role in children's lives in various cultures. Hortacsu (1995) investigated the relationships between parents' education levels, parents' beliefs concerning children's cognitions related to themselves and their relationship, and academic achievement in a sample of Turkish 4th grade children. Hortacsu (1995) found that the level of mother's education was directly related to child perceptions of external control, and academic achievement. The level of father's education was directly related only to child perceptions of efficacy.

There is also evidence to support the importance of parental education on children's academic achievement from underdeveloped countries. A significant relationship was also found between parental education and academic achievement of Xhosa children from South Africa, regardless of whether the family was polygynous or monogamous (Cherian, 2001).

Perceptual Differences Between Parents and Their Children

Many parents and educators believe that the teaching of higher-level thinking skills is contingent on the mastery of basic skills. Research findings focus on integration of critical and creative thinking and subject matter assimilation as a means to foster greater student achievement. Parents and educators are instrumental in influencing critical and creative thinking skills. The enduring problem that plagues the educational system is the perceptual difference between students and their parents as to the parenting style.

A comparison of willingness to conform to academic expectations of parents to student academic achievements for American, Chinese–American, and Chinese high school students was provided by Chen and Lan (1998). The results indicated that American students were less likely than their Chinese and Chinese–American peers to heed parental advice and cared less about fulfilling academic expectations. The authors concluded the students' achievement in all three groups was related to their perception of independence. They support the notion that future studies should examine parental influence or parental expectation and the students' perception of it as it relates to academic achievement. Studies focusing on adolescent perception of independence would provide stronger support for student achievement based on parenting styles.

In a related longitudinal research on patterns of parenting during adolescence, Paulsen and Sputa (1996) established three distinct areas of study: (1) differences in parenting styles and involvement between mothers and fathers, (2) differences in perception of parenting style and involvement between adolescents and parents, and (3) parents involvement in changes between 9th and 12th grade. Results indicated that during 9th and 12th grades, mothers were seen as being more involved than fathers in parenting. Values related to achievement were found to be the same for both mothers and fathers and both rated themselves higher on all aspects of parenting than they were rated by their 9th and 12th grade adolescents. The results support further research on the ability of parents to create optimum environments to nurture adolescent independence.

The independence factor between parents and their children has a basis in perceptual differences. In a study of parent/child ratings of warmth and negativity to the negative adjustment of adolescents, Feinberg, Howe, Hetherington, and Mavis (2000) found that, independent of parenting behavior, perceptual differences (PDs) were clearly linked with adolescents' adjustment. They also found that the correlation between maladjustment in older adolescents and PDs related to parental negativity disappeared over time. They established several caveats for clinical practice: (1) healthy development is more dependent on lower levels of PD in late adolescence than in early adolescence; (2) families need to express divergent views; (3) families may not benefit from decreasing PDs in clinical intervention. In examining family conflict, Bradley and Corwyn (2000) studied its effect on the relation between environmental processes and adolescent well-being. They recommended a long-term "holistic approach" to parenting style to decrease family conflict and facilitate adolescent well-being. The mixed signals of perceptual differences increase the volatility of conflict and decrease the potential for independence. Establishing clinical practices through research implications would provide a sound basis for change within the family constellation.

Ethnicity and Diversity in Parenting Styles

The ethnic identity of an individual is established after the navigation through channels of cultural issues in a society. The parenting style of an individual follows a similar course through acculturation, assimilation, and actualization based on ethnicity. The role of parenting evolves over time, and is influenced by circumstances and by ethnic differences. Research studies have implicated ethnicity in achievement, psychosocial, and other mediating differences as it relates to parenting styles.

Peer group formation can be affected by parenting style. In a longitudinal study, Chen, Chang, He, and Liu (2005) found that children's susceptibility to peer pressure was related to parenting styles and practices for Chinese children. The findings illustrate that children's susceptibility to peer pressure is related to parenting styles and practices. They suggest parenting styles affect children's choices in forming groups. The specific cultural nature of their findings on the effects of parenting and selection of peer groups did not have a comparable match in Western research.

Family composition and parenting style affect gender-role socialization. Crouter, Manke, and McHale (1995) hypothesized that "gender differential socialization" would increase in young adolescents, particularly in families that maintain a traditional division of labor. They found a trend in "gender intensification" in families where there was an increase in maternal involvement with their daughters and paternal involvement with their sons during early adolescence. This intensification was even more evident in families where the adolescent had a younger sibling of the opposite gender.

Cultural influences have significant impact on parenting practices. Chao (1994) looked at the differences in "cultural systems" for Chinese and European Americans through the cultural notion of training. The research provided a basis to characterize Chinese parenting as "restrictive" and "controlling" or "authoritarian". Although poor school achievement has been linked with these parenting styles, Chinese–Americans have shown no decrease in achievement under such styles. The concept of *Chiao shun* is introduced as a term that includes "the idea of training children in the appropriate or expected behaviors." The concept of training is further expanded with the use of the term *guan* which means "to govern". It also has the additional meanings of "to care for" and "to love." The concepts of *guan* and *chiao shun* do not have an equivalent concept in Western style and equating them with "authoritarian" style does not adequately capture Chinese parenting. Chao cites Lau and Cheung (1987) to explain that the concept of training is not intended to lead to parental domination over a child, but to help establish and maintain harmony while maintaining the integrity of the family.

Parents differ in their involvement with their children which impacts student achievement. Chang and McBride-Chang (1998) focused on the effects of parenting style differences on adolescents in Hong Kong and concluded that adolescents who rated highest in life satisfaction tended to be more "parent-oriented" and less "peer-oriented." In addition, their view is such that Chinese and Western parents may be more involved with their children's achievement in school at different stages. Chinese parents may be more involved in the early grades to establish expectations of high achievement, whereas Western parents may be more involved during later grades. There is particular emphasis in the irrelevance of using the categories of authoritative, authoritarian, or permissive parenting styles for the adolescent group in Hong Kong. The parental belief system between the Western and Eastern cultures is targeted as the main reason for the differing outcomes for U.S. adolescents versus Hong Kong adolescents.

The belief system also influences psychological distress as examined by Hong Lorenz, and Veach (2005) in school age boys and girls in Taiwan. They found a strong connection between an adolescents' gender and their psychological distress. The only significant indicator of psychological distress for boys was their lack of self-esteem; whereas for girls the significant indicators were GPA, family income, self-esteem, and parenting practices. The researchers recommend additional case studies to explore additional variables related to psychological distress.

In a longitudinal study focused on multidimensional parental involvement across ethnic groups (White, Hispanic, African–American, and Asian–American), Hong and Ho (2005) found that communication and parental aspiration had both immediate and long-lasting effects on achievement in the White sample. Achievement in the Asian–American sample was most affected by parental participation and involvement. Student achievement in the African–American sample was affected by parental educational aspiration only for a short term. Long-term effects were observed only when there was increased parental supervision for African–American students. However, student achievement in the Hispanic sample was affected primarily by parental communication. The varied results in the targeted ethnicities emphasize the need for methodological considerations.

Finally, in studying ethnic differences in parenting styles as they affect adolescent outcomes, Garg, Levin, Kauppi, and Urajnik

(2005) chose a sample of East Indian and Canadian adolescents. The authors implicate methodological considerations as being "central" to the "cross-cultural studies" of parenting styles as it affects academic achievement. The studies of Western-based parenting styles do not necessarily coincide with studies of parenting styles in other ethnicities. However, studies of ethnic differences in adolescent behavior appear to have some similarity.

Discussion

Behavioral control and psychological control are two inherent features of parenting style. The research on behavioral control clearly indicates that authoritative parenting has the most positive influence on student academic achievement. Of interest to parents, educators, and researchers are (1) what are the positive constructs of authoritative parenting and (2) what is the optimal time of intervention so as to prevent the decline in achievement. Researchers uncovered an interesting finding concerning children's progress in mathematics where psychological control in the absence of affection may be less enmeshing and less harmful. According to Aurola and Nurmi (2004), both a high level of affection and a high level of psychological control sends an inconsistent message to the child and guilt-producing mothers who show high affection may be emotional and impulsive themselves and incapable of providing advice and support to their children.

The traditional gender stereotypes favoring boys in mathematics has been examined and found to have an effect on adolescent girls' perceptions of ability to succeed in mathematics (Bleeker & Jacobs, 2004; Jacobs, 1991; Jacobs & Eccles, 1992) and mothers' beliefs about their adolescent girls' abilities in math and science are shaped by these gender stereotypes and have been shown to have an effect on the adolescent's self-perceptions in those domains. This was found to ultimately affect self-efficacy and the decision to pursue careers in certain areas of math and science.

Parental education may not always affect children's performance; however, it does play a strong indirect role in how children are raised including the amount of parental involvement. There is research to substantiate the need for early interventions for children from impoverished backgrounds. It was found that children whose mothers had some employment are likely to have higher math scores than those whose mothers are consistently unemployed (Jackson, 2003).

Fathers and mothers rate themselves higher than their children in all aspects of parenting (Paulsen & Sputa, 1996). The differences in style between mothers and fathers are apparent in the stages of academic achievement of the adolescents. Children often need the influence of a particular parent when faced with challenges of academic achievement. A broad spectrum of clinical difficulties is realized by families where the perceptual differences of both parents and their children are in conflict. The adolescents' perceived level of independence when interacting with their parents seems to have a direct relationship to their academic achievement (Chen & Lan, 1998). The challenge seems to develop in daily events where parenting style has to nurture the development of independence. In clinical settings, parents often seek assistance to create the appropriate style to elicit independence in their adolescents.

According to Hong and Ho (2005) direct and indirect parental involvement practices can have a combined result based on ethnic differences. The multidimensional phenomenon of diversity and ethnicity issues point toward the need for methodological considerations in research design. For example, research studies designed to identify parent-peer influences of Western parenting styles would provide much needed data to understand their relationship and establish recommendations for clinical practice.

The concepts of *"chiao shun"* and *"guan"* assist in understanding the subtle differences in parenting style of Chinese–Americans (Chao, 1994) and the author additionally establishes the absence of equivalent Western concepts for comparison purposes. The belief system supporting the parenting style can be an additional factor that would produce differing results across ethnic lines (McBride-Chang & Chang, 1998). The inclusion of belief systems in research studies expands the challenge for research design. The advantage of such an inclusion would enable the practitioner to address gender and ethnic differences in psychological distress as seen in clinical settings.

Implications for Couple and Family Counseling

Family events and social exchanges increase the potential for family conflict. Therefore, the ability to see the systemic nature or circular aspect of these social exchanges can enhance the holistic realm. Parental concern for their children's independent functioning can be the driving force leading to family conflict. Conversely, the children's desire for independence can lead to family conflict as well. It appears that while perceptual differences between parents may not directly contribute to family conflict, it does affect the manner in which the perceptual differences are resolved (Bradley & Corwyn, 2000).

The decision made by both parents and their children to cooperate or confront each other is likely to impact the progress toward independence and student achievement. Parents and their children have to examine their belief systems and attitudes which act as the foundation for parenting style and student achievement. Parenting style focuses on engaging the student to become a responsible stakeholder in their own achievement. The challenge for clinicians is to assist families in recognition of their individual strengths and facilitate group action to benefit their unique system. Turbulence generated by the inadequacy in families may best be managed in clinical settings. Couples have to be encouraged to maintain a cohesive parenting style as families are supported to increase student achievement. Family narratives of experience and meaning need to be explored in order to identify and understand processes and generate new hypotheses. Clinicians with their subjective in-depth knowledge related to assisting families, must provide contextual framework, going beyond theory-based views of phenomena and illuminate possible new areas for research study.

Implications for Future Research

Student achievement and parenting styles as they relate to child and adolescent development have been a focus of research for several decades. Cognitive development and reasoning theories specifically have provided insights into how individuals have multiple points of view, personal decision-making schemata, and learning styles. Specifically, children develop learning preferences and parents develop parenting styles that continue to be redefined as a child develops through adolescence and adulthood.

Sociological theorists contribute to the understanding of individual development through theories of environment and interaction. Children and adolescents have an invested physical and psychological energy in their experiences in the learning environment. Furthermore, children need to feel that they "matter" and that people care about them. Through their parenting styles, parents have to create such a caring environment in order to promote a positive learning experience.

Family activities and parents' behavior have a direct influence on children's academic motivation and behavior. The pattern suggests that when parents interact in a fun and loving way during children's homework time, there is a positive outcome for both. A process of academic disengagement and problem behavior results when parents are neglectful. Skowron (2005) found that those mothers who were better at modulating emotion and capable of both intimacy and autonomy had children who demonstrated higher verbal and math achievement scores and were less aggressive. Western-based studies on parenting styles do not have reliability across ethnicities.

CONCLUSION

As a society we are enamored with student achievement. Parents frequently emphasize achievement at the risk of alienating the young achiever. In an act of desperation they enforce penalties and sanctions as a means of dealing with the sagging achievement history of their child. The sanctions can cause psychological distress for the child as well as the parents. In understanding the dynamics of the forces at play, the real problem of student achievement morphs into self-beliefs, self-esteem, self-efficacy, and emotional issues which may provide deterrents to achievement.

Parenting style has contributing influences from parent education, perceptual differences, gender, ethnicity, and diversity. The research on parenting style has focused on comparison of models (Baumrind, 1978; Lamborn et al., 1991; Maccoby & Martin, 1983; Steinberg et al., 1994) and the quest for an optimum style to suit all parents. This may have resulted from the realization of common attributes empirically. The recognition that parenting style has to evolve to meet the challenges of each situation as it surfaces results in a broader conceptualization. Additionally, each situation requires its own unique blend of style. Parents have to meet their child at the crossroads and address circumstances effectively to enhance achievement.

Researchers of parenting style and its relation to academic achievement have to increase methodological considerations for factoring multidimensional variables in their design. The considerations should include variables for family structure, expectations, communication and involvement. Additionally variations need to be established across ethnicities and cognitive abilities. The measures should address cognitive processes that influence achievement. An additional consideration might be focusing on role models. Do children look at their parents as effective role models? What is the process that influences children in selecting their role model? And what strengthens either parent as a role model?

Local communities have experienced profound demographic and socioeconomic changes as demonstrated by shifts in the 1990 and 2000 U.S. Census reports (United States Census 2000 Gateway). The demarcations between various socioeconomic and cultural groups have shifted resulting in increasing levels of impoverished families. Parents are required to work multiple jobs with pressures of seasonal and low wages. They are often required to share cramped quarters in neighborhoods that provide little safety for their children. The mental health delivery systems in these communities are overwhelmed by the high risk factors and inability to meet the challenges of these families. The need for applied research is strong in these communities. Researchers need to examine their agendas to execute best practice methods to assist these communities. Academic institutions need to partner with each other and community entities to develop and implement projects to address parenting styles and its influence on academic achievement.

REFERENCES

Alnabhan, M., Al-Zegoul, E., & Harwell, M. (2001). Factors related to achievement levels of education students at Mu'tah University. *Assessment & Evaluation in High Education, 26*, 593–604.

Aunola, K., & Nurmi, J. (2004). Maternal affection moderates the impact of psychological control on a child's mathematical performance. *Developmental Psychology, 40*, 965–978.

Bandura, A. (1997). *Self-efficacy: The exercise of control.* New York: W.H. Freeman.

Barber, B. K. (1996). Parental psychological control: Revisiting a neglected construct. *Child Development, 67*, 3296–3310.

Barber, B. K., & Harmon, E. L. (2002). Violating the self: Parental psychological control of children and adolescents. In B. K. Barber (Ed.), *Intrusive parenting: How psychological control affects children and adolescents* (pp. 15–52). Washington, DC: American Psychological Association.

Baumrind, D. (1966). Effects of authoritative parental control on child behavior. *Child Development, 37,* 887–907.

Baumrind, D. (1967). Child care practices anteceding three patterns of preschool behavior. *Genetic Psychology Monographs, 75,* 43–88.

Baumrind, D. (1968). Authoritarian vs. authoritative parental control. *Adolescence, 3,* 255–272.

Baumrind, D. (1971). Current patterns of parental authority. *Developmental Psychology Monographs, 4,* 1–102.

Baumrind, D. (1978). Parental disciplinary practices and social competence in children. *Youth and Society, 9,* 239–276.

Bleeker, M. M., & Jacobs, J. E. (2004). Achievement in math and science: Do mothers' beliefs matter 12 years later? *Journal of Educational Psychology, 96,* 97–109.

Bradley, R. H., & Corwyn, R. F. (2000). Moderating effect of perceived amount of family conflict on the relation between home environmental processes and the well being of adolescents. *Journal of Family Psychology, 14,* 349–364.

Bronstein, P., Ginsberg, G. S., & Herrera, I. S. (2005). Parental predictors of motivational orientation in early adolescence: A longitudinal study. *Journal of Youth and Adolescence, 34,* 559–576.

Chang, C., McBride, & Chang, L. (1998). Adolescent-parent relations in Hong Kong: Parenting styles, emotional autonomy, and school achievement. *Journal of Genetic Psychology, 159,* 421–430.

Chao, R. K. (1994). Beyond parental control and authoritarian parenting style: Understanding Chinese parenting through cultural notion of training. *Child Development, 65,* 1111–1119.

Chao, R. K., & Sue, S.(1996). Chinese parental influence and their children's school success: A paradox in the literature on parenting styles. In S. Lau (Ed.), *Growing up the Chinese way: Chinese child and adolescent development* (pp. 93–120). Hong Kong: Chinese University of Hong Kong.

Chen, H., & Lan, W. (1998). Adolescents' perceptions of their parents expectations: Comparison of American, Chinese–American, and Chinese high school students, *Adolescence, 33,* 385–391.

Chen, X., Chang, L., He, Y., & Lui, H. (2005). The peer group as a context: Moderating effects on relations between maternal parenting and social and school adjustment in Chinese children. *Child Development, 76,* 417–434.

Cherian, V. I. (2001). Relationship between parental education and academic achievement of Xhosa children from monogamous and polygynous families. *The Journal of Social Psychology, 132,* 681–683.

Crouter, A., Manke, B., & McHale, S. (1995). The family context of gender intensification in early adolescence. *Child Development, 66,* 317–329.

Davis-Kean, P. E. (2005). The influence of parent education and family income on child achievement: The indirect role of parental expectations and the home environment. *Journal of Family Psychology, 19,* 294–304.

Demo, D. H., Small, S. A., & Savin-Williams, R. C. (1987). Family relations and the self-esteem of adolescents and their parents. *Journal of Marriage and the Family, 49,* 705–715.

Dodge, K. A., Bates, J. E., & Criss, M. M. (2001). Antecedents and behavior-problem outcomes of parental monitoring and psychological control in early adolescence. *Child Development, 72,* 583–598.

Dornbusch, S. M., Ritter, P. L., Leiderman, P. H., Roberts, D. F., & Fraleigh, M. J. (1987). The relation of parenting style to adolescent school performance. *Child Development, 58,* 1244–1257.

Englund, M. M., Luckner, A. E., Whaley, G. J. L., & Egeland, B. (2004). Children's achievement in early elementary school: Longitudinal effects of parental involvement, expectations, and quality of assistance. *Journal of Educational Psychology, 96,* 723–730.

Feinberg, M., Howe, G., Hetherington, R. D., & Mavis, E. (2000). Relationship between perceptual differences of parenting and adolescent antisocial behavior and depressive symptoms. *Journal of Family Psychology, 14,* 531–555.

Gadeyne, E., Ghesquiere, P., & Onghena, P. (2004). Longitudinal relations between parenting and child adjustment in young children. *Journal of Clinical Child and Adolescent Psychology, 33,* 347–358.

Garg, R., Levin, E., Urajnik, D., & Kauppi, C. (2005). Parenting style and academic achievement for East Indian and Canadian adolescents. *Journal of Comparative Family Studies, 36,* 653–662.

Georgiou, S. N. (1999). Parental attributions as predictors of involvement and influences on child achievement. *British Journal of Educational Psychology, 69,* 409–429.

Hill, N. E., Castellino, D. R., Lansford, J. E., Nowlin, P., Dodge, K. A., Bates, J. E., & Pettit, G. S. (2004). Parental academic involvement as related to school behavior, achievement, and aspirations: Demographic variations across adolescent. *Child Development, 75,* 1491–1509.

Hong, H. (2005). Direct and indirect longitudinal effects of parental involvement on student achievement: Second-order latent growth modeling across ethnic groups. *Journal of Educational Psychology, 97,* 32–42.

Hong, Z. R., McCarthy-Veach, P. M. C. & Lawrenz, F. (2005). Psychosocial predictors of psychological distress in Taiwanese Secondary School Boys and Girls. *Sex Roles, 53,* 419–431.

Hortacsu, N. (1995). Parents' education levels, beliefs, and child outcomes. *Journal of Genetic Psychology, 156,* 373–383.

Jackson, A. P. (2003). Mothers' employment and poor and near-poor African–American children's development: A longitudinal study. *Social Service Review, 3,* 93–109.

Jacobs, J. E. (1991). Influence of gender stereotypes on parent and child mathematics attitudes. *Journal of Educational Psychology, 83,* 518–527.

Jacobs, J. E., & Eccles, J. S. (1992). The impact of mothers' gender-role stereotypic beliefs on mothers' and children's ability perceptions. *Journal of Personality and Social Psychology, 63,* 932–944.

Jeynes, W. (2005). A meta-analysis of the relation of parental involvement to urban elementary school student academic achievement. *Urban Education, 40,* 237–269.

Kerr, M. E., & Bowen, M. (1988). *Family evaluation*. New York: Norton.

Lamborn, S., Mounts, N. Steinberg, L., & Dornbusch, S. (1991). Patterns of competence and adjustment amount adolescents from authoritative, authoritarian, indulgent and neglectful families. *Child Development, 62*, 1049–1065.

Leventhal, T., & Brooks-Gunn, J. (2004). A randomized study of neighborhood effects on low-income children's educational outcomes. *Developmental Psychology, 40*, 488–507.

Livaditus, M., Zaphiriadis, K., Samakouri, M., Tellidou, C., Tzavaras, N., & Xenitidis, K. (2003). Gender differences, family and psychological factors affecting school performance in Greek secondary school students. *Educational Psychology, 23*, 223–231.

Maccoby, E. E., & Martin, J. A. (1983). Socialization in the context of the family: Parent-child interaction. In P. H. Mussen (Series Ed.) & E. M. Hetherington (Vol. Ed.), *Handbook of child psychology: Vol. 4. Socialization, personality, and social development* (4th ed., pp. 1–101). New York: Wiley.

Noack, P. (2004). The family context of preadolescents' orientations towards education Effects of maternal orientations and behavior. *Journal of Educational Psychology, 96*, 714–722.

Paulson, S. E., & Sputa, C. L. (1996). Patterns of parenting during adolescence: Perceptions of adolescent parents. *Adolescence, 31*, 369–382.

Pomerantz, E. M., Wang, Q., & Ng, F. F. (2005). Mothers' affect in the homework context: The importance of staying positive. *Developmental Psychology, 41*, 414–427.

Riggio, R. E., Watering, K. P., & Throdmorton, B. (1993). Social skills, social support, and psychosocial adjustment. *Personality & Individual Differences, 15*, 275–280.

Robbins, S. B., Lese, K. P., & Herrick, S. M. (1993). Interactions between goal instability and social support on college freshman adjustment. *Journal of Counseling & Development, 71*, 343–348.

Skowron, E. A. (2005). Parent differentiation of self and child competence in low-income urban families. *Journal of Counseling Psychology, 52*, 337–346.

Slicker, E. K. (1998). Relationship of parenting style to behavioral adjustment in graduating high school seniors. *Journal of Youth and Adolescent, 27*, 345–372.

Smetana, J. G. (1995). Parenting styles and conceptions of parental authority during adolescence. *Child Development, 66*, 299–316.

Smetana, J. G., & Daddis, C. (2002). Domain-specific antecedents of parental psychological control and monitoring: The role of parenting beliefs and practices. *Child Development, 73*, 563–580.

Steinberg, L., Elmen, J. D., & Mounts, N. S. (1989). Authoritative parenting, psychosocial maturity, and academic success among adolescents. *Child Development, 60*, 1424–1436.

Steinberg, L., Lamborn, S. D., Darling, N., Mounts, N., & Dornbusch, S. (1994). Over-time changes in adjustment and competence among adolescents from authoritative, authoritarian, indulgent, and neglectful families. *Child Development,* *65,* 754–770.

Steinberg, L., Lamborn, S. D., Dornbusch, S. M., & Darling, N. (1992). Impact of parenting practices on adolescent achievement: Authoritative parenting, school involvement, and encouragement to succeed. *Child Development, 63,* 1266–1281.

Steinberg, L., Mounts, N., Lamborn, S., & Dornbusch, S. (1991). Authoritative parenting and adolescent adjustment across various ecological niches. *Journal of Research on Adolescence, 1,* 19–36.

Tavani, C. M., & Losh, S. C. (2003). Motivation, self-confidence, and expectations as predictors of the academic performances among our high school students. *Child Study Journal, 33,* 141–151.

Titelman, P. (Ed.). (1998). *Clinical applications of Bowen family systems theory.* New York: Haworth Press.

U.S. Dept. of Commerce, Census Bureau (2006). *United States Census 2000 Gateway,* retrieved http://www.census.gov/main/www/cen 2000.html.

Updegraff, K. A., McHale, S. M., & Crouter, A. C. (1996). Gender roles in marriage: What do they mean for girls' and boys' school achievement? *Journal of Youth and Adolescence, 24,* 73–88.

Zea, M. C., Jarama, S. L., & Bianchi, F. T. (1995). Social support and psychological competence: Explaining the adaptation to college of ethnically diverse students *American Journal of Community Psychology, 23,* 509–531.

Families, Their Children's Education, and the Public School: An Historical Review

Diana B. Hiatt-Michael

ABSTRACT. This analysis focuses on parent involvement in public schooling within the United States of America from the colonial period to present. The analysis is framed by four major forces that influence the kind and degree of parent involvement: the cultural beliefs of families; the social structure of families; economic influences; and political pressures within the nation. The contemporary institutional and legal structure of schools tends to disconnect teachers and families. A tension appears to exist between professionals, on the one hand, who espouse the concept that they alone are qualified to make complex decisions affecting the education of our nation's children, and parents, on the other hand, who believe that they should have a voice in their children's compensatory public education.

Diana B. Hiatt-Michael, EdD, is Professor of Education, Graduate School of Education & Psychology, Pepperdine University, Los Angeles, CA.

FORCES AFFECTING FAMILY INVOLEMENT IN SCHOOLS

An increasing body of research during the past 20 years supports the benefits of parent involvement in their child's schooling. A summary of studies in this research area confirms the importance of parent involvement across cultures, school types, and geographic area (Epstein, 2001; Henderson & Mapp, 2002; Hiatt-Michael, 2005). Findings reveal that teachers' and principals' efforts to involve families promotes higher student attendance rates, lower suspension and expulsion rates, higher graduation rates, more accurate diagnosis of students for educational placement, higher satisfaction with the school, student improved goal-setting and pride in school work, and higher academic achievement in reading and math. This research has reached the attention of public policymakers, and parent involvement was included as one of President Clinton's *Goals 2000 in* 1994 (U.S. Department of Education, 1994), and a cornerstone of President Bush's *No Child Left Behind* (Bush, 2005).

Although this information is readily available, the gap between knowledge of good practice and the actual implementation across most public schools in America continues to be wide. In order to understand this gap, this analysis focuses on parent involvement in public schooling within the United States of America from the colonial period to present.

Contemporary families value education for their children (Cutler, 2000; Rose & Gallup, 2006). To support this parental value, the public school has emerged in countries around the world as the central place for children's basic education (Hiatt-Michael, 2005, pp. 1–12). This ubiquitous institution was developed and is maintained to provide parents, local communities, and governments with compulsory education for all children (Cremin, 1961). Communities and governmental entities pride themselves in school rankings, academic testing scores, graduation rates to describe the social status of communities and countries. Parents select new homes in neighborhoods or send children to distant schools based upon the perceived quality of schooling. In 2003, 24% of parents in America indicated their primary reason to select a neighborhood was the quality of education (National Center for Educational Statistics, 2006).

However, the contemporary American public school, a government social agency, usually operates outside the direct control of the children's families as teachers, administrators, and staff are state-licensed and employed workers. The organizational and legal structure of the state bureaucracy oftentimes separates the child's life in the school from the child's life within the family (Cutler, 2000; Epstein, 2001; Sarason, 1995). Thus, families and school personnel may become distant and even hostile towards one another (Cutler, 2000, p. 199; Gibbs, 2005). Neither may know the life experiences of the other. To help parents understand the school, popular books, such as *No Parent Left Behind*, are written to provide parents with a guide to enter and navigate the complex system of public schools (Petrosino & Spiegel, 2006). But, the school seldom acknowledges what the parents may contribute to the educational process. The family has the opportunity to directly involve themselves with their offspring from conception to adulthood; school teachers interact with their assigned classes for a limited period of time. Family members have knowledge of the individual child across many types of experiences; teachers know the child as a member of a group within the classroom and school. The teacher brings to the situation professional knowledge of teaching and learning; the family brings a lifelong commitment to the child's well-being and deep caring. Both share hopes and dreams for the future of these children, but a distance between the two groups seems to exist in many communities.

This apparent distance may be explained by four major forces, forces that influence the kind and degree of parent involvement (Hiatt-Michael, 2005, pp. 1–12). The four forces are: the *cultural beliefs* of families coupled with *social structure* of families, *economic influences*, and *political pressures* within the nation. Figure 1 illustrates these four primary forces upon the effect of family involvement in schools. For example, cultural beliefs impinge upon the type and quality of education for different groups. The cultural beliefs of parents and schools include, among others, the level of parental expectations on school achievement, desire for upward mobility, what is the education for boys and girls, which language shall be the dominant language spoken in school, which ethnic group attends what schools, and the source of power within the community, such as the counsel of community leaders. Social forces include changes in family structure, differing roles of family members, and the degree of population growth. Economic forces consist of the degree of industrialization

FIGURE 1. Four Forces Influencing Family-School Involvement.

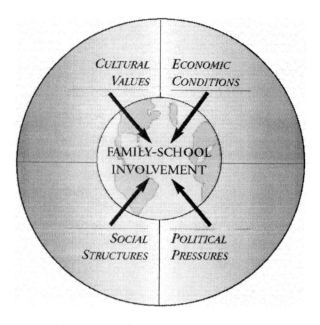

or modern influences, employment opportunities, economic growth, and Gross National Product allocated to education. Political forces are governmental power struggles among local, state, and national levels, governmental perspectives on education, governmental mandates, and changes of power in the country.

The following general description of how the four forces influence the power relationship between parents and the school describes the forces as part of America's desire for economic progress. A democratic way of life and continuing economic progress is hinged on increased education for the general population (Spring, 2004, pp. 3–30). Governments support the development of human capital across the country through financial support of local schools. Holding the financial power, the government can place education in the hands of "experts in the region" that determine valued educational knowledge and skills for the schools' curriculum. Such power directs who receives this schooling, how much schooling is received by various individuals, and the nature of the schooling. Parents' power is manifested by cultural values parents hold for schooling and their children, their belief that social mobility is connected to level of education, and parental economic limitations that hinder school attendance.

HISTORICAL ROLE OF PARENTAL CONTROL IN CHILDREN'S EDUCATION

Historically, parents assumed the responsibility for the education of their children (Berger, 1981; Shostak, 1967). Parental responsibilities included activities related to discipline, basic skills, work skills, ethics, and value inculcation. These educational activities were carried out privately within the family rather than publicly through school attendance. Advanced education for most youth was typically acquired through trade apprenticeships, arranged by the youth's parents, rather than through extensive public education in secondary schools.

During the early years in America, the colonies were granted local control of education (Spring, 2005). The first schools were created by religious leaders and later placed under governance of townships. Under townships, boards comprised lay citizens, who were parents in the community. As many immigrants had left Europe in order to openly practice their religious beliefs, these schools represented the religious beliefs of each particular community. Religion, reading, and writing comprised the curriculum for these schools. Since each colony was founded by a different religious sect and most colonies soon had more than one sect, colonial America was dotted with many small schools representing the religious view of the parental lay board.

Many schools were also organized along social class; this was especially so for the plantation states which attempted to emulate the class structure of Britain (Pulliam, 2003, pp. 84–90). The upper class and growing middle class created schools which catered to the social demands of these parents. These schools were supported by fees paid by parents. In response to concerns of philanthropists, charity schools were organized to provide rudimentary education to children who could not afford fees. In brief, the American scene in elementary education was one of local parental control of school governance, parental support of curriculum, parental choice of teachers, and parental support of religious teachings of the school.

CHANGE IN THE INFLUENCE OF THE FAMILY IN THEIR CHILDREN'S EDUCATION

However, as public education developed and spread across America, family involvement in education diminished (Hiatt-Michael, 2001). The press of social forces on child labor and urban gangs, economic changes for skilled workers, legal mandates supporting the rights of children and laborers, and cultural attitudes toward the value of schooling combined to reduce family control over their children's education. Public educational institutions usurped and supplanted this parental function, some say, to the detriment of the children and the family (Cutler, 2000; Sarason, 1995). Recognizing this during the late twentieth century, many parents, as well as businessmen, politicians, and educators, began to express renewed concern about choice and parent involvement in public education as a possible option to what many see as an outmoded and ineffective public education system. During the early 1980s a series of national task force reports, epitomized by *A Nation at Risk* (National Commission on Excellence in Education, 1983), reiterated the rising need to connect the child's home life with school expectations. These reports expressed the importance of parent involvement in a child's school life.

What caused the apparent separation between the child's parents and schooling? Answering this question is the focus of this historical examination of parent involvement in American public schooling.

THE EMERGENCE OF AMERICAN PUBLIC EDUCATION

The late sixteenth and early seventeenth century was a fertile period of exploration of ideas concerning the social contract and public education as espoused by Comenius, Locke, Rousseau, and other European philosophers (Spring, 2005). Perhaps as a result, the shift from parent education to public education occurred first in Europe and then was transmitted to America. During this period, in the North American colonies under British rule, local colonial authorities had jurisdiction over education. Separated from their mother country, the new colonies translated their European ideas to meet the local situation. For example, as early as 1642, Massachusetts colony, the leading colony regarding educational issues, passed a law which required all parents to provide their children with education in reading, religion, and a trade.

However, families had large families to assist the agrarian culture and their primary family focus was on economic benefit of farm labor. Thus, town leaders noted that some parents were not teaching their children to read and acquire religious knowledge. Therefore, in 1647, this colony pressed for a law which mandated that all towns of 50 families or more hire a teacher who could be paid out of local funds. Towns with 100 or more households had to build and support a grammar school. This act, commonly referred to as *Old Deluder Satan Act*, marks the beginning of public schools in America.

In the eighteenth century many American leaders, such as Noah Webster, Benjamin Rush, and George Washington, advocated national elementary education supported by federal or state taxes (Rippa, 1988, pp. 119–129; Spring, 2005). However, according to the U.S. Constitution, education was a state matter. The Bill of Rights, in Title X, notes that "The powers not delegated to the United States by the Constitution, nor prohibited by it to the States, are reserved to the States respectively, or to the people" (*The Constitution of the United States of America*, 1791). Thus, Thomas Jefferson (Jefferson & Lee, 1961) eloquently argued for public education for all children in the Commonwealth of Virginia. His argument was that America's citizens required certain basic skills in order to function in a democratic society. These skills included reading, writing, and rhetoric. Because most of America's European immigrants did not possess such skills, and were, therefore, incapable of properly educating their own children in them, Jefferson stated that Virginia should provide public schooling for every child. He believed that citizens required the ability to read the printed word and communicate clearly in both oral and written form in order to be free to make rational decisions in the community and nation. He feared that uninformed citizens could easily become pawns of political activists. His bill supported 3 years of public schooling under local control. However, his notion of universal public elementary education was not supported by the legislators of Virginia. The legislators preferred that parents maintain personal choice of private and religious schools rather than the state funds support public schools.

In nineteenth century America, Jefferson's view of universal public education with equal educational opportunity for every child regardless of ability to pay captured the sentiment of the American public and polity. DeTocqueville (1835/1946) noted after a nineteenth-century visit to America, "There reigns an unbelievable outward equality in America." This apparent value placed on equality among the classes noted during the late colonial period continued as the nation developed.

The interest in tax-supported universal education continued following the Revolutionary War. The eloquent voices of numerous educational reformers were heard throughout the nineteenth and twentieth century in support of public education and equality of opportunity (Coleman, 1966; Cutler, 2000; Ravitch, 1995). In the mid-1800s, the leadership of Horace Mann and Henry Barnard influenced educational reform across America (Mann, 1957). Mann's vision of the common school led to the development of a public school system in almost every state by 1860.

However, as analyzed by noted historian Lawrence Cremin (1961) in *Transformation of the American School,* the public school administrators of the 1800s crafted the public school system of the twentieth century. Their work rested on the belief that public schooling provided the forum in which all the diverse elements of America's native and immigrant society acquired a common culture. Their efforts were exemplified by William Torrey Harris, Superintendent of St. Louis Public Schools and later U.S. Commissioner of Education. Faced with ever-increasing student enrollments, he met this rising demand for schools with scientifically managed, graded elementary and secondary schools (Tyack, 1974).

John Dewey, an early twentieth-century philosopher, captured continuing interest in his "progressive" community schools, a concept which rested on public schooling. His beliefs were modified by Ralph W. Tyler, who fervently expounded free universal public schooling, providing the major influence on all students throughout the 1900s (Tyler, 1979–1993). As late as the mid-twentieth century, many supported the egalitarian Jeffersonian model as one that would serve the educational desires of all parents for their children, not only that of the poor, minority, and immigrant population of the United States. By the second half of the nineteenth century, only a percentage of elementary children were educated in private schools (Coleman, Huffer, & Kilgore, 1982). Most parents of lower, middle, and upper middle classes considered the graded public school to be the educational choice. Because children from all ethnic groups and social backgrounds attended the public schools, they served the nation as the "melting pot" for the diverse cultures that immigrated to America.

However, the opposing view, differential educational opportunity or public school choice, appears in recent years to have attracted a strong following (Chubb & Moe, 1990; Forster, 2006; Miron & Nelson, 2002). Supporters of this view believe that choice relates to greater parent involvement in the kind of education their children receive. These proponents support differential education not only among America's moneyed intellectual and business elite, who have always possessed the option of private education for their children, but also increasingly among the rising middle class who are the product of what is now seen by many as an outmoded and ineffective public education system (Gates, 2005). Therein lays the source of the tension and friction between the advocates of free universal public education and the proponents for parental school choice.

COMPULSORY EDUCATION AND CHILD LABOR LAWS

Pre-Revolutionary educational practices occurred on a state-by-state basis. State control of education continued during the Revolutionary period under the Articles of Confederation. For example, in Massachusetts, educational practices continued to evolve along new and broader patterns of public instruction. Virginia differed as private school options were more prevalent. These differences among the states in post-Revolutionary America were accepted by the creators of *The Constitution of the United States of America* and placed the responsibility for the education of each state's citizens to the individual state (*The Constitution of the United States of America*, 1789).

The watershed year 1852 marks the passage of America's first compulsory education law in Massachusetts (Blumenfeld, 1991). Gradually, other states followed Massachusetts' lead. However, as late as 1885, only sixteen out of the then 38 states had similar compulsory education laws.

Throughout the nineteenth century, immigrant parents placed their unemployed children into the mines, mills, and factories of the industrial revolution in order to supplement the family's subsistence wages (Rippa, 1988). These families needed the money to survive in the urban environment, an economic imperative. Likewise on the family farm, parents required the daily labor of the children for planting and harvesting crops, tending the farm animals, helping in the household, and other necessary survival chores. Consequently, parents had little or no motivation and could ill afford economically to send their children to school.

As a result of prevalent low-wage child labor, factories had cheap labor (Tyack, 1974). Thus, the primary political pressure to change this situation came from the working men who formed labor unions and went on strike for higher wages. In order for such strikes to be successful, labor unions enlisted politicians to enact child labor laws. These laws limited an industrialist's ability to utilize the labor of children. But, these laws alone proved insufficient to keep children out of the workplace and gangs of unemployed urban children roamed the city streets, often creating civil disturbances. The City Marshall's survey of the number of children who were vagrant in Boston resulted in 1,066 children or 5% of those ages 6 to 16 who were not in school (Blumenfeld, 1991). Most children were attending some school, but politicians in Boston and elsewhere argued for a compulsory education law as a means to require students to be in school.

Compulsory school attendance coupled with truancy laws compelled the remaining parents to relinquish their children's wages and send them to school. By 1918, all states had passed such legislation (Rippa, 1988). These laws made it illegal for a parent to keep a child out of school without the permission of school authorities and carried stiff fines for noncompliance. To further assure compliance, names of new immigrants were reported to school authorities by immigration authorities. These laws reduced parental control over their children's lives and education.

During early 1900s, children were required to attend public schools for increasingly longer periods of time (Ravitch, 1995). This lengthy institutionalization of children was supported by social reformers who argued the advantages of public education for the betterment of society. To this end, coercion of students into classrooms was condoned. Others supported the compulsory education and truancy laws because of fear of large numbers of unsupervised, unemployed immigrant children who roamed the streets. This fear is exemplified in this district superintendent's comment:

> Citizens should support compulsory education to save themselves from the rapidly increasing herds of non-producers... to

save themselves from the wretches who prey upon society like wild beasts. For such children, the state should establish labor schools so that children can be taught not only how to read but how to work. (Tyack, 1974, p. 69)

THE DEVELOPMENT OF SCHOOL BUREAUCRATIZATION AND PROFESSIONALIZATION OF TEACHERS

The bureaucratization of the American educational system emerged as a result of four combined forces-the growing American population, the growth of the industrial centers, the urbanization of the nation, and the utilization of scientific management techniques in business and industry (Hiatt-Michael, 2001). Bureaucratization is commonly defined as the formation of a hierarchical organization of an institution with defined procedures, roles, and functions of personnel. The early American schools were generally large single-room, multi-age schoolhouses organized and operated by the locally hired teacher (Beisaw & Gibb, 2004). In 1848, Quincy School designed as a novel graded elementary school was opened in Massachusetts. This new organization represented the factory model of schooling and utilized a graded curriculum. The teacher in each classroom focused on content assigned to that grade. Children were classified by grade. The haphazard individualized instruction of early schooling was replaced with an efficient systems approach to specialized curriculum for each grade. The graded school concept spread across states where it was quickly adopted in all modern schools in response to the increasing numbers of children in urban areas (Cremin, 1961).

The early democratic volunteerism of local schools was replaced with "incipient bureaucracy" (Katz, 1971, Summer). In conjunction with the graded school plan, many teachers were required to staff each school and the office of principal was added for efficient management of the school's operation. The increased numbers of schools within a town led to the formation of the superintendent's position, a role developed to assure uniformity across schools.

Mann and Barnard's instrumental leadership throughout in the 1800s promoted the bureaucratization of public schools and the professionalization of faculty (Cremin, 1961; Katz, 1971). Their intent was to bring the scientific management of the industrial age to the education of children. They recommended processes of standardization and systemization so that the growing public schools could operate effectively in the industrialized society. Mann recommended professional education of teachers in normal schools. Both men supported the notion that education of children should be in the hands of the professional teacher and administrator. Their belief was that parents did not possess the time, knowledge, or talents necessary for a child to meet the challenges of the emerging technology. Therefore, the parent should turn over the process of education to professionals hired by the state.

Barnard argued for the reduction of lay control of public schools (Cremin, 1961). Instead of schools directly reporting to financial boards, Barnard felt that there should be general state financial support for public schooling. As Commissioner of Education in the states of Rhode Island and Connecticut, Barnard worked with evangelical fervor to increase state control and reduce local control of schools.

The developing bureaucratization of schools was intended to make the operation more equitable (Tyack, 1974). For example, teachers and administrators would be hired on professional qualifications rather than on personal favoritism or nepotism. However, the stress on equity and systems management increased layers of bureaucracy. These layers separated the parents from the daily decision-making operations of the educational process. The control of schools by lay parent boards was subsumed by school superintendents. Boards of Education evolved into figureheads who were manipulated by the professional superintendent. Davies (2002–2006) commented that the "Professionalism of administrators and teachers led to keeping parents out of power influence." Michael Katz (1971), as part of his analysis of control of education, stated:

> The development of more elaborate and specific written regulations was intended to make the operation of the school system more routine, that is, more impartial and equitable, and the removal of the school board from ward politics was designed to remove the schools from partisanship as well as to foster increased coordination through centralization.... It offered specific advantages to practicing schoolmen in their quest for "professionalism." (p. 70)

The trend in government toward the improvement of social equity in schooling added to the status of the public school in American society (Miron & Nelson, 2002, p. 21).

Professionalization may be defined as the process by which the administrators of the bureaucracy credential themselves as well as those practitioners (teachers, counselors, school nurses) who seek a license to practice within the bureaucracy. Prior to 1800s, few schools required that teachers possess specific professional skills as parent/community boards appeared more concerned about the moral qualifications of teachers (Spring, 2005). In the latter 1800s, normal schools were developed to educate young people, especially women, for the increasing demand for qualified teachers (Pulliam, 2003, pp. 146–148). At the same time, states had begun to require licensing of teachers to assure quality control. In this professional education of teachers, teachers acquired shared standards of professional practice.

In the latter 1800s, 4-year colleges added programs to prepare teachers and administrators for roles in public schooling. During the beginning of the twentieth century, the normal schools, considered acceptable professional education in the 1800s, were gradually absorbed by colleges and universities. During the second half of the 20th-century, requirements to secure a state teaching license increased from the 4-year baccalaureate degree to completion of a 5-year approved college program (Tyler, 1992). Policymakers across many states believed that teachers should be better educated because the quality of the next generation of American citizens was in the hands of the public school teacher.

As the public schools acquired layer after layer of administrative bureaucracy both at the local and state levels, families and community groups were disconnected from the decision-making within public schools (Davies, 2000–2006). In particular, parents felt powerless over this increasingly complex system. The system controlled governance of the schools as well as the professional requirements for those who sought employment in these schools. In addition, the continued press for more education for teachers separated the social and cultural level of the teacher from that of the school's parents in many communities and urban centers. Shipman (1987–2006) reported that lower class parents were hesitant to enter schools because schools belonged to the middle and upper class professionals.

This rapid increase in the number of schools, development of a supporting hierarchy of administration, and rising requirements to serve as a teacher or administrator changed the human relationships between the family and the public schools. The United States education system evolved into a widespread agency with bureaucratization and professionalization of personnel. This bureaucratization of the educational system and increased professionalization of teachers have reduced parental control over school administration, curriculum content, and hiring faculty. In addition, the professionalization of faculty has separated the teacher from the parent, placing teachers and school administrators in the roles of expert educators. The door between the public school and the families the school served was shut (Goodlad, Klein, & Associates, 1970).

PARENTAL CHALLENGES TO PUBLIC SCHOOL BUREAUCRACY

The Development of the Parent/Teacher Association

The change in the power relationship between family and public school was perceived by parents in late 1800s. Mothers sought intervention and formed the National Congress of Mothers (NCM) in 1897. This group, comprising middle and upper class mothers, met with teachers on Saturdays and expressed their concerns to the school principal through petitions. These mothers studied school curricula, became informed about child growth and development, and encouraged other parents to be active in the school. They were particularly active in securing public school kindergarten programs and health programs. The NCM worked for children and youth programs through national, state, and local volunteer units.

The influence of NCMs spread rapidly and formed the basis of the Parent/Teacher Association (PTA). Across the country, PTAs quickly captured the interest of families, who were deeply devoted to improving the schools (Butts & Cremin, 1953). PTAs connected the home and school during the first part of the twentieth century. The PTA helped to "Americanize newcomers to the country and to teach middle class parenting" (Davies, 2002–2006). By the 1940s, parents of all social classes considered the monthly PTA meeting a mandatory community event.

During the second half of the twentieth century, PTAs added students to become PTSA, a group that existed on almost every American school site. The PTA or PTSA actively remain at school sites across the country. Local, state and national offices of this organization are an unharnessed force to promote policy and legislative support for diverse types of parental involvement.

Court Challenges

During the last three decades of the twentieth century, parents increasingly have resorted to courts in order to effect changes within the bureaucracy of the public schools. These parents began to hammer at the public school monolith, created by a century of increasing school bureaucracy. They were joined by social reformers. Their concerted efforts were loud and demanding. Rivlin (1964) remarked that:

> As parents became more enlightened with more education they became more vocal in their demands as to what schools should offer. The parents of American school children are increasingly vocal. It is to be expected that parents who hear the spectacular charges that are made by critics of education should wonder why changes are not made in the way schools are run. (n.p.)

Parents became involved in legal battles which focused on equality of educational opportunities (Wirt & Kirst, 1975). In a landmark court case, Brown v. Board of Education (1954) of Topeka, Kansas, the court ruled that separate schools for black and white children were not providing equality of educational opportunity. The importance of family involvement connected to student achievement was placed in the forefront of U.S. public policy by a large research study that was a direct response to the Civil Rights Act of 1964 (Coleman, 1966). This national survey was commissioned to focus on problems related to academic achievement by children from lower socioeconomic homes or "disadvantaged" homes. This data provided the evidence on which federal legislation was crafted. This report noted significant differences among student academic achievement across socioeconomic levels–namely, children from middle and upper class families had higher GPAs and higher graduation rates from high school and college. In 1966, Coleman's report to U.S. Department of Education, known commonly as the Coleman Study, provided results from a series of data analyses from this national survey. Findings revealed that the effect of outside school factors on student academic achievement was greater than inside school factors. This significant finding led to dialogue on the merits of parent involvement in schooling and connected that dialogue to future political action and educational research.

In conjunction with court rulings, parent involvement was assisted by the diligent labors of educational researchers whose studies pointed out the positive influence parent involvement and parent education had upon student achievement in schools. This knowledge was incorporated into educational legislation, which mandated parent involvement components. The first federally funded legislation, namely Project Head Start in 1964 for disadvantaged children in the inner cities and the Elementary and Secondary Education Act of 1965 required that parents serve on school advisory boards and participate in classroom activities (The Economic Opportunity Act, 1964). Education of the Handicapped Children Act (1975) required parents be an active partner in determining their child's educational program. Each handicapped student was to have an individually developed program. This program was to be developed by teacher, parent, child, and specialists. Parents were mandated to initiate the child's entrance and exit from the program.

Following the development of Head Start programs, there was increased growth in early childhood education programs for all social classes. This increase was directly related to increased numbers of mothers, single and married, participating in the workforce outside the home while their children were still very young. Information generated by Head Start and other federally funded research studies promoted parent involvement in these programs (The Economic Opportunity Act, 1964). Forms of parent involvement included serving on advisory boards, acting as a teacher assistant in the classroom, participating in school events, working in the school office and other related school activities, and participating in parent education classes. The early childhood programs encouraged an open dialogue between the professional teacher and the parent. Many policymakers of the 1990s advocate that the model of parent involvement developed in early childhood programs be emulated in the elementary and secondary schools (Tyler, 1992).

The ruling from Brown v. Board of Education (1954) led to several desegregation cases in major cities such as Boston, Detroit, and

Los Angeles, which forced public schools to reorganize student populations to reflect ethnic diversity. Serrano v. Priest of 1971, a suit involving Serrano, a public school parent, resulted in a decision ordering statewide equalization of school funding. Lau v. Nichols (1974) promoted bilingual education programs so that non-English speaking students equally benefited from public education. The ruling on *Pennsylvania Association for Retarded Children v. Commonwealth of Pennsylvania* (Pennsylvania Assn. for Retarded Children v. Pennsylvania, 1972) led to legislation for equal access for handicapped children. Families acting as activists in the courtroom were regaining their power in the educational opportunities of their children.

PROFESSIONAL SUPPORT FOR FAMILY INVOLVEMENT IN SCHOOLS

Support for parent involvement emerged within schools of higher education. Educators observed the educational advantage of parent involvement. The efforts of Davies, an influential educator and researcher on parent involvement, promoted the development of organized activity on family-community involvement throughout the United States and beyond. Davies founded the Institute for Responsive Education (2002), a forerunner of contemporary associations involved in research and practice in family and community involvement. Davis, Shipman, Moles, and others met at the American Educational Research Association (AERA) and formed the Special Interest Group (SIG) Parents as Educators (Shipman, 1987–2006). This group, later renamed as the Family-School-Community Partnership SIG to incorporate the emerging wider scope of family-community involvement, has continued to connect researchers and educators. Beginning in 2001, members of the group under the guidance of Hiatt-Michael have created practitioner-friendly monographs supported by research. In the 1980s at John Hopkins, Epstein brought together research and researchers with practice and practitioners through the National Network of Partnership Schools. Her models—*Overlapping Spheres of Influence* and *Six Types of Parent Involvement*-continue to influence research and practice across the country (Simon & Epstein, 2001, pp. 1–24). Redding (2005) and the Academic Development Institute in Lincoln, Illinois, has provided a series of activities promoting parent involvement within the region and, since 1991, is expanding the influence of research with a scholarly journal to disseminate research findings across the nation.

A summary of research literature on parent involvement across cultures, school types, and geographic area confirms the importance of parent involvement (Epstein, 2001; Henderson & Mapp, 2002). Teachers' and principals' efforts to involve families promotes higher student attendance rates, lower suspension and expulsion rates, higher graduation rates, more accurate diagnosis of students for educational placement, higher satisfaction with the school, student improved goal-setting and pride in school work, and most notably, higher academic achievement in reading and math.

FAMILY INVOLVEMENT OPTIONS

Homeschooling

In response to desegregation rulings, school districts created plans publicly to transport children from neighborhood schools in order to create ethnically diverse schools. Many parents became so enraged with this situation that they removed their children from public schools and enrolled them in private schools, created new schools, or began home schooling. Home schooling, ardently advocated by John Holt in the 1970s, has become a powerful parental involvement outcome of the desegregation movement (Fantini, 1986–1989; Meighan, 1995). Armed with knowledge of court cases and parents' rights over their child's education, these parents are teaching their children at home (Home School Legal Defense Association, 2006; Millard, 1989). In many states, the parents work under the auspices of a licensed public school teacher. Although the number of children in home schools (less than 2% of K-12 school age population) is small in comparison to the number in public schools, a federal report indicates that their numbers are increasing (National Center of Educational Statistics, 2003). As part of a national survey of parents regarding schooling, those parents who were home schooling their children replied that they chose to home school because they were concerned about the school environment (31%), they were dissatisfied with academic instruction (16%), or they wanted to provide religious and moral instruction (30%) for their children.

Public School Restructuring and Site-based Management

School restructuring, a major movement expressed in educational literature and professional addresses, commenced in the mid-1980s. This movement opens the doors of all public schools to increased family involvement. School restructuring advocates site-based management, in which school districts return significant decision-making control to local schools. Chicago Public Schools is the beacon of school restructuring and site-based management (Chicago Public Schools, 2006). The movement commenced in 1989 and has become an expected school governance model in that city. Each school is to have a Local School Council whose membership must include a majority of local school parents. Members are elected by their peers at each school. This council determines curriculum, creates budgets, and hires the site administrator and faculty. This movement holds promise to restore local parental control. Funds to support the development of school restructuring have been provided by many states. However, No Child Left Behind's (NCLB) (2005) mandates for state standards and high stakes testing for accountability have decreased efforts in school restructuring during the past 5 years.

School Vouchers and Charter Schools

Vouchers and charter schools are viewed in the long term as a legacy of the *Brown* court case (Stulberg, 2006). Twelve states have supported parental choice in the form of voucher plans and others are considering various forms of school vouchers (Forster, 2006). Milton Friedman (1955; Sipchen, 2006), an ardent believer in an open and free economy, convincingly argues for pubic choice and support of private schools. He supports minimum state-regulated standards for all schools and government-supported vouchers that should be used by parents to select the appropriate school for their children. In the states of Maine and Vermont, rural families have utilized local tuition programs to send their children to non public schools since 1800s (Peterson, 2005). Other states vary in the restrictions regarding parental voucher programs; these state or local programs may offer a tuition voucher, state tax credit, or a scholarship to students who are attending low achieving public schools. When provided the option of using a school voucher, parental participation varies from a low of

2%, such as Washington DC, to moderate of 8% as Cleveland to a high of 21% in Milwaukee, a city which has utilized vouchers for over 30 years. About 130,000 children utilize vouchers for public education across United States (Forster, 2006).

While school vouchers had received limited widespread appeal, the charter school concept has captured national attention. Charter schools are "a new breed of public school-a hybrid that mixes traditional public schools (universal access and public funding) with elements associated with private schools (choice, autonomy, and flexibility) (Miron & Nelson, 2002, p. 2). Magnet schools became the popular public school response to desegregation in 1970s and 1980s and served as the catalyst for the 1990s charter school movement. Cutler (2000) reported that between 1991 and 1999, 35 states passed laws approving charter schools, schools that should involve parents in all aspects of school decision-making. In 2006, 40 states and DC have laws providing for charter schools, and none have removed an existing law (Center for Education Reform, 2006). No state's charter law permits selective admissions so charter schools serve as public schools.

Moe, as cited by Merrifield (2006), touts "Charters have become the consensus approach to school choice in American education" (p. 4). Over 4,000 charter schools exist across all 50 states, and approximately 1.1 millon children attend these schools (Center for Education Reform, 2006). During 2005–2006, the number of charter schools increased 13%. Arizona has the most charter schools for the population followed by California, Florida, Ohio, Texas, and Michigan. Although the charter school movement is fraught with debate, charter schools hold the best promise for public school choice for all types of families (Brouillette, 2002; Sarason, 1998; Vergari, 2002). A Harvard University report indicated that the longer a charter school existed, the higher student achievement scores became (Hoxby, 2004). A comparison of student achievement scores between charter schools who had existed nine years or more and local comparison schools revealed that charter school student scores were 10% higher than the regular public school student test scores.

Under *No Child Left Behind* (U.S. Department of Education, 2002), these options are listed for school choices: supplemental educational services for special needs and at-risk children, charter schools, magnet schools, private education, home schooling, and public school choice. This law requires that states and local school districts provide information to parents so that parents can make informed choices about schooling options for their children.

A REVIEW OF PAST AND LOOKING FORWARD

Review

The pivotal role played by families in the education of their children during the colonial period of America changed to that of legislated bystander during the industrial revolution of the 1800s and 1900s. The economic forces that kept children on the farm to assist their families, and acquire the knowledge and trade of farming diminished. As America became industrialized, youth as well as families moved to urban areas to seek work. Immigrants fed the increasing factories' requirement for cheap labor. Both parents and children supported the family economic unit. Unions pushed for child labor, compulsory education, and truancy from school laws to remove the option of inexpensive child labor to factories and businesses.

At the same time, families observed that education changed the economic conditions of others. Length and quality of education assumed increasing worth during 1900s. The common school education espoused by Jefferson in early 1800s was replaced by serious widespread concern for "at-risk" students, those who did not graduate from high school in the second half of the 1900s. Family size decreased throughout the 1900s and parents assumed the full financial support of their offspring.

The press toward opening the schools again to parental control and school choice came from several forces. Politically, the government became concerned about human capital, not simply material capital. Quality education for all children was in the best interests of any country as well as any family engaged in economic competition with other countries and their children. The government and parent legal cases of the second half of 1900s created the foundation for change to desegregation of publicly-funded schools and equal access to educational opportunities for all children. Families were becoming better educated and closing the gap between the education of public school teachers and parents. The fulltime level of parent involvement in their children's education of the agrarian seventeenth century changed to the absentee partner during the bureaucratic factory model schools of the industrial revolution in 1800s and 1900s. The rapid growth of urban centers and rapidly increasing school population led to increased numbers of school administration and large bureaucratic public school districts.

The doors of the public schools appear to be opening again, slowly at first, but gathering momentum, towards schooling which increasingly involves families. This movement is propelled by the social force of the changing lives and structure of families plus the political and economic imperatives for an educated and skilled workforce.

Social and Cultural Forces

Governmental policy seems to be ignoring current social realities of families in America. The changing demographics of families and communities are seldom considered by schools that operate within a structure and system established in 1800s. Educators' expectations regarding family involvement in schools must take into account these changing demographics in the diversity of families. These changing demographics affect every part of American, not simply ports of entry or border towns (Girard, 2005). Waves of immigration that had been more confined to larger cities are now spreading to even pockets in rural and suburban areas. Schools cite dealing with families in which English is the second language as a rising challenge.

Family composition, size, leadership, diversity, type of work, hours of work, and communication patterns have been changing during the past century, especially since 1960 (Meyers, 2005). Families are smaller, averaging 1.8 children per household (U. S. Census, 2001). Divorce has increased the number of families headed by a single parent, nearing one-third of families. Immigration across the globe has altered diversity of most schools. For example, approximately 5.5 million English Language Learners are enrolled in public schools, a change from 2 million in 1993 (Girard, 2005). More mothers and fathers share family leadership, more jobs exist in cubicles with social interaction occurring through technology, hours of work have lengthened and diversified throughout the day, and, increasingly, more parents are employed in different patterns of work hours.

Meyers (2005) shared that a greater number of Americans report that they work more than 100 hours a week, an increase from prior years. The 24/7 demand for service has increased positions for both semiskilled and skilled workers at all hours. Some parents must be away from the home because their employment is nationally or more likely internationally based, with their services needed after standard work hours to accommodate the business needs in various time zones around the world.

Economic Forces

The movement is affected by the emerging culture based on information technology and telecommunications on the lives of children, parents, and schools. Critical information is available to families on the Internet in a moment; the elevation of teachers' expertise over parents is being diminished.

Educators are stressing a change in teacher preparation toward teaching children to be prepared to lives in a global and self-directed work world. Parents and teachers should be preparing children for "an education that teaches students to frame their own problems, organize themselves, and persevere in complex project" (Spring, 2004, p. 28). The service-oriented, knowledge-directed economy will depend on every citizen utilizing their own unique set of talents. Minimum standards, promoted in the past for citizenship and employment in the areas of reading, writing, and math, have become basic requirements to handle everyone's life. In addition, searches on the Internet for banking, shopping, health needs, and the like require knowledge and skills of technology, categorization, and accepted business processes. Modern life is complex and demands so much more than in the 1800s that the schools must open the doors to parents, all family members, and the community in order to meet public demands for educated students that can compete in the world market. Public schooling is a significant economic operation, accounting for about 4% of gross domestic process, in America (National Center for Educational Statistics, 2005).

Political Force

Armed with the research data provided by educators, national politicians consider parent involvement as a major issue in public schooling. *Goals 2000* (1994) included parent involvement as one of eight national goals and NCLB (2005) mandates that all schools provide families information on their rights and educational opportunities and educational achievements of their children. The politics of site-based management, school choice, home schooling, and equal educational opportunity affect all elements of American education-school organization, governance, school finance, curriculum, and teacher education. These are options that have promise to alter the tight bureaucracy of the contemporary public schools and open the doors to families and educational reform.

CONCLUDING REMARKS

The debate over the role of public schools and the degree of parent involvement continues (Tyack, 2004). At present a tension often exists between professionals, on the one hand, who espouse the concept that they alone are qualified to make complex decisions affecting the education of our nation's children, and parents, on the other hand, who believe that they should have a voice in their children's compensatory public education. The late 1990s witnessed other open forums for dialogue between the two groups, such as site-based management meetings, development of school-based parent centers, local meetings to discuss charter school options, home-schooling contracts, and discussion regarding parent vouchers. Such forums will provide opportunities to bridge the gap between the two groups and create new ways for parents and public school professionals to interact. Collaboration among the various constituencies is critical to mutual understanding and support between the school and home, as interdependent not independent entities.

REFERENCES

Beisaw, A. M., & Gibb, J. G. (2004). Beyond slate pencils: Schoolhouse artifacts and community history. Paper presented at the Annual Meeting of the Society for Historical Archeology Conference, St. Louis, MO. Retrieved October 10, 2006, from http://bingweb binghamton.edu.

Berger, E. H. (1981). *Parents as partners*. St. Louis: The C.V. Mosby Co.

Blumenfeld, S. L. (1991, April). *Are compulsory school attendance laws necessary?* Retrieved June 25, 2006, from http://www.fff.org/freedom/0491c.asp.

Brouillette, L. (2002). *Charter schools: Lessons in School reform*. Mahwah, NJ: Lawrence Erlbaum Associates.

Brown, V. Board of Educ., 347 U.S. 483 (1954).

Bush, G. W. (April, 2005). The Whitehouse. Retrieved on October 18, 2007, from http://whitehouse.gov/news/reports/no-child-left-behind.html.

Butts, F. R., & Cremin, L. A. (1953). *A history of education in American culture.* New York: Henry Holt and Company.

Center for Education Reform. (2006). *Charter schools.* Retrieved July 3, 2006, from http://edreform.com/index.cfm?fuseaction=statestats&psectionid=15&csectionid=44.

Chicago Public Schools. (2006). *Local school councils.* Retrieved June 1, 2006, from http://www.cps.k12.il.us/aboutcps/departments/oscr/local_school_councils.html.

Chubb, J. E., & Moe, T. M. (1990). *Politics, markets & America's schools.* Washington, DC: The Brookings Institution.

Coleman, J. S. (1966). *Equality of educational opportunity.* Washington, DC: U.S. Government Printing Office.

Coleman, J. S., Huffer, T., & Kilgore, S. (1982). *High school achievement: Public, catholic and private schools.* New York: Basic Books.

Cremin, L. A. (1961). *Transformation of the American school: Progressivism in American Education.* New York: Vintage Books.

Cutler, W. W. III. (2000). *Parents and schools: The 150-year struggle for control in American education.* Chicago: The University of Chicago Press.

Davies, D. (2002–2006). Interviews with author. Institute of Responsive Education. Marblehead, MA.

DeTocqueville, A. (1946). *Democracy in America.* (H. Reeve, Trans.). London: Oxford University Press, Inc. (Original work published in 1835).

Education of the Handicapped Children Act, P.L. 94–142 (1975).

Elementary and Secondary Education Act, 20 U.S.C. § 6301 (1965).

Epstein, J. L. (2001). *School, family, and community partnerships: Preparing educators and improving schools.* Boulder, CO: Westview Press.

Fantini, M. (1986–1989). *Interviews with author.* University of Massachusetts.

Forster, G. (2006). *Using school choice: Analyzing how parents access educational freedom.* Alliance for School Choice, Milton and Rose D. Foundation. Retrieved July 3, 2006, from http://www.allianceforschoolchoice.org/research_school_choice.aspx?IIcatid=12&iiid=2414.

Friedman, M. (1955). The role of government in education. *In Economics and the public interest.* New Brunswick, NJ: Rutgers University Press.

Gates, W. (2005). *Remarks at national education summit on high schools.* Retrieved December 10, 2005, from http://www.gatesfoundation.org/mediacenter/speeches/billgspeeches/bgspeechnga-050226.htm.

Gibbs, N. (2005, February 21). What teachers hate about parents. *Time, 165.*

Girard, K. (2005, November). Lost in translation: How do you say, "Tomorrow's assignment is..." in 460 languages? *Edutopia, 1,* 34–38.

Goodlad, J. I., Klein, M. F., & Associates. (1970). *Behind the classroom door.* Worthington, OH: Charles A. Jones Publishing Company.

Henderson, A. T., & Mapp, K. L. (2002). *A new wave of evidence: The impact of school, family, and community connections on student achievement.* Austin, TX: Southwest Educational Development Laboratory, National Center for Family & Community Connections with Schools.

Hiatt-Michael, D. B. (2005). *Promising practices for family involvement in schooling across the continents.* Greenwich, CT: Information Age Publishing.

Hiatt-Michael, D. B. (2001). Parent involvement in American public schools: A historical perspective, 1642–2000. In S. Redding & L. Thomas (Eds.), *The community of the school* (pp. 247–258). Lincoln, IL: Academic Development Institute.

Home School Legal Defense Association. (2006). *A fifteen year perspective.* Retrieved July 3, 2006, from http://www.hslda.org/about/history/perspective.asp.

Hoxby, C. (2004, December 14). *New Harvard study shows charter schools are working: charter school students more likely to be proficient in reading and math than their regular public school counterparts.* Retrieved July 3, 2006, from http://www.ed.gov/news/newsletters/extracredit/2004/12/1214.html

Jefferson, T., & Lee, G. C. (1961). *Crusade against ignorance: Thomas Jefferson on education.* New York: Teachers College Press. (Original work published 1779).

Katz, M. B. (1971). *Class bureaucracy and schools.* New York: Praeger Publishers.

Katz, M. B. (1971, Summer). From voluntarism to bureaucracy in American education. *Sociology of Education, 44,* 297–332.

Lau v. Nichols, 414 U.S. 563 (1974).

Mann, H. (1957). *The republic and the school* L. Fremin (Ed.), New York: Bureau of Publications, Teachers College, Columbia University.

Meighan, R. (1995). *John Holt: Personalized education and the reconstruction of schooling.* Nottingham, UK: Educational Heretics Press.

Merrifield, J. (2006). Charter laws: Disaster, detour, irrelevant or reform tool? *Journal of School Choice, 1,* 3–22.

Meyers, M. K. (2005, March). *The intersection of child care and low-wage employment.* Panelist at the Annual Meeting of the Child Care Policy Research Consortium. Baltimore, MD.

Millard, A. W. (1989). *Home schools and the law.* Unpublished manuscript, Pepperdine University.

Miron, G., & Nelson, C. (2002). *What's public about charter schools? Lessons learned about choice and accountability.* Thousand Oaks, CA: Corwin Press.

National Center for Educational Statistics. (2005). *Public efforts to fund elementary and secondary education.* Retrieved June 26, 2006, from http://nces.ed.gov/programs/coe 2005/section4/indicator39.asp.

National Center for Educational Statistics. (2006). *Parental choice of schools.* Retrieved June 26, 2006, from http://nces.ed.gov/programs/coe2006/section4/indicator36.asp.

National Center for Educational Statistics. (2003). *Homeschooling in the United States: 2003: Executive summary.* Retrieved June 30, 2006, from http://nces.ed.gov/pubs2006/homeschool/.

National Commission on Excellence in Education. (1983). *A nation at risk: The imperative for educational reform.* Washington, DC: U.S. Government Printing Office.

Pennsylvania Assn. for Retarded Children v. Pennsylvania, 343F. Supp. 279 (E.D. Pa. 1972).

Peterson, K. (2005). School vouchers slow to spread. Retrieved June 30, 2006, from http://nces.edgov/programs/coe2005/section4/indicator39.asp.

Petrosino, P., & Spiegel, L. (2006). *No parent left behind: A guide to working with your child's school*. Lanham, MD: Rowman & Littlefield Education.

Pulliam, J. D. (2003). *History of education in America* (8th ed.). Columbus: Merrill Publishing Company.

Ravitch, D. (1995). *Learning from the past: What history teaches us about school reform*. Baltimore, MD: John Hopkins University Press.

Redding, S. (2005, Spring/Summer). From the executive editor: Rallying the troops. *The School Community Journal, 15*, 7–13.

Rippa, S. A. (1988). *Education in a free society: An American history* (6th ed.). New York: Longman.

Rivlin, H. N. (1964). *The professional responsibility for educational change. Changes in teacher education: An appraisal report*. Washington, DC: National Commission on Teacher Education and Professional Standards, Columbus Conference, National Education Association of the U.S.

Rose, L. C., & Gallup, A. M. (2006). The 38th annual Phi Delta Kappa/Gallup poll of public's attitudes toward the public schools. *Phi Delta Kappan, 88*, 42–53.

Sarason, S. B. (1998). *Charter schools: Another flawed educational reform?* New York: Teachers College Press.

Sarason, S. B. (1995). *Parental Involvement and the political principle*. San Francisco: Jossey-Bass.

Serrano v. Priest, 5 Cal.3d 584 (1971)

Shipman, V. (1987–2006). *Interviews with author.*Department of Family Studies, University of New Mexico.

Shostak, A. B. (1967, February). Education and the family. *Journal of Marriage and the Family, 29*, 124–139.

Simon, B. S., & Epstein, J. L. (2001). School, family, and community partnerships: Linking theory to practice. In D. B. Hiatt-Michael (Ed.), *Promising practices for family involvement in schools*. Greenwich, CT: Information Age Publishing.

Sipchen, B. (2006, July 3). Are public schools worth the effort? *Los Angeles Times*, A1.

Spring, J. (2005). *The American school 1642–2004* (6th ed.). New York: McGraw Hill.

Spring, J. (2004). *American education* (11th ed.). Boston, MA: McGraw Hill.

Stulberg, L. M. (2006). School choice discourse and the legacy of Brown. *Journal of School Choice, 1*, 23–46.

The Constitution of the United States of America (1789). Retrieved June 25, 2006, from http://www.gpoaccess.gov/constitution/html/conamt.html.

The Constitution of the United States of America, Amendments, Article X. (1789). Retrieved June 25, 2006, from http://www.gpoaccess.gov/constitution/html/conamt.html.

The Economic Opportunity Act of 1964, 6 U.S.C.A. § 2701 *et seq.*

Tyack, D. B. (2004). *Seeking common ground: Public schools in a diverse society*. Cambridge, MA: Harvard University Press.

Tyack, D. B. (1974). *The one best system: A history of American urban education*. Cambridge, MA: Harvard University Press.

Tyler, R. W. (1979–1993). *Interviews with author*. University of Chicago.

U. S. Census. (2001). Retrieved July 3, 2006, from http://census.gov/prod/2001pubs/c2kbr018.pdf.

U.S. Department of Education. (1994). *National education goals*. Washington, DC: Author.

U.S. Department of Education. (2002). *No child left behind act*. Retrieved December 10, 2005, from the National Education Association website: http://www.nea.org/esea/index.html.

Vergari, S. (2002). *The charter school landscape*. Pittsburgh, PA: University of Pittsburgh Press.

Wirt, F. M., & Kirst, M. W. (1975). *Political and social foundations of education*. Berkeley, CA: McCutcheon Publishing Corp.

Father Involvement and Children's Early Learning: A Critical Review of Published Empirical Work from the Past 15 Years

Jason Downer
Rodrigo Campos
Christine McWayne
Tara Gartner

ABSTRACT. Parent involvement research predominantly focuses on the involvement of mothers in children's educational experiences, and rarely speaks to the role of the "other" parent – fathers. Yet, there is building interest in the role that fathers play in children's development, and how this role may be especially salient during early childhood and the transition into formal schooling. This review critically evaluates father involvement literature from 1990 to 2005 within this early childhood population. In particular, it provides systematic evidence that to some degree researchers have been responsive to recent critiques, and lays out a path of sampling, methodological and conceptual challenges still left to be tackled.

Jason Downer, PhD, is affiliated with Center for Advanced Study of Teaching and Learning, Charlottesville, MA. Christine M. McWayne, PhD, and Tara Gartner are affiliated with Department of Applied Psychology, New York University, New York NY.

INTRODUCTION

More than ever, young children are entering kindergarten and 1st grade without the requisite academic, social, emotional, and language skills to make use of classroom resources and successfully adjust to school (National Center for Education Statistics [NCES], 2000; Rimm-Kaufman, Pianta, & Cox, 2000). These early difficulties occur disproportionably for children from economically disadvantaged families and tend to persist through elementary school and beyond (Alexander, Entwisle, & Kabbani, 2001; Consortium of Longitudinal Studies, 1983; National Center for Education Statistics, 2002; Reynolds, 1994; Stevenson & Newman, 1986). However, several have argued from a developmental/ecological perspective that "school readiness" is as much about the contextual and relational supports available to children prior to and during the transition into school as it is about children's actual cognitive and social skills (Kagan & Kauerz, 2007; Meisels, 1999; Rimm-Kaufman & Pianta, 2000). Recent research in early childhood, therefore, has focused on understanding variability in young children's environment and relational experiences from preschool to early elementary school, in order to identify contextual inputs that could be targets for intervention (e.g., Ripple, Gilliam, Chanana, & Zigler, 1999).

Family involvement, in its many forms and conceptualizations (Christenson, 1999; Epstein, 1996; Fantuzzo, Tighe, & Childs, 2000), has surfaced as an especially important relational resource during early childhood and elementary school, especially for low-income and minority children (Jeynes, 2003; Lee & Bowen, 2006). Recent meta-analyses substantiate that the association between parent involvement and academic achievement is both positive and relatively strong across many studies of school-aged children (Fan & Chen, 2001; Jeynes, 2005; Jeynes, 2007). And yet, family involvement research throughout the years has predominantly referred to the involvement of mothers in children's educational experiences, meaning that the general parent involvement literature rarely speaks to the role of the "other" parent – fathers. Importantly, father-specific studies suggest that men may be involved with children in ways that are distinct from mothers (Hawkins & Palkovitz, 1999; Marsiglio, Day, & Lamb, 2000; Roggman, Fitzgerald, Bradley, & Raikes, 2002) and that fathering behaviors can contribute uniquely to children's development (Grossmann, Grossmann, Fremmer-Bombik, Kindler, Scheuerer-Englisch, & Zimmerman, 2002; Lamb & Tamis-LeMonda, 2004; Paquette, 2004). Such findings, combined with the well-publicized rise in the number of "fatherless" families in the United States (Blankenhorn, 1995), have sparked rising empirical inquiry into the extent to which fathers may be involved in the lives and, particularly, early education of young children.

Contemporary father involvement researchers have been heavily influenced by developmental/ecological theory, leading to increased recognition of the complexity of male involvement in families. Within such a model, children's interactions within dyads (e.g., father-child interactions) and settings (e.g., families, classrooms) are conceptualized as the primary means by which early learning occurs (Bronfenbrenner & Morris, 1998). And yet, developmental/ ecological theory acknowledges the transactional nature of interactions between dyads and settings, highlighting the indirect means through which fathers might bolster the developmental and educational progress of young children. Guided by this theoretical lens, the objective of this review is to summarize and critically appraise father involvement research conducted from 1990 to 2005 within the early childhood population (ages 0–6). This work distinguishes itself from other recent reviews of father involvement research in its systematic approach, focus on published empirical articles, inclusion of diverse father samples, and exclusive emphasis on young children.

Early Childhood Education Context

Nation-wide focus on early childhood education has amplified in recent years, leading to greater public investment in providing high quality preschool experiences for all children (National Institute for Early Education Research, 2005; West, Denton, & Germino-Hausken, 2000) and prompting some to consider preschool for 3- and 4-year-olds to be the "new" kindergarten (Pianta, 2005). This interest has been fueled in part by growing evidence that the transition into elementary school is a sensitive period for children's development (Entwisle & Alexander, 1998; Shonkoff & Phillips, 2000) *and* the formation of connections between families and schools (Christenson, 1999; Pianta & Kraft-Sayre, 2003). In fact, a final report from the National Governors' Association Task Force on School Readiness in 2005 affirmed that the "responsibility for school readiness lies not with children, but with the adults who care for them and the systems that support them" (p. 31).

Another major contributor to the enhanced focus on early childhood is the *No Child Left Behind Act*, which in 2001 set forth mandatory standardized testing in third grades across the country in order to hold schools accountable for student progress. Given these academic expectations in early elementary school, superintendents, principals, and teachers are paying more attention to children's socioemotional and academic skills upon entrance into kindergarten. Unfortunately, strong empirical evidence indicates that many young children, and in particular those from economically disadvantaged families, are entering kindergarten and first grade without essential skills that provide a solid foundation for early learning and success (National Center for Educational Statistics, 2000). In addition, children from low-income families tend to have less access to potentially supportive relationships, interactions and educational resources, such as high quality classroom environments (Pianta, Howes, Burchinal, Bryant, Clifford, Early, & Barbarin, 2005), language- and literacy-rich households (National Institute of Child Health and Human Development, Early Child Care Research Network, 2000), and regular contact with a residential father (Coley, 2001).

Importance of Fathers During Early Childhood

Paralleling the fervor around early childhood education has been a growing interest in the role that fathers play in children's development and how this role may be especially salient during early childhood and the transition into formal schooling. Why is the study of fatherhood in early childhood worthy of special attention? As early as 1975, Lamb suggested that, in contrast to a mother's role of caretaker, a father's socializing role might involve introducing children to the world and realities outside the home. For a growing number of youth today, preschool is one of their first forays into the world outside of their family household and therefore a propitious moment for their fathers to take on a unique caretaking role. Fathers appear poised to offer assistance to children during this early childhood

period by providing linguistically challenging communicative environments (Lamb & Tamis-LeMonda, 2004; Leaper, Anderson, &
Sanders, 1998) and everyday interactions that place demands on children's self-regulatory capacities (Grossmann et al., 2002; Paquette,
2004). By taxing children's language capacity and self-regulatory
skills in new and unforeseen ways, theorists have suggested that
fathers may uniquely prepare children to enter classrooms in which
interactions with unfamiliar peers and teachers can be both novel
and demanding. In addition, fathers appear to be most engaged with
and accessible to children during these early childhood years (Yeung,
Sandberg, Davis-Kean, & Hofferth, 2001). Given that fathers who
are involved early tend to remain so over time (Aldous, Mulligan,
& Bjarnason, 1998; National Institute of Child Health and Human
Development, Early Child Care Research Network, 2000), early
childhood becomes a logical period during which to learn more about
father involvement and its influences.

Recent Historical Context of Father Involvement Research

The 1980s and 1990s constituted a major shift in attention toward
fathers, beginning with efforts to improve child support responsibilities and leading toward multiple non profit and federal initiatives
to increase awareness of the importance of fatherhood (Annie E.
Casey, 2002). In 1994, the National Fatherhood Initiative (NFI),
organized around the goal of making father involvement a national
priority, sponsored its first National Summit on Fatherhood in
Dallas. Around the same time, the Annie E. Casey Foundation funded
the National Center on Fathers and Families (NCOFF) and the
National Practitioners Network for Fathers and Families (NPNFF)
to dually lead the empirical and practical realms of the fatherhood
movement. President Clinton, shortly thereafter, issued an Executive
Memorandum that directed all federal agencies to "engage and mean-
ingfully include fathers" and resulted in the Department of Health and
Human Services Fatherhood Initiative (Annie E. Casey, 2002). Riding
the momentum of so much national interest in fatherhood, a flurry of
empirical work at the turn of the century, including a father-specific
special issue in *Marriage & Family Review* (Peters, Peterson,
Steinmetz, & Day, 2000), reflected on how the research community
brought notice to, expanded, and improved the quality of fatherhood
research in the 1990s. Since then, fatherhood scholarship has continued

to flourish with multiple edited volumes (e.g., *Conceptualizing and Measuring Father Involvement* [Day & Lamb, 2004] and *Handbook of Father Involvement* [Tamis-LeMonda & Cabrera, 2002]) and the establishment of a new peer-reviewed journal entitled *Fathering*.

Notable Recent Reviews: Lessons Learned and Shortcomings

A handful of published manuscripts at the turn of the century made a substantial contribution to our understanding of fatherhood literature, in large part by representing a wide range of issues that included both macro level and group-specific foci. For instance, Cabrera and colleagues (Cabrera, Tamis-LeMonda, Bradley, Hofferth, & Lamb, 2000) offered a somewhat comprehensive analysis, which focused primarily on articulating a conceptualization of fatherhood within a dynamic sociocultural context. As the most systematic review of empirical work on fatherhood in the 1990s, Marsiglio and colleagues (Marsiglio, Amato, Day, & Lamb, 2000) summarized relevant theoretical and measurement issues in fatherhood research, reviewed 72 studies of two-parent households linking father involvement with child outcomes (55 of which included children between the ages of 0–19), and examined 38 studies of nonresidential fathers. The most recent reviews, by Nelson (2004) and Coley (2001), cover literature on particular subgroups, namely low-income, unmarried, and minority fathers of children across all age groups.

Several recommendations were forwarded by these authors to guide future inquiry. For example, it was suggested that greater consideration be given to the context within which fathering occurs. Specifically, more empirical study is needed to identify barriers and supports to fathering behaviors within the diverse ethnic, cultural, and family contexts. Another commonly cited recommendation from these reviews was to broaden the conceptualization of father involvement to more accurately reflect the "entire range of fathering experience" (Nelson, 2004, p. 446) thus moving further away from the absence-presence dichotomy popularized in the 1980s and recognizing the nuances and distinct contributions of fathering roles and behaviors. Other methodological issues were also raised such as the need for inclusion of fathers in large, national, and longitudinal studies and more attention to multi method, multi source assessment of both father involvement and child outcomes.

Despite playing a considerable role in the synthesis of fatherhood literature, there were limitations in the scope and/or approach of these recent reviews. Although comprehensive in their articulation of a new conceptualization of fatherhood, Cabrera and colleagues (2000) did not provide a systematic review of the literature. Marsiglio and colleagues (2000) did present a systematic analysis of the literature, yet, even this review was limited in its coverage of fatherhood "types," neglecting non-married and social fathers (i.e., males who are involved, but not the biological father or even necessarily a blood relative of the child), and could not comment upon literature in the early part of the 21st century or specific to early childhood. Finally, the two most recent reviews by Coley (2001) and Nelson (2004) were focused on specific subgroups, but collapsed the literature across all ages, not allowing for analysis within specific developmental periods.

These limitations have opened the door for the current review to make a distinct contribution to the field. First and foremost, whereas all previous reviews referenced studies of fathers with children of all ages, this review only examines studies that address father involvement during early childhood, thus allowing for an explicit focus on fathering during a critical developmental period. Second, we utilized a systematic approach to collecting published articles across the past 15 years, which extends the Marsiglio et al. (2000) review by 5 years and allows for a thorough, critical appraisal of whether the landscape of fatherhood scholarship for this group of children and their fathers has changed in ways recommended by lead scholars at the turn of the century. Finally, this review was all-inclusive when it came to defining the role of a father, thus encompassing studies with samples of mixed and underrepresented fathering subgroups (e.g., minority, social) so that conclusions might be reached about patterns of studies within and/or across groups.

Focus of Review

A developmental/ecological perspective of young children's transition from home into preschool, and then preschool into elementary school, recognizes the utility of identifying and examining relational assets to better understand children's early educational successes or challenges. Fathers are an often neglected piece of the relational puzzle within families and may serve a particularly important role in helping children venture successfully out of the family and into a school context. This literature review provides a systematic and critical examination of literature emphasizing father involvement with young children (ages 0–6) over the last 15 years. In a first step, the entire landscape of father involvement literature within this child population is described, in particular examining the extent to which turn of the century recommendations about methodology and sampling may be reflected in more recent publications. Then, a spotlight is trained on 90 empirical articles that focus exclusively on children ages 3–6 who are experiencing the all-important transition to school. Initially, these studies are examined for conceptual and methodological advances over time, followed by an in-depth review of findings from 32 studies concerning the link between father involvement and children's academic and socioemotional competence.

METHODS

Article Identification

An exhaustive literature search of the last 15 years (1990–2005) targeted peer-reviewed journal articles on father involvement with young children (ages 0–6). The selection criteria at this stage of the search were intentionally broad, with initial search efforts producing 1,210 article titles. The following keywords were used both independently and in combinations: father, male involvement, father involvement, Head Start, early childhood, and preschool. The keywords father, male involvement and father involvement served as anchors for each search combination. For the purposes of initial article identification, early childhood was defined as birth through the end of first grade. The following nine online databases were used for this investigation: *Education: A SAGE Full-Text Collections in Education, Psychology, and Sociology; ERIC; IBBS: International Bibliography of the Social Sciences; Linguistics & Language Behavior Abstract; Psych Info; Social Services Abstracts; and Sociological Abstracts.*

All article reference listings, including abstracts, were imported into *RefWorks*, a web-based bibliographic management software program. Duplicate articles were eliminated from the database, reducing the number of entries to 1,125 (see Figure 1 for a flowchart of how articles were identified for this review).

Key Exclusion Criteria

In the next phase of organization, all abstracts in *RefWorks* were reviewed for relevance and certain articles were excluded based on

FIGURE 1. Flowchart for Article Identification Procedure.

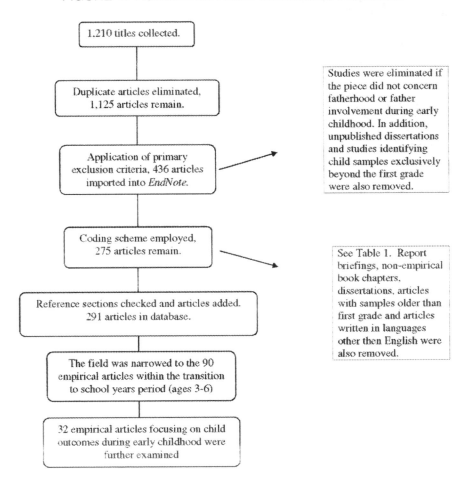

the following criteria. Studies were eliminated from the review if they exclusively focused on samples of children beyond first grade or did not directly address father involvement with children (e.g., position piece on why there are so few male teachers in early grades). Also, publication in a peer-reviewed journal was a central criterion for inclusion. Although some have argued for inclusion of unpublished work in reviews, such as dissertations (Cooper, 2003), this review provides a stringent focus on published articles that have reached the highest levels of scholarly and public scrutiny. Subsequent to excluding articles based on these three criteria, 436 references were exported from *RefWorks* into *EndNote*, a program which allowed for greater flexibility in coding and sorting.

Coding Approach

A coding scheme was used to organize the body of work into nine categories, related to a study's emphasis, content focus, methodology, and sampling (See Table 1); these codes were entered into the *EndNote* database for each article, which also offered coders the opportunity to further eliminate superfluous works. Articles were first coded according to their "Emphasis," including—Conceptual, Empirical, Review or meta-analysis, and Other (comprised position papers, policy pieces, editorials, etc.). Any article coded as "Empirical" was then specifically coded for content focus, methodological approach, and sample characteristics. For any of the coded categories, when sample information was omitted (e.g., many empirical articles did not report if their sample was made up of biological fathers or whether the father lived with the child) or ambiguous (e.g., loose language, such as "school-aged children" was common) an "NA" classification was used.

"Content focus" was organized into seven subcategories: Determinants, Child outcomes, Intervention, Well-being and identity, Descriptive, Perceptions, and Other. Articles were classified under the *Determinants* subcategory if results were presented from a study dedicated to examining determinants or correlates of father involvement (e.g., Is there a relationship between a father's level of education and the time he spends with his child?). The subcategory of *Intervention* was used for articles that reported results from evaluations of father involvement programs. Studies were coded under the *Child outcomes* subcategory when they examined how father involvement was associated with child competence and skills (e.g., academic, socioemotional). *Well-being and identity* articles were focused on characteristics of fathers as outcomes (e.g., anger, depression) or self-perceptions of fathering identity. There were also a set of articles coded as *Descriptive* in that they simply provided a description of what certain fathering behaviors looked like, or made comparisons of fathering to mothering. A small set of articles were coded as *Perceptions,* which includes studies that examined mothers' and

TABLE 1. Coding Categories for Father Involvement Articles.

1. Emphasis
   a. Theoretical/conceptual
   b. Empirical
   c. Literature review or meta-analysis
   d. Other (Position/Policy/Interview)
2. Content focus
   a. Determinants of father involvement
   b. intervention
   c. Child outcomes
   d. Well-being and identity
   e. Descriptive
   f. Perceptions
   g. Other
3. Methods
   a. Qualitative
   b. Quantitative
   c. Mixed methods
   d. NA
4. Age (Code a, b, c or d only if reports 90% or more of that variable)
   a. Infant (Below 3)
   b. Preschool (3–5)
   c. Kindergarten
   d. First
   e. Mix of early childhood
   f. NA
5. Relationship to child (Code a or b if reports 90% or more of that variable)
   a. Biological father
   b. Non-biological father or other relative
   c. Mixed
   NA
6. Residential status (Code a or b if reports 90% or more of that variable)
   a. Residential
   b. Non-residential
   c. Mixed
   d. NA
7. SES (Use poverty table) (Code a or b if reports 90% or more of that variable)
   a. Low SES
   b. Mid to high
   c. Mixed SES
   d. NA
8. Ethnicity (Code a or b if reports 90% or more of that variable)
   a. Minority
   b. Non-minority
   c. Mixed
   d. NA

(*Continued*)

TABLE 1. Continued.

9. Sample size
a. Small (<50)
b. Medium (50–300)
c. Large (>300)
NA

children's perceptions of the fathering role. All remaining articles fell into the subcategory of *Other*.

"Methods" were organized into three subcategories: Qualitative, Quantitative, and Mixed. *Qualitative* studies used methods such as open-ended interviews and focus groups, whereas *Quantitative* referred to methods such as surveys, observations, standardized interviews, etc., that resulted in quantitative data. Studies coded as *Mixed* incorporated both qualitative and quantitative methods.

Articles were organized around the following six sample characteristics: child age, father's relationship to the child, residential status of father, family socioeconomic status, father race/ethnicity, and sample size. Child age was categorized as: Infant/toddler (0–2), Preschool (3–4), Kindergarten (5), First grade (6), and Mixed. Father's relationship to the child was categorized as: Biological, Non biological/other relative, and Mixed. Residential status was coded as: Residential, Nonresidential, and Mixed. Socioeconomic status was categorized as Low, Mid to High, and Mixed, whereas race/ethnicity was coded as Minority, Nonminority, and Mixed. In order to determine whether the subcategory *Mixed* should be coded, a study's sample could not include 90% or more of any other coding subcategory. For example, in the case of "Child age," an article that reported a study sample consisting of 75% preschoolers and 25% first graders was coded *Mixed*. In contrast, an article that reported a sample including 91% preschoolers and 9% school-aged children was coded *Preschool*. This 90% criterion was established with the following in mind: when represented within 90% of the study's sample, a variable likely can be analyzed quantitatively with enough power (e.g., Analysis of Variance).

Reliability and Final Checks

Two trained independent coders performed coding duties. A preliminary check on intercoder reliability was performed on 15% of the first 100 articles, and reliability was established at 95%. Intercoder reliability was further assessed on 25% of the articles throughout the coding process, and reliability continued to be at or above 95%. Identified coding errors, only 1% of the total coding, were corrected ($n = 23$). Also, in order to ensure that the search was exhaustive, the reference sections of articles published from 2004 to 2005 were reviewed, as these articles were expected to be the most inclusive of related references. Titles were earmarked for relevance to the subject matter and cross-referenced against the existing review database. Articles that did not exist in the database were more closely examined and coded, leading to the addition of 13 articles (4%) and bringing the total number of articles in the database to 291 (see Table 2 for a summary of the coding results).

FINDINGS OF THE REVIEW

Findings based on a review of these 291 articles are organized into three sections. The first section provides a landscape view of literature focusing on father involvement with young children ages birth to 6 and examines the degree to which researchers have responded over time to earlier critiques of father-related empirical inquiry. The second section then concentrates on 90 articles specifically emphasizing children who are experiencing the transition into a school environment (ages 3–6) in order to systematically review conceptual and methodological advances and shortcomings (see articles in Reference section with asterisks). And finally, the third section provides a focused, critical review of findings from the 32 studies that examined the association between father involvement during the transition to school and young children's academic and socioemotional outcomes, with a particular emphasis on fathers typically underrepresented in the literature–those of ethnic minority and low-income status.

Landscape of Literature on Father Involvement with Young Children: 1990–2005

The primary intent of this section is to broadly appraise the state of the literature base for father involvement with young children and, in doing so, ascertain whether science has responded to the concerns and recommendations voiced by previous researchers and review articles. To begin with, one of the more pervasive concerns a decade ago was that fathers were receiving little attention in the general literature

TABLE 2. Coding Categories, Totals and Percentages for Father Involvement Articles: 1990–2005 (N = 291).

Emphasis	Theoretical/conceptual	1541	5%
	Empirical	220	76%
	Literature review/meta analysis	15	5%
	Other	41	14%
Content focus	Determinants of father involvement	84	29%
	Father involvement intervention studies	25	8%
	Father involvement related to child outcomes	61	21%
	Other	121	42%
Methods	Qualitative	15	5%
	Quantitative	198	68%
	Mixed methods	8	3%
	NA[a]	70	24%
Age	Infant (Birth-3 years old)	57	20%
	Preschool (3 years old-5 years old)	78	27%
	Kindergarten	3	1%
	First grade	4	1%
	Mixed	58	20%
	NA	91	31%
Relationship to child	Biological	96	33%
	Non-biological	2	1%
	Mixed	34	12%
	NA	159	54%
Residential status	Residential	100	34%
	Non-residential	25	9%
	Mixed	31	11%
	NA	135	46%
SES[b]	Low	50	17%
	Mid-high	46	16%
	Mixed	52	18%
	NA	143	49%
Ethnicity	Minority	41	14%
	Non-minority	56	19%
	Mixed	64	22%
	NA	130	45%
Sample size	Small ($n < 50$)	46	16%
	Medium ($n = 50$ to 300)	117	40%
	Large ($n > 300$)	56	19%
	NA	72	25%

[a]The "NA" category was used if the articles did not provide the respective information, or if the study was not an empirical article.

[b]U.S. census poverty levels were used to establish the low-income criteria for each year.

on families and young children (Marsiglio et al., 2000; Nelson, 2004). Given the energy exerted to bring more attention to the inclusion of fathers in research with young children, are fathers better represented

FIGURE 2. Early Childhood Father Involvement Articles Published from 1990 to 2005.

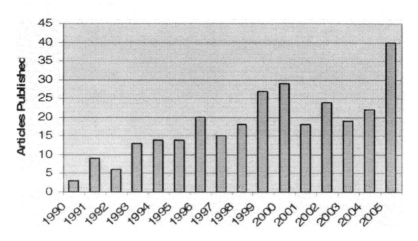

in the early childhood literature now than they were 15 years ago? Correlational analyses were used to assess the association between years of publication and the number of articles published in peer-reviewed journals. Results indicate a strong positive correlation between the two variables ($r = .80$), indicating that efforts to include fathers in early childhood research have indeed increased over time (see Figure 2).

Given confirmation that more father involvement research has occurred in recent years, the question then becomes–what focus has this growing literature taken and do trends reflect suggestions by leading experts since the turn of the century? An overall description of trends in the literature over the last 15 years is presented in Table 2 with respect to study emphasis, content focus, basic methods, and approach to sampling. Of the 291 journal articles gathered, 220 were identified as empirical studies, far outnumbering even the combination of conceptual articles, literature reviews, and meta-analyses. Most empirical studies in the early childhood literature examined determinants of father involvement, while a sizeable number also focused on child outcomes related to father involvement; far fewer articles examined the effectiveness of father involvement interventions. This pattern of approach and content focus suggests that father involvement literature remains in the early stages of development. The field has emphasized basic science to generate an early understanding of what factors are related to fathers' involvement with young children in addition to testing this involvement's association with children's early learning. Published intervention studies typically require a solid foundation of basic science, perhaps helping to explain the lower number of this type of work. Interestingly, the vast majority of empirical studies employed quantitative methods, whereas relatively few utilized qualitative or mixed methods. Given that the field appears to just now be building a research base about father involvement with young children, one might expect to find more in-depth, emic studies that can help to stimulate scientific discussion and may result in more refined research questions that can be examined through quantitative methods.

Several trends in the literature are also clear with respect to sample characteristics, when examining the entire 15-year span from 1990 to 2005. Within the birth to first grade time period, preschoolers and infant/toddlers are most commonly included in father involvement research, though mixed age samples also occur frequently. A look at father and family characteristics demonstrates a preponderance of biological and residential fathers in these studies, perhaps reflecting samples of convenience that are less challenging to access. However, there is far more diversity across studies in terms of socioeconomic status and race/ethnicity of families. To some degree, this pattern may reflect concern for young children in low-income and ethnic/racial minority families who are entering school already behind their peers. There is a lot of energy in education science and child development research devoted to identification of factors contributing to early achievement gaps, and the role of fathers is a natural extension of this work.

In addition to describing the landscape of father involvement research over the last 15 years, it is important to ascertain the extent to which this literature may have responded to critiques and recommendations over time. In particular, early empirical work on father involvement largely focused on samples of Caucasian, middle-class men in intact families (Cabrera et al., 1999; Marsiglio et al., 2000; Parke, 2000), which fails to reflect the growing cultural and structural diversity of families in the United States (Cabrera et al., 2000; Marsiglio et al., 2000; Nelson, 2004). Therefore, as part of this review, changes in publication patterns and foci over time were explored by dividing articles into two equal time periods, 1990–1997 and 1998–2005. Nonparametric analyses were then

TABLE 3. Comparisons of Empirical Early Childhood Literature Sample Characteristics Between Time Periods: 1990–1997 versus 1998–2005 (N = 220).

Minority[a]	Minority	Non-Minority	Mixed	Total
Period 1: 1990–1997	13	20	14	47
Period 2: 1998–2005	26	31	46	103
Totals	39	51	60	150
SES[b]	Low Income	Mid-High Income	Mixed	Total
Period 1: 1990–1997	9	18	22	49
Period 2: 1998–2005	42	23	28	93
Totals	51	41	50	142
Place of Residence[c]	Residential	Non-Residential	Mixed	Total
Period 1: 1990–1997	45	8	4	57
Period 2: 1998–2005	51	17	25	93
Totals	96	25	29	150
Biological[d]	Biological	Non-Biological	Mixed	Total
Period 1: 1990–1997	39	0	7	46
Period 2: 1998–2005	52	2	28	82
Totals	91	2	35	128
Sample Size[e]	Small	Medium	Large	Total
Period 1: 1990–1997	24	33	10	67
Period 2: 1998–2005	22	76	42	140
Totals	46	109	52	207

[a]$\chi^2 = 3.33$, p = .189; [b]$\chi^2 = 10.01$, p = .007; [c]$\chi^2 = 10.80$, p = .005; [d]$\chi^2 = 6.88$, p = .032; [e]$\chi^2 = 12.56$, p = .002.

used to test shifts in approaches to sampling over time, focusing on ethnic/racial minority families, low-income fathers, nonresidential fathers, nonbiological fathers, and sample sizes (see Table 3). Important to note up front is that the number of studies incorporating these underrepresented groups have increased between these two time periods, paralleling the increase in father involvement literature as a whole. However, the following chi-square results provide a distinct test of whether studies of underrepresented groups constitute a larger proportion of the total number of studies in a given time period.

Many leading researchers argue that the father involvement literature should account for differences in ethnic and cultural backgrounds by focusing on a variety of minority populations, in contrast to past research practices which largely employed non-minority populations (Cabrera et al., 1999; Hofferth, Pleck, Stueve, Bianchi, &

Sayer, 2002; Marsiglio et al., 2000). There is also concern in the field that studies have too often conflated socioeconomic status and family structure with race/ethnicity, thus perpetuating negative stereotypes about minority fathering practices (Hernandez & Brandon, 2002; Parke, 2000). Of studies in this review that distinguished between minority and nonminority samples, 26% of the articles gathered over the last 15 years reported samples solely comprising of minority fathers, whereas 34% exclusively focused on non-minority men. Further exploration of the descriptive data showed that of the 41 articles that fell into the minority group subcategory, 19 reported samples comprised of 90% or more African American participants. Although chi-square analysis revealed no significant difference between the early and recent periods in the proportion of articles that focused exclusively on minority fathers ($\chi^2 = 3.33$, $p = .189$), the proportion of studies that have included groups other than African American fathers has indeed increased over time ($\chi^2 = 5.83$, $p = .016$). So to a subtle degree the field has responded to the aforementioned critiques, but studies of fathering within minority populations could still be greatly improved. For example, there continues to be a need to explore within-group differences to gain a fuller understanding of the range of father involvement behaviors among all minority groups.

In spite of the well-recognized importance of income as it relates to children's academic success, relatively little is known about the fathering practices of low-income men and the impact that these practices may have on child outcomes (Cabrera et al., 2000; Nelson, 2004). Of articles in this review that described the income levels of families with young children ($n = 148$), 34% focused on low-income fathers and 35% incorporated a mixed sampling of low-income to high-income fathers. A chi-square test revealed that there was a significant difference in the proportion of studies published on low-income men between the early and recent time periods ($\chi^2 = 10.01$, $p = .007$), with far greater representation during the 1998–2005 time period.

Given the nation's shifting demography toward larger numbers of nonresidential fathers, calls for research to incorporate nonresidential fathers into study designs have become more prevalent (Amato & Gilbreth, 1999; Cabrera et al., 2000; Marsiglio et al., 2000). Sixty-four percent of the studies in this review that accounted for fathers' residential status concentrated wholly on residential fathers, whereas 17% reported samples comprised exclusively of nonresidential fathers.

Chi-square analysis indicated that there is a difference in the proportion of articles that have focused solely on non-residential fathers between the two time periods ($\chi^2 = 10.80, p = .005$), with an increase in recent years.

It is increasingly recognized that considerable numbers of young children experience contact with a nonbiological father figure, such as stepfathers, adoptive fathers, or nonmarital partners of mothers (Harris & Ryan, 2004; Hernandez & Brandon, 2002), suggesting the need for an "inclusive approach" toward sampling of fathers (Day & Lamb, 2004; Marsiglio, Day, & Lamb, 2000). Of the articles that distinguished between samples of biological and nonbiological fathers, the overwhelming majority (71%) focused solely on biological fathers, whereas 27% employed a mix of biological and nonbiological fathers. Chi-square analysis revealed that a significant difference exists in the proportion of publications between the two time periods ($\chi^2 = 6.88, p = .032$), with the number of publications incorporating nonbiological fathers on the rise.

Finally, among the methodological concerns researchers have raised, inadequate sample sizes and their resulting inability to yield robust effect has consistently been cited (Amato & Gilbreth, 1999; Marsiglio et al., 2000; Nelson, 2004). Twenty-two percent of the publications gathered over the last 15 years included a relatively small sample size ($n < 50$), 53% employed a medium size sample ($n = 50$–300), and 25% included a relatively large sample ($n > 300$). Results indicated a significant difference in sample sizes for studies of father involvement between the early and recent periods ($\chi^2 = 12.56, p = .002$), with studies utilizing medium and large sample sizes increasing in number. Larger sample sizes mean greater power to detect associations between father involvement and determinants or child outcomes; this bodes well in particular for those hard-to-reach fathers for whom samples are typically too small to detect effects or make generalizable comparisons with the majority group.

Conceptual and Methodological Rigor for Studies of Father Involvement Across the School Transition

In this section, we summarize issues related to the conceptualization of father involvement and methodological characteristics of the 90 studies that incorporated only children ages 3 to 6 years. We chose a more in-depth examination of studies pertaining to this age group in order to understand what the literature currently posits concerning the nature and effects of father involvement during this sensitive developmental period of transition to school. In particular, we examined the extent to which these studies addressed previously identified shortcomings in fathering literature: (1) over reliance on dichotomous characterizations of fathering (i.e., present vs. absent), (2) single source methods (particularly, exclusive reliance on mothers' ratings of fathers' involvement), (3) absence of guiding theories for empirical work, and (4) the use of one-dimensional constructs rather than attention to the multidimensional nature of father involvement. Therefore, we created categories to address these criticisms and engaged in second level coding with this refined sample (following procedures outlined in the previous section).

Subsequent to coding, cross-tabulations were run on the following categories: dichotomous versus continuous measure of father involvement, father-rated involvement, multiple raters of involvement, presence of guiding theory, and presence of multidimensional constructs for measuring father involvement. As before, these 90 studies were divided according to two equivalent time periods (1990–1997 and 1998–2005) and chi-square analyses were conducted (see Table 4). Although none of the chi-square analyses were statistically significant (indicating that across these two time periods, the proportions of studies taking into account these methodological and conceptual recommendations did not significantly increase), several trends are noteworthy and, for many of these categories, proportions are moving in the right directions according to recent recommendations.

For example, although proportionally, studies which employed continuous measures of father involvement do not appear to have increased, the sheer number is worth mention. In the first time period, 24 out of 28 studies employed continuous measures of father involvement, but in the second time period, 48 out of 51 did, indicating that, overall, the vast majority of studies employ continuous measures of father involvement and the proportion is steady over time. Whereas, with respect to the number of studies that have employed multiple raters of father involvement, although the sheer number has increased, the gap between those that include single raters and multiple raters actually expanded slightly (i.e., 14 out of 31 employed single raters in the first time period; 22 out of 53 did so in the second time period). This clearly goes against the recommendations of Marsiglio et al. (2000), who advocate for more multisource studies.

TABLE 4. Conceptual and Methodological Characteristics Among Empirical Articles Examining the Transition to Elementary School Period: Comparisons between Time Periods 1990–1997 versus 1998–2005 (N = 90, Ages 3–6).

Variable Scale[a]	Dichotomous/Categorical	Continuous
Period 1: 1990–1997	4	24
Period 2: 1998–2005	3	48
Totals	7	72
Father Rater of Involvement[b]	No	Yes
Period 1: 1990–1997	11	20
Period 2: 1998–2005	20	34
Totals	31	54
Multiple Raters of Involvement[c]	No	Yes
Period 1: 1990–1997	17	14
Period 2: 1998–2005	31	22
Totals	48	36
Presence of Guiding Theory[d]	No	Yes
Period 1: 1990–1997	16	13
Period 2: 1998–2005	21	33
Totals	37	46
Multidimensional Study[e]	No	Yes
Period 1: 1990–1997	10	19
Period 2: 1998–2005	16	38
Totals	26	57

[a]$\chi^2 = 1.58$, p = .209; [b]$\chi^2 = .021$, p = .886; [c]$\chi^2 = .107$, p = .744; [d]$\chi^2 = 2.03$, p = .155; [e]$\chi^2 = 2.07$, p = .649.

There is an increase in the trend to recognize the multidimensional nature of father involvement. In the 1990–1997 period, 19 of the 29 studies (65.5%) included multifaceted constructs. However, 38 of 54 studies (70.4%) included these constructs in 1998–2005. However, as can be seen from these numbers, there are still many studies that continue to treat father involvement unidimensionally, warranting more attention to Nelson's (2004) call for more comprehensive measurement. Finally, with respect to those studies guided explicitly by some theoretical framework, the numbers have actually reversed across time periods, with a more promising trend emerging. During the first time period, more studies ignored this need (16 did not include a guiding theory, while 13 did) as opposed to the second time period, where more studies have incorporated explicit theories to guide their work (33 studies included guiding theory, while 21 did not). Again, this trend indicates that more recent studies have heeded recommendations by Lamb and Tamis-LeMonda (2004), although we have still failed to create a more unifying theory of father involvement.

Our qualitative coding also indicated some interesting trends related to the issues of guiding theory and multidimensional assessment. In nearly 50% of studies (48.9%) no theoretical framework was mentioned as guiding the work. Among the theoretical frameworks chosen for the remaining half, 11% were guided primarily by attachment theory, 11% by some form of the tripartite model of fathering (Lamb, Pleck, Charnov, & Levine, 1987), 3% by Belsky's (1984) process model of parenting, 3% by some form of cultural ecology, and 2% by Patterson's (1982) model of coercive parenting. Among other theoretical conceptualizations included (but not to any significant degree) were: Baumrind's (1971) typology of parenting, Bronfenbrenner's (1986) developmental-ecological theory, Weisner's (2002) ecocultural theory, Pleck's (1997) model of relationship quality, social learning theory, and evolutionary biology (Palkovitz, 1997). These findings indicate that relatively speaking, there are few father-specific theories guiding father involvement research. Rather, the preponderance of studies are either guided by no theoretical framework at all or by theory derived from the historical study of mother-child interactions (e.g., attachment). On the upside, 69% of these 90 studies incorporated multidimensional assessment of father involvement, which is encouraging for the field.

Father Involvement During the Transition to School and Children's Academic and Social Outcomes

As families and educators work together to ensure young children's early school success, the ultimate question to be asked of the burgeoning fatherhood literature is this–do fathers play a significant role during the transition to school in promoting children's academic and socioemotional outcomes? Thirty-two articles from 1990 to 2005 focusing on 3 to 6-year-old children reported findings that address this link between child outcomes and a wide variety of father involvement constructs. Four studies focused exclusively on academic outcomes, 22 studied only socioemotional outcomes, five examined both types of outcomes, and one study focused only on physical health outcomes. The following sections separately review patterns across these studies in terms of methodological rigor, children's academic and socioemotional competence, and racial/ethnic minority and low-income fathers.

Methodological rigor. Since a particular focus of this review was to examine the literature that relates fathers' involvement to children's educational well-being, we engaged in a final level of coding for the 32 empirical studies which addressed child outcomes, in order to comment on any content-specific advances that exist across time. The coding categories at this level were specifically targeted at understanding methodological rigor and included examination of whether studies: (1) controlled for mothers' involvement, (2) modeled growth in child outcomes, (3) modeled bidirectionality, (4) measured indirect effects, or (5) attended to the issue of shared source variance.

As with the 90 studies above, chi-square analyses did not indicate any statistically significant differences across the two time periods (1990–1997 and 1998–2000), indicating that advances toward more methodologically rigorous studies are not increasing in proportion over time for this group of studies (see Table 5). However, again, certain trends are worth noting. For example, approximately half of the analyses were found to control for mother involvement and, over time, the number of these studies has increased even though the proportional increase has not yet approached statistical significance. Only two studies among the 32 modeled growth in child outcomes over time and five included predictive designs; therefore the majority of child outcome studies are concurrent in nature. Only two studies in this group included measurement of bidirectional effects of father-child interaction, and these studies resided in the earlier time period. However, approximately equal numbers of studies across the two time periods measured indirect effects, with a trend toward more of these studies in the later period. Finally, the preponderance of studies has attended to the need for multiple raters across independent and dependent variables, with 72% of the 32 studies doing so, indicating that, at least within this age group, the majority of researchers reflect the recommendation forwarded by Marsiglio et al. (2000). Therefore, with respect to controlling for mother involvement and attending to source variance issues, the field is moving in the right direction toward more careful research. However, we need to build on our current state of knowledge

TABLE 5. Conceptual and Methodological Rigor in Empirical Articles Examining the Associations Between Father Involvement and Child Outcomes: Comparisons Between Time Periods 1990–1997 versus 1998–2005 (N = 32, Ages 3–6).

	No	Yes
Controlled for Mother Involvement[a]	No	Yes
Period 1: 1990–1997	9	4
Period 2: 1998–2005	9	9
Totals	18	13
Modeled Bidirectionality of Effects[b]	No	Yes
Period 1: 1990–1997	11	2
Period 2: 1998–2005	18	0
Totals	29	2
Modeled Growth of Child Outcomes[c]	No	Yes
Period 1: 1990–1997	12	1
Period 2: 1998–2005	17	1
Totals	29	2
Modeled Moderation/Mediation[d]	No	Yes
Period 1: 1990–1997	9	4
Period 2: 1998–2005	10	8
Totals	19	12
Different Rater for Involvement and Outcome[e]	No	Yes
Period 1: 1990–1997	3	10
Period 2: 1998–2005	4	14
Totals	7	24

[a]$\chi^2 = 1.15$, p $= .284$; [b]$\chi^2 = .057$, p $= .811$; [c]$\chi^2 = 2.96$, p $= .085$; [d]$\chi^2 = .595$, p $= .440$; [e]$\chi^2 = .003$, p $= .995$.

concerning concurrent and direct effects of fathering on children's outcomes, and design more rigorous studies that test the indirect, bidirectional and longitudinal interactions of father involvement and child outcomes over time.

Fathers and children's academic development. Only nine studies focused on the extent to which father involvement is associated with academic-related child outcomes, including cognitive abilities, educational attainment, language abilities, and school readiness. Five of these studies found that fathering was significantly associated with academic competence in a positive direction, whereas four studies reported nonsignificant results. Types of involvement that were positively related to children's academic outcomes included: mere presence, warmth, responsibility, parenting satisfaction, nurturance, financial contribution, and use of language. Of the three most rigorous studies that controlled for mothers' involvement, two indicated that fathers made a unique contribution to children's language abilities. More in-depth appraisal of the four studies with nonsignificant results indicates that half of them operationalized involvement as merely fathers' presence or absence, which is considered a simplistic, potentially misleading construct given that the quality of involvement is unknown (Amato & Gilbreth, 1999). These limited results are promising and in line with past reviews of fathering that cover a broader age range; however, there is clearly not enough relative attention being paid to children's academic-related outcomes when studying father involvement.

Fathers and children's social and emotional development. Twenty-seven studies examined the link between father involvement and young children's socioemotional competence. The disparity in the number of studies that focused on academic and socioemotional outcomes is perhaps best explained by how "school readiness" is defined for those youth about to enter elementary school; there is an emphasis during this early childhood period on the importance of children's development of self-regulatory and social skills in order to be able to fully take advantage of learning opportunities within early classroom environments. Twenty-five of the 27 studies (93%) found a significant association between father involvement and children's socioemotional skills, in the expected, positive direction. The most common pattern revealed that some form of paternal supportiveness related to fewer problem behaviors, and in particular externalizing behaviors. There is a parallel pattern of findings for the same types of fathering behavior being linked with diverse measures of children's social competence, such as social skills, peer acceptance, and empathy in the expected directions. As noted above, however, the methodological rigor of these studies as a whole is mediocre at best, with the majority reporting concurrent correlational findings without controlling for maternal involvement. It is therefore important to emphasize findings from the eight studies with more rigorous, controlled designs in order to discern the direction of effects and disentangle father and mother involvement.

Five studies controlled for mother involvement and used a different rater for father involvement and children's outcomes, all of which reported father involvement accounting for unique variance in children's social competence and problem behaviors, above and beyond the level and quality of involvement by mothers. Three additional studies addressed the directionality of effects between father involvement and children's outcomes, using prediction models in which paternal behavior at an earlier point in time was linked with later child behavior. All of these studies indicated that early measures of fathering characteristics were associated with children's later socioemotional outcomes, though one finding was in an unexpected direction.

Racial/ethnic minority and low-income fathers. A small body of research has addressed racial/ethnic minority and low-income fathers' involvement with young children and the association with child outcomes. In particular, six outcome studies were conducted with samples of racial/ethnic minority fathers, five of which largely focused on African American fathers and one on Mexican American fathers. Interestingly, these same six studies were the only ones that focused exclusively on low-income families, reflecting Parke's (2000) concerns about conflation of race/ethnicity and socioeconomic status in fathering studies. Out of these studies, those that measured a continuously scaled fathering behavior during the transition to school reported a positive link to children's outcomes, such as receptive language, cognitive abilities, emotional maturity, and lower problem behaviors. For example, Black, Dubowitz and Starr (1999) found that low-income, African American fathers' financial contributions and nurturing behavior were positively associated with children's receptive language skills, after controlling for maternal characteristics.

Another 12 studies utilized mixed race/ethnicity samples, all of which included a large enough percentage of ethnic/minority fathers to allow cross-group comparisons of the involvement and child outcome association. And yet, only three of these studies controlled for race/ethnicity in analyses, and just one study tested the interaction of race/ethnicity and father involvement in predicting children's outcomes, with no significant findings. Six other studies also reported a mixed sample in terms of family socioeconomic status (SES). Again, while four of these studies controlled for socioeconomic status in analyses, two did not incorporate SES into analyses at all and none of the six tested for moderation. So, few studies have actually examined race/ethnicity or socioeconomic status as a moderator, making it difficult to conclude one way or another whether there is a differential link between father involvement and child outcomes across certain groups. Studies of racial/ethnic minority and low-income fathers that use a strength-based approach to measurement of involvement (i.e., Black, Dubowitz, & Starr, 1999), however, suggest that the positive influence of fathering behaviors, such as nurturance and complexity of language use, on language and socioemotional competencies parallel those findings in the literature as a whole.

SUMMARY OF FINDINGS

In this review, we sought to explore the landscape of father involvement literature within an early childhood population and describe its current state and growth in response to the recommendations of key scholars and seminal reviews. As a whole, this literature appears to have engaged primarily in the quantitative exploration of the determinants of father involvement, followed by questions exploring father involvement related to children's academic, cognitive and socioemotional outcomes. Our findings also indicate that father involvement articles have begun to utilize larger samples and more regularly address questions related to certain underrepresented father samples (e.g., low-income, nonbiological and nonresidential fathers), but not others (e.g., racial/ethnic minority).

More nuanced trends were explored with the 90 studies specifically targeting children ages 3–6 during the transition to school period. We found that there is a trend toward the use of more continuous variables (contrary to the historical use of dichotomous notions of involvement), as well as the use of multi-dimensional paradigms of involvement. Additionally, there seems to be increasing use of a guiding theory of father involvement in studies for this age group. Yet, the proportion of studies using multiple raters of father involvement has remained mostly stable with a slight decrease. For the 32 studies that directly addressed fathers' involvement in relation to children's developmental outcomes, there were trends toward a greater proportion of studies over time controlling for mother involvement and avoiding shared method variance. However, the majority of these child outcome studies lacked a predictive or longitudinal design, and the proportion of studies measuring indirect effects of father involvement stayed about the same over time. Findings from these 32 studies indicated that father involvement was consistently associated with both academic and socioemotional child outcomes, and this pattern generally held true across race/ethnicity and socioeconomic status.

This summary is qualified by the following limitations of the current review. First, only published works were included, thereby limiting the conclusions that we can draw to the body of empirical work that is published and circulated relatively widely. Therefore, the findings presented here, and our proceeding discussion of the implications, will be inherently biased toward statistically significant findings. Although arguably a limitation, we posit that these findings represent what is most visible and influencing the direction of future research, practice, and policy. Second, this review was characterized by less emphasis on certain content types of studies than others. For example, our substantive focus was on the father-child dyad as much as possible, rather than on issues such as how average levels of father involvement compare to mother involvement or fathers' perceptions of fatherhood. Third, with so few studies incorporating nonresidential and nonbiological fathers into samples, it was not possible to describe patterns of findings for these fathers with the 3 to 6-year-old group in any detail. This, however, is a general weakness in the literature (and less a weakness of this particular review) and underscores the continued need to find innovative and successful ways to recruit these men into studies. Fourth, it is important to note that the range of assessable child outcomes is restricted in a sample of young children, given developmental limitations to reliably self-report feelings and motivation. Finally, although systematic in nature, the current review is not a meta-analysis, and therefore, we could not comment on the strength of relationships between variables overall or for different groups. This is clearly a direction for future reviews.

IMPLICATIONS FOR FUTURE RESEARCH WITHIN EARLY CHILDHOOD POPULATIONS

In 1990, fewer than five published articles addressed father involvement with young children. Compared to the almost 40 relevant articles published in the 2005 edition of peer-reviewed journals, there is no doubt that research on father involvement with young children has come a long way in the last 15 years. This review provides systematic evidence that researchers have been responsive to past critiques to some degree, and lays out a path of persistent sampling, methodological and conceptual challenges still left to be tackled.

Methodological

Past critiques of father involvement literature have harped repeatedly on the lack of nationally representative samples and in particular a shortage of work that reflects the increasing diversity of families in the United States (Cabrera et al., 2000; Coley, 2001; Lamb & Tamis-LeMonda, 2004). This review suggests movement in the field toward larger samples and a greater proportion of studies inclusive of non-biological, nonresidential, and low-income fathers. Larger, more diverse samples provide greater power to detect hypothesized associations of father involvement with either determinants (e.g., relationship with child's mother, paternal self-efficacy) or child outcomes. These samples also offer the opportunity to apply more complicated analytical models, such as those that include tests for moderation, mediation, bidirectional effects, and even hierarchical linear modeling, which were rarely evident in this set of reviewed articles. For example, questions of moderation, beyond gender differences, were atypical, despite samples with a substantial mix of demographic characteristics such as socioeconomic status. This is unfortunate because of the powerful implications of asking questions such as whether the correlates of authoritative parenting may be different for African American, Caucasian and Latino men, or whether a father's involvement is uniquely associated with his child's literacy skills in kindergarten only under certain family conditions (e.g., positive coparenting relationship). More nuanced research questions must be asked to refine our understanding of father involvement in a way that holds promise for informing intervention and policy.

Although fatherhood samples appear to be diversifying, there continues to be a shortage of studies that include and/or exclusively focus on racial/ethnic minority fathers. This is particularly concerning for several reasons. First, the demography of American families is changing at a rapid pace, in particular toward greater numbers of Latino and immigrant families, which has yet to be fully reflected in the literature on father involvement with young children. This reduces the generalizability of existing evidence and renders related conceptualizations inadequate for the population at-large. Second, racial/ethnic minority children in the United States are often under-resourced during early years of development and therefore can face greater risk for early school problems. Knowledge about how fathers serve as a resource, or a deterrent, to early learning for youth in these families would be invaluable as school systems attempt to determine ways to improve the readiness of children for the increasing demands of early classroom experiences. Third, as was evident in the set of studies that examined child outcomes, too often the combination of race/ethnicity and socioeconomic status in studies on fatherhood is restricted to groups such as Caucasian, middle-class families or African American, low-income families (Nelson, 2004). Such studies lend themselves to misinterpretation and perpetuate negativistic stereotypes, because the full range of families is not represented. For example, what looks like a race/ethnicity effect may actually be a socioeconomic status effect, or vice versa. Given the limitations of the field in covering the diverse nature of American families in regards to race/ethnicity, far more attention must be paid to conducting emic, qualitative studies to provide a clear sense of how certain groups may be similar or distinct from others in terms of what fathers are doing and how their behaviors operate within a family context.

In the past, father involvement research has been characterized by a number of key methodological shortcomings, to some extent restricting the field's knowledge base. This review supplies evidence of trends in a positive direction for addressing many of these limitations within research during this early childhood developmental period, yet illustrates how methodological rigor continues to lag behind best practices in some ways. Clearly, the field has moved beyond an oversimplified, polarized view of father involvement as either present or absent, with the vast majority of studies during the transition to school including some continuous measure of involvement. However, many studies continue to use only a single source for reports of this involvement, leaving reporter bias left unacknowledged and untested. Plus, many unanswered questions remain about how perceptions of father involvement may be impacted differently by family context and father attributes depending on the rater.

In contrast to the shared source variance issue raised above, when addressing the foundational question of whether father involvement makes a difference for children's early school readiness and success, studies appear to be adequately addressing previous concerns about shared method variance between independent and dependent variables, as well as isolating unique father involvement effects by controlling for mothers' involvement. Yet, along the lines of the critique offered above for the larger group of early childhood studies, more sophisticated modeling of growth, moderation, and bidirectional effects continue to be less prevalent when testing fathers' influence on child outcomes (as evident in Table 5). For instance, how are father involvement and child development related to one another over the course of time, and in particular during this all-important transition from the home into preschool and then from preschool into the public school system? Although it appears clear that the two are positively linked regardless of the race/ethnicity and socioeconomic status of fathers, what is the direction of this effect– does children's behavior influence fathering behavior, or vice versa? And, are certain types of father involvement more central at some points of early childhood than others? These questions represent the next level of inquiry requiring attention from the field, in order to move beyond simple concurrent associations of fathering behavior and children's socioemotional and academic competence.

Conceptual

The conceptual work of Lamb and others does appear to have left a permanent stamp on the field of father involvement research, mainly in terms of increasing awareness of the multifaceted nature of how fathers can be involved in the lives of young children. In fact, multidimensional measurement models of involvement appear to be somewhat more commonplace now than in the past. And yet, there is still no "Grand Unifying Theory" of fatherhood (Hofferth et al., 2002), which integrates parenting literature based on mother-child dyad research with father-specific roles and behaviors and recognizes family diversity. In fact, nearly half of the studies in this review failed to report a clear theory that guided the choice of a father involvement measurement, and those that did provide a conceptual justification often used a more general model of parenting. Parenting literature as a whole, though largely developed through empirical inquiry with mothers, clearly applies to fathers and has served as a useful foundation for inquiry. However, in order to isolate what might be unique about father involvement in relation to support of children's early learning and development, the field must step outside of the typical parenting literature box and apply a fresh perspective to fathering that is unencumbered by preconceived notions informed by a maternal template and patterns in Caucasian, middle-class, two-parent households.

As reported in the National Academies book *Scientific Research in Education* (Shavelson, Towne, & the Committee on Scientific

Principles for Education Research, 2002), the development of any given science occurs through a "dynamic interplay among methods, theories, and findings" (p. 2). Similarly, development of fathering theory (particularly as it relates to the learning/education of young children) must progress through a series of discrete steps–the posing of significant questions, applying and integrating theories, and conducting direct investigation–in order to continue building a distinct *science of fathering*. As mentioned above, direct investigation of father involvement is on the rise, yet questions must move beyond asking the degree to which fathers matter and instead emphasize identification of the processes through which fathers exert their influence on children's early competencies. And, ultimately, the progression of fathering research in early childhood and other developmental periods requires integration of relevant theories, such as developmental/ ecological, family systems, attachment, and social learning to name just a few, and generation of novel ideas to help guide future research.

CONCLUSIONS

The education of our nation's young children as they enter preschool and early elementary school has received unprecedented attention in recent years, given a growing understanding of how crucial early success can be to later educational achievement. As family systems, developmental, and education sciences work toward identifying all of the supports available to children during this time period, fathers are being recognized as an important socializing adult for whom far too little information is available. Although this review identifies a rise in empirical inquiry about fathers during early childhood that seems to have substantiated their positive influence on developmental outcomes, it is not a time for the field to rest on its laurels. Much more work is left to be done as father involvement researchers build upon the momentum created over the past 15 years and work toward developing a meaningful *science of fathering* relevant for all young children and their families.

REFERENCES

*Ahmeduzzaman, M., & Roopnarine, J. L. (1992). Sociodemographic factors, functioning style, social support, and fathers' involvement with preschoolers in African-American families. *Journal of Marriage & the Family, 54*, 699–707.

*Aldous, J., Mulligan, G. M., & Bjarnason, T. (1998). Fathering over time: What makes the difference? *Journal of Marriage and the Family, 60,* 809–820.

Alexander, K. L., Entwisle, D. R., & Kabbani, N. S. (2001). The dropout process in life course perspective: Early risk factors at home and school. *Teachers College Record, 103,* 760–822.

Amato, P. R., & Gilbreth, J. G. (1999). Nonresident fathers and children's well-being: A meta-analysis. *Journal of Marriage and the Family, 61,* 557–573.

Annie, E. (2002). Casey Foundation. *Making fathers count.* Baltimore: Author.

*Bagner, D. M., & Eyberg, S. M. (2003). *Father involvement in parent training: When does it matter?* Annual Parent Child Interaction Therapy Conference, 3rd, Sacramento, CA.

Baumrind, D. (1971). Current patterns of parental authority. *Developmental Psychology Monograph, 4,* 1–103.

Belsky, J. (1984). The determinants of parenting: A process model. *Child Development, 55,* 83–96.

*Belsky, J. (2005). Intergenerational transmission of warm-sensitive-stimulating parenting: A prospective study of mothers and fathers of 3-year-olds. *Child Development, 76,* 384–396.

*Bernadett-Shapiro, S., Ehrensaft, D., & Shapiro, J. L. (1996). Father participation in childcare and the development of empathy in sons: An empirical study. *Family Therapy, 23,* 77–93.

*Black, M. M., Dubowitz, H., & Starr, R. H. (1999). African American fathers in low income, urban families: Development, behavior, and home environment of their three-year-old children. *Child Development, 70,* 967–978.

Blankenhorn, D. (1995). *Fatherless America: Confronting our most urgent social problem.* New York: Basic Books.

*Bouchard, G. V., & Lee, C. M. (2000). The marital context for father involvement with their preschool children: The role of partner support. *Journal of Prevention & Intervention in the Community, 20,* 37–53.

*Bowey, J. A. (1995). Socioeconomic status differences in preschool phonological sensitivity and first-grade reading achievement. *Journal of Educational Psychology, 87,* 476–487.

*Bright, J. (1996). Child rearing and education in urban environments: Black fathers' perspectives. *Urban Education, 31,* 245–260.

Bronfenbrenner, U. (1986). Ecology of the family as a context for human development: Research perspectives. *Developmental Psychology, 22,* 723–742.

Bronfenbrenner, U., & Morris, P. A. (1998). The ecology of developmental processes. In W. Damon & R. M. Lerner (Eds.), *Handbook of child psychology: Vol. 1: Theoretical models of human development* (pp. 993–1028). Hoboken, NJ: John Wiley & Sons, Inc.

*Brooks-Gunn, J., Guo, G., & Furstenberg, F. F. (1993). Who drops out of and who continues beyond high school? A 20-year follow-up of black urban youth. *Journal of Research on Adolescence: Special Late Adolescence and the Transition to Adulthood, 3,* 271–294.

*Burgos, L. (2003). The effect of the father-child relationship on the social conduct of 2 1/2 year old children in preschool. *European Journal of Psychology of Education, 18,* 136–155.

Cabrera, N. J., Tamis-LeMonda, C. S., Bradley, R., Hofferth, S., & Lamb, M. E. (2000). Fatherhood in the twenty-first century. *Child Development, 71,* 127–136.

Cabrera, N. J., Tamis-LeMonda, C. S., Lamb, M. E., & Boller, K. (1999). *Measuring father involvement in the early head start evaluation: A multidimensional conceptualization.* Paper presented at the National Conference on Health Statistics, Washington, DC.

Christenson, S. L. (1999). Families and schools: Rights, responsibilities, resources, and relationships. In R. C. Pianta & M. J. Cox (Eds.), *The transition to kindergarten* (pp. 143–177). Baltimore, MD: Paul H. Brooks Publishing Co.

*Cohn, D. A., Cowan, P. A., Cowan, C. P., & Pearson, J. (1992). Mothers' and fathers' working models of childhood attachment relationships, parenting styles, and child behavior. *Development & Psychopathology, 4,* 417–431.

Coley, R. L. (2001). (In)visible men: Emerging research on low-income, unmarried, and minority fathers. *American Psychologist, 56,* 743–753.

*Coley, R. L., & Chase-Lansdale, P. L. (1997). Stability and change in paternal involvement among urban African American fathers. *Fathering in Urban Families: The Role of Men in the Lives of Minority Children and Adolescents.* Symposium presentation at the biennial meeting of the Society for Research in Child Development. Washington, DC.

Consortium of Longitudinal Studies. (1983). *As the twig is bent...lasting effects of preschool programs.* Hillsdale, NJ: Erlbaum.

Cooper, H. (2003). Psychological Bulletin: Editorial. *Psychological Bulletin, 129,* 3–9.

*Crain-Thoreson, C., Dahlin, M. P., & Powell, T. A. (2001). Parent-child interaction in three conversational contexts: Variations in style and strategy. *New Directions for Child and Adolescent Development, 92,* 23–37.

*Cugmas, Z. (1998). The correlation between children's personal behavioural characteristics and indicators of children's attachment to their mother or father, respectively. *Early Child Development & Care, 143,* 65–78.

*Culp, R. E., Schadle, S., Robinson, L., & Culp, A. M. (2000). Relationships among paternal involvement and young children's perceived self-competence and behavioral problems. *Journal of Child and Family Studies, 9,* 27–38.

*Curtner-Smith, M. E., Bennett, T. L., & O'Rear, M. R. (1995). *Fathers' occupational conditions, values of self-direction and conformity, and perceptions of nurturant and restrictive parenting in relation to young children's depression and aggression.* Biennial Meetings of the Society for Research in Child Development. Indianapolis, IN.

Day, R. D., & Lamb, M. E. (2004). *Conceptualizing and measuring father involvement.* Mahwah, NJ: Lawrence Erlbaum Associates.

Day, R. D., & Lamb, M. E. (2004). Conceptualizing and measuring father involvement: Pathways, problems, and progress. In R. D. Day & M. E. Lamb (Eds.), *Conceptualizing and measuring father involvement* (pp. 1–16). Mahwah, NJ: Lawrence Erlbaum Associates.

*DeKlyen, M., Biernbaum, M. A., Speltz, M. L., & Greenberg, M. T. (1998). Fathers and preschool behavior problems. *Developmental Psychology, 34*, 264–75.

*DeKlyen, M., Speltz, M. L., & Greenberg, M. T. (1998). Fathering and early onset conduct problems: Positive and negative parenting, father-son attachment, and the marital context. *Clinical Child & Family Psychology Review, 1*, 3–21.

*Denham, S. A., Workman, E., Cole, P. M., Weissbrod, C., Kendziora, K. T., & Zahn- Waxler, C. (2000). Prediction of externalizing behavior problems from early to middle childhood: The role of parental socialization and emotion expression. *Development & Psychopathology, 12*, 23–45.

*Downer, J. T. (2005). African American father involvement and preschool children's school readiness. *Early Education and Development, 16*, 317–340.

*Dubowitz, H., Black, M. M., Cox, C. E., Kerr, M. A., Litrownik, A. J., Radhakrishna, A., English, D. J., Schneider, M. W., & Runyan, D. K. (2001). Father involvement and children's functioning at age 6 years: A multisite study. *Child Maltreatment: Journal of the American Professional Society on the Abuse of Children, 6*, 300–309.

Entwisle, D. R., & Alexander, K. L. (1998). Facilitating the transition to first grade: The nature of transition and research on factors affecting it. *Elementary School Journal, 98*, 351–364.

Epstein, J. L. (1996). Perspectives and previews on research and policy for school, family, and community partnerships. In A. Booth & J. F. Dunn (Eds.), *Family-school links: How do they affect educational outcomes?* (pp. 209–246). Mahwah, NJ: Erlbaum.

*Fagan, J. (1996). A preliminary study of low-income African American fathers' play interactions with their preschool-age children. *Journal of Black Psychology, 22*, 7–19.

*Fagan, J. (1998). Correlates of low-income African American and Puerto Rican fathers' involvement with their children. *The Journal of Black Psychology, 24*, 351–367.

*Fagan, J. (1999). Predictors of father and father figure involvement in pre-kindergarten Head Start. *National Center on Fathers and Families*, 1–21.

*Fagan, J. (2000). African American and Puerto Rican American parenting styles, paternal involvement, and Head Start children's social competence. *Merrill-Palmer Quarterly, 46*, 592–612.

*Fagan, J. (2000). Head Start fathers' daily hassles and involvement with their children. *Journal of Family Issues, 21*, 329–346.

*Fagan, J., & Fantuzzo, J. W. (1999). Multirater congruence on the social skills rating system: Mother, father, and teacher assessments of urban Head Start children's social competencies. *Early Childhood Research Quarterly, 14*, 229–242.

*Fagan, J., & Iglesias, A. (2000). The relation between fathers' and children's communication skills and children's behavior problems: A study of Head Start children. *Early Education and Development, 11*, 307–320.

*Fagan, J., Jay, & Iglesias, A. (1999). Father involvement program effects on fathers, father figures, and their Head Start children: A quasi-experimental study. *Early Childhood Research Quarterly, 14*, 243–269.

*Fagan, J., Newash, N., & Schloesser, A. (2000). Female caregivers' perceptions of fathers' and significant adult males' involvement with their Head Start children. *Families in Society, 81*, 186–196.

Fan, X., & Chen, M. (2001). Parental involvement and students' academic achievement: A meta-analysis. *Educational Psychology Review, 13*, 1–22.

Fantuzzo, J., Tighe, E., & Childs, S. (2000). Family Involvement Questionnaire: A multivariate assessment of family participation in early childhood education. *Journal of Educational Psychology, 92*, 367–376.

*Flouri, E., & Buchanan, A. (2002). What predicts good relationships with parents in adolescence and partners in adult life: Findings from the 1958 British birth cohort. *Journal of Family Psychology, 16*, 186–198.

*Frosch, C. A., Mangelsdorf, S. C., & McHale, J. L. (2000). Marital behavior and the security of preschooler-parent attachment relationships. *Journal of Family Psychology, 14*, 144–161.

*Girolametto, L., & Tannock, R. (1994). Correlates of directiveness in the interactions of fathers and mothers of children with developmental delays. *Journal of Speech and Hearing Research, 37*, 1178–91.

*Grbich, C. (1992). Societal response to familial role change in Australia: Marginalisation or social change? *Journal of Comparative Family Studies, 23*, 79–94.

*Grbich, C. F. (1995). Male primary caregivers and domestic labour: Involvement or avoidance? *Journal of Family Studies, 1*, 114–129.

*Greene, A. D., & Moore, K. A. (2000). Nonresident father involvement and child well-being among young children in families on welfare. *Marriage and Family Review, 29*, 159–180.

*Grietens, H., Onghena, P., Prinzie, P., Gadeyne, E., Van Assche, V., Ghesquire, P., & Hellinckx, W. (2004). Comparison of mothers', fathers', and teachers' reports on problem behavior in 5- to 6-year-old children. *Journal of Psychopathology & Behavioral Assessment, 26*, 137–146.

Grossmann, K., Grossmann, K. E., Fremmer-Bombik, E., Kindler, H., Scheuerer-Englisch, H., & Zimmerman, P. (2002). The uniqueness of the child-father attachment relationship: Fathers' sensitive and challenging play as a pivotal variable in a 16-year longitudinal study. *Social Development, 11*, 307–331.

*Haden, C. A., Haine, R. A., & Fivush, R. (1997). Developing narrative structure in parent-child reminiscing across the preschool years. *Developmental Psychology, 33*, 295–307.

Harris, K. M., & Ryan, S. (2004). Father involvement and the diversity of family context. In R. D. Day & M. E. Lamb (Eds.), *Conceptualizing and measuring father involvement* (pp. 293–320). Mahwah, NJ: Lawrence Erlbaum Associates.

Hawkins, A. J., & Palkovitz, R. (1999). Beyond ticks and clicks: The need for more diverse and broader conceptualizations and measures of father involvement. *Journal of Men's Studies, 8*, 11–32.

*Hay, D. F., Pawlby, S., Sharp, D., Schmucker, G., Mills, A., Allen, H., & Kumar, R. (1999). Parents' judgments about young children's problems: Why mothers and fathers might disagree yet still predict later outcomes. *Journal of Child Psychology & Psychiatry, 40*, 1249–1258.

Hernandez, D. J., & Brandon, P. D. (2002). Who are the fathers of today? In C. S. Tamis-LeMonda & N. Cabrera (Eds.), *Handbook of father involvement: Multidisciplinary perspectives* (pp. 33–62). Mahwah, NJ: Erlbaum.

Hofferth, S. L., Pleck, J., Stueve, J. L., Bianchi, S., & Sayer, L. (2002). The demography of fathers: What fathers do. In C. S. Tamis-LeMonda & N. Cabrera (Eds.), *Handbook of father involvement: Multidisciplinary perspectives* (pp. 63–90). Mahwah, NJ: Erlbaum.

*Hong, G. S., & White-Means, S. I. (1995). Health care use by preschool children: Effects of maternal occupation and household structure. *Family And Consumer Sciences Research Journal, 24*, 117–138.

*Hwang, C. P., & Lamb, M. E. (1997). Father involvement in Sweden: A longitudinal study of its stability and correlates. *International Journal of Behavioral Development, 21*, 621–632.

*Isley, S., O'Neil, R., & Parke, R. D. (1996). The relation of parental affect and control behaviors to children's classroom acceptance: A concurrent and predictive analysis. *Early Education and Development, 7*, 7–23.

*Jackson, A. P. (1999). The effects of nonresident father involvement on single Black mothers and their young children. *Social Work, 44*, 156–166.

*Jayakody, R., & Kalil, A. (2002). Social fathering in low-income, African American families with preschool children. *Journal of Marriage & Family, 64*, 504–516.

Jeynes, W. (2003). A meta-analysis: The effects of parental involvement on minority children's academic achievement. *Education and Urban Society, 35*, 202–218.

Jeynes, W. (2005). A meta-analysis of the relation of parental involvement to urban elementary school student academic achievement. *Urban Education, 40*, 237–269.

Jeynes, W. (2007). The relationship between parental involvement and urban secondary school student academic achievement: A meta-analysis. *Urban Education, 42*, 82–110.

Kagan, S. L., & Kauerz, K. (2007). Reaching for the whole: Integration and alignment in early education policy. In R. C. Pianta, M. J. Cox, & K. Snow (Eds.), *School readiness, early learning, and the transition to kindergarten.* Baltimore, MD: Paul H. Brooks.

*Karther, D. (2002). Fathers with low literacy and their young children. *Reading Teacher, 5*, 184–193.

*Keown, L. J., & Woodward, L. J. (2002). Early parent-child relations and family functioning of preschool boys with pervasive hyperactivity. *Journal of Abnormal Child Psychology, 30*, 541–553.

*Kerns, K. A., & Barth, J. M. (1995). Attachment and play: Convergence across components of parent child relationships and their relations to peer competence. *Journal of Social & Personal Relationships, 12*, 243–260.

*Kuersten-Hogan, R., & McHale, J. P. (2000). Stability of emotion talk in families from the toddler to the preschool years. *Journal of Genetic Psychology, 161*, 115–121.

*LaFreniere, P. J., Provost, M. A., & Dubeau, D. (1992). From an insecure base: Parent-child relations and internalizing behaviour in the pre-school. *Early Development & Parenting, 1*, 137–148.

Lamb, M. E. (1975). Fathers: Forgotten contributors to child development. *Human Development, 13*, 245–266.

Lamb, M. E., Pleck, J. H., Charnov, E. L., & Levine, J. A. (1987). A biosocial perspective of paternal behavior and involvement. In J. B. Lancaster, J. Altman, & A. Rossi (Eds.), *Parenting across the lifespan: Biosocial perspectives* (pp. 11–42). New York: Academic Press.

Lamb, M. E., & Tamis-LeMonda, C. S. (2004). The role of the father: An introduction. In M. E. Lamb (Ed.), *The role of the father in child development* (4th ed., pp. 1–31). New York: Wiley.

*Lavigueur, S., Saucier, J. F., & Tremblay, R. E. (1995). Supporting fathers and supported mothers in families with disruptive boys: Who are they? *Journal of Child Psychology and Psychiatry and Allied Disciplines, 36*, 1003–1018.

Leaper, C., Anderson, K. J., & Sanders, P. (1998). Moderators of gender effects on parents' talk to their children: A meta-analysis. *Developmental Psychology, 34*, 3–27.

Lee, J., & Bowen, N. K. (2006). Parent involvement, cultural capital, and the achievement gap among elementary school children. *American Educational Research Journal, 43*, 193 218.

*Liang, S., & Sugawara, A. I. (1996). Family size, birth order, socioeconomic status, ethnicity, parent-child relationship, and preschool children's intellectual development. *Early Child Development and Care, 124*, 69–79.

*Lindsay, E. W., Mize, J., & Pettit, G. S. (1997). Differential play patterns of mothers and fathers of sons and daughters: Implications for children's gender role development. *Sex Roles, 37*, 643–661.

*Lindsey, E. W., & Mize, J. (2001). Contextual differences in parent-child play: Implications for children's gender role development. *Sex Roles, 44*, 155–176.

*Lindsey, E. W., Mize, J., & Pettit, G. S. (1997). Mutuality in parent-child play: Consequences for children's peer competence. *Journal of Social and Personal Relationships, 14*, 523–538.

*McBride, B. A. (1990). The effects of a parent education/play group program on father involvement in child rearing. *Family Relations, 39*, 250–256.

*McBride, B. A. (1991). Parental support programs and paternal stress: An exploratory study. *Early Childhood Research Quarterly, 6*, 137–149.

*McBride, B. A., & Darragh, J. (1995). Interpreting the data on father involvement: Implications for parenting programs for men. *Families in Society, 76*, 490–497.

*McBride, B. A., & Mills, G. (1993). A comparison of mother and father involvement with their preschool age children. *Early Childhood Research Quarterly, 8*, 457–477.

*McBride, B. A., & Rane, T. R. (1997). Role identity, role investments, and paternal involvement: Implications for parenting programs for men. *Early Childhood Research Quarterly, 12*, 173–197.

*McBride, B. A., & Rane, T. R. (1998). Parenting alliance as a predictor of father involvement: An exploratory study. *Family Relations, 47*, 229–236.

*McBride, B. A., Rane, T. R., & Bae, J. H. (2001). Intervening with teachers to encourage father/male involvement in early childhood programs. *Early Childhood Research Quarterly Special Issue, 16*, 77–93.

*McBride, B. A., Schoppe, S. J., & Rane, T. R. (2002). Child characteristics, parenting stress, and parental involvement: Fathers versus mothers. *Journal of Marriage and the Family, 64*, 998–1011.

*Magill-Evans, J., & Harrison, M. J. (2001). Parent-child interactions, parenting stress, and developmental outcomes at 4 years. *Children's Health Care, 30*, 135–150.

Marsiglio, W., Amato, P., Day, R., & Lamb, M. E. (2000). Scholarship on fatherhood in the 1990s and beyond. *Journal of Marriage and the Family, 62*, 1173–1191.

Marsiglio, W., Day, R., & Lamb, M. E. (2000). Exploring fatherhood diversity: Implications for conceptualizing father involvement. *Marriage and the Family Review, 29*, 269–293.

*Maurer, T. (2003). Methodological considerations in measuring paternal identity. *Fathering, 1*, 117–129.

Meisels, S. J. (1999). Assessing readiness. In R. C. Pianta & M. J. Cox (Eds.), *The transition to kindergarten* (pp. 39–66). Baltimore: Paul H. Brookes.

National Governor's Association (2005). *Final report of the NGA task force on school readiness.* Washington, D.C.: Author.

National Center for Education Statistics. (2000). *The kindergarten year.* Washington, D.C.: National Center for Education Statistics.

National Center for Education Statistics. (2002). *Early Childhood Longitudinal Study—Kindergarten class of 1998–99 (ECLS-K), Psychometric report for kindergarten through first grade.* Washington, DC: National Center for Education Statistics.

National Institute for Early Education Research. (2005). *The state of preschool: 2005 state preschool yearbook.* Retrieved November 30, 2006, from http://nieer.org/yearbook/pdf/yearbook.pdf

National Institute of Child Health and Human Development, Early Child Care Research Network. (2000). Factors associated with fathers' caregiving activities and sensitivity with young children. *Journal of Family Psychology, 14*, 200–219.

National Institute of Child Health and Human Development, Early Child Care Research Network. (2005). Duration and developmental timing of poverty and children's cognitive and social development from birth through third grade. *Child Development, 76*, 795–810.

Nelson, T. J. (2004). Low-income fathers. *Annual Review of Sociology, 30*, 427–451.

*Ortiz, R. W. (2001). Pivotal parents: Emergent themes and implications on father involvement in children's early literacy experiences. *Reading Improvement, 38*, 132–144.

*Ozgun, O. (2005). Parental involvement and spousal satisfaction with division of early childcare in Turkish families with normal children and children with special needs. *Early Child Development and Care, 175*, 259–270.

*Page, T., & Bretherton, I. (2001). Mother- and father-child attachment themes in the story completions of pre-schoolers from post-divorce families: Do they predict relationships with peers and teachers? *Attachment & Human Development, 3*, 1–29.

*Page, T., & Bretherton, I. (2003). Representations of attachment to father in the narratives of preschool girls in post-divorce families: Implications for family relationships and social development. *Child & Adolescent Social Work Journal, 20*, 99–122.

Palkovitz, R. (1997). Reconstructing "involvement": Expanding conceptualizations of men's caring in contemporary families. In A. J. Hawkins & D. C. Dollahite (Eds.), *Generative fathering: Beyond deficit perspectives* (pp. 200–216). Thousand Oaks, CA: Sage.

Paquette, D. (2004). Theorizing the father-child relationships: Mechanisms and developmental outcomes. *Human Development, 47*, 193–219.

Parke, R. D. (2000). Father involvement: A developmental psychological perspective. *Marriage & Family Review. Fatherhood: Research, interventions and policies. Part I, 29*, 43–58.

Patterson, G. R. (1982). *Coercive family process.* Eugene, OR: Castalia.

*Peretti, P. O., & di Vitorrio, A. (1993). Effect of loss of father through divorce on personality of the preschool child. *Social Behavior & Personality, 21*, 33–38.

*Pettit, G. S., Brown, E. G., Mize, J., & Lindsey, E. (1998). Mothers' and fathers' socializing behaviors in three contexts: Links with children's peer competence. *Merrill-Palmer Quarterly, 44*, 173–193.

Peters, H. E., Peterson, G. W., Steinmetz, S. K., & Day, R. D. (Eds.). (2000). *Fatherhood: Research, Interventions, and Policies.* New York: Haworth. Published simultaneously as *Marriage & Family Review, 29* (2–4).

Pianta, R. C. (2005). Standardized observation and professional development: A focus on individualized implementation and practices. In M. Zaslow and I. Martinez-Beck (Eds.), *Critical issues in early childhood professional development* (pp. 231–254). Baltimore: Paul H. Brookes Publishing.

Pianta, R. C., & Kraft-Sayre, M. (2003). *Successful kindergarten transition.* Baltimore: Paul H. Brookes Publishing Co.

Pianta, R. C., Howes, C., Burchinal, M., Bryant, D., Clifford, R., Early, C., & Barbarin, O. (2005). Features of pre-kindergarten programs, classrooms, and teachers: Do they predict observed classroom quality and child-teacher interactions? *Applied Developmental Science, 9*, 144–159.

Pleck, J. H. (1997). Paternal involvement: Levels, sources, and consequences. In M. E. Lamb (Ed.), *The role of the father in child development* (3rd ed., pp. 66–103). New York: John Wiley & Sons.

*Raikes, H. H. (2005). Father involvement in early head start programs. *Fathering, 3*, 29–58.

*Rane, T. R., & McBride, B. A. (2000). Identity theory as a guide to understanding fathers' involvement with their children. *Journal of Family Issues, 21*, 347–66.

Reynolds, A. J. (1994). Effects of a preschool plus follow-on intervention for children at risk. *Developmental Psychology, 30*, 787–804.

*Rimm-Kaufman, S. E. (2005). Father-school communication in preschool and kindergarten. *School Psychology Review, 34*, 287–308.

Rimm-Kaufman, S. E., & Pianta, R. C. (2000). An ecological perspective on the transition to kindergarten: A theoretical framework to guide empirical research. *Journal of Applied Developmental Psychology, 21*, 491–511.

Rimm-Kaufman, S. E., Pianta, R. C., & Cox, M. J. (2000). Teachers' judgments of success in the transition to kindergarten. *Early Childhood Research Quarterly, 15,* 147–166.

Ripple, C. H., Gilliam, W. S., Chanana, N., & Zigler, E. (1999). Will fifty cooks spoil the broth? The debate over entrusting head start to the states. *American Psychologist, 54,* 327–343.

*Roer-Strier, D. (2005). Fatherhood and immigration: Challenging the deficit theory. *Child & Family Social Work, 10,* 315–329.

Roggman, L. A., Fitzgerald, H. E., Bradley, R. H., & Raikes, H. (2002). Methodological, measurement, and design issues in studying fathers: An interdisciplinary perspective. In C. S. Tamis-LeMonda & N. Cabrera (Eds.), *Handbook of father involvement: Multidisciplinary perspectives* (pp. 1–30). Mahwah, NJ: Erlbaum.

*Roopnarine, J. L., & Ahmeduzzaman, M. (1993). Puerto Rican fathers' involvement with their preschool-age children. *Hispanic Journal of Behavioral Sciences, 15,* 96–107.

*Roopnarine, J. L., Church, C. C., & Levy, G. D. (1990). Day care children's play behaviors: Relationship to their mothers' and fathers' assessments of their parenting behaviors, marital stress, and marital companionship. *Early Childhood Research Quarterly, 5,* 335–346.

*Seltzer, J. A. (1991). Relationships between fathers and children who live apart: The father's role after separation. *Journal of Marriage and the Family, 53,* 79–101.

Shavelson, R. J., & Towne, L. (2002). Committee on Scientific Principles for Education Research. *Scientific research in education.* Washington, DC: National Academy Press.

Shonkoff, J. P., & Phillips, D. A. (2000). *From neurons to neighborhoods: The science of early childhood development.* Washington, DC: National Academy Press.

*Siantz, M., & Smith, M. S. (1994). Parental factors correlated with developmental outcome in the migrant head start child. *Early Childhood Research Quarterly, 9,* 481–503.

*Stevens, M., Golombok, S., Beveridge, M., & Study Team, A. (2002). Does father absence influence children's gender development?: Findings from a general population study of preschool children. *Parenting: Science & Practice, 2,* 47–60.

Stevenson, H. W., & Newman, R. S. (1986). Long-term prediction of achievement and attitudes in mathematics and reading. *Child Development, 57,* 646–659.

*Stover, C. S., Van Horn, P., Turner, R., Cooper, B., & Lieberman, A. F. (2003). The effects of father visitation on preschool-aged witnesses of domestic violence. *Journal of Interpersonal Violence, 18,* 1149–1166.

*Stright, A. D., & Bales, S. S. (2003). Coparenting quality: Contributions of child and parent characteristics. *Family Relations: Interdisciplinary Journal of Applied Family Studies, 52,* 232–240.

*Stueve, J. (2003). Fathers' narratives of arranging and planning: Implications for understanding paternal responsibility. *Fathering, 1,* 51–70.

*Suppal, P., & Roopnarine, J. L. (1999). Paternal involvement in child care as a function of maternal employment in nuclear and extended families in India. *Sex Roles, 40,* 731–744.

Tamis-LeMonda, C. S., & Cabrera, N. (2002). *Handbook of father involvement: Multidisciplinary perspectives*. Mahwah, NJ: Lawrence Erlbaum Associates.

*Tudge, J., Hayes, S., Doucet, F., Odero, D., Kulakova, N., Tammeveski, P., Meltsas, M., & Lee, S. (2000). Parents' participation in cultural practices with their preschoolers. *Psicologia: Teoria e Pesquisa, 16*, 1–11.

*Tulananda, O., & Roopnarine, J. L. (2001). Mothers' and fathers' interactions with preschoolers in the home in Nothern Thailand: Relationships to teachers' assessments of children's social skills. *Journal of Family Psychology, 15*, 676–687.

*Volling, B. L., & Elins, J. L. (1998). Family relationships and children's emotional adjustment as correlates of maternal and paternal differential treatment: A replication with toddler and preschool siblings. *Child Development, 69*, 1640–1656.

Weisner, T. S. (2002). Ecocultural understanding of children's developmental pathways. *Human Development, 45*, 275–281.

West, J., Denton, K., & Germino-Hausken, E. (2000). *America's kindergartners*. NCES 2000-070. Washington, DC: National Center for Education Statistics.

*Winsler, A. (2005). Correspondence between maternal and paternal parenting styles in early childhood. *Early Childhood Research Quarterly, 20*, 1–12.

Yeung, W. J., Sandberg, J. F., Davis-Kean, P. E., & Hofferth, S. L. (2001). Children's time with fathers in intact families. *Journal of Marriage and Family, 63*, 136–154.

*Young, D. M., & Roopnarine, J. L. (1994). Fathers' childcare involvement with children with and without disabilities. *Topics in Early Childhood Special Education, 14*, 488–502.

Note: Asterisks denote the 90 empirical articles (1990–2005) addressing father involvement with children experiencing the transition to school (ages 3–6).

Community Literacy Resources and Home Literacy Practices Among Immigrant Latino Families

Leslie Reese
Claude Goldenberg

Leslie Reese is Professor with California State University, Long Beach, CA. Claude Goldenberg is Professor with the School of Education, Stanford University, Stanford, CA.

The authors wish to express their deepest thanks to the families and school personnel who made this work possible, as well as to their colleagues on the Project 4 research team: Bill Saunders, Coleen Carlson, Elsa Cárdenas Hagen, Sylvia Linan Thompson, Elizabeth Portman, Ann Adam, Liliana De La Garza, and Hector Rivera. Their thanks is also to Paul Cirino and David Francis for assistance with database preparation. This work was supported by a grant from the National Institute of Child Health and Human Development and the Institute of Education Sciences, P01 HD39521, "Oracy/Literacy Development in Spanish-Speaking Children."

ABSTRACT. This paper reports relationships among communities, families, and Spanish-speaking children's language and literacy development in kindergarten and grade 1. Findings from a study of 35 communities show that communities with greater concentrations of Latinos are less likely to have printed materials, and available materials are more likely to be in Spanish. Communities with higher income and education levels have more literacy materials in English. Contrary to predictions, there are few associations among community literacy resources, frequency of children's home reading activities, and children's literacy achievement. This lack of association is due to within-community variation in home literacy practices and to schools' impact on home literacy. However, there are associations among community and family *language* characteristics and child literacy outcomes in Spanish and English, suggesting that at least in the early stages of literacy development, communities' influence on Spanish-speaking children's literacy development is through language-learning opportunities rather than literacy-learning opportunities per se.

INTRODUCTION

This article examines the communities in which Spanish-speaking children of immigrants are growing up and the opportunities these communities offer for the acquisition of English, maintenance of Spanish, and the development of literacy skills in both languages. Ultimately, these opportunities will influence children's integration into U.S. society and their ability to maintain the language and culture of their families. The tension between social integration and linguistic and cultural maintenance is palpable. The massive "Day Without Immigrants" demonstrations on May 1, 2006, urging Congress to enact legislation designed to facilitate the legal incorporation of undocumented immigrants into the workforce and ultimately into American society (Gorman, Miller, & Landsberg, 2006), brought to the forefront a debate about the nature of the United States as a pluralistic and multicultural nation of immigrants. Newspapers carried stories focusing on the impact of immigration on local communities and expressing considerable concern about the incorporation of present-day immigrants into the American social fabric. In particular, there was concern that contemporary immigrants, mainly from

Latin America and Asia, are not learning English and thus not assimilating into American society as quickly as immigrants in the past (McKay & Wong, 2000). How these children fare in school and work will affect them, their families, and the society as a whole.

Spanish-speakers are by far the largest language-minority group in the United States, comprising more than 10% of the total U.S. population and 60% of the language-minority population (Shin & Bruno, 2003). The focus of our analysis is on the relationship between Spanish-speaking children's out-of-school literacy-learning opportunities (community and home) and their early literacy achievement in both English and Spanish. We look at ways in which the language characteristics of the communities where Spanish-speaking children live might influence patterns of home language and literacy use, which in turn influence early literacy achievement in English and Spanish. We pay particular attention to access to oral and written language in the children's first language (L1) and second language (L2) in different types of communities.

For immigrants and children of immigrants, full and equitable incorporation into American society involves at least moderately high levels of English language proficiency and literacy attainment. These accomplishments, in turn, require access to quality schooling and learning opportunities outside of school. As a group, children from non-English-speaking homes tend to lag behind their mainstream peers on both state (e.g., California Department of Education, 2005) and national (e.g., Institute of Education Sciences, 2005) tests of academic achievement. Yet, as might be expected, there is a considerable range of outcomes among these children. On the National Assessment of Educational Progress (NAEP), for example, most English learners score below basic. However, 27% score at or above basic and 7% score at or above proficient (Institute of Education Sciences, 2005). Clearly, some English learners do very well in school and beyond, while others lag far behind. What explains this variability, and can understanding its sources help us understand how to improve learning outcomes for more children from Spanish-speaking homes?

FAMILY AND COMMUNITY INFLUENCES ON LITERACY DEVELOPMENT

Family practices associated with children's literacy development have been widely studied over the past 25 years. In general, greater amounts of literacy and oral language in the home are associated with higher levels of children's language and literacy development (Booth & Dunn, 1996; Hart & Risley, 1995. However, for the nearly 10 million children in the United States who come from homes where a language other than English is spoken–70% of whom are Spanish speakers–the dynamics of language and literacy use in the home and literacy attainment at school are necessarily more complex than are those for monolingual speakers of English. These children experience literacy at home in a language other than the one that ultimately they must master in order to succeed in school and beyond. Moreover, even in homes where a language other than English is used, there is generally at least some level of English use as well.

How children growing up in multilingual communities acquire and develop literacy in one, two, or several languages have received increasing scholarly attention over the past two decades (Bayley & Schecter, 2003; Martin-Jones & Jones, 2000; McCarty, 2005). Families' literacy practices include both the activities involving use of text themselves, but also the cultural values, attitudes, feelings and relationships that shape and give meaning to those activities (Barton & Hamilton, 2000; Street, 1993). With respect to immigrant Latino families, studies have documented ways in which parents' cultural experiences guide literacy practices with their children. For example, Valdés (1996) noted that Mexican immigrant parents of kindergartners did not anticipate that the school expected children to know their ABCs by the time they began first grade, since in Mexico ability to recite the alphabet is not considered particularly important. Findings from a longitudinal study of second-generation Latino students in the greater Los Angeles area indicated that families' home country experiences, including grandparents' level of education and parents' experience growing up in a rural versus an urban community, continued to influence children's literacy development as late as middle school (Reese, Garnier, Gallimore, & Goldenberg, 2000). Home country experiences of these Latino immigrant parents also served to shape the ways in which they engaged in oral reading with their children, including their motivations for reading and their understandings, or cultural models, of the nature of literacy itself. However, these cultural models were not static; rather, they changed over time as families adapted to U.S. environments and school demands (Reese & Gallimore, 2000).

Ecocultural theory (Gallimore et al., 1989; Reese, Kroesen, & Gallimore, 2000; Weisner 1984; Whiting & Whiting, 1975) provides a useful orientation for analyzing family practices within and across contrasting settings, taking into account cultural influences on family practices. This approach focuses on the everyday routines constructed and sustained by families. A family's routine is seen as a compromise between the structural and ecological constraints that families must live with on one hand, and the cultural values, understandings, models and beliefs which guide and give meaning to people's lives. Thus, ecocultural analyses encompass both the structural and the cultural forces shaping daily life and influencing decisions and accommodations made by individuals and families (Gallimore, Goldenberg & Weisner, 1993). An important feature of this perspective is that distal environmental influences such as the socioeconomic status or ethnic homogeneity of the community are conceptualized as exerting an indirect influence on children's developmental outcomes by influencing the more proximal environment with which children and families are engaged. With respect to literacy development, ecocultural theory predicts that family literacy practices will influence children's literacy development and will be shaped and/or constrained by proximal environmental factors such as the availability of literacy resources in L1 and/or L2 in the community where families live.

Recent literacy research has documented literacy practices in a wide variety of communities and out-of-school settings, emphasizing the notion of "literacies," that is, that there are different literacies associated with different domains of life (Barton & Hamilton, 1998; Barton, Hamilton & Ivanic, 2000; Moss, 1994; Street; 1993). In a study of the uses of written language among immigrant families in Chicago, Farr (1994) described literacy practices in terms of the domains in which these literacy acts occurred, identifying the five domains of religion, commerce, politics/law, family/home, and education. Participation in community literacy practices can fulfill a variety of purposes including reinforcement of ethnic pride and identity (Pak, 2003), participation in religious services and observations (Reese, Linan Thompson, & Goldenberg, 2005), or navigation of demands by government agencies such as the IRS or INS (Farr, 1994). It is likely, then, that children's engagement in activities making use of text material in one or both languages may influence their literacy development in general and in the long term. However, in "nonmainstream communities . . . literacy practices might–or more likely–might not match literacy practices in mainstream academic communities" (Moss, 1994, p. 2). Therefore, the extent to which community literacy resources contribute to specific academic outcomes is not a given and has yet to be documented.

The present study addresses this issue through the following questions regarding communities with large populations of Spanish-speaking children and families:

1. What is the relationship between community sociodemographic characteristics (e.g., income, educational level, and ethnic heterogeneity) and the language and literacy resources that exist in the community?
2. What is the relationship between community language and literacy resources and family literacy practices in English and Spanish?
3. What is the relationship between family literacy practices in English and Spanish and children's early reading achievement in English and Spanish?

Ultimately the question we are addressing is to what extent community sociodemographics (distal influences on family literacy practices) and community language and literacy resources and opportunities (proximal influences) facilitate or constrain family literacy practices, which then predict child literacy outcomes.

METHODS

This study is part of larger longitudinal study of language and literacy development among Spanish-speaking children carried out in 35 schools and communities in California and Texas. The Oracy/Literacy study developed a common set of data collection protocols for examining literacy development in English and Spanish, classroom instruction, family practices, and community characteristics. The present study focused on literacy development outside of school. Measures include individual assessments of children's early literacy and oral language proficiencies in English and Spanish, neighborhood observational surveys, parent surveys, and principal, parent and child interviews, and teacher focus group interviews.

Sample Selection

We selected a total of 35 schools in urban California (12) and urban and border Texas (12 and 11, respectively). Schools were selected in order to maximize variability with respect to school program and community characteristics. Yet we had to select schools with substantial Latino/ELL populations so that there would be sufficient children at each school (approx. 40 Spanish speaking ELLs/school in kindergarten) to permit meaningful inferences for schools and communities. (Since this was to be a longitudinal sample, we also had to take attrition into account.) Therefore, selection criteria required that schools have at least 40% Latino enrollment overall and at least 30% English language learner (ELL) enrollment in grades K and 1. These minimum percentages provided assurance of a sufficiently large Spanish-speaking population at the school and in the community. Sixty percent of ELLs in California and Texas attend schools that have greater than 30% ELL enrollment (August & Shanahan, 2006), so our sample schools were well within the typical range of ELL concentration in the two states where the study was conducted.

We furthermore sampled schools from a range of language programs for ELLs: English immersion, transitional bilingual education, developmental (or maintenance) bilingual education, and dual-language bilingual education (see Genessee, 1999, for more information on each of these program models). Finally, we sampled schools in diverse community types: ethnically heterogeneous, ethnically homogeneous (i.e., almost exclusively Latino), mixed-income and low-income communities.

Because we wanted to study at least adequate exemplars within each of these program categories, schools were rank ordered by achievement (Academic Performance Index, or API, in California; Texas Education Agency, TEA, ratings in Texas), within program (English immersion, etc.) and geographic site (urban and border Texas; urban California). In one case, we recruited a California school that had a relatively low API score but that had high scores in Spanish reading in grades 2–5 (64th–67th national percentile on the Spanish Assessment of Basic Skills; CTB-McGraw Hill).

Data Collection

Parent survey. Parents were surveyed using a written questionnaire sent home through the child's classroom teacher. This protocol included questions in Spanish on family sociodemographics (occupation, length of time in the local community, education), parents' expectations regarding their children's academic attainment and performance, school-related interactions, reported home literacy and homework practices, and the child's behavioral adjustment. Of the 1,865 parents we attempted to survey, 1,418 (76%) returned the surveys with at least some responses. Numbers are lower for the analyses due to missing data.

Parent interviews with key informant families. A subset of families at each school was selected to be interviewed in greater depth, participating in three home interviews over the course of the school year. Children's academic performance was rated by the teacher as high, medium, or low. For each school or program, four families were randomly selected for participation–one from the high group, two from the medium group, and one from the low group. Each interview lasted approximately 90–120 minutes. Most interviewees were the children's mothers; however, one family was headed by a single father, and fathers participated in some of the other interviews with the mothers. Project-trained interviewers were bilingual; most were themselves first- or second-generation Latino immigrants. The interviews focused on family language and literacy practices, attitudes, and materials. Also included was information on how long parents had lived in the local community, their perceptions about community resources and safety, and their participation in church and other community organizations. Parents were also asked about their own schooling experiences in their home countries, their school and job-related experiences in the United States, and ways in which they believed that their experiences might influence their children. Detailed data about the children's daily activities outside school, on both weekends and weekdays, and the opportunities for children's participation in literacy activities of different types in the community were collected, as well as parents' perceptions of neighborhood patterns of language and literacy use and potential barriers to children's literacy development and academic progress.

School attendance area surveys (SAAS & SAAS-L). We surveyed the school attendance neighborhood to assess languages heard and observed in different neighborhood settings. We also collected data on the types and condition of dwellings, the types and density of commercial enterprises, the presence and condition of recreational facilities such as parks and swimming pools, and the presence of organizations (such as sports clubs) and institutions (such as churches, libraries, health facilities etc.). Project investigators drove or walked each street in the neighborhood and stopped to observe key areas such as parks, grocery stores, libraries, and recreation centers (as available). Samples of free materials were collected. Observational data were recorded in two ways: on precoded forms and in relatively open-ended (but structured according to a common format) field notes where we made extensive notes on the characteristics described above. Field notes and coded survey protocols were augmented by photos and video footage taken to facilitate coding and write-up. Each survey took approximately 8 hours in the field, followed by approximately 10 hours of coding and field note write up.

Following completion of the SAAS and identification of key locales in which literacy materials were most likely to be available (e.g., markets, bookstores, libraries, community centers), a second survey focusing on literacy (SAAS-L) was carried out. In this survey, language use by participants in the setting was noted and textual materials (books, magazines, fliers, newspapers, greeting cards, and environmental print such as signs and notices) were coded for quantity, language, and type.

Principal interview and survey. Each school principal was interviewed for approximately 2 hours about characteristics of school functioning and culture that might influence students' achievement. Specifically, principals were asked to describe the community in which the school was located, the families and children who attended the school, changes in the community and school over time, learning resources available or lacking in the local area, and school attempts to involve parents and the community. Principals also filled out a detailed survey about student performance and a variety of factors that may be associated with performance: family and staff demographic profiles, class size, policies involved in academic tracking and retention in grade, scheduling, available resources, and so on.

Teacher focus group interview. A focus group interview of approximately 2 hours in length was carried out with 5–8 teachers from each school site. The teachers were chosen by the principals to represent a range of grade levels, number of years of experience in the teaching profession, and, where applicable, to include both bilingual and monolingual teachers. The teacher focus group protocol included the same questions and topics as those discussed with the principals.

U.S. census. U.S. Census data from 2000 were also gathered to provide background demographics such as ethnic distribution, home ownership, family size, and so on for the census tract in which each school attendance area was located.

Student achievement. Trained research assistants administered the Woodcock Language Proficiency Battery-Revised in English and Spanish (Woodcock, 1991; Woodcock & Muñoz-Sandoval, 1995). The WLPB-R is perhaps the most widely used assessment of language and literacy achievement in the United States. It has parallel forms in English and Spanish, thereby permitting comparisons of achievement within and across languages. We report scores on first grade basic reading (decoding and word recognition) and passage comprehension.

Family Sample Description

The total sample included 1,418 students selected at random from classrooms at the school with at least 50% Spanish-speaking ELLs. A large majority of parents were immigrants from Latin America, with 76% of mothers (female head of household) and 75% of fathers (male head of household) from Mexico. Seventeen percent (17%) and 18% of mothers and fathers, respectively, were born in the United States. Mothers averaged 11.4 years and fathers averaged 13.9 years in the United States. The mean number of years of schooling parents received was 9.1.

ANALYSIS

The analyses reported here represent a first step in trying to understand the complex relationships between family and community factors on the one hand and Spanish-speaking children's early reading attainment on the other. Although many possible analytical strategies are available (e.g., regression, structural equation modeling) and other variables could be included in analyses (e.g., family demographics), at this initial stage we use simple correlations to explore bivariate relationships that exist among community sociodemographics, community language and literacy resources, and family literacy practices in English and Spanish. We also examine the relationship between family literacy practices and children's first-grade reading achievement in English and Spanish. Our goal in this paper is to report plausible, empirically grounded hypotheses that future analyses will confirm or reject.

The data exist at two levels: community and family (including child level test data). Correlations involving community-level variables were calculated at the community level with all 35 communities. Interpretation of these correlations is straightforward–the degree of association between pairs of variables characterizing the communities in the study (e.g., mean income level and language heard in the community). We report correlations that reached the standard .05 level of significance.

Correlations involving family and child variables were calculated at the family/child level; their interpretation is also straightforward– the degree of association between family literacy practices (e.g., language in which parents read) and children's reading achievement (e.g., passage comprehension in Spanish). Because of our very large sample, many weak correlations (below .10) were statistically significant at beyond the .001 level. In order to prevent interpreting trivial associations (less than 1% of explained variance), we set the threshold for reporting correlations at the family/child level at .15, indicating a bivariate relationship in which one variable accounts for more than 2% of the variance in the other.

Analyses that involved both community-level (e.g., percent of English-only speakers in the census tract) and family-level (e.g., frequency of parents' reading) variables present more of a challenge, since interpretation of the correlations is less straightforward. We must be particularly mindful of the "ecological fallacy" (Sirin, 2005), that is, making individual-level inferences from group-level data. Group-level and individual-level analyses address subtly different questions, even when they use the same variables. We therefore calculated the correlations involving community and family-level variables in two ways:

1. At the community level, by aggregating family-level data up, that is, averaging values of all families within the community and using the resulting average as a community-level value. These correlations involve an N of 35 cases. They tell us the degree of association between community characteristics and *average* values in the community on the family variables; but they tell us nothing about whether community variables are associated with *individual* family characteristics.
2. At the individual family level, by assigning to each family the community-level value that corresponds to the community-level variable. These correlations involve Ns of approximately 1,000, depending on missing family-level data. They tell us the degree to which community characteristics are associated with family-level

FIGURE 1. Conceptual Model of Hypothesized Relationships

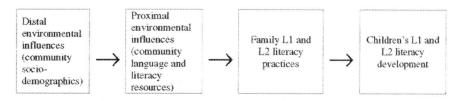

characteristics. Although seemingly more meaningful intuitively, it is this type of analysis that is most prone to the "ecological fallacy," since "an individual-level inference is made on the basis of group aggregated data" (Sirin, 2005, p. 419).

The general conceptual model underlying our analyses is depicted in Figure 1. A complete list of variables comprising each of the boxes in the conceptual model is provided in Table 1.

We hypothesized that more distal features of the environment, such as concentrations of speakers of one language or another, would be associated with more proximal influences on children's literacy development such as availability of text materials or the language of environmental print. The type, quantity, frequency and quality of the text materials in L1 and L2 in the surrounding community would then influence the frequency and types of literacy practices carried out in the home in ways that ultimately would influence the children's literacy development (see Figure 1).

RESULTS

Community Characteristics and Language and Literacy Resource Availability

The communities are located in urban, suburban, and semi-rural settings in Southern California, border Texas, and in two centrally located Texas cities. Some neighborhoods are almost exclusively Latino, where Spanish is the language heard. In other communities, Latinos occupy neighborhoods that include African American, White, Asian, and Pacific Islander populations as well. In some settings Spanish is heard but rarely seen in signage and printed materials available for sale, while in other settings Spanish print predominates.

TABLE 1. Community and Family Variables Used in the Analysis.

Community Socio-Demographics	Community Language and Literacy Resources	Family L1 and L2 Literacy Resources, Practices	Children's L1 and L2 Literacy Development
• % Latino population HS grads • % Latino population below poverty • Median income, adjusted for COL • % Latino population • Commercial/residential heterogeneity	*Language resources* • % Eng only speakers • % Spanish, little/no English • Language heard in community • Language used by children • Language used by adults • Language used by all *Literacy resources* • Total books, magazines for sale (except library, bookstores) • Total books, magazines • # libraries • # bookstores • % places w/newspapers • % places w/free print	*Literacy practices* • # of adult books • # children books • Frequency child reads on own • Frequency father reads books, magazines, etc. • Frequency mother reads books, magazines, etc. • Frequency child goes to library (not school library) *Language of literacy practices* • Frequency someone reads in English w/child • Frequency someone reads in Spanish w/child • Language child reads in • Language parents read in	*Basic reading* English • Letter sound identification • Word reading Spanish • Letter sound identification • Word reading *Passage comprehension* • English • Spanish (Woodcock Language Proficiency Battery-Revised)

(Continued)

TABLE 1. Continued.

Community Socio-Demographics	Community Language and Literacy Resources	Family L1 and L2 Literacy Resources, Practices	Children's L1 and L2 Literacy Development
	Language of literacy • Language of environmental print • % books, magazines in Spanish • % books for adults in Spanish (except library) • % magazines in Spanish (except library, bookstores) • % child consumables in Spanish • Overall community language of literacy • Language of commercial signs • Language of social service signs		

TABLE 2. Community Descriptive Statistics.

Vriable	N	Mean	SD	Min	Max
Community socio-demographic characteristics (distal)					
% Latino	35	72.6	25.1	14.0	98.7
% Latinos who are HS graduates	35	38.3	15.2	12.33	74.9
Commercial/residential heterogeneity	35	2.9	.7	2	4
Median COL-adjusted income	35	$29,408	$8,843	$11,808	$44,127
Community literacy resources (proximal)					
Printed material for sale (excl. libraries, bookstores)	35	65.9	94.0	0	432.5
Number of books and magazines	35	50,896	194,787	0	1,043,682
# of libraries	35	.2	.4	0	1
# of bookstores	35	.4	.8	0	3
Community language of literacy resources (proximal)					
Lang of signs, newspapers, free printed material*	35	3.6	.8	1.6	5.0
% of reading material for sale in Spanish	35	12.9	21.9	0	100
Language of commercial signs*	35	4.0	.7	2	5
Language of social services signs*	35	3.8	1.0	1	5
Community language resources (proximal)					
% population speaks only English	35	29.8	22.8	3.0	85.4
% population speaks Spanish; little or no English	35	22.5	11.4	1.3	50.4
Language heard around the community*	34	2.7	1.0	1	5
Language used in stores and other establishments*	35	3.2	1.0	2	5

*1 = only Spanish, 2 = mostly Spanish, 3 = Spanish and English equally, 4 = mostly English, 5 = only English.

In some communities, families live in quiet, predominantly residential neighborhoods; other communities include shopping malls, small businesses, and public service locales such as community centers, municipal buildings, courthouses, and hospitals. Table 2 reports descriptive statistics for the community-level variables used in this part of the analysis.

Table 3 summarizes the associations between community socio-demographic characteristics (distal influences) and language and

TABLE 3. Relationship Between Community Socio-Demographic (Distal) Factors and Literacy and Language Resources (Proximal Influences).

Community Literacy and Language Resources (Proximal Environmental Influences)		Community Socio-Demographics (Distal Environmental Influences)			
		% Latino	% Latinos who are HS Graduates	Residential/ Commercial Heterogeneity	Median COL-Adjusted Income
Literacy resources	Printed material for sale (excluding libraries, bookstores)	-.34	.56		.37
	Number of books and magazines			.41	
	# of libraries	-.46		.36	
	# of bookstores	-.41		.45	
Language of literacy materials	Language of signs, newspapers, free printed material*	-.59	.59		
	% of reading material in Spanish	.42			
	Language of commercial signs*	-.48	.49	.38	
	Language of social service signs*	-.53	.36	.48	
Community language	% population speaks only English	-.96	.47		.44
	% population speaks Spanish; little, no Eng	.76	-.72	-.33	-.34
	Language heard around the community*	-.78			.35
	Language used in stores and other establishments*	-.73			.34

Note: All correlations significant at p ≤ .05.
*1 = only Spanish, 2 = mostly Spanish, 3 = Spanish and English equally, 4 = mostly English, 5 = only English.

literacy resources in the community (proximal influences) across the 35 communities. Community language and literacy resources, such as languages heard and seen, availability of books, and access to a library, vary according to community sociodemographics. The single most important variable among the community sociodemographic characteristics was percent of the census tract that is Latino. Percent Latino was correlated with 11 of the 12 languages and literacy resources shown in Table 3. Communities with greater concentrations of Latino residents are less likely to have printed materials for sale, libraries, and bookstores. What materials are available have a greater likelihood of being in Spanish when a community has a higher concentration of Latinos. Finally, and not surprisingly, concentration of Latinos is associated with more use of Spanish in the community, among individuals, and inside stores and other establishments.

Higher income communities are more likely to have printed material for sale, but income level had no relationship with any other literacy indicators. Communities with a greater percentage of high school graduates among the Latino populace are also likely to have more literacy materials than communities with fewer high school graduates. Greater percentage of high school graduates is also associated with more materials in English and with more English use in the community. Communities with greater residential/commercial heterogeneity (i.e., greater percentage of commercial land use in comparison to residential) are more likely to have a greater number of books, magazines, libraries, and bookstores; English is also more likely to be heard in these communities.

Findings by Neuman and Celano (2001) and a three-case analysis by Smith, Constantino and Krashen (1997) that more literacy materials are available in higher SES neighborhoods are partly supported by our findings. The income level of the community and the educational level of the Latino population predict the amount of printed material for sale in the community, but they do not predict any other measure of quantity of print available such as number of books and magazines and number of libraries and bookstores. Higher educational attainment among the Latino community, however, was associated with more printed material in English. A contrastive case analysis carried out in a pilot year of work in two of our participating communities also indicated that availability of text material in Spanish did not follow the same pattern as that observed in English. More Spanish materials were available in the lower income,

Latino neighborhood than in the higher income, predominantly Anglo and English-speaking neighborhood (Reese & Goldenberg, 2006). All three of the studies cited above are premised on the assumption that community availability of resources can/will play a role in children's literacy development. Testing this assumption forms the basis for the questions posed in the sections to follow.

Community Language and Literacy Resources (Proximal Influences) and Family Literacy Practices

Are proximal community language and literacy resources associated with families' literacy practices in English and Spanish? The answer varies by category of resource: Community *literacy resources* show very little relationship with family literacy practices. Community *oral language characteristics*, in contrast, show stronger relationships with family literacy practices, particularly family literacy practices analyzed at the community (rather than individual) level.

In this section we first report the *absence of an association* between community literacy and family literacy practices, followed by an illustrative case study of one of our communities that suggests an explanation for the absence of the predicted association. In the next section, we report on the one domain of proximal community resources–language use in the community–where we do see an association with family literacy practices, although in an unexpected direction.

Table 4 reports descriptive statistics for selected family-level variables (at the family level).

At the family level, we found very few correlations between community literacy resources (identified in Table 2) and family literacy practices (shown in Table 4) high enough to meet our .15 threshold. Of the approximately 200 possible correlations, only 5 met the criterion: The number of books and magazines in the community was correlated with the frequency of reading to the child in English (.16) and the frequency that the child reads or looks at books in English on his or her own (.25). The number of bookstores was associated with the child's reading or looking at books more in English (.18). The quality of Spanish literacy materials was associated (.21) with children's reading or looking at books more in Spanish. One correlation was counterintuitive: The percentage of magazines in Spanish was associated (.19) with children reading more in English.

TABLE 4. Family Literacy Practices.

Variable	N	Mean	SD	Min	Max
Frequency of reading to child in English**	1,314	2.4	1.4	0	4
Frequency of reading to child in Spanish**	1,351	2.5	1.4	0	4
Child reading language*	893	2.4	1.4	1	5
Parents' reading language*	1,402	2.1	1.2	1	5
# Adult books in the home	1,064	17.2	40.3	0	900
# Child books in the home	1,287	30.0	46.2	0	700
Frequency child reads on own**	862	3.0	1.2	0	4
Frequency Mother reads***	1,384	2.8	1.2	0	4
Frequency Father reads***	1,288	2.2	1.4	0	4

*1 = only Spanish, 2 = mostly Spanish, 3 = Spanish and English equally, 4 = mostly English, 5 = only English.

**0 = almost never, 1 = less than once a month, 2 = 1–2 times a month, 3 = 1–2 times a week, 4 = daily.

***0 = never, 1 = less than once a month, 2 = 1–2 times a month, 3 = 1–2 times a week, 4 = almost daily, 6 = more than once a day.

Expected relationships, such as the number of books available in the community or presence of a library, on the one hand, and frequency of reading at home or books for children and adults at home, on the other, did not emerge.

When we did the analysis aggregated at the community level, we found only 4 significant correlations: language of commercial and social service signs each correlated (.37 and .32, respectively) with the average number (across project participants in the community) of children's books in the homes. Total books available in the community predicted average frequency with which children were read to (.47); and the percentage of visited establishments that had free printed material predicted the frequency with which mothers report reading (.34).

Why do we find relatively little evidence for the effects of proximal community factors on home family literacy practices? Of course, it is possible that the ecocultural theory upon which the hypotheses were based is flawed (or only partially true), and, in fact, family practices operate relatively independently from the contexts in which families live. Or it might be that, although family practices are shaped by ecological and cultural factors, other processes might be at work in which diminish potential relationships between community influences and family practices. In the following section we will use one community case study to illustrate ways in which family agency works to counter structural influences reflected in the distal and proximal community factors described above.

Community Case Study of Family Use of Available Literacy Resources

The 35 communities included in our study include a wide range of characteristics–from urban to semirural, from exclusively Latino to predominantly Anglo and English-speaking, from exclusively residential neighborhoods to neighborhoods surrounded by strip malls, industrial parks, and shopping centers. While selection of a single representative community is close to impossible, the community surrounding Bell School, described below, is more or less typical of the Southern California communities in our study. It is mixed with regard to ethnicity and language, while the school program has switched to English immersion as a result of California legislation passed in 1998.

Community description. Bell Elementary School is located in the downtown area of a mid-sized coastal city in Southern California. The community is predominantly Latino and low income, but at the same time it is highly diverse with respect to ethnicity, language, SES and land use (residential/commercial/industrial). The neighborhood includes the civic center, with the city hall, court building, police department, and public library.

The major literacy resource in the community is the main library. A two-story building located in the civic center, it contains a large selection of books, magazines, and media materials in English and some materials in Spanish. Very little environmental print (such as signs, fliers) is in evidence in Spanish, or any language other than English. There are no bookstores in the school attendance area neighborhood, but two are located close by; however, each of these contains very few books in Spanish. Few materials in the local discount grocery stores are available in either L1 or L2, but there is a Wal-mart close by with materials in English. Again, however, there are limited titles available in Spanish.

Survey data for the 40 participating families living in the Bell community indicated that all parents were native speakers of Spanish and were born outside of the United States. Parents averaged 7.4 years of schooling. Mothers averaged 9.7 years in the United States, and fathers slightly more (11 years). The great majority of families (92.5%) earned under $30,000/year, with 67% earning under $20,000/year.

Accessing "available" materials. Although materials may be available in what we have determined to be the "community" (School Attendance Area), they might not be equally accessible to all families. For example, three families described walking to the library because it was close; however, one family did not go because the children *"no tienen credencial ellos para sacar [libros], se me ha hecho muy dificil para ellos"* ("they don't have a credential [library card] to be able to take out [books], I have found it to be very difficult for them'). The school principal explained that one of the requirements for a library card was a social security number and that this was a problem for parents who were in the United States illegally.

Role of the school in providing materials for home use. At Bell School, all four interviewees took advantage of the school library to check out materials for their children, stating that reading materials were not hard to obtain in their community because the school provided them. One mother volunteered at school and checked out books: *"Yo allí me voy de voluntaria y allí agarro el que yo quiero también"* ("I go there as a volunteer and there I take the books I want too'). Daily homework is a school policy, and many teachers send books home regularly. Another mother commented that her son *"está estudiando los libros y haciendo lo que le dejan de tarea"* ("is studying the books and doing what they send as homework'). In addition, the school periodically gives away books that it no longer uses. *"En la escuela también así les dan. De repente les dan su libro de los que ya no ocupan, que ya tienen de más, les dan que dos, que tres y así."* ("At school they also give them out. At times they give them a book from those that they don't need any more, since they have others, they give out two or three, like that"). The pattern of the school's providing of take-home reading materials and books, through the school or classroom libraries, was found across schools in the study.

It may be that because schools included in our study were higher achieving schools, they were more proactive than normal in compensating for lack of availability of books in the community. One teacher described the role of the school as a service provider in the inner city neighborhood where it is located: "If they have any questions about, you know, police, or being evicted, or welfare, or social security, they come to school first even for help, even if they're sick. They come to school to get the answers or get referred to somewhere, to some agency for some assistance; so, they really value our school being in this location." It is possible that if there were a wider range in achievement levels represented in the schools participating in the study, we might also see greater variation in the extent to which the schools provided reading material to families. Regardless, in this sample of 35 schools we consistently heard reports of schools sending home homework and reading materials and making the school libraries available for parents and children to use. We suspect these actions by schools help mitigate the effect of low levels of literacy materials available in the community. Absent this school effect, we expect we would have seen a greater impact of availability of community literacy resources on children's home literacy opportunities.

Accessing resources outside of the community. Although aspects of families' daily routines may be constrained within the neighborhood by what is within walking distance, particularly for low-income families with a single vehicle that is used by one of the parents to go to work, families can and do go outside of their immediate neighborhoods for a variety of purposes and activities. Church attendance is an example of an activity that takes some families outside of the neighborhood. Most families in the study report attending church; all four Bell families attend Catholic mass at St. Mark's, about 10 blocks outside of their school attendance area neighborhood. As Catholics, the families do not attend one of the three Protestant churches located closer and within the neighborhood. At St. Mark's, the church services are separated by language, which results in separation by ethnicity. *"Hay misa para los Latinos y hay misa para los gabachos"* ("There is one mass for Latinos and one mass for white people"), and families in our study all attend the Spanish mass. Children also attend catechism classes on Saturdays in the church's education building, with classes available in Spanish for the younger children and English for the older children. Some families report driving to neighboring communities on occasion to attend church with relatives. The church serves not only a spiritual role but also is a setting for language and cultural maintenance. Church attendance appears to motivate families to go outside of their immediate neighborhood to access resources. We do not have evidence that literacy motivates families in a similar way.

Differential accessing of literacy materials by families and children. Regardless of how much is available in the community with respect to books and print materials for sale or how easy or difficult it is to access a public library, families vary in how much they take advantage of these local resources. For example, one of the case study mothers is a volunteer at school in a program called Partners in Print. Although concerned that her own level of schooling is not high (she has a second grade education), Mrs. Salinas nonetheless participated in training to enable her to read with children at school, and she faithfully volunteered once a week to read in her daughter's classroom. She reported being able to bring home books for her child to use at home. Another mother reported buying books often because her child requested them. On the other hand, one of the mothers stated that she did not take her children to the library because it was too far away.

The actions and responses of these different parents illustrate how family activities, choices, and decisions operate either to offset the potential constraints of the literacy environment in which they live or to bypass literacy opportunities that do exist. Some parents choose to participate in school parent activities, to take their children to the library, and obtain second-hand books from the school. Families are not bound by the limits of their neighborhood, traveling outside of the neighborhood to attend church, for example. At the same time, not all families seek out or take advantage of literacy opportunities in the community. This variability in family practices that exists within communities will of course tend to diminish the correlation between community literacy resources and family literacy practices. Added to this variability, then, is the role the school plays in providing books and materials for take-home use, further weakening the link between community literacy resources and children's literacy experiences at home. The fact is that communities themselves are not monolithic; individuals within them, supported by a key institution–the school–make choices and take actions that influence children's learning opportunities.

Community Language Resources and Family Literacy Practices

While the availability of print materials per se appears to have no influence on family literacy practices, community *language* use and *language* characteristics show more of an association. Table 5 reports correlations between community language resources and family literacy practices, *at the family level*, that meet our .15 threshold for reporting.

TABLE 5. Community Language Use and Family Language of Literacy (Family Level Correlations).

		Community Language			
		% Population Speaks Only English	% Population Speaks Spanish, with Little/No English	Language Heard Around the Community*	Language Used in Stores and Other Establishments*
Family language of literacy	Parents' reading language*	−.22		−.17	−.24
	Child's reading language*	−.15			
	Frequency of reading with child in Spanish				.15

Note: All correlations significant at p ≤ .05.
*English = high.

When relationships between language use in the community and family practices are examined at the family level, correlations are relatively few and of low magnitude. The correlations that do appear are between community language use and family language of literacy; however, no correlations between community language use and other family practices, such as frequency of reading by child or parents, are evident. A somewhat stronger pattern emerges when the data are examined at the community level. Table 6 reports correlations between community language resources and family literacy practices, *at the community level.*

Tables 5 and 6 report surprising and complex findings for which we have no clear explanation. In brief, the tables suggest that

(a) *more English speakers* in the community are associated with *more reading in Spanish* by parents (row 1 of Tables 5 and 6) and *more reading in Spanish* to children (row 3 of Table 6); however,
(b) *more English heard* in the community has essentially *no bearing* on reading by children (row 2 of Table 6);
(c) *more English* heard in the community (but not language as gauged by census data) is associated with *less reading* by parents (rows 4 and 5 of Table 6).

TABLE 6. Community Language Use and Family Literacy (Community Level Correlations).

		Community Language			
		% Population Speaks Only English	% Population Speaks Spanish, with Little/No English	Language Heard Around the Community*	Language Used in Stores and Other Establishments*
Family language of literacy	Parents' reading language*	−.49		−.39	−.55
	Child's reading language* Frequency of reading with child in Spanish	.35			.41
Family literacy practices	Frequency father reads			−.38	−.51
	Frequency mother reads				−.41

Note: All correlations significant at $p \leq .05$.
*English = high.

Finding (b) is probably due to the fact that children's reading (and the language of their reading) is more likely motivated by the school rather than any community characteristics. But what are we to make of findings (a) and (c)? Our qualitative data provide no insights to help explain these findings. Analyses currently underway using multilevel analytical models might shed more light. All we can say with assurance is that community language characteristics bear some relationship to family language and literacy practices. The nature of that relationship is yet to be fully understood.

Family Practices and Student Literacy Achievement

Finally we turn to the association between family experiences and first-grade reading achievement. Table 7 shows the descriptive statistics for the WLPB-R standard scores. Overall, children are scoring right at the national mean (100). Scores are higher in basic reading than in reading comprehension and higher in Spanish than English.

TABLE 7. WLPB-R First Grade Standard Scores, Reading Clusters.

Variable	N	Mean	SD	Min	Max
Basic reading-English	1,353	104.5	18.3	50	181
Passage comprehension-English	1,439	98.0	15.4	47	137
Basic reading-Spanish	1,341	123.6	28.9	45	185
Passage comprehension-Spanish	1,431	100.0	18.9	33	131

Tables 8 and 9 report the correlations between family literacy practices and children's reading scores. What is most striking is that there
is virtually no correlation with measures of home literacy practices
that are language-neutral, that is, with measures that index literacy
experiences, independent of language. However, there are moderate
correlations between literacy practices *in either English or Spanish*
and reading outcomes. As we saw in the relationships between community literacy and family literacy, the *language of literacy* is a
key dimension. *Language of literacy*–not *literacy per se*–connects
community influences, family influences, and child outcomes. See
Tables 8 and 9.

TABLE 8. Correlations Between Family Literacy Practices and Basic
Reading.

Family Language of Literacy (More Eng = High*)	Correlation with	
	English *Basic Reading*	Spanish *Basic Reading*
Frequency of English reading with child	–	−.15
Frequency of Spanish reading with child	–	.30
*Child's reading language	.31	−.53
*Parents' reading language	.20	−.20
Family literacy practices		
# adult books in the home	–	–
# child books in the home	–	–
Frequency child reads on own	–	–
Frequency father reads books, magazines, newspaper	–	–
Frequency mother reads books, magazines, newspaper	–	–
Frequency child goes to library	–	–
Frequency reading to child, any language	–	–

Note: All correlations significant at p ≤ .001.

TABLE 9. Correlations Between Family Literacy Practices and Reading Comprehension.

Family Language of Literacy (More Eng = High*)	Correlation with	
	English *Passage Comprehension*	Spanish *Passage Comprehension*
Frequency of English reading with child	.19	− .19
Frequency of Spanish reading with child	− .16	.27
*Child's reading language	.45	− .54
*Parents' reading language	.28	− .20
Family literacy practices		
# adult books in the home	−	−
# child books in the home	−	−
Frequency child reads on own	.16	.15
Frequency Father reads books, magazines, newspaper	−	−
Frequency Mother reads books, magazines, newspaper	−	−
Frequency child goes to library	−	−
Frequency reading to child, any language	−	−

Note: All correlations significant at p ≤ .001.

DISCUSSION

The analyses reported above represent an initial step in exploring relationships among community and family inputs and children's literacy development in two languages. Our analyses were limited to simple bi-variate correlations, which were sufficient for our purposes, but fail to control for confounds and variables measured at the individual and community levels. In addition, conducting a large number of correlations raises the risk of spurious findings, since some small percentage of correlations will always appear statistically significant. We partly addressed this problem by setting a minimum threshold of magnitude (±.15) before reporting and interpreting correlations. Moreover, we attempted to find broad patterns among correlations involving groups of variables (e.g., community characteristics, community language, family literacy, family language of literacy; see Table 1), rather than interpreting individual correlations. Analyses currently underway will test hypotheses the current analyses have generated while addressing the methodological limitations of what we report here.

The findings are complex and not necessarily what we expected. First, and not surprisingly, community characteristics–ethnicity, education levels, residential/commercial mix, and income–are associated with literacy and language resources in the community (Table 3). Second, and very surprising, there is no association between literacy resources in the community and literacy practices in families. In other words, families in relatively "high literacy communities" did not report more literacy in the home than did families in "low literacy communities." The Bell case study material suggests two possible explanations: (1) schools' outreach efforts, including sending homework, making libraries available, etc., tended to increase literacy inputs into the families, regardless of the disparities in the community resources from one community to the next and (2) parent agency–parents might or might not take advantage of literacy resources in their communities and in nearby communities, so there was no direct line between community literacy resources and family literacy practices.

Patterns of language use in the community, however, including the language of literacy materials that were available, appear to be a greater influence (to the extent correlations can be interpreted causally) on home reading practices. The patterns of relationships we observed reveal the importance of considering what language is being used in the community and in which language texts are available. These are what have a bearing on home literacy practices. Finally, home literacy practices appear to have language-specific effects on early literacy development. For children of immigrants growing up bilingually, it is not enough to examine the quantity of materials or frequency of literacy activities in general. It is necessary to take into account the language in which these occur, since the language influences home language and literacy practices, which in turn influence children's literacy development.

The study also found that communities with higher percentages of Latino residents are more likely to include fewer English-only speakers and fewer literacy resources such as books and magazines for sale. This implies that Spanish-speaking families may have to work harder to access books to read to and with their children than do families living in more affluent and English-speaking environments.

The children in our study live in communities that are surprisingly different in terms of socioeconomic status, ethnic heterogeneity, and residential/commercial mix. These communities offered varying opportunities for resident families to use and hear English and/or Spanish and to obtain literacy materials in each language. However, as we have seen, the community context does not determine family practices. Families demonstrate considerable variability with respect to the frequency, types, and language(s) of literacy activities carried out by parents and children, exhibiting agency in taking advantage of materials available locally as well as outside of their immediate neighborhoods.

Despite the puzzling findings about community language and family language and literacy activities, the take-home message for educators and practitioners is, therefore, a cautionary one: Children's home literacy opportunities cannot be predicted by the communities in which they live and by the resources that those communities offer. The families in the study vary considerably in the literacy opportunities they provide their children, but this variability has little to do with literacy resources in the communities where they live. Rather, agency at both the family level and the school level–what parents, children, and teachers do and the decisions they make–makes a difference in terms of children's performance in school.

The findings reported here represent an initial attempt to organize and interpret data on a complex set of processes, and findings should be seen as preliminary. Further data are needed to see if the patterns identified here continue as children progress in school and in their literacy development. Lack of correlation between family literacy practices (not tied to a specific language) and children's literacy performance may hold true for the early literacy measures used in our study of children in kindergarten and grade one but may not be the case when reading tasks become more demanding and measures of reading comprehension become more complex. Future research must therefore study language and literacy development into middle elementary grades and beyond.

In addition, comparative research is needed with monolingual English samples. This would help clarify the role of dual-language settings in the processes of community and family influences on the literacy development of the children in our sample. The bilingual environments in which Spanish-speaking children live introduce a layer of complexity in the study of language and literacy development; parallel comparative studies with monolingual populations could help clarify more precisely the role these bilingual contexts play.

Finally, there is a great need for the sort of detailed micro-analysis among bilingual populations that Hart and Risley (1995) conducted with a monolingual population. In the absence of such data, we can only guess about the quality and quantity of linguistic input these children receive and what its cognitive and linguistic consequences are. Given the large and growing language-minority population in the United States, and the large number of bilinguals world–wide, this is a gap we should address.

REFERENCES

August, D., & Shanahan, T. (Eds.). (2006). *Developing literacy in second-language learners: Report of the national literacy panel on language-minority children and youth.* Mahwah, NJ: Lawrence Erlbaum.

Barton, D., & Hamilton, M. (1998). *Local literacies.* NY: Routledge.

Barton, D., & Hamilton, M. (2000). Literacy practices. In D. Barton, M. Hamilton, & R. Ivanic (Eds.), *Situated literacies: Reading and writing in context* (pp. 7–15). London: Routledge.

Barton, D., Hamilton, M., & Ivanic, R. (2000). *Situated literacies.* London: Routledge.

Bayley, R., & Schecter, S. (2003). *Language socialization in bilingual and multilingual societies.* Clevedon, UK: Multilingual Matters.

Booth, A., & Dunn, J. (Eds.) (1996). *Family and school links: How do they affect educational outcomes?* Mahwah, NJ: Erlbaum.

California Department of Education (2005). *California STAR program.* Retrieved June 20, 2006 from http://star.cde.ca.gov/star2005.

Farr, M. (1994). En los dos idiomas: Literacy practices among Chicago mexicanos. In B. Moss (Ed.), *Literacy across communities* (pp. 9–47). Cresskill, NJ: Hampton Press.

Gallimore, R., Weisner, T., Kaufman, S., & Bernheimer, L. (1989). The social construction of ecological niches: Family accommodation of developmentally delayed children. *American Journal of Mental Retardation, 94,* 216–230.

Genesee, F. (Ed.). (1999). Program alternatives for linguistically diverse students (Educational Practice Report #1). Santa Cruz, CA: Center for Research on Education, Diversity and Excellence.

Gorman, A., Miller, M., & Landsberg, M. (2006). Immigrants demonstrate peaceful power. *Los Angeles Times,* May 2, 2006.

Hart, B., & Risley, T. R. (1995). *Meaningful differences in everyday experiences of young American children.* Baltimore, MD: Paul H. Brookes.

Institute of Education Sciences. (2005). *2005 assessment results.* Retrieved August 15, 2006 from http://nces.ed.gov/nationsreportcard/nrc/reading_math_2005.

Martin-Jones, M., & Jones, K. (2000). *Multilingual literacies: Reading and writing different worlds.* Philadelphia: John Benjamins.

McCarty, T. (2005). *Language, literacy, and power in schooling.* Mahwah, NJ: Lawrence Erlbaum.

McKay, S., & Wong, S. (2000). *New immigrants in the United States.* Cambridge, UK: Cambridge University Press.

Moss, B. (Ed.). (1994). *Literacy across communities.* Cresskill, NJ: Hampton Press.

Neuman, S., & Celano, D. (2001). Access to print in low-income and middle-income communities: An ecological study of four neighborhoods. *Reading Research Quarterly, 36,* 8–26.

Pak, H. (2003). When MT is L2: The Korean church as a context for cultural identity. In N. Horberger (Ed.), *Continua of biliteracy* (pp. 269–290). Clevedon: Multilingual Matters.

Reese, L., & Gallimore, R. (2000). Immigrant Latinos' cultural model of literacy development: An evolving perspective on home-school discontinuities. *American Journal of Education, 108,* 103–134.

Reese, L., Garnier, H., Gallimore, R., & Goldenberg, C. (2000). A longitudinal analysis of the ecocultural antecedents of emergent spanish literacy and subsequent english reading achievement of Spanish-speaking students. *American Educational Research Journal, 37,* 633–662.

Reese, L., & Goldenberg, C. (2006). Community contexts for literacy development of Latina/o children: Contrasting case studies. *Anthropology and Education Quarterly, 37,* 42–61.

Reese, L., Kroesen, K., & Gallimore, R. (2000). Agency and school performance among urban Latino youth. In R. Taylor & M. Wang (Eds.), *Resilience across contexts: Family, work, culture and community.* New Jersey: Erlbaum.

Reese, L., Linan Thompson, S., & Goldenberg, C. Variability in Community, Home Language, and Literacy Opportunities among Spanish-Speaking Children. Poster Presented at the International Reading Association 2005 Annual Convention, San Antonio, Texas, May, 2005.

Sirin, S. (2005). Socioeconomic status and academic achievement: A meta-analytic review of research. *Review of Educational Research, 3,* 417–453.

Smith, C., Constantino, R., & Krashen, S. (1997). Differences in print environment for childrenin Beverly Hills, Compton and Watts. *Emergency Librarian, 24,* 8–9.

Street, B. (1993). *Cross-cultural approaches to literacy.* Cambridge: Cambridge University Press.

Shin, H., & Bruno, R. (2003). *Language use and English-speaking ability: 2000* (C2KBR-29). Washington, DC: U.S. Department of Commerce, U.S. Census Bureau.

Valdés, G. (1996). *Con respeto: Bridging the distances between culturally diverse families and schools.* New York: Teachers College Press.

Weisner, T. S. (1984). Ecocultural niches of middle childhood: A cross-cultural perspective. In W. A. Collins (Ed.), *Development during middle childhood: The years from six to twelve* (pp. 335–369). Washington, DC: National Academy of Sciences.

Whiting, J., & Whiting, B. (1975). *Children of six cultures: A psychocultural analysis.* Cambridge, MA: Harvard University Press.

Woodcock, R. W. (1991). *Woodcock language proficiency battery-revised* (English form). Chicago, IL: Riverside.

Woodcock, R., & Muñoz-Sandoval, A. F. (1995). *Woodcock language proficiency battery-revised* (Spanish form). Chicago, IL: Riverside.

Examining Familial-Based Academic Success Factors in Urban High School Students: The Case of Puerto Rican Female High Achievers

René Antrop-González
William Vélez
Tomás Garrett

ABSTRACT. This article works to dispel the myth that Puerto Rican female urban high school students living in poverty are not capable of performing at high academic levels. This article attempts to counteract these beliefs by describing the four success factors that seven Puerto Rican female high school students attribute to their high academic achievement. These success factors are: (1) religiosity and extracurricular activities as sources of social capital, (2) affirming and maintaining a Puerto Rican identity, (3) maternal influences on students' academic achievement and, (4) the potential for caring teachers and other school staff to influence high academic achievement. Finally, our findings suggest that opportunities for Latinas and other youth of color are still inequitably structured in large, comprehensive

René Antrop-González, PhD, is Associate Professor of Curriculum and Instruction/Second Language Education, School of Education; William Vélez, PhD, is Professor of Sociology with the Department of Sociology and Tomás Garrett is currently a doctoral student in the Urban Studies Program, University of Wisconsin-Milwaukee, WI.

high schools. Hence, we argue that schools must continue to bridge the large gap between themselves and the families/communities they serve and utilize the funds of knowledge and social capital that their students already bring to school.

INTRODUCTION

Puerto Rican female high achievers are largely invisible in traditional, public urban high schools and in educational research. Over the last three decades, numerous scholars have written about the connections between the academic *underachievement* of Puerto Rican colonial subjects educated in the United States and socioeconomic/academic barriers like internal and direct colonialism, single-parent households, poverty, culturally irrelevant curricula, and the non academic tracking these students face within traditional public urban schools on a continual basis (Díaz, 1998; Nieto, 1998, 2000; Spring, 1994).

Díaz (1998), for instance, recently explored the self and environmental factors that led to the academic underachievement of six talented, Puerto Rican urban high school students. In turn, she found that that there were five school-related factors, which influenced their underachievement. They were (1) a lack of exposure to appropriate and challenging curricular experiences at the elementary school level, (2) an absence of opportunities to develop or improve a schoolwork discipline, (3) negative interactions with teachers, (4) an unrewarding curriculum, and (5) questionable experiences with guidance counselors. Moreover, the self and environmental factors that these six students felt fueled their underachievement and hindered their academic success were directly related to the above school-related factors and included low self confidence and low levels of motivation. Hence, Díaz concluded that "educators, practitioners, administrators, and the public in general must recognize the existence of talented students of Puerto Rican descent despite the negative stereotypes of intellectual inferiority, low achievement, and laziness about Puerto Ricans that may exist" (Díaz, 1998, p. 119).

Although the above-mentioned scholarship is important, it places overdue emphasis on the academic underachievement of these students. Furthermore, this academic underachievement has been exacerbated by the fact that Puerto Rican and other Latina/o students are disproportionately represented in special education programs that academically miscategorize them and espouse watered-down curricula (Artiles & Trent, 1994; MacMillan & Reschly, 1998; Obiakor, 2001). This academic (mis)categorization and subsequent overrepresentation of urban youth of color in special education programs often stems from the gravely erroneous and racist belief that being poor equates to being unintelligent. Consequently, some teachers mislabel their students of color (Obiakor, 2001). To counteract the overabundance of scholarly literature that discusses reasons why Puerto Rican students drop out of school and/or academically underachieve, we felt that it was important to explore the factors that Puerto Rican female students who are enrolled in traditional urban high schools may attribute to their academic success in spite of the previously mentioned socioeconomic barriers.

BACKGROUND

Scholars have recently produced research that serves to deconstruct, reconstruct, and transcend the scholarship on academic underachievement by examining factors that foment the high academic achievement of Puerto Rican/Latino students. These factors include the importance of these students' families, especially the role of the mother and/or grandmother, as support systems (Díaz, 1998; Gándara, 1995; Hidalgo, 2000; Hine, 1992; Rolón, 2000), these students' acquisition of social capital and their participation in social networks, including churches and extracurricular activities with institutional agents (Flores-González, 1999, 2002; Hine, 1992; Reis & Díaz, 1999; Sikkink & Hernández, 2003; Stanton-Salazar, 2001), and the importance of caring teachers and culturally relevant curricula within schools (Ladson-Billings, 1995; Nieto, 1998; Valenzuela, 1999).

Hine (1992) interviewed 10 gifted Puerto Rican urban high school students and their families to understand factors that contributed to their high achievement. The students and their families revealed the importance of mothers and the support they offered their children. This support included monitoring their child's success in school by checking their schoolwork, offering help with their child's homework and/or finding someone who could help if they were not able to, and showing interest in topics being studied in school. The students also belonged to families who strongly encouraged their children to develop their linguistic skills in both Spanish and English, held their children to high academic expectations, and encouraged their children to use negative cultural stereotypes and low teacher expectations as a motivating tool. In other words, they encouraged their children to prove to others that Puerto Ricans can achieve academic success. Finally, these families strongly encouraged their children to participate in extracurricular activities and socially bond with their classmates.

Hidalgo (2000) interviewed four working-class Puerto Rican mothers of kindergarten students in Boston whom teachers identified as high achievers. These mothers used a variety of strategies to start their children on the path to academic success: monitoring strategies, communication strategies, motivational strategies, and protective strategies. The monitoring strategies included checking children's schoolwork on a daily basis, checking their book bags daily, doing homework with them, and attending open house meetings at school. The communication strategies consisted of maintaining family bonds that nurtured the maintenance of Puerto Rican values like the use of Spanish at home and encouraging a strong sense of Puerto Rican ethnicity. This communication and transmission of cultural values between mother and child also included the establishment of behavioral parameters like counseling against drug use and other negative peer influences like gang membership. The motivational strategies these mothers provided for their children consisted of positive messages like trying their best, working hard, and to keep trying even if their child received low grades.

Flores-González (1999, 2002) used role identity theory to explain the multiple ways in which urban high schools structure inequitable opportunities for Puerto Rican students by influencing whether they adopt either a "school kid" or "street kid" identity. The high-achieving Puerto Rican students whom she interviewed and classified as having a "school kid" identity were more likely to be sheltered in safe social niches with other school kids and encouraged by school staff to actively participate in extracurricular activities like athletic teams, church-related activities, and academic-based school clubs. These extracurricular activities also enabled these students to set themselves apart from the "street kids." Moreover, these school kids were more likely to view postsecondary education as a way through which they could become a member of the middle class.

On the contrary, the low achieving Puerto Rican students who adopted a "street kid" identity found it difficult to situate themselves within school oriented peer social networks and the school staff neither encouraged nor facilitated these students' participation in school-related activities. Hence, the self-concept that children and young adults develop reflects their images of their future and what they hope to become, and thus guides their actions in schools and other social institutions. Additionally, unlike the schooling experiences of high-achieving African–American students in previous studies (Fordham & Ogbu, 1986), the high-achieving Puerto Rican students interviewed by Flores-González (1999, 2002) voiced a strong Puerto Rican ethnic identity, revealing that they neither perceived themselves nor were perceived by other school peers as "acting White." Additionally, recent quantitative research has provided explanations regarding the connection between religiosity as a source of social capital and the high academic achievement of Latina/o and other youth of color (Jeynes, 2003; Muller & Ellison, 2001; Park, 2001; Sikkink & Hernández, 2003).

Religiosity and active participation in church-related activities have also been found to be an important source of social capital for two reasons. First, church membership provides mentoring relations between adults and youth that instill positive attitudes, values, and behaviors that promote school success and serve as protective measures against oppositional youth behaviors like gang membership, drug use, and truancy. Second, participating in church activities like retreats and conventions facilitates intergenerational closure (Carbonaro, 1998; Sikkink & Hernández, 2003). Intergenerational closure is valuable because it helps these students, through the relationships they have with their friends and their friends' parents, gain access to important resources like advice, mentorship, and other positive help-seeking behaviors that encourage them to pursue and maintain their high academic achievement.

The above scholarship is important because it has seriously worked to offer an alternative scholarly perspective to the more abundant underachievement literature that exists pertaining to the schooling experiences of Latina/o students and other urban youth of color. However, much work remains to be done because, with the exception of a few recent studies (Reis & Díaz, 1999; Rolón, 2000), very few scholars have attempted to describe and make sense of the experiences of Puerto Rican female high achievers schooled in urban high schools in the United States.

Like Hine (1992), other researchers have recently revealed the powerful influence of mothers and/or grandmothers on the high academic achievement of Puerto Rican elementary school-aged children and female urban high school students (Hidalgo, 2000; Rolón, 2000). Rolón (2000) interviewed 10 high-achieving, Puerto Rican females who attended an urban high school. These students revealed three key elements that contributed to their school success. First, they all perceived their mothers to be their driving forces for their academic achievement because they strongly encouraged them to succeed so they could better themselves economically. Second, they saw their school as being a second home because they had female teachers who embraced their ethnic and linguistic realities. In fact, these students referred to these teachers as "second mothers." Third, they all aspired to earn a college education so they could obtain a middle class lifestyle and become role models for their families and communities. Thus, this study continues to test and build upon the aforementioned findings. The main purpose of this article, then, is to describe the four success factors that seven Puerto Rican female urban high school students living in poverty attributed to their high academic achievement. We conclude with a discussion of implications of our findings for practice.

METHODS

Research Questions

The study was guided by the principal research question, "According to the experiences of Puerto Rican 11th and 12th grade female students who are enrolled in a traditional comprehensive urban high school, what factors are linked to their high academic achievement?" This research also allowed us to explore three additional areas of inquiry because we wanted to determine the extent to which these affected our participants' high academic achievement:

1. What types of roles do institutional agents (e.g., guidance counselors, teachers, community members, and administrative staff) within this school assume in the personal/scholastic lives of these students?

2. What kinds of classes are these students taking (academic vs. vocational tracking)?
3. To what extent, if any, do the descriptions of the students' schooling/home experiences and post graduation aspirations follow traditional gender roles?

Setting and Participants

This study was conducted at University High School (a pseudonym), a large comprehensive high school located in a large Midwestern city, during the 2001–2002 academic year. This high school enrolls 1,500 students from grades 9–12 of which 55% fall below the federal poverty line. Approximately 70% of the high school's students are of color with 15% of these students being Puerto Rican. This school is regarded as one of only two of the district's best high schools out of 20 because its curriculum offers many advanced placement and honors level courses and because 70% of its graduates go on to pursue some sort of post-secondary education. As a result, this high school attracts many students of color from around the city because of its reputation as a college preparatory high school. We specifically selected this high school for the study because of this reputation.

The students recruited for this study had to meet three criteria that would help us purposefully select students who could best speak about their schooling and home experiences and how these impacted their high academic achievement. First, they had to be enrolled in grades 11 or 12 because the majority of Puerto Rican students drop out of school by the 10th grade (Nieto, 1998). Second, the students had to have a cumulative GPA of 3.0 or higher because we determined this GPA to be indicative of a high-achieving student. Third, the students could not have dropped out of school at any time because we wanted this study to focus on nondropouts. Using these three criteria, a Puerto Rican guidance counselor at the school facilitated the recruitment and selection process of the participants because she knew the Latina/o students well. A total of seven female students met these three criteria and they all agreed to participate after we explained the purpose of the study to them.

Data Collection

In the philosophical tradition and method of phenomenology, in-depth interviews and observations were the primary methods of data collection used to conduct this study. Phenomenology "attempts to understand participants' perspectives and views of social realities" (Leedy, 1997). Because the main data collection tool of phenomenology is the in-depth interview (Merriam, 1998; Tesch, 1994), we (Antrop-González and Vélez) structured our conversations with each student using the three-interview series (Seidman, 1998). Each of the three semistructured interviews lasted approximately one hour and was spaced one week apart. All interviews were audiotaped and transcribed verbatim by one of the members (Garrett) of the study team. Approximately 3 students each week were interviewed in "interview blocks" meaning that we focused on completing the three-interview series with 3 students at a time until all seven students completed their three series interview blocks.

The first interview, called the "focused life history" interview, elicited the students' descriptions regarding their family backgrounds and previous schooling experiences. The second interview, known as the "details of experience" interview, focused on each student's current schooling experiences. Thus, they were asked questions meant to elicit descriptions of their current relationships with teachers, their peers, other school staff, and community members. Finally, the purpose of the third "reflection on the meaning" interview was to have each student compare and contrast their previous and current school and home experiences and discuss their future life aspirations.

The second data collection method we used for this study consisted of documenting our observations of participants as they interacted with their teachers and peers during and in between classes so we could learn more firsthand about their everyday school experiences and compare them with what they told us in their interviews. These observations were conducted separately from the interviews by Antrop-González once a week during the school year. Each of the seven students was observed for approximately three class periods each for a total of thirty hours of observations. In total, the data collection period lasted 12 weeks.

Data Analysis

The objective of the phenomenological data analysis process is to identify and examine recurring meaning units, which are the "the smallest segments of texts that are understandable by themselves" (Tesch, 1994, p.148). Moreover, phenomenological researchers "do not establish categories, but aim at discovering the 'themes' in the data" (Tesch, 1994, p. 148). Thus, our data analysis consisted of the three study team members reading and analyzing all the interviews to discover meaningful recurring themes and the ways in which our participants linked them to their high academic achievement. When these recurring themes were discovered within the interview data, we proceeded to color code them and place them into distinct categories called "success factors." We also triangulated the interviews with the observations to determine if there were any major inconsistencies between what students told us in their interviews and what we observed as they interacted with their teachers and peers in school.

PARTICIPANT PROFILES

The seven Puerto Rican female high achievers who shared their experiences with us had a grade point average (GPA) of 3.0 or higher. Additionally, all of them were enrolled in advanced placement (AP) or honors classes and they all considered themselves to be English-dominant bilinguals. Moreover, with the exception of one student, all the participants commented that their parents had either dropped out of high school or had not had a college experience. Although all the students we spoke with came from working-class backgrounds, their personal backgrounds varied in many ways, including the neighborhoods where they resided and how they described their families. In the following section, we provide a brief glimpse into their school, community, and family lives.

Lisa was an 11th grader who was born and raised in Brew City. She lived with her extended family, which was comprised of her mother, father, maternal grandmother, sister, and maternal uncle. She mentioned that she hoped to be the first in her family to attend college. Lisa was enrolled in Honors Chemistry and Pre-Calculus. Her mother was a bill collector and her father a construction worker; both were high school graduates. She described her neighborhood as a quiet one with residents who were of different racial/ethnic backgrounds. She chose to attend Brew City High School because her mother had studied there. Most of Lisa's social networks were largely African–American and Latina/o. Her postgraduation aspiration was to become a social worker.

Erica was an 11th grader who moved to Brew City from Puerto Rico when she was 10 years old. Her family consisted of her mother, father, several sisters and brothers. She described herself as a "second mother" to her siblings because she took a central role in cooking, cleaning, and caring for them because her parents worked long hours. Her mother was employed as a custodial crew supervisor and her father worked with an auto parts supplier. Neither of Erica's parents graduated from high school. As a result of her parents' long work hours, she also mentioned that her social life outside school and home was nonexistent. Her closest friend, however, was another Puerto Rican girl who attended a Catholic high school. Erica's post-high school aspirations included finding her place in the world of work.

An eleventh grader who was born and raised in Brew City, Cecilia lived with her parents, two brothers, and a sister in the city's East side. She quickly pointed out that her brother was an "outpost student." In other words, he had been expelled from Brew City High School and referred to an alternative high school. When asked to describe her neighborhood surroundings, she remarked that there was a very prominent drug culture and that prostitution was rampant. She mentioned that her father was a construction worker and her mother a licensed practical nurse. She chose Brew City High School because of its academic reputation and diverse student body. She was enrolled in various honors classes, such as English and Trigonometry. She was also very involved in school-sponsored extracurricular activities. For example, she played flute and was on the high school's varsity softball and basketball teams. She talked about how her grandparents, who lived in Brew City, facilitated her academic accomplishments because they offered her continual mentorship in times of need. She also mentioned the influence of her "school kid" friends who helped her with homework. Cecilia's life aspirations included being a physical education teacher and having her own family of a husband and three children.

Ivelisse moved to Brew City from Puerto Rico when she was 8 years old. Her mother, who had 2 years of college, was employed with the Brew City public school district as a teacher's aide and her father was a high school graduate and a farmer in Puerto Rico. She was enrolled in the school district's bilingual education program for 6 years. Ivelisse resided in the city's Latino south side, which she described as being a rough area due to the high crime rate and overt gang presence. Like many of her Puerto Rican peers we spoke with, she stated that she chose Brew City High School because of its reputation regarding a strong college prep curriculum. In 11th grade, she was taking advanced Spanish and English classes and saw herself as a mother and teacher in the future. In addition to her regular academic course load, Ivelisse held a part-time job and considered herself very active in her church.

Rachel was a senior who, like many Puerto Ricans, had experienced circulatory migration. Although she was born in Brew City and her first 4 years of her formal schooling experiences were in public schools in the United States, her family later moved to Puerto Rico where she attended public schools from the fifth through eighth grades. Rachel described her family as working class because her mother was a high school graduate and a factory worker. She had three sisters who lived at home and ranged in age from 16 to 23 years. Her father had an eighth grade education, was disabled, and unable to work. Rachel resided in the East side of the city and chose to attend Brew City High School because it was close to her home. She was enrolled in various honors classes and hoped to become an elementary school teacher. Rachel remarked that a majority of her social networks at school were multiracial/ethnic. Like a number of the students we interviewed, she mentioned being active in church.

Alexia was born and raised in Brew City. She was a junior who alternated between living with her mother and her boyfriend. Her mother dropped out of high school in the 10th grade and was employed as a receptionist. Her father, who also did not finish high school, worked with a maintenance company. She described her neighborhood as a tough one and she expressed the desire to leave it when she finished college. Although she was 6 months pregnant, she was determined to remain in school, go to college, and obtain a career in high school teaching. She was enrolled in honors classes in United States history and chemistry, and was active in the Latino community where she volunteered her time at various social agencies like the YMCA, the Salvation Army, the Latino Community Center, and the Christian Center.

Finally, Limari was a senior who arrived in Brew City from Puerto Rico when she was 11 years old. Neither of her parents completed high school. Her mother was a lunchroom worker with the local public school district and her father worked in a shoe factory. Limari spoke of the many racist teachers she had encountered over the years. For Limari, these teachers did not believe in her potential to be a stellar student. Her academic load was demanding–she was enrolled in several honors classes–but she still found time to play on the high school's varsity softball team. On more than one occasion, she credited her church friends and her mother for encouraging her to realize her potential as a student. She credited this encouragement with her ability to obtain a full academic scholarship to a major private university.

It is interesting to note that while all the students we spoke with desired a middle class lifestyle, we noticed that our participants' life and career aspirations followed traditional gender roles. Hence, all the female students voiced their desire for academic achievement around the idea of one day being able to raise families and/or become a teacher or social worker.

FINDINGS

Religiosity and Extracurricular Activities as Sources of Social Capital

Many of the participants we interviewed voiced a connection between their high academic achievement and access to sources of social capital through their ties to a religious organization and/or other extracurricular activities. When asked which religious faith or church they professed or belonged to, our participants stated that they were either Catholic or Pentecostal. They mentioned that the main benefit of participating in these activities consisted of targeted recreational activities for youth that steered them away from antischool, oppositional youth culture like gang membership and truancy. These high degrees of social capital also facilitated their access to school-related resources like homework help and mentorship.

As evidenced in recent studies (Flores-González, 1999, 2002; Hébert & Reis, 1999), several of our participants suggested that multicultural peer networks consisting of other high-achieving urban youth were valuable assets that influenced their academic achievement. Cecilia remarked that she valued her church involvement and its impact on her academic achievement because of the multicultural peer networks she belonged to. These networks were highly conducive to supportive relationships and to her strong sense of belonging. In fact, although the majority of the students were English-dominant bilinguals, they spoke about their multicultural approach in their school peer networks, as they expressed the importance of their friendships with Latinas/os and other friends of color like African Americans and Mexican Americans. This finding suggests that students seek friends who possess diverse cultural and linguistic backgrounds because who positively support their academic achievement. Cecilia shared:

> Ever since I was in the ninth grade, I have been going to church regularly. I also sing in the church choir. The people at church have always been friendly and supportive of me. I feel like I really belong. I have also met a lot of people at church. I have a lot of friends from different backgrounds. I have Hispanic, White, Asian, and Black friends. We all treat each other as friends and we keep each other in line. I really think going to church has helped me become a better student.

Estrella also talked about her involvement in a church and connected it with her high academic achievement. Like Cecilia, she was able to participate in church activities with peer networks consisting of other Latina/o youth. She also felt that these friendships and her participation in religious-based activities had a positive impact on her academic achievement. Estella remarked:

> I'm involved in church very much. I have lots of friends of church in church. We do lots of things together. We do retreats and we invite other youths to come. We also evangelize together. We want other youths to know God and Jesus. There are also lots of camps in the summer and conventions in the Midwest. There are lots of Latinos that get together for these conventions and we have lots of fun. I really think that these church things have helped me be a good student.

While Cecilia and Estrella talked about the importance of receiving mentorship and informational resources through their social networks at church, several other students specifically mentioned the influence of spirituality in their scholastic lives. This particular finding is consistent with recent research (Cook, 2000; Jeynes, 2003), which shows that religious people are more likely to have an internal locus of control because they feel that the spirit of God resides within them and steers them to positive things like high academic achievement. Rachel commented:

God has helped me become a good student. He has helped me keep focused. I know he helps me do the best I can in school.

Likewise, Limari also commented:

God had helped me become a good student because He has been with me through all my struggles.

While these participants credited their high academic achievement with their participation to church and school-related activities, other participants spoke about their involvement with community-based agencies and how it facilitated their engagement with school and meeting people from different walks of life. Alexia stated:

I do all kinds of work with people in the community. I work with the Private Industry Council and help people get jobs. I also work with the Historical Society. These jobs keep me busy and focused on school and help me meet lots of interesting people.

Just like the recent research that shows religiosity (Jeynes, 2003; Muller & Ellison, 2001; Park, 2001; Sikkink & Hernández, 2003) and participation in extracurricular activities (Flores-González, 1999, 2002; Hébert & Reis, 1999) have a positive impact on academic achievement for students of color, our participants also suggested that involvement in church and other school and community-based extracurricular activities served an important dual function. First, church involvement served as a protective measure by discouraging them from participating in oppositional youth culture (i.e., gang life and truancy) because it impinges on their scholastic endeavors. Second, involvement in these kinds of activities also contributed to their high degrees of social capital through the intergenerational closure between these students, their friends, and their friends' parents (Carbonaro, 1998). This high degree of intergenerational closure was valuable because it insured that these students gained access to important resources like good advice through adult mentorship and other positive help-seeking behaviors that encouraged them to pursue academic excellence and a school kid identity (Flores-González, 2002).

Affirmation and Maintenance of a Puerto Rican Identity

All the high achieving students with whom we spoke were very clear about their Puerto Rican identity, always stating to their friends that they were *Boricua* or *puertorriqueña* and proud of it. This particular finding challenges the belief held by other researchers (Fordham & Ogbu, 1986; Ogbu, 1978) that, for many students of color, being a good student is essentially tantamount to "acting White." Contrary to these beliefs, Flores-González (1999) documented that the high-achieving students she interviewed did not hide their Puerto Rican ethnicity. In fact, Hine (1992) found that the negative stereotypes held by teachers and peers served as a motivating tool for the Puerto Rican high achievers in her school to do well in school. Additionally, we also believe this phenomenon reflects the successful utilization of our participants' ethnic identities because they were able to easily make the transition between their home and school worlds.

This finding compels us to believe that our participants' sense of school-based marginalization, rather than cause them to resist the idea of schooling, actually worked to motivate them to academically perform well. Thus, we have decided to name this finding the "marginalization as motivation concept." This concept also works to support previous research (Flores-González, 1999, 2002) that challenges the commonly held belief that involuntary migrant group status, often associated with the sociopolitical reality of Puerto Ricans, is a strong and predictable indicator of low academic achievement (Ogbu, 1978). A majority of our respondents frequently expressed their frustration about how Puerto Ricans were often negatively represented in the city. In turn, they thought that their high academic achievement could have the potential of dispelling these negative stereotypical images.

Jasmine commented on the negative stereotypes that white students in her advanced placement classes held towards her by virtue of being the only minority student in the class. In turn, she also felt compelled to use her high academic performance as a way to prove others wrong about the academic potential of Puerto Ricans.

Sometimes in my AP [advanced placement] classes, like AP English and AP History, some of the white students make you feel really small because you're the only Latino student in the class. I remember one time when a boy asked me what I was doing in the class. He said that he didn't think that people like us could be in these kinds of classes. I told him that he shouldn't be so stereotypical and that we can be smart, too.

These students expressed pride in their Puerto Rican ethnicity. It became evident that many of the students used their education as a tool with which to prove to their peers they had the potential to be good students. Our observations also clearly revealed that our participants were subjected to a highly subtractive curriculum (Valenzuela, 1999) because very little effort was made to weave these students' linguistic, historical, and sociocultural realities into the curriculum.

Maternal Influences on Students' Academic Achievement

All the Puerto Rican females we spoke with talked about the three distinct roles that their mothers played in their school and home lives. First, these mothers often took it upon themselves to help their daughter or son with schoolwork. When the mother felt she could not directly help with schoolwork, she actively sought out the necessary resources that would facilitate her child's learning process. Second, several of the students felt compelled to make their mothers proud of them by getting good grades. Third, several of the students commented that their mothers served as their friends or mentors in times of need or personal crisis. When asked to elaborate on her mother's role in her education, Lisa stated:

> Ever since I was in middle school, my mom has been sending me to pre-college programs and doing things like getting me stuff on the ACT and the kinds of questions they ask on that test. I also go to my mom for personal problems that come up. My mom is always coming down hard on me to do well in school. So if she can't help me with my school stuff she finds somebody who can.

Lisa's mother, like other mothers of students in this study, "went the extra mile" to counsel her daughter and seek informational resources that would aid in the college application and general learning processes. This finding supports the work of several scholars and their discussions pertaining to the influence of Latina/Puerto Rican mothers in the academic lives of their children (Hidalgo, 2000;

Hine, 1992; Gándara, 1995; Reis & Díaz, 1999; Rolón, 2000) because our participants' mothers also held their children to high academic expectations and actively sought out human resources that could help their children (e.g., with homework) in the event that they were not able to.

Erica was unique from the other participants in that she contrasted the roles that both her parents played in her school success. While she perceived that her father played a limited role as an authority figure that demanded she follow the "rules of the house," she commented on the words of encouragement and friendship that were character-istic of her mother's role as a nurturing supporter.

> My mother is the best. She supports me in everything I do. She is always willing to support me at whatever I do at school. She is always very excited about helping me with my work and she always talks to me more like a friend than a mom. My father is very different. He always comes across as the authority figure.

Cecilia also relied exclusively on her mother for her trust and sup-port in times of personal need and remarked that teachers and friends could not be trusted for revealing or seeking support in times of crises. It was evident, then, that she was involved in a high quality interpersonal relationship with her mother.

> When I have a personal problem, I don't really trust my teachers or friends. I usually go to my mother who is always willing to be there for me because I know she won't go around spilling my personal life to everyone.

Rachel also spoke about her mother encouraging her to do her best in school so she would not be a high school dropout like her. Rachel's mother never had the experience of going to college; nonetheless, she knew the importance of after-school programs, tutoring services, and having access to college information because these things would greatly facilitate her daughter's entry into college. Rachel commented:

> My mom dropped out of high school in the 10th grade. So she doesn't want me to have the hard life that she has had. For her, it's a top priority that I stay in school and go to college. She has gotten me in after school programs and found me jobs. She

makes a lot of phone calls to people and asks about the kinds of programs that exist to get me help with school work and information I need to get into college.

Based on these statements, it was clear that mothers felt much more obligated to take on substantial roles in the schooling lives of these high achievers and that fathers were not as willing to assume these types of roles. In the next section, we highlight how students described good teachers and the potential they could have on their high academic achievement.

The Potential for Caring Teachers and Other School Staff Members to Influence High Academic Achievement

All the participants in our study talked about the potential impact that caring teachers could have on their high academic achievement. The recurring theme of caring was especially prevalent in their descriptions of good teachers. Our participants, like the high school students in previous studies (Antrop-González, 2003; Nieto, 1998; Valenzuela, 1999), defined caring teachers as those individuals who were interested in getting to know them on a personalized basis, who could be trusted enough to talk about their personal problems and seek advice, and who would hold them to high academic expectations. Our participants also mentioned they felt it was important for students to be able to rely on teachers, guidance counselors, and administrators for obtaining information or assistance with important tasks like applying for college, tutoring, or successfully securing part-time employment. Erica defined a caring teacher in the following way:

A good teacher is one who knows you, cares about what you do, pushes students, and cares about the stuff going on in your life. A good teacher also wants you to absorb information and understand it.

Cecilia also defined a caring teacher as one who held their students to high academic expectations and being constantly encouraged to do high quality schoolwork.

A good teacher is someone who cares enough not to accept low quality work. I like being pushed and told that I can do better. Some of my better teachers are like this.

Ironically, although these students had clear definitions of what it meant to be a caring teacher, only one Puerto Rican Spanish teacher and a Puerto Rican guidance counselor qualified as caring teachers and/or staff members. These students' other teachers, per se, were not described as caring. Consequently, our participants did not feel compelled to seek nor maintain meaningful, interpersonal relationships, advice, or mentorship with the rest of their teachers.

DISCUSSION

This study's findings add to the recent contributions of research that examines factors that facilitate the high academic achievement of urban youth, particularly Latinas. Moreover, our participants' voices are important because they enable us to conceptualize a three-tiered framework that consists of personal/familial, cultural/community-based, and school-based success factors. This framework will enable general and special education teachers, administrators, and education students to understand ways to understand and address the sociopedagogical needs of underachieving and/or academically talented Puerto Rican students educated in urban high schools.

The personal/familial success factors that students described in relation to their high academic achievement reinforce recent research (Flores-González, 1999, 2002; Hébert & Reis, 1999, Muller & Ellison, 2001; Park, 2001; Sikkink & Hernández, 2003) that discusses the connection between religiosity and extracurricular activities as sources of social capital and high academic achievement. These sources of social capital encourage students to seek adult mentorship, homework help, and seek and maintain peer networks that consist of other high-achieving students of color while discouraging them to adopt anti-school behaviors like truancy and gang membership. These sources of social capital also greatly facilitated high degrees of intergenerational closure (Carbonaro, 1998), which was characterized by the sharing of human and material resources between these students' friends and their parents. These resources can include such things as information about the college admission process, access to computers, and valuable adult mentorship. What is also interesting to note is that these resources, and the social networks that made their access possible, were also coupled with their collective desire for upward social mobility.

Furthermore, like in other studies (Cook, 2000; Jeynes, 2003), several of our students described that religiosity was an important source for their spirituality, which also drove them to succeed academically. Again, while many schools have the tendency to discount or simply not address religion, it is important for school personnel to realize that churches of all faiths sponsor and encourage urban youth to participate in psychologically and physically healthy after-school and weekend youth groups and recreational activities that encourage them to adopt "school kid identities" (Flores-González, 2002). Therefore, school workers should strongly encourage participation in faith-based organizations.

The cultural/community success factors that students attributed to their academic success were the maintenance and affirmation of Puerto Rican identity and maternal influences. These factors are consistent with recent research (Flores-González, 1999; Hidalgo, 2000; Hine, 1992; Reis & Díaz, 1999; Rolón, 2000) that highlights the importance of these factors on high academic achievement. Rather then hide their Puerto Rican identity, our students affirmed and maintained it. Their identity proved to be an important motivating tool for their academic success because it allowed them to dispel stereotypes held by some of their peers and teachers regarding their potential to be good students. Furthermore, our students' mothers were important sources of inspiration for their children because they held their children to high academic expectations, helped them with their homework, and provided guidance and mentorship in times of personal crisis. Even when these mothers could not help their children with homework or did not have direct access to informational resources that would help them in the college application process, they would actively seek people who did have this knowledge or access.

The school-based success factors that our participants described as having an impact on their academic achievement were virtually non-existent and only consisted of their definitions of caring teachers and the potential they could have on their academic achievement. Similar to student voices in previous educational scholarship (Antrop-González, 2003; Valenzuela, 1999), our students defined caring teachers as those who held their students to high academic expectations, were interested in getting to personally know their students, and who could be trusted enough for students to share their emotional needs with them and receive advice in return. Although students were precise in their definitions of caring teachers, they also pointed out that most of their teachers did not fit these definitions. This perceived lack of caring teachers who value personal relationships with their students raises a serious concern for this high school and many others like it because it is only when these types of reciprocal student-teacher relationships exist that students feel a high sense of belonging in school. Furthermore, as documented in recent studies involving urban high school youth of color (Conchas, 2006, 2001; Gibson, 1988; Lee, 2001), our participants' schooling experiences seem to support the "accommodation and acculturation without assimilation" concept. Hence, although they were willing to accommodate themselves in mainstream curricular classes while having to subject themselves to racially, ethnically, and culturally hostile conditions instigated by some of their teachers and peers, they did so with the express intent of dispelling negative stereotypes while maintaining their Puerto Rican identity and not succumbing to ethnic and/or cultural assimilation.

CONCLUSION

Our participants taught us that their academic success was not mostly attributable to school-related factors like teachers and other institutional agents but to familial sources of social capital, which consisted of home and community-related factors like the influence and advocacy of their mothers, the importance of their ethnic identity, and their acquisition of social capital through community-based social networks like churches and extracurricular activities. Hence, the experiences of these high-achieving Puerto Rican students lead us to believe that even "good" large comprehensive urban high schools (Obiakor, 2001) are still inequitably structuring opportunities for Puerto Rican/Latino students because they do not tap into the funds of knowledge that these students bring to school (Moll et al., 1992).

It is important that we encourage schools to examine the ways in which their students' lives and familial sources of social capital are reflected both inside and outside schools. Broader partnerships with community based agencies, families, and area universities should be encouraged. Through these types of school-community partnerships, high schools can further reinforce the social and cultural capital these students are already receiving in their homes and communities and which our students need to graduate from high school, enter college, and eventually obtain a career that will increase their life chances and structures of opportunities.

Finally, teachers and administrators must begin to unlearn their erroneous assumptions pertaining to the lives of urban youth of color. Coming from a working-class background or being Puerto Rican/Latino does not equate to being unintelligent or labeled as a student in need of special education. Only when general and special educators begin to strongly believe that all urban youth of color can academically flourish, if provided the necessary mentorship and guidance on behalf of their schools in conjunction with their caring communities, will more underachieving and high achieving Puerto Rican female students be acknowledged for their vast potential rather than assuming that they cannot succeed by virtue of their racial, ethnic, and socioeconomic backgrounds.

REFERENCES

Antrop-González, R. (2003). "This school is my sanctuary:" The Dr. Pedro Albizu Campos alternative high school. *Journal of the Center for Puerto Rican Studies, 15,* 232–255.

Artiles, A., & Trent, S. C. (1994). Overrepresentation of minority students in special education: A continuing debate. *Journal of Special Education, 27,* 410–438.

Carbonaro, W. J. (1998). A little help from my friend's parents: Intergenerational closure and educational outcomes. *Sociology of Education, 71,* 295–313.

Conchas, G. (2006). *The color of success: Race and high-achieving urban youth.* New York: Teachers College Press.

Conchas, G. (2001). Structuring failure and success: Understanding the variability in Latino school engagement. *Harvard Educational Review, 71,* 475–504.

Cook, K. V. (2000). "You have to have somebody watching your back, and if that's God, then that's mighty big": The church's role in the resilience of inner-city youth. *Adolescence, 35,* 717–730.

Díaz, E. I. (1998). Perceived factors influencing the academic underachievement of talented students of Puerto Rican descent. *Gifted Child Quarterly, 42,* 105–122.

Flores-González, N. (2002). *School kids/street kids: Identity development in Latino students.* New York: Teachers College Press.

Flores-González, N. (2000). The structuring of extracurricular opportunities and Latino student retention. *Journal of Poverty, 4,* 85–108.

Fordham, S., & Ogbu, J. U. (1986). Black students' school success: Coping with the burden of 'acting White.' *The Urban Review, 18,* 176–206.

Gándara, P. (1995). *Over the ivy walls: The educational mobility of low-income Chicanos.* New York: SUNY Press.

Gibson, M. (1988). *Accommodation without assimilation: Sikh immigrants in an American high school.* Ithaca, NY: Cornell University Press.

Hébert, T. P., & Reis, S. M. (1999). Culturally diverse high-achieving students in an urban high school. *Urban Education, 34,* 428–457.

Hidalgo, N. M. (2000). Puerto Rican mothering strategies: The role of mothers and grandmothers in promoting school success. In S. Nieto (Ed.), *Puerto Rican students in U.S. schools* (pp. 167–196). Mahwah, NJ: Lawrence Erlbaum.

Hine, C. Y. (1992). The home environment of gifted Puerto Rican children: Family factors which support high achievement. *Proceedings of the third national research symposium on limited english proficient student issues: Focus on middle and high school issues* (pp. 1–20). Washington, DC: United States Department of Education.

Jeynes, W. H. (2003). The effects of Black and Hispanic 12th graders living in intact families and being religious on their academic achievement. *Urban Education, 38,* 35–57.

Ladson-Billings, G. (1995). Toward a theory of culturally relevant pedagogy. *American Educational Research Journal, 32,* 465–491.

Lee, S. J. (2001). More than "model minorities" or "delinquents": A look at Hmong American high school students. *Harvard Educational Review, 71,* 505–528.

Leedy, P. D. (1997). *Practical research: Planning and design* (6th ed.). Upper Saddle River, NJ: Merrill.

MacMillan, D., & Reschly, D. J. (1998). Overrepresentation of minority students: The case for greater specificity or reconsideration of the variables examined. *Journal of Special Education, 32,* 15–25.

Merriam, S. B. (1998). *Qualitative research design and case study applications in education.* San Francisco: Jossey-Bass.

Moll, L., Amanti, C., Neff, D., & González, N. (1992). Funds of knowledge for teaching: Using a qualitative approach to connect homes and classrooms. *Theory into Practice, 31,* 132–141.

Muller, C., & Ellison, C. G. (2001). Religious involvement, social capital, and adolescents' academic progress: Evidence from the national education longitudinal study of 1988. *Sociological Focus, 34,* 155–182.

Nieto, S. (2000). Puerto Rican students in U.S. schools: A brief history. In S. Nieto (Ed.), *Puerto Rican students in U.S. schools* (pp. 5–38). Mahwah, NJ: Lawrence Erlbaum.

Nieto, S. (1998). Fact and fiction: Stories of Puerto Ricans in U.S. schools. *Harvard Educational Review, 68,* 133–163.

Obiakor, F. E. (2001). *It even happens in "good" schools: Responding to cultural diversity in today's classrooms.* Thousand Oaks, CA: Corwin Press.

Ogbu, J. U. (1978). *Minority education and caste: The American system in cross-cultural perspective.* New York: Academic Press.

Park, H. (2001). Religiousness as a predictor of academic performance among high school students. *Journal of Research on Christian Education, 10,* 361–378.

Reis, S. M., & Díaz, E. (1999). Economically disadvantaged urban female students who achieve in schools. *The Urban Review, 3,* 31–54.

Rolón, C. A. (2000). Puerto Rican female narratives about self, school, and success. In S. Nieto (Ed.), *Puerto Rican students in U.S. schools* (pp. 141–166). Mahwah, NJ: Lawrence Erlbaum.

Seidman, I. (1998). *Interviewing as qualitative research: A guide for researchers in education and the social sciences* (2nd ed.). New York: Teachers College Press.

Sikkink, D., & Hernández, E. (2003). *Religion matters: Predicting schooling success among Latino youth* (Vol. 2003.1). Notre Dame, IN: University of Notre Dame, Institute for Latino Studies.

Spring, J. (1994). *Deculturalization and the struggle for equality: A brief history of the education of dominated cultures in the United States.* New York: McGraw-Hill.

Stanton-Salazar, R. D. (2001). *Manufacturing hope and despair: The school and kin support networks of U.S.–Mexican youth.* New York: Teachers College Press.

Tesch, R. (1994). The contribution of a qualitative method: Phenomenological research. In M. Lagenbach, C. Vaughn, & L. Aagaard (Eds.), *An introduction to educational research* (pp. 143–157). Boston: Allyn & Bacon.

Valenzuela, A. (1999). *Subtractive schooling: U.S.–Mexican youth and the politics of caring.* Albany: SUNY Press.

Expectations, Aspirations, and Achievement Among Latino Students of Immigrant Families

Dick M. Carpenter II

ABSTRACT. This study examines the relationship between various measures of parental and student expectations and aspirations and math achievement among Latino 12th graders of immigrant parents in the Educational Longitudinal Study (ELS): 2002 database. Findings indicate parental expectations and aspirations were not significant predictors of student achievement after controlling for an index of covariates. Moreover, neither were student expectations, agreement between student and parent expectations, nor student perceptions of parental aspirations. The analyses of the secondary questions likewise indicated only one strong relationship between aspirations, expectations, and parents' time in the United States – parental aspirations and expectations.

Dick M. Carpenter II, PhD, is Assistant Professor of Educational Leadership, Research, and Foundations, University of Colorado, Colorado Springs, Co.

INTRODUCTION AND/OR REVIEW
OF THE LITERATURE

In the perpetual quest to identify variables that improve academic achievement, none have proven more consistently influential than those that originate in the home. According to Rumberger (1995), "family background is widely recognized as the most significant important contributor to success in schools" (p. 587). Family background can be defined many different ways, from parental involvement to socioeconomic status, and each definition shows varying degrees of significance. However, one has shown repeated importance in student achievement: parental expectations.

"It is clear that high achieving children tend to come from families which have high expectations for them" (Boocock, 1972, p. 60). Moreover, Henderson (1988) found this holds true across various social, economic, and ethnic backgrounds, which has been confirmed in numerous studies over multiple decades (Alexander, Entwisle, & Horsey, 1997; Casanova, García-Linares, Torre, & Carpio, 2005; Frome & Eccles, 1998; Goyette & Xie, 1999; Hao & Bonstead-Bruns, 1998b; Räty, 2006; Seginer, 1983; Singh, Bickley, Keith, Keith, Trivette, & Anderson, 1995; Steinberg, Lamborn, Dornbusch, & Darling, 1992; Trusty, 2000, 2002; Trusty & Harris, 1999; Vollmer, 1986; Wang & Wildman, 1995; Wright, Horn, & Sanders, 1997). Parental expectation is routinely defined as the conviction a parent holds in his or her child's future level of achievement. Often this is measured by asking a parent how far in school (in terms of grade levels) she/he expects the child to progress. However, it is sometimes measured by asking a parent her/his expectations for the child's performance in a certain course or on a particular test. To further understand parental expectation, an important distinction must be made. Parental expectation differs from parental aspiration. The latter is regularly defined as the *desire* a parent holds about his or her child's future level of achievement, as opposed to a belief in the child's likely future achievement. Sometimes the answers to the questions are the same, but often they are not.

The link between parental expectations and student achievement has been examined by researchers in different ways, from basic small sample correlation studies (Sanders, Field, & Diego, 2001) to sophisticated cross-cultural examinations of student performance using large datasets (Tsui, 2005). In all, the findings appear quite consistent.

For example, using multiple regression analysis, Jacobs and Harvey (2005) studied a sample of Australian students and found parental expectation was the strongest predictor of student success. Trusty, Plata, and Salazar (2003) applied structural equation modeling to the NELS: 88 database and found parental influence, in the form of expectations and involvement, was the greatest influence on student success. In fact, parental influence dominated the effects of other variables, including SES, student self-perceptions, and prior achievement.

The effects of parental expectations are manifest in studies of elementary-aged students (Gill & Reynolds, 1999) through upper secondary school (Räty, 2006) and using both quantitative (Ma, 2001) and qualitative methods (Lara-Alecio, Rafael, & Ebener, 1997). The latter authors interviewed parents, teachers, and children to discern the parental behaviors or practices most important in student success. High expectations were among the top three.

Of course, the linear relationship of parental expectations and achievement passes though the student, yet few studies of parental expectations take into account student perceptions of parental expectations or aspirations (Gill & Reynolds, 1999). Those that have predictably show that children's perceptions of parental expectations influence children's school success (Alexander, Entwisle, & Bedinger, 1994; Jacobs, 1991; Parsons, Adler, & Kaczala, 1982) and that those perceptions depend on interactions between parents and children (Chin & Kameoka, 2002; Yan & Lin, 2005).

Another limitation in this line of inquiry exists in the composition of the samples. That is, much of this research has been conducted with predominantly Caucasian, middle class children but comparatively fewer with ethnically diverse student groups. As a result, numerous authors conclude the effects of parental expectations among diverse ethnic and racial populations remains unclear (Elliott, Hufton, Illushin, & Willis, 2001; Mau, 1995; Yan & Lin, 2005). This is particularly true for the Latino population (Okagaki & Frensch, 1998). Of those that have studied diverse populations, researchers have paid particular interest to differences between Caucasians, Asians, and/or African Americans (Gill & Reynolds, 1999; Goyette & Xie, 1999; Yan & Lin, 2005). Yet, studies involving Latino families have played a surprisingly small role-surprising given the growth of the Latino community in the United States. And precious few of those utilize national samples, longitudinal analyses, randomization, or other sophisticated methods (Trusty et al., 2003).

Nevertheless, among studies on Latino populations, the relationship between parental expectations and student achievement parallels those in other populations (Trusty et al., 2003). For example, Fisher and Padmawidjaja (1999), through interviews of Mexican–American college students, found that parents' high expectations had a strong and lasting influences on students' educational and career development.

Ramos and Sanchez (1995) studied the postsecondary educational expectations of Mexican–American high school students from a school in Northern California. They found that students' reports of parents' educational expectations had significant effects on students' expectations. Hao and Bonstead-Bruns (1998a) further found that *agreement* between parents and children about expectations played an important role in achievement among Mexican families. Specifically, low levels of agreement led to lower achievement, even after controlling for parent SES.

A particularly salient recent study examined parental expectations and student achievement specifically among Latino immigrant families (Goldenberg, Gallimore, Reese, & Garnier, 2001). In the current context, such research has significant practical implications. While exact numbers remain unknown, estimates put the number of immigrants to the United States at more than one million per year, many of whom are Latino (Dillin, 2001). Although this presents challenges to schools that serve immigrant families, some postulate that immigrant parents are actually the school's "best friends" (Henderson, 1988) in that immigrant parents hold high expectations in an attempt to maximize educational opportunities for upward social mobility (Sue & Okazaki, 1990). As a result, children of immigrant parents should exhibit greater academic achievement.

Yet, expectations and achievement among immigrant families appears uneven. For example, although Hao and Bonstead-Bruns (1998a) found a significant relationship between parental expectations and student achievement, they also discovered that Asian immigrant parents held higher expectations than their Latino peers, and Asian students significantly outperformed their Hispanic peers.

Goldenberg et al.'s (2001) study further challenges previous findings in that they found no significant relationship between parental expectations and student achievement among Latino immigrant families. That is, while the parents in this study held high expectations and aspirations, those did not translate into higher performance. Given contemporary immigration patterns, this is an important finding. Yet, the study's limitations necessitate further research in this area.

Specifically, the Goldenberg and colleagues sample included 81 Latino children in Los Angeles. Clearly, other studies with larger, if not national samples would contribute to this line of inquiry. In addition, their study measured parental expectations but not student perceptions, students' own expectations, or the agreement between them. As referenced earlier, these are important factors in research of this type. Finally, this sample only included elementary-aged students. This line of inquiry would greatly benefit from a sample comprised of older students.

Given the importance of this research and the limitations noted, our research expands on Goldenberg et al. and other studies of parental expectations and student achievement among Latino high school students of immigrant parents included in the ELS:2002 database. Findings indicate parental expectations and aspirations are not significant predictors of student achievement after controlling for an index of covariates. Moreover, neither were student expectations, agreement between student and parent expectations, nor student perceptions of parental aspirations. The analyses of the study's secondary questions likewise indicated only one strong relationship between aspirations, expectations, and parents' time in the United States – parental aspirations and expectations. The remaining correlations never exceeded a moderately weak relationship.

METHODS

This study begins with the following primary questions.

1. What is the relationship between parental expectations and student achievement among Latino students with at least one immigrant parent?
2. What is the relationship between student expectations and achievement among Latino students with at least one immigrant parent?

3. What is the relationship between parental aspirations and student achievement among Latino students with at least one immigrant parent?
4. What is the relationship between student perceptions of parental aspirations and student achievement among Latino students with at least one immigrant parent?
5. Is there a significant difference in student achievement based on agreement of expectations between parents and students?

Secondarily, this research asks:

1. What is the relationship between parental expectations and student expectations?
2. What is the relationship between parental aspirations and student perceptions of parental aspirations?
3. What is the relationship between the length of time immigrant parents have been in the United States and their expectations?
4. What is the relationship between parental aspirations and parental expectations?

This study's data came from the Educational Longitudinal Study (ELS):2002 database. ELS:2002 is the fourth in a series of longitudinal studies conducted by the National Center for Education Statistics (NCES). This iteration began in 2002 with a national sample of 15,362 10th graders in 752 public and private schools and is expected to gather data on these participants for 10 years. Currently, data are available for 10th grade, herein called base year (BY), and 12th grade, referred to as first follow-up (F1).

The ELS:2002 schools were selected from a population of approximately 25,000 public and private schools. For the 752 public and private schools with 10th grades that were randomly sampled and agreed to participate in ELS:2002, complete 10th-grade rosters were produced for each school. From this roster, approximately 25 students per school, on average, were randomly selected, with Asian and Hispanic students selected at a higher rate than others.

In the first year of data collection, ELS:2002 measured students' achievement in reading and math and obtained information from students about their attitudes and experiences. The students who remained in their base year schools were tested (in math only) and surveyed again in 12th grade. A freshened sample was also included in 12th grade, making the study representative of spring 2004 high school seniors nationwide. Although the practice of freshening samples draws mixed opinions, NCES has successfully used freshened samples in earlier longitudinal studies. In ELS:2002, the sample was freshened with students who did not have the opportunity to be selected into the sample during the 10th grade (e.g., they may have been out of the country or out of grade sequence). In so doing, this reflects the actual context common in schools (i.e., students who leave the country in one grade but return in another) and strengthens the database in cross-sectional research. However, those completing longitudinal research must take steps to ensure that the sample is a panel composed of students present in all waves, thus eliminating students included in the freshening. The panel sample herein is just that-students who were present in both 10th and 12th grade.

ELS:2002 also gathered information from students' parents, their teachers, and the administrators (principal and library media center director) of their schools. Students who transferred to a different school, switched to a home school environment, graduated early, or dropped out were administered a customized questionnaire tailored to their first follow-up status. School administrators at the participating schools were surveyed once again. For further information about ELS:2002, see Burns et al. (2003).

Sample. The sample in this study includes 1,050 Latino students with at least one immigrant parent. This equals a weighted sample of 260,320. The students in this sample were present in both 10th and 12th grade.

Instrumentation. The instruments used in ELS:2002 include questionnaires and student tests. Each of the components underwent field-testing prior to administration. Questionnaires were designed to be self-explanatory and gathered a wide range of information on student interests, uses of time, involvement in activities, etc. Teacher, parent, and administrator questionnaires gathered descriptive information pertinent to their respective fields of involvement and influence.

The cognitive tests measured achievement at grade 10 in reading and math and grade 12 in math. There were different versions (forms) of the mathematics cognitive test of varying difficulty designed to meet different levels of student ability. The purpose of the multilevel design was to guard against ceiling and floor effects, which may occur when testing spans multiple years of schooling. The tests contained a mix of multiple choice and open-ended items addressing simple mathematical skills, comprehension of mathematics concepts, and problem solving ability. Some of the open-ended items required setting up formulas, solving equations, or writing explanations.

Variables. Because only math was measured in both grades, it was used as the dependent variable in this study, as measured by the ELS variable: FITXM1IR Math IRT Estimated Right. Although a detailed explanation of Item Response Theory (IRT) lies outside of this treatment, some description is helpful in understanding this measure.

Raw scores achieved on different tests that vary in average difficulty are not comparable to each other. IRT was employed to calculate scores that could be compared regardless of which test form a student took. A core of items shared among the different test forms made it possible to establish a common scale. IRT uses the pattern of right, wrong, and omitted responses to the items actually administered in a test form, and the difficulty, discriminating ability, and "guess-ability" of each item, to place each student on a continuous ability scale. It is then possible to estimate the score the student would have achieved for any arbitrary subset of test items calibrated on this scale.

Independent variables included parental expectations, parental aspirations, student expectations, student perceptions of parental aspirations, and agreement of parent and student expectations. Consistent with Goldenberg et al. (2001) and others referenced above, the ELS questionnaire measured expectation by asking how far in school the parent expected the child to go (or how far the student expected to go) in school on a Likert-type scale, where 1 was noncompletion of high school and 7 was a PhD, MD, or equivalent. Aspiration was measured using the same scale. Agreement was created as a yes/no dichotomous variable using the aforementioned parent and student expectation variables.

Fourteen covariates were included based on prior research and the study's theoretical framework: family SES (Chen & Lan, 1998; Chin & Kameoka, 2002; Der-Karabetian, 2004; Gill & Reynolds, 1999; Hao & Bonstead-Bruns, 1998a; Smith-Maddox, 1998; Trusty et al., 2003; Tsui, 2005; Yan & Lin, 2005), prior math achievement (Bandura, 1982; 1995; Gill & Reynolds, 1999; Trusty et al., 2003), students' sex (Chen & Lan, 1998; Der-Karabetian, 2004; Gill & Reynolds, 1999; Hao & Bonstead-Bruns, 1998a; Räty, 2006; Yan & Lin, 2005), length of parents' time in United States (Hao & Bonstead-Bruns, 1998a), child is interested in school (Goldenberg et al., 2001),

TABLE 1. Coding of Nominal Variables.

Variable	Coding
Students' sex	0 = male, 1 = female
Child's is interest in school	0 = no, 1 = yes
Parents take children to educational/ cultural activities	0 = no, 1 = yes
Parent/child interactions	0 = never, 1 = sometimes, 2 = frequently
Number of parents/guardians in the home	0 = single parent/parents, 1 = two parents/guardians
Parents' religion	0 = none, 1 = Christian, 2 = other
Parents' command of English	0 = not well, 1 = well
School type	0 = private, 1 = public
Urbanicity	0 − urban, 1 = suburban, 2 − rural
Geographic location of the school	0 = Northeast, 1 = Midwest, 2 = South, 3 = West

hours per week spent on homework (Smith-Maddox, 1998), parents taking children to educational/cultural activities (Smith-Maddox, 1998), number of siblings (Gill & Reynolds, 1999; Hao & Bonstead-Bruns, 1998a), parent/child interactions (Gill & Reynolds, 1999; Hao & Bonstead-Bruns, 1998a), number of parents/guardians in the home (Hao & Bonstead-Bruns, 1998a), parents' religion (Hao & Bonstead-Bruns, 1998a), parents' command of English (Hao & Bonstead-Bruns, 1998a), school type (Hao & Bonstead-Bruns, 1998a), urbanicity (Hao & Bonstead-Bruns, 1998a), and geographic location of the school (Hao & Bonstead-Bruns, 1998a).

Five of the control variables-SES, prior achievement, hours spent on homework, length of parents' time in United States, and number of siblings-were continuous (ordinal or scalar). The remainder was nominal. Table 1 indicates how the latter variables were coded.

Analysis. All analyses utilized the American Institutes for Research AM software program. The AM software is designed specifically for analyzing the complex sampling designs inherent within NCES datasets, such as ELS:2002.

The primary research questions were analyzed using the enter method of multiple regression. Separate analyses were performed for each independent variable using the same dependent variable and covariates described above. The secondary research questions were examined using simple correlations.

For comparison purposes, these same analyses were performed on a sample of non-Latino students with at least one immigrant parent

($N = 2,150$). While comparing results across different groups is not the thrust of this article, the comparison provides a useful point of reference in understanding results from the Latino sample.

RESULTS

Table 2 includes descriptive statistics for both the Latino and non-Latino samples. Looking specifically at the Latino sample, some variables indicate mean differences in math achievement that are inconsistent with some of the aforementioned findings. For example, students who expressed interest in school scored lower ($M = 39.95$) than those who did not ($M = 42.17$). Likewise, students who interacted with parents scored lower ($M = 40.29$) than those who interacted only sometimes ($M = 42.21$) or rarely ($M = 44.42$) with parents.

However, other variables indicated mean differences as expected. In particular, students who accompany parents to educational/ cultural activities showed greater math performance ($M = 42.12$) than those who did not attend such activities ($M = 38.52$). The same pattern held for those whose parents indicated a greater command of English (Well $M = 43.97$, Not Well $M = 38.61$). Moreover, students in private schools ($M = 51.91$) outperformed those in public schools ($M = 40.13$), and students in two parent homes ($M = 40.73$) enjoy greater math achievement than those in single parent homes ($M = 39.90$).

In the non-Latino sample, almost all of the same patterns were consistent with the Latino sample. One difference of note was in the parents' command of English. Among non-Latinos, students with parents who did not indicate a strong command of English demonstrated slightly greater math achievement ($M = 54.51$) than students of parents with a stronger command of English ($M = 54.05$). Finally, a comparison of the grand mean shows that Latino students demonstrated significantly lower math achievement ($M = 40.54$) than their non-Latino peers ($M = 51.38$), $t(2770) = -12.40$, $p = .000$.

Primary Questions

1. *What is the relationship between parental expectations and student achievement among Latino students with at least one immigrant parent?*

TABLE 2. Descriptive Statistics of Nominal Variables for Latinos and Non-Latinos.

	Latino		Non-Latino	
	M	*SD*	*M*	*SD*
Students' sex				
Male	41.70	13.76	51.86	15.76
Female	39.56	13.27	50.89	14.80
Child is interested in school				
Yes	39.95	13.65	51.23	15.57
No	42.17	13.30	51.81	14.20
Parents take children to educational/cultural activities				
yes	42.12	13.29	52.74	14.64
No	38.52	13.60	50.82	15.81
Parent/child interactions				
Rarely	44.42	16.20	53.21	13.73
Sometimes	42.21	13.93	52.98	15.59
Frequently	40.29	13.28	51.67	14.82
Number of parents/guardians in the home				
Single parent	39.90	12.95	48.19	15.17
Two parents	40.73	13.70	52.00	15.28
Parents' religion				
None	39.84	11.53	59.88	15.65
Christian	40.63	13.55	51.42	14.57
Other	44.81	14.23	52.83	15.64
Parents' command of English				
Not well	38.61	12.56	54.51	15.08
Well	43.97	14.40	54.05	15.00
Urbanicity				
Urban	40.13	13.81	49.37	15.08
Suburban	40.71	13.00	52.34	15.50
Rural	41.93	15.08	53.06	14.49
School type				
Public	40.13	13.34	50.79	15.41
Private	51.91	14.05	56.70	13.16
Geographic location of the school				
Northeast	41.31	12.77	50.40	15.23
Midwest	38.77	12.29	48.74	16.18
South	42.59	14.25	53.44	14.37
West	39.63	13.51	51.80	15.38
Grand Mean	40.54	13.54	51.38	15.31

In the full regression model, parental expectations proved not to be a significant predictor of student achievement ($B = .148$, $p = .51$). Among the covariates, only three proved to be significant-prior performance $(B = 1.04, \ p = .000)$, hours spent on homework $(B = .709, \ p = .007)$, and number of siblings $(B = -.430, \ p = .03)$. The model with this independent variable accounted for a substantial amount of variance $(R^2 = .79)$.

2. *What is the relationship between parental aspirations and student achievement among Latino students with at least one immigrant parent?*

Results for parental aspirations paralleled those of parental expectations. Like expectations, parental aspirations proved not to be a significant predictor of student achievement $(B = .416, \ p = .07)$. Among the covariates, the same three proved to be significant-prior performance $(B = 1.03, \ p = .000)$, hours spent on homework $(B = .695, \ p = .01)$, and number of siblings $(B = -.419, \ p = .02)$. The model with this independent variable accounted for a substantial amount of variance $(R^2 = .79)$.

3. *What is the relationship between student expectations and student achievement among Latino students with at least one immigrant parent?*

When student expectations are used as the independent variable, the results are largely the same as parental expectations, but with one difference. As with parents, student expectations proved not to be a significant predictor of student achievement $(B = -.015, \ p = .95)$. Among the covariates, prior performance $(B = 1.03, \ p = .000)$ and hours spent on homework $(B = .792, \ p = .009)$ again were significant, but number of siblings was not. And nearly identical to the previous model, this accounted for a substantial amount of variance $(R^2 = .78)$.

4. *What is the relationship between student perceptions of parental aspirations and student achievement among Latino students with at least one immigrant parent?*

Student perceptions followed the pattern set above. Perceptions of neither mother's $(B = -.018, \ p = .94)$ nor father's $(B = -.140, \ p = .64)$ aspirations proved significant, but prior performance $(B = 1.05, \ p = .000)$ and hours spent on homework $(B = 1.01, \ p = .003)$ were. And as before, the model accounted for a notable amount of variance $(R^2 = .81)$.

5. *Is there a significant difference in student achievement based on agreement of expectations between parents and students?*

Results from the final question mirrored those in other questions. Agreement between student and parent expectations proved not to be a significant predictor of student achievement ($B = .049$, $p = .781$). But, as before, prior performance ($B = 1.03$, $p = .000$) and hours spent on homework ($B = .747$, $p = .014$) were significant. This model, too, accounted for a substantial amount of variance ($R^2 = .78$).

For point of comparison, these analyses were also completed with non-Latino students of immigrant parents. As Table 3 indicates, only one of the independent variables, parental aspirations, proved to be a significant predictor of achievement ($B = .776$, $p = 01$). The remainder, as with Latino students, was not significant. Moreover, the models with non-Latino students accounted for substantial variance, similar to the Latino sample. However, more of the covariates in the non-Latino sample were significant, specifically SES, the mothers' number of years in the United States, and parents' command of English.

Secondary Questions

As Table 4 indicates, only one pair of variables under consideration in the secondary questions indicates a strong relationship-parent aspiration and parent expectation ($r = .70$). The next strongest correlation was only a moderately weak relationship between student expectation and parent expectation ($r = .33$). The remaining variables under question-parental aspirations, student perceptions of parental aspirations, and number of years parents have been in the United States and their expectations-appear to be essentially unrelated. Although not included in the secondary research questions, one relationship is worth noting. What parents want for their children appears unrelated to how long the parents have been in the United States.

Table 5 indicates some of the same patterns in the Latino sample appear in the non-Latino sample. Specifically, there appears to be no relationship between parental expectations and the number of years in the United States (Mother $r = .008$, Father $r = .07$). Moreover, parental aspirations and expectations are strongly related ($r = .67$). However, a notable difference between the samples appears in the relationship between student and parent expectations. While somewhat weak among Latino families, the relationship appears stronger among non-Latino families ($r = .33$), although the relationship is still only moderate in the latter sample.

TABLE 3. Expectation, Aspirations, and Significant Covariates for Regression Analyses of Non-Latino Sample.

	R^2	Independent Variables		SES		Prior Achievement		Hours on Homework		# Years Mother in United States		Parent Command of English	
		B	p	B	p	B	p	B	p	B	p	B	p
Parental expectations	.85	.389	.23	1.90	.00	1.06	.00	.528	.00	.109	.04	−2.51	.00
Student expectations	.85	.487	.23	1.83	.00	1.05	.00	.521	.00	.135	.02	.067	.92
Parental aspirations	.85	.776	.01	1.82	.00	1.05	.00	.541	.00	.135	.01	−2.26	.01
Student perceptions of parental aspirations	.84	M = −.014 F = .725	M = .97 F = .07	1.72	.01	1.01	.00	.597	.00	.170	.00	−3.37	.00
Agreement of expectations	.86	−.426	.57	1.98	.00	1.06	.00	.594	.00	.121	.03	−3.02	.00

TABLE 4. Intercorrelations of Expectations, Aspirations, and Time in the United States for Latino Students.

	# Years Mother in United States	# Years Father in United States	Parent Aspiration	Parent Expectation	Student Perception of Mother Aspiration	Student Perception of Father Aspiration
Student expectation	.09	.03	.27	.33	.32	.28
# Years mother in United States		.71	.00	−.05	.06	.05
# Years father in United States			−.02	−.06	.01	.003
Parent aspiration				.70	.15	.05
Parent expectation					.20	.07
Student perception of mother aspiration						.75

TABLE 5. Intercorrelations of Expectations, Aspirations, and Time in the United States for Non-Latino Students.

	# Years Mother in United States	# Years Father in United States	Parent Aspiration	Parent Expectation	Student Perception of Mother Aspiration	Student Perception of Father Aspiration
Student expectation	.03	.06	.42	.46	.43	.33
# Years mother in United States		.85	.07	.008	−.04	−.02
# Years father in United States			.11	.07	.01	.03
Parent aspiration				.67	.30	.30
Parent expectation					.23	.19
Student perception of mother aspiration						.71

DISCUSSION

This study examined the relationship between various measures of parental and student expectations and aspirations and math achievement among Latino 12th graders of immigrant parents in the ELS:2002 database. Consistent with Goldenberg et al. (2001), parental expectations and aspirations were not significant predictors of student achievement after controlling for an index of covariates. Moreover, neither were student expectations, agreement between student and parent expectations, nor student perceptions of parental aspirations.

The analyses of the secondary questions likewise indicated only one strong relationship between aspirations, expectations, and parents' time in the United States – parental aspirations and expectations. The remaining correlations never exceeded a moderately weak relationship.

Although not central to this study, findings related to some of the covariates are notable. First, prior achievement and hours spent on homework were both significant predictors of math achievement, which is consistent with previous findings (Bandura, 1982; 1995; Gill & Reynolds, 1999; Smith-Maddox, 1998; Trusty et al., 2003). Second, these were the only consistently significant covariates herein. Number of siblings was significant for some of the independent variables but not all. Third, several variables that have proven influential in numerous other studies were not significant in this one, particularly SES, school type, and urbanicity.

The nonsignificant effect of SES deserves some discussion here. An examination of the data used herein reveals this noneffect is largely a function of the rather homogenous quality of the Latino immigrant sample in terms of SES, particularly compared to the non-Latino immigrant comparison group. As Figure 1 illustrates, the mean SES in the Latino sample ($M = -.655$, $SD = 668$) is considerably less than that of the non-Latino group ($M = .117$, $SD = .773$), $t(3025) = -18.84$, $p = .000$. But the distribution of the Latino group is far from normal, as the demonstrable positive skew illustrates. Moreover, as the standard deviations indicate, the Latino scores show less variance.

Yet, the same is not the case for parental expectations between the Latino and non-Latino samples. Specifically, Latino ($M = 5.27$, $SD = 1.38$) and non-Latino ($M = 5.27$, $SD = 1.32$) parents hold nearly identical expectations, $t(2615) = -1.06, p = .288$. And as both Figure 2 and the standard deviations indicate, the distributions are quite similar. Thus, the weak correlation between SES and parental expectations among Latino parents ($r = .09$) reflects the homogeneity of SES in the Latino sample, not randomness in expectations. Indeed, Latino parents hold the same expectations for their children as do non-Latino parents regardless of their SES.

FIGURE 1. SES Distribution of Latino and Non-Latino Families.

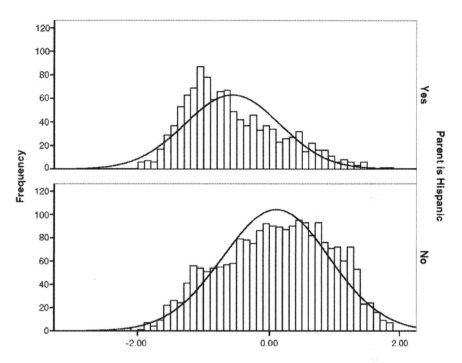

Some of the findings related to the primary and secondary questions challenge prevailing wisdom, previous findings about immigrant parents' expectations and aspirations, agreement between parents and children, and the relation of those to academic achievement. To begin, there remains a popular belief that immigrant parents hold high expectations for their children, since they see education as a means to social acculturation and economic success. Those expectations are then expected to translate into children's greater educational achievement (Sue & Okazaki, 1990).

The first part of that wisdom remains uncontested here. Indeed, 46% of the Latino parents in this sample *expected* their children to complete a four year degree, and 25% expected their child to complete a PhD, MD, or equivalent. The numbers for aspiration differed little-45% for a four year degree and 30% for a PhD, MD, or equivalent. What is not supported herein is the idea that those expectations or aspirations predict or effect greater academic achievement.

FIGURE 2. Expectations Distribution of Latino and Non-Latino Parents.

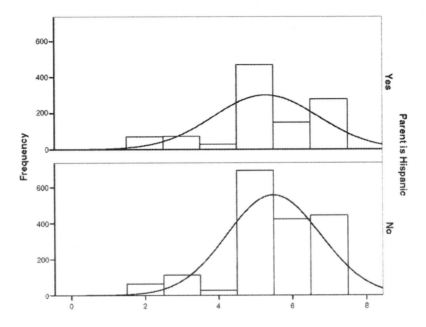

Likewise, the findings concerning agreement between students and parents challenge earlier propositions about its influence on achievement (Hao & Bonstead-Bruns, 1998). Considering the moderately weak relationship ($r = .33$) between parent and student expectations, the non-significant effect is not surprising in these data.

While those findings challenge many prevailing ideas, at least one result herein confirms earlier findings. Specifically, previous studies have found acculturation variables (such as length in the United States or command of English) exhibit weak or nonsignificant influence on student achievement (Goldenberg et al., 2001; Trusty et al., 2003). Among Latino parents the same proved true in these data. Thus, the notion that educational expectation diminishes with one's lack of facility with English, potential experiences with racism, or the simple passage of time appears unsubstantiated.

If most of these findings challenge conventional wisdom concerning the influence of parental expectations among the children of Latino immigrants, they should not be interpreted to mean that parental factors have no influence. Indeed, Table 2 indicates there are achievement differences among students based on several parent factors, such as the number of parents in the home or parent and child attendance at educational/cultural events. Yet, when controlling for other factors, these parental variables do not act as significant predictors of achievement.

This could reflect the age of the children under question here. As Yan (2005) asserts, late adolescence is a time of changing child-parental relationships and the growth of teens' independence. Thus, parental influence in the lives of 16- to 18-year-olds may be more subtle and indirect than the Pygmalion-like notion of expectations and performance.

Future research should examine such indirect relationships within this population specifically, as well as other student groups. For example, it could be that parental expectations influence achievement indirectly through the significant covariates in this study. Moreover, future research would benefit from expanding the types of outcome variables in this line of inquiry. While achievement measured by reading, math, or content tests provides valuable information, few studies consider the relationship between expectations/aspirations and the actual level of education attained.

Finally, specific to limitations in this article, subsequent research is needed in the creation of models to understand the factors significant in predicting or influencing achievement in Latino immigrant families. This study essentially expanded on and applied the work of others to a national, random sample of Latino students from immigrant families. To date, however, little exploratory research has experimented with diverse variables in the creation of models that then could be tested on other samples and populations. Given recent immigration patterns involving Latino families, such research clearly would be salient.

REFERENCES

Alexander, K. L., Entwisle, D. R., & Bedinger, S. D. (1994). When expectations work: Race and socioeconomic differences in school performance. *Social Psychology Quarterly, 57,* 283–299.

Alexander, K. L., Entwisle, D. R., & Horsey, C. S. (1997). From first grade forward: Early foundations of high school dropout. *Sociology of Education, 70,* 87–107.

Bandura, A. (1982). Self-efficacy mechanism in human agency. *American Psychologist, 37,* 122–147.

Bandura, A. (1995). Exercise of personal and collective efficacy in changing societies. In A. Bandura (Ed.), *Self-efficacy in changing societies* (pp. 1–45). New York: Cambridge University Press.

Boocock, S. P. (1972). *An introduction to the sociology of learning*. Boston: Houghton Mifflin.

Burns, L. J., Heuer, R., Ingels, S. J., Pollack, J., Pratt, D. J., Rock, D. et al. (2003). *Education longitudinal study of 2002 base year field test report* (No. NCES 2003-03). Washington, DC: National Center for Education Statistics.

Casanova, P. F., García-Linares, M. C., de la Torre, M. J., & de la Villa Carpio, M. (2005). Influence of family and socio-demographic variables on students with low academic achievement. *Educational Psychology, 25*, 423–435.

Chen, H., & Lan, W. (1998). Adolescents' perceptions of their parents' academic expectations: Comparison of American Chinese–American, and Chinese high school students. *Adolescence, 33*, 385–391.

Chin, D., & Kameoka, V. A. (2002). Psychosocial and contextual predictors of educational and occupational self-efficacy among Hispanic inner-city adolescents. *Hispanic Journal of Behavioral Sciences, 24*, 448–464.

Der-Karabetian, A. (2004). Perceived family process factors and mathematics performance among Latino, African, and European American middle school students. *Educational Research Quarterly, 28*, 38–47.

Dillin, J. (2001, March 20). USA: An open border?: Immigration proposals get mixed reviews. *Christian Science Monitor, 93*, 3.

Elliott, J. D., Hufton, N., Illushin, L., & Willis, W. (2001). The kids are doing all right: Differences in parental satisfaction, expectation, and attribution in St. Petersburg, Sunderland, and Kentucky. *Cambridge Journal of Education, 31*, 179–204.

Fisher, T. A., & Padmawidjaja, I. (1999). Parental influences on career development perceived by African American and Mexican American college students. *Journal of Multicultural Counseling and Development, 27*, 136–152.

Frome, P., & Eccles, J. (1998). Parents' influence on children's achievement related perceptions. *Journal of Personality and Social Psychology, 74*, 435–452.

Gill, S., & Reynolds, A. J. (1999). Educational expectations and school achievement of urban African American children. *Journal of School Psychology, 37*, 403–424.

Goldenberg, C., Gallimore, R., Reese, L., & Garnier, H. (2001). Cause or effect? A longitudinal study of immigrant Latino parents' aspirations and expectations, and their children's school performance. *American Educational Research Journal, 28*, 547–582.

Goyette, K., & Xie, Y. (1999). Educational expectations of Asian American youths: Determinants and ethnic differences. *Sociology of Education, 72*, 22–36.

Hao, L., & Bonstead-Bruns, M. (1998a). Parent–child differences in educational expectations and the academic achievement of immigrant and native students. *Sociology of Education, 7*, 175–198.

Hao, L., & Bonstead-Bruns, M. (1998b). Parents' extrafamilial resources and children's school attainment. *Sociology of Education, 71*, 175–198.

Henderson, A. (1988, October). Parents are school's best friends. *Phi Delta Kappan, 70*, 149–153.

Jacobs, J. E. (1991). Influence of gender stereotype on parent and child mathematics attitudes. *Journal of Educational Psychology, 83*, 518–527.

Jacobs, N., & Harvey, D. (2005). Do parents make a difference to children's academic achievement? Differences between parents of higher and lower achieving students. *Educational Studies, 31,* 431–448.

Lara-Alecio, Rafael, I. J. B., & Ebener, R. (1997). Developing academically supportive behaviors among Hispanic parents: What elementary teachers and administrators can do. *Preventing School Failure, 42,* 27–33.

Ma, X. (2001). Participation in advanced mathematics: Do expectation and influence of students, peers, teachers, and parents really matter? *Contemporary Educational Psychology, 26,* 132–146.

Mau, W.-C. (1995). Educational planning and academic achievement of middle school students: A racial and cultural comparison. *Journal of Counseling & Development, 73,* 518–535.

Okagaki, L., & Frensch, P. A. (1998). Parenting and children's school achievement: A multicultural perspective. *American Educational Research Journal, 35,*123–144.

Parsons, J. E., Adler, T. F., & Kaczala, C. M. (1982). Socialization of achievement attitudes and beliefs: Parental influences. *Child Development, 53,* 310–321.

Ramos, L., & Sanchez, A. R. (1995). Mexican–American high school students: Educational aspirations. *Journal of Multicultural Counseling and Development, 23,* 212–221.

Räty, H. (2006). What comes after compulsory education? A follow-up study on parental expectations of their child's future education. *Educational Studies, 3,* 1–16.

Rumberger, R. W. (1995). Dropping out of middle school: A multilevel analysis of students and schools. *American Educational Research Journal, 32,* 583–625.

Sanders, C. E., Field, T. M., & Diego, M. A. (2001). Adolescents' academic expectations and achievement. *Adolescence, 36,* 795–803.

Seginer, R. (1983). Parents' educational expectations and children's academic achievement: A literature review. *Merrill-Palmer Quarterly, 29,* 1–23.

Singh, K., Bickley, P. G., Keith, T. Z., Keith, P. B., Trivette, P., & Anderson, E. (1995). The effects of four components of parental involvement on eighth-grades student achievement: Structural analysis of nels-88 data. *School Psychology Review, 24,* 299–317.

Smith-Maddox, R. (1998). Defining culture as a dimension of academic achievement: Implications for culturally responsive curriculum, instruction, and assessment. *Journal of Negro Education, 67,* 302–317.

Steinberg, L., Lamborn, S. D., Dornbusch, S. M., & Darling, N. (1992). Impact of parenting practices on adolescent achievement: Authoritative parenting, school involvement and encouragement to succeed. *Child Development, 63,* 1266–1281.

Sue, S., & Okazaki, S. (1990). Asian–American educational achievements. *American Psychologist, 45,* 913–920.

Trusty, J. (2000). High educational expectations and low achievement: Stability of educational goals across adolescence. *Journal of Educational Research, 93,* 356–365.

Trusty, J. (2002). African Americans' educational expectations: Longitudinal causal models for women and men. *Journal of Counseling & Development, 80,* 332–345.

Trusty, J., & Harris, M. B. C. (1999). Lost talent: Predictors of the stability of educational expectations across adolescence. *Journal of Adolescent Research, 14,* 359–382.

Trusty, J., Plata, M., & Salazar, C. F. (2003). Modeling Mexican Americans' educational expectations: Longitudinal effects of variables across adolescence. *Journal of Adolescent Research, 18,* 131–153.

Tsui, M. (2005). Family income, home environment, parenting, and mathematics achievement of children in China and the United States. *Education and Urban Society, 37,* 336–355.

Vollmer, F. (1986). The relationship between expectancy and academic achievement—How can it be explained? *British Journal of Educational Psychology, 56,* 64–74.

Wang, J., & Wildman, L. (1995). An examination of effects of family commitment in education on student achievement in seventh grade science. *Journal of Research in Science Teaching, 32,* 833–837.

Wright, S. P., Horn, S. P., & Sanders, W. L. (1997). Teacher and classroom context effects on student achievement: Implications for teacher evaluation. *Journal of Personnel Evaluation in Education, 11,* 57–67.

Yan, W., & Lin, Q. (2005). Parent involvement and mathematics achievement: Contrast across racial and ethnic groups. *Journal of Educational Research, 99,* 116–127.

Family, Denomination, and the Adolescent World View: An Empirical Enquiry Among 13- to 15-Year-Old Girls in England and Wales

Leslie J. Francis

ABSTRACT. The present study draws on a large survey of 16,581 13- to 15-year-old girls representative of the school population in England and Wales to examine the power of family denominational affiliation to predict the adolescent world view. World view was illustrated by reference to nine areas: personal well-being, worries, counseling, school, social concern, religious beliefs, paranormal beliefs, sexual morality, and attitudes toward substances. Comparisons were made between those who claimed no religious affiliation and those who claimed affiliation as Anglicans, Roman Catholics, Methodists, Baptists, Presbyterians, Pentecostals, and Jehovah's Witnesses. The data demonstrated that each of these seven denominational groups offered a distinctive profile in areas of personal and social importance. These findings were interpreted as offering support for views advanced in Canada by Bibby, in Australia by Bouma, and in the United Kingdom by Fane regarding the continuing social significance of religious and denominational affiliation and as offering critique of the British Government's decision

The Revd Canon Professor Leslie J. Francis is affiliated with the University of Warwick, Coventry, UK.

not to include denominational subdivision of the Christian category within the 2001 census conducted in England and Wales.

INTRODUCTION

Religious denomination has been a relatively neglected variable within research intended to identify sources of individual differences within the adolescent world view in England and Wales. No reference has been made to this factor by a number of studies (see, for example, Barry, 2001). Two main reasons underpin this neglect. The first reason reflects the more general influence of the secularization thesis that assumes the marginality of religion in personal and social life and consequently eclipses dimensions of religiosity from research concerned with contemporary world views. Other studies have clearly indicated the erroneous nature of this judgment by demonstrating the continuing influence of a number of dimensions of religiosity on aspects of adolescent development in England and Wales, including prayer (Francis, 2005), bible reading (Francis, 2000), church attendance (Kay & Francis, 2006), God images (Robbins, Francis, & Kerr, 2006), and attitude (Francis, 2006).

The second reason underpinning the neglect of religious denomination in empirical research in England and Wales concerns uncertainty regarding what it is that is being accessed by the straightforward denominational question. There are both theological and empirical bases for this uncertainty. The theological argument is based on an examination of what properly counts as "religion." True religion, some might argue, is reflected in what people believe (e.g., claim Jesus as their personal savior), in what people do (e.g., attend church), and in how people behave (e.g., display love for their neighbor), not in self-assigned labels of affiliation. The empirical argument is based on an examination of the general evidence for a lack of clear association between self-assigned religious affiliation and those other indicators of religiosity generally included in social surveys (belief, practice, and behavior).

The debate about the usefulness or uselessness of religious affiliation as an indicator in social research was brought into particular prominence in England and Wales in the 6-year period before the 2001 national census, when the introduction of a religious affiliation question within the census was seriously debated for the first time (Francis, 2003; Weller, 2004).

The major argument against accepting religious affiliation as a useful variable in the census in England and Wales is based on a failure to understand affiliation as a serious social indicator in its own right but rather to see it as a poor predictor of other religious dimensions. The same problem was voiced in other countries. For example, an information paper produced in preparation for the 2001 Census of Population and Dwellings in New Zealand argued as follows (Statistics New Zealand, 1998):

> The practical value of census information on religion is questionable, particularly in view of the fact that it does not provide an accurate indication of either the churchgoing practices of the population or the depth of a person's commitment to their specified religions.

A number of empirical studies in England drew attention to the way in which affiliation is a poor predictor of practice and to how the relationship varies from denomination to denomination (Francis, 1982). For example, although most self-assigned Baptists may well be regular churchgoers, most self-assigned Anglicans appear never to consider going to church. Herein is the problem of "religious nominalism."

For a question on religious affiliation to be included as a valid social indicator in the national census, affiliation needed to be understood in its own right and not merely as a poor approximation for other dimensions of religion. An important and powerful attempt to rehabilitate self-assigned religious affiliation as a theoretically coherent and socially significant indicator was advanced by Fane (1999), drawing on Bouma's (1992, p. 110) sociological theory of religious identification, according to which religious affiliation is defined as a "useful social category giving some indication of the cultural background and general orientating values of a person." Then Bouma (1992) posits a process through which cultural background and general orientating values are acquired. Importantly, this process of acquisition is exactly the same for religious identity as it is for political or sporting or philosophical identifies and consists of meaning systems and plausibility structures. Bouma (1992) describes meaning systems as "a set or collection of answers to question

about the meaning and purpose of life" (p. 106) and plausibility structures (borrowed from Berger, 1967, 1971) as "social arrangements
which serve to inculcate, celebrate, perpetuate and apply a meaning
system" (p. 107). He maintains that people possess meaning systems
from which they derive their existential purpose. He cites a living church
as being one example of a plausibility structure through which a
meaning system is made plausible and then disseminated. Although a
self-assigned religious identity might also imply commitment to a plausibility structure (practice) and adherence to its relating meaning system
(belief), Bouma (1992) suggests that it might be equally, perhaps more,
significant in terms of the exposure to the particular cultural background that it represents. Crucially, this alternative conceptualization
avoids the difficult terrain of religious affiliation as proxy for practice
and belief by recognizing that even non-churchgoers and nonbelievers
"may still show the effect of the meaning system and plausibility
structure with which they identify" (Bouma, 1992, p. 108).

The value of Bouma's (1992) sociological theory of religious
identification is that it allows self-assigned religious affiliation to be
perceived, and thus analyzed, as a key component of social identity,
in a way similar to age, gender, class location, political persuasion,
nationality, ethnic group, and other factors (Zavalloni, 1975).
Religious affiliation informs our attitudes and, in turn, our modes
of behavior by contributing to our self-definition both regarding
who we are and, equally importantly, regarding who we are not.
This type of analysis is especially advantageous when interpreting
census data, because it is inclusive of all those who claim a religious
affiliation, not only of the minority who also attend church.

Alongside Bouma's (1992) theory of religious identification, Fane
also draws on Bibby's (1985, 1987) theory of "encasement"
developed from his empirical surveys in Canada. Bibby argues that
Canadian Christians are "encased" within the Christian tradition.
In other words, this tradition has a strong influential hold over both
its active and latent members from which affiliates find it extremely
difficult to extricate themselves. Contrary to the claims of secularization theorists that low levels of church attendance are indicative of
the erosion of religion's social significance (Wallis & Bruce, 1992),
Bibby (1985, 1987) would argue that this trend is actually a manifestation of the repackaging of religion in the context of late 20th
century consumer-orientated society. Consumers are free to select
"fragments" of faith, and they are encouraged to do this by the

way in which the churches have simulated the marketing strategies of the wider society.

The central point to glean from Bibby's (1985, 1987) analysis is that the potential for religion, in this case Christianity, to be a socially significant attitudinal and behavioral determinant has not necessarily disappeared. If anything, the Christian "casing" may have been strengthened, because the accommodationist stance adopted by the Christian churches has, according to Bibby (1985, 1987), reduced the need for affiliates to look elsewhere.

The flaw in the question eventually introduced to the 2001 census in England and Wales was that religious affiliation was conceptualized only in terms of the major faith traditions (Christian, Buddhist, Hindu, Muslim, Jewish, Sikh). The Government at Westminster remained unconvinced that any further relevant information would be generated by subdividing the Christian category into the component denominations. The aim of the present study is to expose the fallacy of this flaw, specifically in respect of the world view of young people. Building on Fane's development of Bibby's encasement theory, the thesis of the present study is that information about religious denomination provides key access to the nature of the *family* influences that mold the attitudes and values of the young. At this stage in life religious denomination and family identity remain closely associated.

In another part of the United Kingdom (Northern Ireland) denominational influence has been and remains a powerful predictor of the world view adopted by young people. Empirical evidence for the key difference between young people shaped by Protestant families and by Catholic families has been well-documented by the research tradition pioneered by John Greer (see Francis, 1996). For example, in 1984 Greer administered a broad-ranging questionnaire throughout 10 Protestant and 10 Catholic schools to samples of 14- to 17-year-old pupils. A total of 1,177 pupils participated (606 attending Protestant schools and 571 attending Catholic schools). The findings from this study reported by Greer and Francis (1990) indicated significant difference in the profiles of the two denominational groups.

In a subsequent study in 1998, Francis, Robbins, Barnes, and Lewis (2006) administered a similar and somewhat extended questionnaire throughout seven Protestant and nine Catholic schools to a sample of 16- to 18-year-old pupils. A total of 2,369 pupils participated (1,099 attending Protestant schools and 1,270 attending Catholic schools). The findings demonstrated just how much the young people educated within the segregated system of Protestant and Catholic schools maintained different religious and ethical profiles. Reflecting on their data, Robbins, Barnes, and Lewis (2006, p. 199) concluded the following:

> Protestant and Catholics seem to inhabit somewhat different moral universes, which in turn may reflect somewhat different understandings of the moral values espoused by their God. The God of the Protestant community seems to be more against gambling, drunkenness, smoking, lying, stealing and sexual intercourse before marriage. The God of the Catholic community seems to be more against capital punishment, war, the use of nuclear weapons, color prejudice and religious discrimination.

Although the two studies reported by Greer and Francis (1990) and by Francis et al. (2006) were relatively restricted in terms of the range of issues used, a much more broadly based study comparing the world views of pupils educated in Protestant and Catholic schools in Northern Ireland is reported by Robbins and Francis (in press). Drawing on a sample of 1,585 13- to 15-year-old male pupils, this study highlighted the significant differences in world views between adolescents educated within the two school systems across eight domains, defined as religious beliefs, paranormal beliefs, church-related attitudes, attitudes toward sex and family life, law-related attitudes, school-related attitudes, locality-related attitudes, and personal anxiety and depression.

The cultural context of England and Wales is so different from Northern Ireland that generalizations cannot be made from the one community to the other. However, Francis (2001a,b) provided some relatively recent evidence that Christian denomination may be far from irrelevant in predicting individual differences in the world views of adolescents living in England and Wales. These two studies profiled differences according to the categorization of four Christian groups: Anglican, Catholic, Protestant, and sects. For example, drawing on a sample of 29,124 13- to 15-year-old pupils, Francis (2001a) gave particular attention to ways in which affiliation to these four Christian groups predicted individual differences in moral values. Interesting patterns emerged. Thus, 44% of young people affiliated to Christian sects maintained that it is wrong to become drunk, compared with 26% of Protestants, 19% of Anglicans, and 18% of Catholics; 57% of young people affiliated to Christian sects maintained that it is wrong to have sexual intercourse outside marriage, compared with 19% of Protestants, 15% of Catholics, and 13% of Anglicans; and 65% of young people affiliated to Christian sects maintained that abortion is wrong and so did 50% of Catholics, compared with 38% of Protestants and 31% of Anglicans.

Against this background the aim of the present study is to build on the initial findings presented by Francis (2001a,b) delineating a fuller profile of the adolescent world view and distinguishing between individual denominations rather than by groups of denominations. These new analyses draw on the Religion and Values Today database thoroughly reported and described by Francis (2001c). The database provides a reliable and representative sample of nearly 34,000 year-9 and year-10 pupils (13- to 15-year-olds) across England and Wales. In view of space restrictions, the analyses concentrates on the female pupils only, obviating the need to take sex differences into account.

METHODS

Sample

A sample of 33,982 year-9 and year-10 pupils (between the ages of 13 and 15 years) participated in the project from schools throughout England and Wales, including a proper mix or urban and rural schools and independent and state-maintained schools. Within the state-maintained sector, a correct balance between nondenominational, Anglican voluntary, and Roman Catholic voluntary schools was included. The project was set up in 1990 and progressed at a consistent pace throughout the 1990s. Pupils were assured of confidentiality and anonymity. Although all pupils were given the choice not to participate, very few decided not to take part in the survey, probably in light of the interest of the subject matter.

Instrument

In addition to a number of background questions, the questionnaire included 128 well-focused and easily-understood statements, to which the pupils responded on a five-point Likert-type scale (Likert, 1932): *agree strongly, agree, not certain, disagree,* and *disagree strongly*. Although presented in a thoroughly randomized fashion, the items were designed to profile the adolescent world view through 15 themes defined as personal well-being, worries, counseling, school, work, religious beliefs, church and society, paranormal beliefs, politics, social concerns, sexual morality, substance use, right and wrong, leisure, and the local area.

Analysis

To simply clarify the analysis, this study is based on the responses of the 16,581 girls. Religious affiliation was assessed by the question, "Do you belong to a church or other religious group?" followed by a list beginning with "no," identifying the major Christian denominations and the major world faiths, and ending with "other (please specify)." Responses to this question then allowed eight groups to be identified as useful for comparison in their analysis of family denomination, namely those who self-identified as no religious affiliation (7,132), Baptist (438), Anglican (4,996), Jehovah's Witnesses (91), Methodist (480), Pentecostal (102), Presbyterian (119), and Roman Catholic (1,698). A number of other established Christian denominations were represented by insufficient pupils to sustain independent analysis, including Quaker, Orthodox, Salvation Army, and Seventh-day Adventist. Many New Churches were also represented by small numbers of pupils. Overall, these figures provide a fair indication of the relative strength of denominational affiliation in England and Wales given the persistence of Anglicanism as the Established Church in England (although not in Wales).

From the large quantity of information within the database, the relationship between denominational identity and the adolescent world view was tested and illustrated by selecting just two items each from five themes (personal well-being, worries, counseling, school, and social concerns) and five items each from four themes that were examined in greater detail (religious beliefs, paranormal beliefs, sex and morality, and substance use). In Tables 1 to 3, the responses of the eight groups of young people are presented in the following order: those who self-identified as having no religious affiliation (None), Anglicans (Ang), Roman Catholics (RC), Methodists (Meth), Baptists (Bapt), Pentecostals (Pent), Presbyterians (Pres), and Jehovah's Witnesses (JW). Multiple chi-square tests were used to test the statistical significance of the difference between the endorsement of the nonaffiliates and the endorsement of each denominational group in turn. Endorsement was calculated as the

TABLE 1. Views on Personal Social Life by Denomination

	None (%)	Ang (%)	RC (%)	Meth (%)	Bapt (%)	Pent (%)	Pres (%)	JW (%)
Personal well-being								
I feel my life has a sense of purpose	50	58***	63***	64***	65***	75***	59	73***
I have sometimes considered taking my own life	32	28***	29*	27*	28	28	17***	24
Worries								
I am worried about my attractiveness to the oppposite sex	39	41**	43**	47***	44*	44	44	31
I am worried about getting AIDS	63	64	64	54***	59	41***	62	33***
Counseling								
I find it helpful to talk about my problems with my mother	55	61***	58*	60*	57	63	54	72**
I find it helpful to talk about my problems with my father	23	26***	26**	25	28*	31*	31*	46***
School								
School is boring	37	28***	35	26***	28***	30	33	32
Teachers do a good job	40	48***	48***	55***	53***	60***	55***	56**
Social concern								
I am concerned about the risk of pollution to the environment	63	71***	67**	78***	72***	71	83***	80**
I am concerned about the poverty of the Third World	60	71***	77***	73***	75**	75**	79***	74**

$^*p < .05$; $^{**}p < .01$; $^{***}p < .001$.

product of the "agree strongly" and "agree" responses compared with the product of the "disagree strongly," "disagree," and "not certain" responses on the five-point Likert scale. In view of the complexity of the data, statistical significance tests were not used to compare the responses of the seven denominational groups. In interpreting the levels of probability, it needs to be recognized that statistical significance is highly dependent on the sample size and that in the present study, there is a wide discrepancy between the strength of the different groups, from the two extremes of 4,996 Anglicans to 91 Jehovah's Witnesses.

TABLE 2. Views on Religion and the Paranormal by Denomination

	None (%)	Ang (%)	RC (%)	Meth (%)	Bapt (%)	Pent (%)	Pres (%)	JW (%)
Religious beliefs								
I believe in God	27	50***	73***	58***	71***	88***	66***	95***
I believe that Jesus really rose from the dead	17	37***	57***	47***	61***	84***	51***	91***
I believe that God punishes people who do wrong	14	21***	21***	24***	33***	50***	23*	44***
I believe Christianity is the only true religion	8	16***	21***	20***	35***	68***	22***	33***
I believe that God made the worle in 6 days and rested on the 7th	10	22***	16***	33***	49***	83***	37***	67***
Paranormal beliefs								
I believe in my horoscope	50	45***	47*	42***	36***	16***	41	14***
I believe in ghosts	41	40	43	35*	36*	31*	28**	29*
I believe in black magic	19	16***	16*	15	11***	15	8**	13
I believe that fortune-tellers can tell the future	27	27	27	22*	22*	19	14**	13**
I believe that it is possible to contact the spirits of the dead	35	33**	33	30**	27**	30	25*	21***

*p < .05; **p < .01; ***p < .001.

TABLE 3. Views on Sex and Substances by Denomination

	None (%)	Ang (%)	RC (%)	Meth (%)	Bapt (%)	Pent (%)	Pres (%)	JW (%)
Sex								
It is wrong to have sexual intercourse outside marriage	9	12***	14***	16***	23***	54***	12	70***
Homosexuality is wrong	20	19	20	21	27***	59***	18	81***
Contraception is wrong	3	2***	4	2	5	3	3	9**
Abortion is wrong	38	34***	53***	37	45**	68***	36	82***
Divorce is wrong	13	14*	19***	17**	24***	40***	11	61***
Substances								
It is wrong to smoke cigarettes	35	40***	35	47***	43***	54***	52***	78***
It is wrong to become drunk	15	18***	17	24***	29***	47***	32***	59***
It is wrong to use marijuana	49	58***	52*	59***	54*	69***	69***	76***
It is wrong to use heroin	74	79***	77*	82***	75	89***	87**	87**
It is wrong to sniff glue	79	82***	80	85**	79	83	89**	88*

$*p < .05; **p < .01; ***p < .001.$

RESULTS AND DISCUSSION

Table 1 presents the item endorsement for the eight groups of young girls with respect to the five aspects of personal and social life (personal well-being, worries, counseling, school, and social concern). Two items were selected to illustrate each of these five areas.

In terms of personal well-being, Christian affiliation tends to be associated with an enhanced sense of purpose in life and with lower levels of suicidal ideation. Both findings are consistent with the broader research literature that associated religiosity with purpose in life (as summarized by Francis & Robbins, 2006) and that associated religiosity with lower levels of suicidal ideation (as summarized by Kay & Francis, 2006).

In terms of worries, Christian affiliation is associated with greater anxiety about attractiveness to the opposite sex (except in the case of Jehovah's Witnesses). Anxiety about AIDS is lower among Methodists, Pentecostals, and Jehovah's Witnesses but not among Anglicans, Roman Catholics, Baptists, or Presbyterians. These differences suggest that teaching on sexuality may vary significantly from one Christian group to another.

In terms of counseling, Christian affiliation is, overall, associated with the experience of greater support from both mothers and fathers. In other words, young girls whose family background includes the sense of Christian affiliation feel a significantly closer bond with their parents, in the sense that they are more likely to find it helpful to talk about their problems with their mother or father.

In terms of attitude toward school, Christian affiliation is, overall, associated with a more positive experience and a more positive response. Generally, young girls who identify with a Christian denomination are less likely to find school boring and more likely to rate teachers as doing a good job. These findings are consistent with the broader research literature that finds an association between religiosity and school-related attitudes (see, for example, Francis, 1992; Montgomery & Francis, 1996).

In terms of social concern, Christian affiliation is, overall, associated with a greater commitment to environmental matters and to world development. Young girls who identify with a Christian denomination are more likely to be concerned about the risk of pollution to the environment and more likely to be concerned about the poverty of the Third World. The positive association between religiosity and environmental concern is consistent with earlier research among young people in the United Kingdom reported by Francis (1997).

Table 2 presents the item endorsement for the eight groups of young girls with respect to views on religion and the paranormal. Five items have been selected to illustrate each of these two areas.

In respect of views on religion, it is not surprising that those young people who claim affiliation with a Christian denomination display higher levels of belief than do nonaffiliates. What is of greater interest, however, is the way in which levels of belief vary so greatly between the different denominational groups. Belief in God may provide a broad indication of the level of nominalism within the denominational categories, with Anglicanism (the established religion in England, although not in Wales) carrying the highest level of nominalism. Thus, in ascending order, belief in God was expressed by 50% of Anglicans, 58% of Methodists, 66% of Presbyterians, 71% of Baptists, 73% of Roman Catholics, 88% of Pentecostals, and 95% of Jehovah's Witnesses. An almost identical pattern emerges concerning belief that Jesus really rose from the dead, with just Roman Catholics and Baptists swapping positions. A somewhat different pattern emerges, however, with respect to an item intended to gauge conservatism in belief. The belief that God made the world in 6 days and rested on the 7th was expressed, in ascending order, by 16% of Roman Catholics, 22% of Anglicans, 33% of Methodists, 37% of Presbyterians, 49% of Baptists, 67% of Jehovah's Witnesses, and 83% of Pentecostals.

With respect to views on the paranormal, the situation is somewhat more complex. Different Christian groups seem to vary in the extent to which they tend to steer their young affiliates away from the paranormal and the occult (Boyd, 1996). Overall, however, young girls affiliated to a Christian denomination are less inclined than nonaffiliated young girls to believe in their horoscope, but it is the Pentecostals and Jehovah's Witnesses who are least likely to accept such beliefs. Belief in their horoscopes was expressed, in descending order, by 47% of Roman Catholics, 45% of Anglicans, 42% of Methodists, 41% of Presbyterians, 36% of Baptists, 16% of Pentecostals, and 14% of Jehovah's Witnesses. Belief in the possibility of contacting the spirits of the dead is also lowest among Jehovah's Witnesses. This belief was expressed, in descending order, by 33% of Anglicans, 33% of Roman Catholics, 30% of Methodists,

30% of Pentecostals, 27% of Baptists, 25% of Presbyterians, and 21% of Jehovah's Witnesses.

Table 3 presents the item endorsement for the eight groups of young girls with respect to views on sexual morality and substances. Five items have been selected to illustrate each of these two areas.

Regarding views on sexual morality, some very clear delineation takes place along denominational lines. Anglicans, Presbyterians, Roman Catholics, and Methodists are slightly more conservative in their approach to sexual intercourse outside marriage than young people who claim no religious affiliation. Although 9% of the nonaffiliates believed that it is wrong to have sexual intercourse outside marriage, the proportions rose to 12% among Anglicans, 12% among Presbyterians, 14% among Roman Catholics, and 16% among Methodists. The proportions rose further to 23% among Baptists, 54% among Pentecostals, and 70% among Jehovah's Witnesses. Similar contours are followed regarding attitudes toward homosexuality. The view that homosexuality is wrong was taken by 20% of nonaffiliates, 18% of Presbyterians, 19% of Anglicans, 20% of Roman Catholics, and 21% of Methodists. The proportions rose, however, to 27% among Baptists, 59% among Pentecostals, and 81% among Jehovah's Witnesses. A somewhat different pattern emerges with respect to attitudes toward abortion in light of the clear stance of the Roman Catholic Church on this issue. The view that abortion is wrong was taken by 38% of nonaffiliates, 34% of Anglicans, 36% of Presbyterians, and 37% of Methodists. The proportions rose, however, to 45% among Baptists, 53% among Roman Catholics, 68% among Pentecostals, and 82% among Jehovah's Witnesses.

Regarding views on substances, once again some very clear delineation takes place along denominational lines. A more liberal position was generally taken by Roman Catholics, and a more conservative position was generally taken by Jehovah's Witnesses. In terms of tobacco use, 35% of nonaffiliates believed that it is wrong to smoke cigarettes, and so did 35% of the Roman Catholics. Then, in ascending order, this view was taken by 40% of Anglicans, 43% of Baptists, 47% of Methodists, 52% of Presbyterians, 54% of Pentecostals, and 78% of Jehovah's Witnesses. In terms of alcohol use, 15% of nonaffiliates believed that it is wrong to become drunk. The proportion rose marginally to 17% among Roman Catholics and 18% among Anglicans. The proportion rose further to 24% among Methodists, 29% among Baptists, 32%

among Presbyterians, 47% among Pentecostals, and 59% among Jehovah's Witnesses.

CONCLUSION

Drawing on a large data set of 16,581 female secondary school pupils, between the ages of 13 and 15 years, the present study set out to test two hypotheses: (1) that young people whose families identify with a Christian denomination differ in significant ways in terms of their world view from young people whose families identify with no religious group and (2) that the nature of this difference varies greatly from one Christian denomination to another. Both hypotheses are supported by the data. The considerable variations between the different Christian denominations clearly highlight the inadequacy of the religious operationalizations included in the national census for England and Wales in 2001. In terms of a range of socially significant aspects of the young person's world view, knowledge about denominational affiliation is of considerably greater use than the broad-brush grouping of all Christian denominations together.

Considering the seven denominational groups together, there is broad evidence that compared with young girls whose families hold no religious affiliation, those who claim Christian affiliation (in whatever form) tend to enjoy a greater sense of purpose in life and are less likely to entertain suicidal ideation. They are likely to receive greater support from their parents, hold a more positive attitude toward school, and espouse a higher level of social commitment. They are more likely to hold traditional religious beliefs and less likely to hold paranormal beliefs. They are more likely to take a conservative stance on issues concerning sexual morality and on issues concerning the use and abuse of substances. Behind this global summary, however, there are considerable variations from one denomination to another. Each denomination is reviewed in turn to highlight distinctive features.

On many issues young Anglicans stand closer to the nonaffiliates than young people belonging to other denominations. Nonetheless, there are clear distances between the young Anglicans and the young nonaffiliates. Twice as many Anglicans believe in God (50% compared with 27%). Anglicans are less likely to believe in their horoscope or in the possibility of contacting the spirits of the dead.

Anglicans are likely to take a slightly more conservative view on sex outside marriage, on getting drunk, and on smoking cigarettes.

In many ways young Methodists stand quite close to the young Anglicans. They are slightly more likely than Anglicans to believe in God and slightly less likely to believe in their horoscope. On the other hand, young Methodists take a more conservative stance than young Anglicans on alcohol and on tobacco, positions consistent with the historic roots of Methodism. Young Methodists also display greater concern than young Anglicans for environmental issues, a position consistent with current national programs in the Methodist Church in the United Kingdom.

Young Presbyterians stand a little further away from the nonaffiliates than either Anglicans or Methodists. They are slightly more inclined to believe in God and less inclined to believe in their horoscope. They take a somewhat more conservative view on substances but not on sexual morality. They show a higher level of social concern but not a higher sense of purpose in life.

Compared with the three mainline reformed denominations (Anglicans, Methodists, and Presbyterians), the young Catholics project a distinctive profile. They are more inclined to believe in God but much less inclined to believe in a God who made the world in 6 days and rested on the 7th. They are also more inclined to believe in their horoscope and in other paranormal phenomena. In terms of the use of alcohol and tobacco, young Catholics take a more permissive view than young Anglicans, Methodists, and Presbyterians. In terms of sexual morality, young Catholics are no more likely to reject contraception, but they are much more likely than Anglicans, Methodists, and Presbyterians to reject abortion. Young Catholics are clearly selective regarding the aspect of their denominational teaching they choose to adopt. In terms of social concerns, young Catholics show more concern than young Anglicans and Methodists for world development issues but less concern for environmental issues.

Young Baptists seem to occupy a position midway between the mainline reformed denominations (Anglicans, Methodists, and Presbyterians) and the more sectarian groups (Pentecostals and Jehovah's Witnesses). Compared with the mainline reformed denominations, young Baptists are more inclined to believe in God, more inclined to believe the Genesis account of creation, and less inclined to believe in paranormal phenomena. They are more inclined to take a conservative view on areas of sexual morality (sex outside marriage, homosexuality, abortion, and divorce) and on the use and abuse of alcohol.

Young Pentecostals appear to have a very different world view from that adopted by Anglicans, Methodists, Presbyterians, and Catholics. Young Pentecostals are much more likely to believe in the Genesis account of creation, to believe in a God who punishes people who do wrong, and to believe that Christianity is the only true religion. They are much less likely to believe in their horoscope. Young Pentecostals are much more likely to take a conservative view on areas of sexual morality (sex outside marriage, homosexuality, abortion, and divorce) and on the use and abuse of substances (tobacco, alcohol, marijuana, and heroin). They benefit from a much higher sense of purpose in life and are significantly less likely to be worried about getting AIDS, because their lifestyle seems to protect them from the transmission of such diseases.

Like young Pentecostals, young Jehovah's Witnesses have a highly distinctive world view. Among young Jehovah's Witnesses there is a high level of belief in God and a low level of paranormal belief. Their world view is highly committed to moral absolutes. The vast majority of young Jehovah's Witnesses reject sex outside marriage, homosexuality, abortion, and divorce. The vast majority of young Jehovah's Witnesses reject tobacco and alcohol as well as other substances. For young Jehovah's Witnesses there seems comparatively little fear from AIDS. For young Jehovah's Witnesses there is a significantly higher level of support from talking through problems with their parents.

The findings generated by the present study provide important new data that support the overall contention advanced by Fane (1999), drawing on ideas formulated by Bibby (1985, 1987) and Bouma (1992). Fane (1999, p. 122) summarized her conclusion as follows:

> Self-assigned religious affiliation may also be useful as a predictor of social attitudes and behaviors, particularly when subdivided by denomination.... In analyses of census data, it may prove helpful to conceptualize self-assigned religious affiliation as a component of social identity, rather than as an inadequate indicator of religious practice and belief.

In terms of the present study, this conclusion is consistent with the view that for adolescents, self-assigned religious affiliation conveys really important information about the context in which their family life nurtures their world view, with or without additional information about their religious beliefs and their religious practices.

Because of restrictions on space the present analyses have concentrated specifically and only on young girls. A similar set of analyses are now needed to replicate this study among young boys to test whether the findings are in any ways gender specific.

REFERENCES

Barry, M. (2001). *Challenging transitions: Young people's views and experiences of growing up.* London: Save the Children.

Berger, P. (1967). *The sacred canopy: Elements of a sociology of religion.* New York: Doubleday.

Berger, P. (1971). *A rumour of angels: Modern society and the rediscovery of the supernatural.* Harmondsworth: Penguin Books.

Bibby, R. W. (1985). Religious encasement in Canada: An argument for Protestant and Catholic entrenchment. *Social Compass, 16,* 287–303.

Bibby, R. W. (1987). *Fragmented gods: The poverty and potential of religion in Canada.* Toronto: Irwin Publishing.

Bouma, G. D. (1992). *Religion: Meaning, transcendence and community in Australia.* Melbourne: Longman Cheshire.

Boyd, A. (1996). *Dangerous obsessions: Teenagers and the occult.* London: Marshal Pickering.

Fane, R. S. (1999). Is self-assigned religious affiliation socially significant? In L. J. Francis (Ed.), *Sociology, theology and the curriculum* (pp. 113–124). London: Cassell.

Francis, L. J. (1982). *Youth in transit: A profile of 16–25 year olds.* Aldershot: Gower.

Francis, L. J. (1992). The influence of religion, gender and social class on attitudes toward school among eleven year olds in England. *Journal of Experimental Education, 60,* 339–348.

Francis, L. J. (1996). John E. Greer: Research pioneer in religious education. In L. J. Francis, W. K. Kay, & W. S. Campbell (Eds.), *Research in religious education* (pp. 11–30). Leominster: Fowler Wright Books.

Francis, L. J. (1997). Christianity, personality and concern about environmental pollution among 13- to 15-year olds. *Journal of Beliefs and Values, 18,* 7–16.

Francis, L. J. (2000). The relationship between bible reading and purpose in life among 13–15 year olds. *Mental Health, Religion and Culture, 3,* 27–36.

Francis, L. J. (2001a). Religion and values: A quantitative perspective. In L. J. Francis, J. Astley, & M. Robbins (Eds.), *The fourth R for the third millennium: Education in religion and values for the global future* (pp. 47–78). Dublin: Lindisfarne Books.

Francis, L. J. (2001b). The social significance of religious affiliation among adolescents in England and Wales. In H.-G. Ziebertz (Ed.), *Religious individualisation and Christian religious semantics* (pp. 115–138). Münster: Lit Verlag.

Francis, L. J. (2001c). *The values debate: A voice from the pupils.* London: Woburn Press.

Francis, L. J. (2003). Religion and social capital: The flaw in the 2001 census in England and Wales. In P. Avis (Ed.), *Public faith: The state of religious belief and practice in Britain* (pp. 45–64). London: SPCK.

Francis, L. J. (2005). Prayer, personality and purpose in life among churchgoing and non-churchgoing adolescents. In L. J. Francis, M. Robbins, & J. Astley (Eds.), *Religion, education and adolescence: International empirical perspectives* (pp. 15–38). Cardiff: University of Wales Press.

Francis, L. J. (2006). Attitude toward Christianity and premarital sex. *Psychological Reports, 98,* 140.

Francis, L. J., & Robbins, M. (2006). Prayer, purpose in life, personality and social attitudes among non-churchgoing 13- to 15-year-olds in England and Wales. *Research in the Social Scientific Study of Religion, 17,* 123–155.

Francis, L. J., Robbins, M., Barnes, L. P., & Lewis, C. A. (2006). Religiously affiliated schools in Northern Ireland: The persistence of denominational differences in pupils' religious and moral values. *Journal of Empirical Theology, 19,* 182–202.

Greer, J. E., & Francis, L. J. (1990). The religious profile of pupils in Northern Ireland: A comparative study of pupils attending Catholic and Protestant secondary schools. *Journal of Empirical Theology, 3,* 35–50.

Kay, W. K., & Francis, L. J. (2006). Suicidal ideation among young people in the UK: Churchgoing as an inhibitory influence? *Mental Health, Religion and Culture, 9,* 127–140.

Likert, R. (1932). A technique for the measurement of attitudes. *Archives of Psychology, 140,* 1–55.

Montgomery, A., & Francis, L. J. (1996). Relationship between personal prayer and school-related attitudes among 11–16 year old girls. *Psychological Reports, 78,* 787–793.

Robbins, M., & Francis, L. J. (in press). Still worlds apart: The worldviews of adolescent males attending Protestant and Catholic secondary schools in Northern Ireland. *Research in Education.*

Robbins, M., Francis, L. J., & Kerr, S. (2006). God images and empathy among a group of secondary school pupils in South Africa. *Religion and Theology: A Journal of Contemporary Religious Discourse, 13,* 175–194.

Statistics New Zealand (1998). *2001 Census of population and dwellings: Preliminary views on content.* Wellington: Statistics New Zealand.

Wallis, R., & Bruce, S. (1992). Secularization: The orthodox model. In S. Bruce (Ed.), *Religion and modernization: Sociologists and historians debate the secularization thesis* (pp. 8–30). Oxford: Clarendon Press.

Weller, P. (2004). Identity, politics, and the future(s) of religion in the UK: The case of the religious question in the 2001 decennial census. *Journal of Contemporary Religion, 19*, 3–21.

Zavalloni, M. (1975). Social identity and the recording of reality: Its relevance for cross-cultural psychology. *International Journal of Psychology, 10*, 197–217.

The Influence of Religion on Latino Education, Marriage, and Social Views in the United States

Gastón Espinosa

ABSTRACT. This study analyzes the Hispanic Churches in American Public Life National Survey (n = 2,060) data set to examine the relationship between religious affiliation and commitment and education, marital status, and social views in the U.S. Latino community. The findings indicate that religious affiliation and high rates of religious participation and commitment are important factors that are positively and negatively related to Latino education, marriage, and social action. This study found a positive relationship between high rates of religious participation and commitment and high rates of marriage, social action, and conservative views on church–state relations and social issues like abortion and homosexual relations, but not on other social views like the death penalty and the ordination of women. In general, conservative religiosity (in this case Protestant Evangelicalism and Pentecostalism) is positively related to high rates of marriage and social action. However, the data also suggest that high rates of religious participation and commitment do not necessarily result in higher income and educational levels, although this may be due to the fact that many Latinos recently converted from Catholicism to Protestantism and thus have not had a chance to adopt and benefit from Protestant educational attitudes and resources.

Gastón Espinosa, PhD, is Associate Professor of Religious Studies at Claremont McKenna College, Claremont, CA.

INTRODUCTION

In 2003 the U.S. Census Bureau announced that the Latino community surpassed the African-American community as the nation's largest minority group. It has blossomed from 22.4 million in 1990 to 44.3 million in 2006, a figure that does not include an estimated 11 to 12 million undocumented persons and 4 million people living on the Island of Puerto Rico, the latter of which hold U.S. citizenship. In total, there are almost 60 million Latinos living in the United States and Puerto Rico. Thus, the future of the United States is increasingly yoked to the future of the Latino community.

Most of the research on minority education, marriage, and families has historically focused on the African-American community, with limited attention to other racial–ethnic groups (Patterson, 1998; Tucker & Mitchell-Kernan, 1995; Wilson, 1996). Not withstanding this fact, the current demographic shifts have caught the attention of the scholarly community and have contributed to a burst of research and polling on Latino political party affiliation, economic and employment preferences, and educational attainment (Badillo, 2004; Bean, Berg, & Van Hood, 1996; Crane, 2003; Oropesa, 2004; Phillips & Sweeney, 2005; Suárez-Orozco & Páez, 2002; Wilcox, 2002). Despite this research, we know surprisingly little about the religious profile of the U.S. Latino community and how religious affiliation, practice, and commitment is positively or negatively related to educational and marital status and social views (Crane, 2003). In a forthcoming study, W. Bradford Wilcox and Edwin I. Hernández argue that although religion does have a general positive affect on Latino relationships, it does not promote "high-quality relationships in a uniform manner" (Wilcox & Hernández, 2007). They found that religious attendance of U.S. Latino fathers is positively linked to high-quality relationships for both fathers and mothers because it may soften machismo and make fathers more understanding, affectionate, faithful, and responsible. Religious homogeneity was also linked to positive relationship outcomes if men regularly attend church. They further found (somewhat counterintuitively) "no evidence that the effects of religion vary by marital status." Religious attendance rather than religious affiliation is a greater predictor of the possible positive link between religion and happy and healthy parenting and family relations. Equally important, they note that unmarried parents also benefit from attending church and religious services, thus indicating that religion has a net positive effect on Latinos regardless of their marital status. Finally, they argue that their original hypothesis, that the association between religion and marriage will be strongest for Protestants, did not hold. They found, contrary to some stereotypes, "no evidence that Protestant parents are happier than other parents ... despite the fact that Protestant churches appear to focus more on family life among Latinos" (Wilcox & Hernández, 2007). Their findings would seem to indirectly support the long-held perception that Latino Catholics are more likely than Latino Protestants to promote conservative values like traditional marriage and education through their churches, parochial schools, and colleges and universities. The present research builds on and expands their findings by further analyzing the relationship between religion and marital, educational, and social views.

This study analyzes the Hispanic Churches in American Public Life National Survey (n = 2,060) data set to examine the relationship between religious affiliation and commitment and education, marital status, and social views in the U.S. Latino community. The findings indicate that religious affiliation and high rates of religious participation and commitment are important factors that are positively and negatively related to Latino education, marriage, and social views. This study found a positive relationship between high rates of religious participation and commitment and high rates of marriage, social views, and conservative views on church-state relations but not on social views like the death penalty and the ordination of women. In general, conservative religiosity (in this case Protestant Evangelicalism and Pentecostalism) is positively related to high rates of marriage and social views. However, the data also suggest that high rates of religious participation and commitment do not necessarily result in higher income and educational levels, although this may be because many Latinos recently converted from Catholicism to Protestantism and thus have not had a chance to adopt and benefit from Protestant educational attitudes and resources.

METHODS

The Hispanic Churches in American Public Life (HCAPL) research project (1999–2002) was a nonsectarian study funded by a $1.3 million grant from The Pew Charitable Trusts. It sought to examine the impact of religion on political and civic engagement in the Latino community in the United States and Puerto Rico. It was directed and managed by Virgilio Elizondo, Jesse Miranda, and Gastón Espinosa. They collaborated with Harry Pachon, Rodolfo O. de la Garza, and Jongho Lee of The Tomás Rivera Policy Institute to oversee a national random-sample, bilingual, and Hispanic-framed telephone survey of 2,310 Latino adults across the United States (2,060) and Puerto Rico (250). The 19-minute, 63-question survey was conducted between August 29 and October 31, 2000. Survey samples were drawn from Los Angeles, San Antonio, Houston, Chicago, Miami, New York City, rural Iowa, rural Colorado, and Puerto Rico. Latino households were randomly selected by drawing on a two-tier approach that used samples both from the random digit-dialing method in high-density Hispanic areas and from directory-listed households with Spanish surnames in low-density Hispanic areas. Respondents who self-identified as Hispanic and were at least 18 years of age were surveyed. The resulting sample includes a primary national sample of 1,709 respondents that consists of a metropolitan base sample of 1,404 respondents and a rural sample of 305 respondents, with an over-sample of 351 Protestants and an over-sample of 250 Puerto Rican islanders.

The HCAPL survey has several important limitations. First, it did not survey Latinos without a telephone, which would include a small but important number of economically poor and thus underrepresented Latinos. However, it did sample Latinos that were undocumented, an important segment the community. Second, it only surveyed Latinos that were at least 18 years of age. Thus it does not capture the attitudes of youth. Third, it did not survey Euro-Americans or Blacks for comparability purposes, although it did include questions from the General Social Survey and other survey instruments that can be used for such purposes. Finally, the small cell count on many of these survey responses means that some of the estimates are suggestive rather than conclusive.

Despite these limitations, the HCAPL survey has several advantages over the General Social Survey, the National Survey of Religious Identification, the National Alcohol Survey, the Gallup

Poll, and other national data sets. First, it is Hispanic framed. The survey instrument was created with the Hispanic community in mind by a nationally recognized advisory board of 17 Hispanic and Euro-American scholars in sociology, political science, public policy, education, religious studies, theology, history, and Latino studies. Second, it is a very large sample. It surveyed 2,310 Latinos across the United States (2,060) and Puerto Rico (250). This study focuses exclusively on the U.S. sample. Third, it included a Protestant over-sample, which allows for more in-depth analyses and comparisons with Roman Catholics. This enabled the researchers to further breakdown the rather broad category of Protestant and Alternative Christian into a more refined family classification that included Mainline Protestants, Evangelical Protestants (non-Pentecostal), Pentecostal Protestants, and Alternative Christian (Jehovah's Witness, Mormon, and others). Fourth, the survey was completed in the fall of 2000 and is thus more recent than many other national surveys. This is very important given the massive levels of Latin-American immigration in the 1990s. Fifth, the HCAPL survey was conducted in English (62%) and Spanish (38%). This has the distinct advantage of capturing the values, attitudes, and beliefs of Spanish-speaking dominant Latinos across the United States, along with the ability to compare them with their English-speaking counterparts. Sixth, the religious affiliation survey question includes a list of 21 possible response options, including several indigenous Protestant traditions, something never done before. It also listed open-ended response options and then asked respondents to specify which religious tradition they participated in, thus giving a much more precise read on religious affiliation than is normally available in most national surveys. Finally, it allowed for a wider range of country of origin self-identification possibilities than most surveys, including Mexico, Puerto Rico, Cuba, the Dominican Republic, El Salvador, Guatemala, Colombia, other Latin America, other parts of the world, and more than one ancestry.

RESULTS

U.S. Latino Religious Profile

The religious marketplace is becoming denominationally diverse. The HCAPL national survey found that 93% of all Latinos self-identify as Christian, 6% self-identify as having no religious preference/other, 1% self-identify as practicing a world religion other than Christianity, and less than one-half of 1% self-identify as atheist or agnostic. Of those that self-identified as Christian, 70% are Roman Catholic and 23% are Protestant or Alternative Christian (Jehovah's Witness, Mormon, other). When the Protestant and Alternative Christian grouping was broken down further, we found that 7.72% self-identified with Evangelical traditions, 7.72% self-identified with Pentecostal/Charismatic traditions, 4.41% self-identified with Mainline Protestant traditions, and 3.01% self-identified with Alternative Christian traditions like the Jehovah's Witnesses and Mormonism. Less than 1% of all U.S. Latinos self-identified with a world religion like Islam, Judaism, Buddhism, or Hinduism, and less than one-half of 1% (0.36%) self-identified as Atheist or Agnostic.

One of the most important findings is that the overall percentage of Latino Catholics has remained around the 70% mark since the mid-1980s. Although Greeley noted in 1997 that less than 70% of all Latinos were Roman Catholic and that this was likely to continue to decline over the next 25 years, we found that the proportion of Catholic Latinos was 70% (or 28 million in 2006 projected numbers). This percentage, however, is largely due to the significant influx of Catholics into the United States from Latin America and especially from Mexico, a country that has one of the highest rates of Catholicism (84%) in Latin America and the world. The relatively high overall percentage of Catholics is also due to the creative work of Latino priests, Catholic youth programs, social programs that address the needs of the poor and immigrants, increased lay participation, and especially to the growth in Charisma Missions and in other Catholic Charismatic organizations. The overlay between being Charismatic and born-again was strong as the HCAPL survey found that more than one in four (26%) Catholics in our survey sample (n = 1,422) reported having had a born-again experience with Jesus Christ and more than one in five (22%) Latino Catholics reported being born-again and Pentecostal, Charismatic, or spirit-filled. A full 86% of those that said they were born-again also said they were Charismatic.

These findings are consistent with the work of Andrew Greeley, who noted that one of seven Hispanics had left the Catholic Church in less than a quarter of a century and that as many as 600,000 Latinos may be "defecting" from the Catholic Church every year. He warned that if this "hemorrhaging" continues for the next 25 years, half of all American Hispanics will not be Catholic (Greeley, 1988, 1997). The HCAPL survey confirmed high defection rates because it found that for every one Latino that recently returned to Catholicism, five recently left it. It also found that the Catholic affiliation drops from 74% among first-generation Latinos to 62% by the third generation. Protestant religious affiliation simultaneously increases from one in six among first-generation Latinos to almost one in three by the third generation. Were it not for high Catholic birthrates and the massive numerical influx of largely Catholic immigrants from Latin America over the past decade, Greeley's predictions might have already come to pass. Although we knew that the numbers of Latino Protestants and Alternative Christians were growing, we were surprised to find that almost one-third (30%) of all U.S. Latinos self-identified as something other than Roman Catholic—mostly Protestant or other Christian (Espinosa, 2004a; Espinosa, Elizondo, & Miranda, 2003).

Protestants and Alternative Christians and persons with no religious preference/other constitute, respectively, approximately 23% and 6% of all Latinos. Pentecostals and Evangelicals constitute a majority of the former. The growth of Pentecostal and Evangelical Christianity was evident not only in Latino Catholicism but also in Latino Protestantism. Our survey found that 77% of all Latino non-Catholics are Protestant or Alternative Christian. Of this group, 85% identify as Protestant (i.e., Mainline, Evangelical, Pentecostal). Perhaps more surprising, 88% of all Latino Protestants are associated with an Evangelical denomination and/or self-identify as born-again, and 64% are members of Pentecostal or Charismatic denominations and/or self-identify as Pentecostal, Charismatic, or spirit-filled (Espinosa, 2004a,b).

Our findings refine and expand those of Andrew Greeley, who stated in 1997 that almost half of all Latino Protestants "belong to moderate or even liberal Protestant denominations." We found that Latino Mainline Protestants made up only 14.8% of all Latino non-Catholics, of whom 43% claim to be born-again and 21% claim to Pentecostal, Charismatic, or spirit-filled.

To put the number of Latino Protestants in national comparative perspective, there are now more Latino Protestants in the United States than Jews or Muslims or Episcopalians and Presbyterians combined. The growth of the born-again experience is contributing to this growth across many Latino Christian traditions. This is evident in the finding that 37% of all U.S. Latinos self-identified as born-again

Christian. The growth of born-again spirituality is in turn being driven by the Pentecostal/Charismatic movement, as 28% of all U.S. Latinos self-reported being born-again and Pentecostal, Charismatic, or spirit-filled. All the above trends reveal the profound influence of transdenominational born-again and Pentecostal/ Charismatic spirituality in the U.S. Latino community (Espinosa, 2004a,b).

Latino Catholic and Protestant Religiosity

As the above findings indicate, Latino Protestants are more likely to be Evangelical and Pentecostal than the national U.S. Euro-American Protestant population, which is significantly influenced by liberal Mainline Protestantism (Bader et al., 2006; Lugo et al., 2006). Despite the rich tradition of Catholic spirituality, Confraternity of Christian Doctrine (CCD), and spiritual formation in parochial schools, Latino Protestants were significantly more likely to affirm and engage in spiritual practices than their Catholic counterparts. Latino Protestants were significantly more likely (67%) than Latino Catholics (25%) to say that they read the Bible once a week or more. Latino Protestants were also significantly more likely (69%) to say that they attend church every week or more than once a week than Catholics (48%) and that they (42%) were more likely to have led a Bible study than Catholics (21%). All these practices are a reflection and a measure of religious commitment. However, it is possible that these findings may be biased in favor of Protestants, who are more likely to engage in these kinds of religious practices than Catholics because the latter place a greater emphasis on popular religious practices such as praying to the Virgin Mary and participating in home altar devotions (Díaz-Stevens & Stevens-Arroyo, 1998; Dolan & Figueroa-Deck, 1994; Stevens-Arroyo & Díaz-Stevens, 1994). Despite this fact, the HCAPL national survey also found that Latino Protestants (67%) were significantly more likely than Catholics (48%) to say that religion provides a great deal or quite a bit of guidance for their day-to-day living, a question that measures religious commitment and that is not biased in favor of Protestants. Thus, Latino Protestants are more likely to be Evangelical or Pentecostal/Charismatic than Mainline Protestant and more likely to report higher rates of religious practice than their Catholic counterparts.

Educational Profile of U.S. Latino Catholics and Protestants

The HCAPL national survey found that Latino Protestants have higher rates of educational attainment than Latino Catholics. They are more likely than Catholics to have graduated from high school (27% vs. 23%) or have at least some college (28% vs. 21%). Catholics (19%) are also more likely than Protestants (13%) to have a grade school education or less. Significantly, these higher rates of education are directly shaped by the fact that U.S. Latino Catholics are more likely to be immigrants (54%) than their Protestant counterparts (33%). However, the HCAPL survey also found that contrary to the stereotype that Latino Catholics have the highest poverty rates and that they convert to Protestantism primarily for financial benefits and thus increased social status advantage, Latino Pentecostals (49.2%) and Alternative Christians (56%) have as high or higher poverty rates as Latino Catholics (49%). In light of this fact, it may not be surprising to note that Latino Catholics are also more likely to have graduated from college (14%) or graduate school (4%) than either Pentecostals (10% and 2%) or Jehovah's Witnesses (9% and 0%). Thus, although it is true that Latino Protestants in general have higher rates of educational attainment because Latino Mainline and Evangelical (non-Pentecostal) Protestants are more likely to have graduated from college, this is not true for Latino Pentecostals and Alternative Christian traditions—the two fastest growing segments of the U.S. Latino non-Catholic Christian community today (Espinosa, Elizondo, & Miranda, 2005).

When further broken down by religious family grouping based on shared theological roots, traditions/liturgies, or sectarian outlook, Latino Mainline Protestants (49.62%) and Evangelicals (44.40%) had higher rates of college attendance than Other Religion (38.71%), Pentecostals (35.19%), Catholics (33.73%), Atheists/ Agnostics (33.33%), Alternative Christians (32.63%), and those with no one religious preference (32.48%). Although a higher percentage of Roman Catholics are immigrants than their Protestant counterparts, they did not have the lowest educational attainment rates. Of those stating they had a grade-school level education or less, Alternative Christians (41.05%), those with no religious preference (40.17%), and Catholics (36.53%) were the most likely to say they had a grade-school education or less followed by Pentecostals (33.91%),

Atheists/Agnostics (33.33%), Evangelicals (24.90%), Other Religions (22.58%), and Mainline Protestants (18.32%).

Higher Protestant educational levels are not the only factors shaping these findings, because there are different levels of educational attainment in each Latino country of origin subgroup. Colombians (75%) and Latinos with more than one ancestry (71.42%) have higher educational attainment (college and graduate school) rates than Latinos from other parts of Latin America (56.45%), Cuba (52.38%), Puerto Rico (44.28%), Mexico (31.93%), Guatemala (31.43%), and El Salvador (18.75%). Not surprisingly, Latinos of El Salvadorian (57.81%) and Guatemalan (54.29%) origin (many of which were refugees fleeing civil war) had lower levels of educational attainment than those of Mexican (38.75%), Dominican (34.15%), Puerto Rican (30.73%), Cuban (26.19%), other Latin American (23.56%), more than one ancestry (10.71%), and Colombian (9.09%) origin.

U.S.–Latino Religious Practices

Very little research has been published on the relationship between religious identity and affiliation and educational attainment in the U.S. Latino community in general and the Latino Evangelical born-again population in particular. These data are important because of the growth of born-again Christianity across denominations in the Latino community. For example, 58.45% of all Latinos that self-identified as born-again had a high school education or less. Only 39.59% of all Latino born-again Christians had a college level education or higher. The importance of religion is further evident in the finding that Latinos reporting that a political candidate's personal faith or morals are very relevant to their voting decision are more likely to have a high school education or less (57.26%) rather than college or graduate school (41.26%). Similarly, Latinos that report attending church once a week or more are more likely (57.18%) to have a high school education or less than those that have attended college or graduate school (42.82%). Likewise, those responding that they have taken part regularly in a prayer group, Bible study group, or cell group are more likely to have a high school or less (56.35%) education than those that have attended college or graduate school (41.92%). They are equally more likely to say that they have read their Bible almost every day (56.48%) than those with a college education or more (41.44%). These findings indicate that Latino born-again Christians are more likely to have a high school education or less and that people with a high school education or less are more likely to say that they take part in prayer groups, Bible studies, and/or read their Bible almost every day.

Latinos with lower levels of education are not only more likely to engage in religious practices but also in social action. The HCAPL national survey found that Latinos with a high school education or less are significantly more likely (60.64%) to want their churches or religious organizations to become involved in social, educational, and political issues than those that attended college or graduate school (36.87%). Despite the long tradition of Catholic faith-based activism with César Chávez, PADRES, Las Hermanas, COPS, and other organizations, Latinos attending Protestant churches were also more likely than their Catholic counterparts to state that their churches provide educational social services like reaching out to gangs (44% vs. 36%); helping immigrants establish themselves (39% vs. 35%); starting day-care centers, food co-ops, or child-care centers (48% vs. 43%); starting English as a Second Language and citizenship classes (33% vs. 30%); and starting after school programs for youth (43% vs. 35%). For only one measure—starting drug or alcohol rehabilitation homes—did Catholics slightly surpass (33%) their Latino Protestant counterparts (32%), but given the margin of error the responses were virtually identical (Espinosa et al., 2005).

Marriage and Religious Participation

As with education, there appears to be a positive relationship between high levels of religious participation and marriage. Married Latinos were more likely to report that they attended church or religious services once a week or more (52.04%) than widows (50.32%), divorcees (45.14%), singles (39.41%), and those living together in domestic partnerships (37.04%). Interestingly enough and contrary to arguments that Latinos are becoming more secular (Kosmin, Mayer, & Keysar, 2001), only 8.09% of all Latinos say they never attend church or religious services, thus implying that the other 91.89% of Latinos do at least once a year—the lowest level of church attendance response option on the HCAPL survey outside of not attending church (Kosmin et al., 2001). Furthermore, 71.43% of Latinos stated that they attended church and religious services at least once or twice a month. In fact, when we combine the three response categories of once a week, almost every week, and once or twice a month into one category of at least once or twice a month, the HCAPL survey found that 75.6% of Latino married couples, 69.45% of divorcees, 68.79% of widows, 66.67% of people living together in domestic partnerships, and 64.63% of singles reported that they attended church or religious services at least once or twice a month. Even if we take into account that people over-report their church attendance rates, the high rates nonetheless indicate that Latinos place a value on church attendance.

These findings are buttressed by the fact that almost a third of married Latinos (31.8%) reported that they led a Bible study at a church or a religious organization in the previous 2 years. Although not quite as high, more than one in four in the other relational categories reported similar support, except for those living together: singles (28.5%), widows (28.08%), divorcees (27.61%), or those living together in domestic partnerships (21.09%). The relatively high commitment to attending church and leading religious services may have something to do with the spiritual formation they received in religious schools. Latinos have attended an average of almost 6 years (5.92 years) of religious school education. Widowers (6.29 years) and singles (6.0 years) had more years of religious school attendance than married (5.91 years), those living in domestic relationships (5.7 years), and divorcees (5.64 years).

Religion, Marriage, and Social Views

The positive relationship between high rates of religious practice and faith-based social action may be influenced by the fact that Latino Protestants have higher marriage rates than Latino Catholics, thus providing a more stable context, financial stability, and time in which to engage in social activities. The HCAPL national survey found that Latino Protestants (55.73%) were more likely than Catholics (49.62%) to say they are married. However, it also found that Latino Protestants (9.90%) are also more likely to say they are divorced than Catholics (6.80%). Although not surprising in light of the widespread practice of cohabitation in Mexico and Latin America, Catholics are more likely than Protestants to say they have a domestic partner (9.52% vs. 2.08%). This may be because it is difficult to secure an annulment or a divorce from the Catholic Church as both are frowned upon. They are only slightly more likely to say that they are single (24.47% vs. 23.96%). Interestingly enough, when broken down by religious family groupings, Latino Alternative Christians (57.89%), Pentecostals (57.51%), and Evangelicals (55.60%) are more likely to say they are married than Catholics (49.62%), Mainline Protestants (48.85%), Other Religions (41.94%), and those with no religious preference (41.94%).

Although beyond the scope of a detailed analysis here, there also seems to be a relation between country of origin and marital status. Approximately one-half (50.73%) of Latinos nationwide reported being married. One troubling finding is that second- and third-generation U.S.-born Latinos had the third lowest marriage rate. Latinos born in Mexico (61.48%) had the highest rates of marriage followed by those born in Guatemala (58.62%), Cuba (54.76%), El Salvador (52.46%), Other Latin America (50%), other parts of the world (50%), Colombia (48.57%), the United States (45.74%), the Dominican Republic (40.54%), and Puerto Rico (39.6%). The lower rate of marriage may be the result of U.S.-born Latinos assimilating relatively permissive American attitudes toward marriage and divorce. There is evidence for this in the finding that divorced Latinos lived in the United States longer (25.80 years) than married Latinos (18.05 years) and longer than the national U.S. Latino average (18.04 years).

The influence of the Euro-American value system on Latino social and moral views may also be apparent in the surprising finding that 52.72% of U.S. Latinos stated that women should be ordained and allowed to pastor churches. This is remarkable given the fact that 70% of U.S. Latinos are Roman Catholic, a tradition that prohibits the ordination of women to the pastoral ministry. Only 22.16% of U.S. Latinos stated that women should not be ordained, 10.84% that women should be licensed but not ordained, and 14.29% that women should serve in the lay ministry only. Perhaps not surprisingly given traditional conservative Latin American values, married Latinos were less likely (48.89%) to state that women should be ordained and allowed to pastor churches than either divorcees (59.29%), singles (58.84%), those living together in domestic relationships (55.81%), and widows (51.39%). Congruent with strong support for the ordination of women to the pastoral ministry, a clear majority of U.S. Latinos believe that the church is a place where men and women are treated equally. In fact, 89.5% of all U.S. Latinos stated that men and women are treated equally in their churches and religious organizations. The highest responses were from divorcees (93.13%) and married couples (90.86%) and the lowest from widows (88.89%), singles (86.34%), and those living together in a domestic partnership (85.6%).

In light of this fact, it was surprising to find that 67.02% of Latinos stated that abortion should never be permitted or permitted only in the case of rape, incest, or danger to the woman's life. When broken down by marital status, married Latinos were only slightly less likely (72.57%) than widowers (72.78%) but significantly more likely than singles (57%), divorcees (59.48%), and those living together in domestic partnerships (61.15%) to agree with the statement that abortion should never be permitted or permitted only in the case of rape, incest, or danger to the woman's life. Latinos were equally conservative on homosexual practice, with 67.74% of all U.S. Latino respondents agreeing that sexual relations between two adults of the same sex are always wrong and that the church should not ordain homosexual priests or pastors (69.77%). Married Latinos (75.21%) were more likely to say that homosexual relations were always wrong than widowers (73.97%), divorcees (70.59%), those living together in domestic partnerships (55.73%), and singles (52.02%). Latinos also did not support the ordination of homosexuals. Interestingly enough, divorcees (75.16) were more likely than married couples (74.01%) and widows (73.25%), those living together in a domestic partnership (67.89%), and singles (59.88%) to say they disagreed or strongly disagreed with the statement that "the church should accept homosexuals as priests or ministers." Given their relatively progressive views on the ordination of women, it was surprising to find that Latinos do not support either same-sex relations or the ordination of homosexuals.

U.S. Latinos were not conservative on all controversial social issues as a majority (55.34%) opposed the death penalty. Widows (58.33%) opposed the death penalty more than singles (56.5%), married couples (53.91%), those living together in a domestic partnership (53.21%), and divorcees (48.06%). This may be shaped by the fact that Mexico and many other Latin American countries do not support the death penalty. An even higher percentage of Latinos (66.54%) also agreed (19.89%) or strongly agreed (46.65%) that people who have immigrated to the United States illegally should be eligible for government assistance, such as Medicaid or welfare. An even higher majority (78.38%) agreed (25.04%) or strongly agreed (53.34%) that churches or religious leaders should provide assistance to illegal immigrants even when providing such help is illegal.

The sensitivity to the plight of the undocumented may be due to the fact that almost half of all U.S. Latinos live in poverty. An alarming 47.22% of all U.S. Latinos live below the poverty line ($24,999) and 66.71% earn less than $34,999 per year; one-third (33.28%) earn a total household income before taxes of $50,000 or more per year. Perhaps one positive financial incentive to marry is the fact that married Latinos are significantly less likely (39.47%) to live in poverty ($24,999 or less) than divorcees (53.91%), those living in domestic relationships (53.1%), singles (55.29%), and widowers (60.79%). Married Latinos are also more likely (25.44%) to earn more than $50,000 per year than singles (14.82%), those living together in domestic partnerships (13.26%), divorcees (11.72%), and widows (6.86%). Married Latinos are also almost twice as likely (15.37%) to earn $65,000 per year or more than those living together in a domestic partnership (7.95%), singles (7.94%), and divorcees (7.03%). They are more than six times more likely to do so than widowers (3.98%). The importance of financial stability and marriage for the future of the United States comes into focus when people realize that Latinos are relatively young. The HCAPL national survey found that the average age of Latinos living in the United States was 40.32 years. Perhaps not surprising, widows were the oldest (54.14 years), followed by divorcees (47.43 years), married couples (43.09 years), those living together in domestic partnerships (33.57 years), and singles (29.92 years).

Latino Church–State Views

Perhaps because many live in economically impoverished *barrios* and rural *colonias* where crime, violence, drugs, and gangs are a reality in public schools, Latinos across all relational categories overwhelmingly support prayer in public schools, school vouchers, and the teaching of creationism in public schools. Nationwide, 74.37% of all U.S. Latinos supported prayer in public schools. Interestingly enough, divorcees (87.76%)—those most likely to be single parents and economically impoverished—and widows (85.26%) were significantly more likely to want prayer in public schools than Latinos that were married (76.66%), those living together in a domestic partnership (66.91%), and singles (63.73%). The strong support for prayer in schools should not be surprising given the fact that an equally overwhelming number of Latinos stated that religion provides a great deal or quite a bit of guidance for their lives (75.82%) and that religious leaders should try to influence public affairs (55.84%). When analyzed further by marital status, married (78.65%) and widowed (78.14%) Latinos were more likely than divorcees (77.63%), those living together in domestic partnerships (74.62%), and singles (69.41%) to say that religion provides a great deal or quite a bit of guidance in their day-to-day living.

There was similarly strong support for another controversial church–state issue: school vouchers. Almost two-thirds (63.46%) of all U.S. Latinos stated that they supported school vouchers and that the government should provide parents with funding to send their child to a private school, including a religious school. There was uniform support for vouchers, with divorcees (66.2%)—those most likely to be single parents—offering the most support followed closely by married couples (64.68%), those living together in a domestic partnership (64.44%), widows (64.19%), and singles (59.55%). The strong support for school vouchers may be influenced by the relatively high number of years U.S. Latinos reported attending religious schools (5.92%) and the fact that they report religion provides guidance for their day-to-day living. They may see religious schools as a place where their children can also receive religious guidance and instruction.

The critical influence of religion on Latino attitudes toward church–state controversies is also evident in their strong support for the teaching of creationism in public schools. When asked how creation and evolution should be taught in public schools, the overwhelming majority (87.5%) of U.S. Latinos stated that public schools should either teach creationism (31.58%) or teach both (53.15%) creationism and evolution in public schools. There was strong support across marital status, with 91.61% of divorcees supporting the teaching of creationism or creationism and evolution followed by equally strong support from married couples (89.69%), widows and widowers (89.05%), those living together in domestic partnerships (86.03%), and singles (81.72%). Exactly why there is such broad support for the teaching of creationism in public schools is uncertain. However, their views may be shaped by listening to and watching religious television, where these views are more likely to be supported. A surprising 37.66% of U.S. Latinos reported listening to religious preaching or music on the radio at least once a week (29.23%) or one to three times a month (8.43%). A similarly high percentage (37.56) of all U.S. Latinos reported watching religious programming on television at least once a week (25.7%) or one to three times a month (11.86%). Widows (42.33%), married couples (39.02%), and divorcees (38.96%) were more likely to listen to religious preaching or music on the radio than singles (34.38%) and those living together in domestic partnerships (28.07%). Similarly, widows (47.56%), divorcees (40.91%), and married couples (38.12%) were more likely to watch religious television than those living together in domestic partnerships (34.97%) and singles (32.29%). Because it is well known that religious radio and television is produced primarily by conservative Protestants (e.g., Trinity Broadcasting Network, Christian Broadcasting Network) and Catholics (Eternal Word Television Network), we may surmise that they are partly responsible for shaping the U.S. Latino community's relatively conservative views on moral and church–state issues.

The willingness of U.S. Latinos to bring their faith into the public on matters of school prayer, vouchers, and creationism may be related not only to the fact that religion provides guidance in their day-to-day living, but also to the fact that a majority (54.45%) believe they can have quite a bit (22.72%) or some (31.73%) influence on the U.S. government. A majority (61.19%) of U.S. Latinos also want their churches to be more involved than it is now with social, educational, or political issues. Perhaps not surprising in light of the above findings, a majority of Latinos stated that a candidate's personal faith or morals were relevant to their decision to vote for him or her. Interestingly enough, Latino divorcees (85.03%) and those living together in a domestic partnership (76.65%) were more likely than married (75.87%), widowed (75%), and single Latinos (71.84%) to affirm that a political candidate's personal faith or morals are relevant to their decision to vote for him or her. What is surprising is the relatively strong support across marital status, even for singles—those most likely to be young and independent voters.

DISCUSSION

The findings in this essay refine, challenge, and/or revise a number of major misperceptions and stereotypes about the U.S. Latino community. It challenges the notion that to be Latino is to be Roman Catholic and that most Latino Protestants belong to moderate to liberal Protestant traditions because many are converting not only to Evangelical and Pentecostal traditions but also to Jehovah's Witness, Mormon, and other traditions. It further found that the born-again and Pentecostal/Charismatic movement is not restricted to conservative Protestantism because 21% of all Latino Mainline Protestants and 22% of all U.S. Latino Catholics also self-identified as both born-again and Pentecostal/Charismatic/spirit-filled. Despite this growth, Latino Protestants were overall still more likely than Catholics to state that they attend church, read their Bibles, led a Bible study, and state that religion provides quite a bit or a great deal of guidance in their day-to-day living.

The HCAPL national survey also found that despite a long and rich tradition of Catholic parochial schools in the United States and in Latin America that Latino Protestants had higher rates of educational attainment than Latino Catholics. This, however, may have more to do with nativity, immigration status, income, and class than to a lack of commitment in the U.S. Latino Catholic community. Contrary to widespread arguments that tied Pentecostal conversion to economic and status advantage and upward mobility, Latino Pentecostals and Alternative Christians (two of the fastest growing groups in the U.S. Latino community) had as low or lower income and educational attainment levels than their Catholic counterparts (Greeley, 1994). Latinos want their churches and religious organizations to become more involved in social, educational, and political issues. Protestants were more likely than Catholics to report that their churches provide educational social services like reaching out to gangs, helping immigrants establish themselves, and starting after-school programs for youth. However, Catholics were more likely to report that their churches had started drug or alcohol rehabilitation programs.

The pervasive influence of born-again and Pentecostal/ Charismatic values and spirituality may help explain why Latino Protestants were more likely to report being married than Latino Catholics. They do not, however, explain why they were also more likely to be divorced. The lower marital rates among Catholics may be due to the fact that it is difficult to secure an annulment in the Church. Catholics are five times more likely to report living together in a domestic partnership than Protestants. In light of this reality, it may not be surprising that Latinos born in Mexico had the highest rates of marriage and the longer Latinos lived in the United States, the higher their rate of divorce. Married Latinos were also more likely to earn $50,000 or $65,000 per year than Latinos in any other relational status (i.e., single, divorced, domestic partnership, widow). Married Latinos are also the least likely to live in poverty. This study confirms the finding that marriage provides economic benefits for Latinos and helps reduce poverty (Wilcox, Doherty, Glenn, & Waite, 2005). The average length of time Latinos lived in the United States may also help explain their relatively progressive social views. A majority stated that women should be ordained and allowed to pastor churches, and a smaller majority opposed the death penalty. However, a majority also opposed abortion and stated that abortion should only be allowed in the case of rape, incest, or danger to the woman's life. Similarly, a clear majority of Latinos stated that they do not support same-sex relations or the ordination of homosexuals. A clear majority of Latinos across relationship status support prayer in public schools, school vouchers, and the teaching of creationism in public schools and believe that religious leaders should try to influence public affairs and that a political candidate's personal faith and morals are relevant in their voting decision.

Finally, we have seen that divorcees, singles, and widows were as supportive or in a number of cases more supportive of traditional Latin American moral and cultural values as their married counterparts. This is significant because often public policy analysts working on these issues along with some Latino political activists advocate for positions and views that purportedly represent divorced, single, and married Latinos but that are in fact at odds with their actual views. In light of these findings, it is critical that public policy analysts, educators, and political, civic, and religious leaders listen to the community and adjust their work and advocacy on behalf of Latinos in such a way that accurately represents their grassroots attitudes and views lest they be criticized by the community.

This study confirms the finding by Wilcox and Hernández (2007) that religion in general does have a positive affect on Latino relationships across relationship or marital status. Although this study neither confirms nor denies their finding that Protestants are not necessarily happier in their relationships and families than Catholics because this finding went beyond the purview of the study and data, it does seem to suggest that the level of religious practice does differ by relationship and marital status. In general, married Latinos reported higher rates of religious practice and that religion provides a great deal or quite a bit of guidance for their lives than divorcees, singles, widows, and those living together in domestic partnerships. It also found that Protestants reported higher rates of religious practice and guidance than their Catholic counterparts. The data also suggest a stronger positive correlation between religion and marriage for Protestants than Catholics. However, the data also suggest that higher rates of religious participation and commitment do not necessarily result in higher levels of income and educational attainment, although this may be because many recent converts may not have had the opportunity to benefit from Protestant attitudes and resources.

The findings in this study have only scratched the surface of a vitally important subject. The intersection between religious affiliation, participation, and commitment and education, marriage, and social views is only now beginning to be examined by social scientists, educators, and scholars in the academy. The author hopes that these findings may serve as the basis for further analyses that will not only strengthen the U.S. Latino community, but also the nation. The future of marriage, education, and social action in the United States and in the U.S. Latino community are inextricably connected in an inescapable web of mutuality.

REFERENCES

Bader, C., Dougherty, K., Froese, P., Johnson, B., Mencken, F. C., Park, J. Z., & Stark, R. (2006). *American piety in the 21st century: Select findings from the Baylor religion survey*. Waco, TX: Baylor Institute for Studies of Religion.

Badillo, D. A. (2004). Mexicanos and suburban parish communities: Religion, space, and identity in contemporary Chicago. *Journal of Urban History, 31,* 23–46.

Bean, F. D., Berg, R. R., & Van Hook, J. V. W. (1996). Socioeconomic and cultural incorporation and marital disruption among Mexican Americans. *Social Forces, 75,* 593–617.

Crane, K. R. (2003). *Latino churches: Faith, family, and ethnicity in the second generation*. New York: LFB Scholarly Publishing.

Díaz-Stevens, A. M., & Stevens-Arroyo, A. M. (1998). *Recognizing the Latino resurgence in U.S. religion*. Boulder: Westview Press.

Dolan, J. P., & Figueroa, D. A. (1994). *Hispanic Catholic culture in the U.S.: Issues and concerns*. Notre Dame, IN: University of Notre Dame Press.

Espinosa, G. (2004a). Changements démographiques et religieux chez les hispaniques des Etats-Unis. *Social Compass: International Review of Sociology of Religion, 51,* 303–320.

Espinosa, G. (2004b). The Pentecostalization of Latin American and U.S. Latino Christianity. *Pneuma: The Journal of the Society for Pentecostal Studies, 26,* 262–292.

Espinosa, G., Elizondo, V., & Miranda, J. (2003). *Hispanic churches in American public life: Summary of findings.* Notre Dame, IN: Institute for Latino Studies, University of Notre Dame.

Espinosa, G., Elizondo, V., & Miranda, J. (Eds.). (2005). *Latino religions and civic activism in the United States.* New York: Oxford University Press.

Greeley, A. M. (July, 1988). Defection among Hispanics. *America, 30,* 61–62.

Greeley, A. M. (1994). The demography of American Catholics: 1965–1990. In A. M. Greeley (Ed.), *The sociology of Andrew Greeley.* Atlanta: Scholars Press.

Greeley, A. M. (September, 1997). Defection among Hispanics (Updated). *America, 27,* 12–13.

Lugo, L., Stencel, S., Green, J., Shah, T. S., Grim, B. J., Smith, G., Ruby, R., & Pond, A. (2006). *Spirit and power: A 10-country survey of Pentecostals.* Washington, DC: The Pew Forum on Religion & Public Life.

Kosmin, B. A., Mayer, E., & Keysar, A. (2001) *American religious identification survey, 2001 report.* New York: The Graduate Center of the City University of New York.

Oropesa, R. D. (2004). The future of marriage and Hispanics. *Journal of Marriage and Family, 66,* 901–920.

Patterson, O. (1998). *Rituals of blood: Consequences of slavery in two American centuries.* New York: Basic Books.

Phillips, J., & Sweeney, M. (2005). Premarital cohabitation and marital disruption among white, black, and Mexican American women. *Journal of Marriage & Family, 67,* 296–314.

Stevens-Arroyo, A. M., & Diaz-Stevens, A. M. (1994). *An enduring flame: Studies on Latino popular religiosity.* New York: Bildner Center for Western Hemisphere Studies.

Suárez-Orozco, M. M., & Páez, M. M. (Eds.). (2002). *Latinos: Remaking America.* Berkeley: University of California Press.

Tucker, M. B., & Mitchell-Kernan, C. (Eds.). (1995). *The decline in marriage among African Americans.* New York: Russell Sage Foundation.

Wilcox, W. B. (2002). *Then comes marriage: Religion, race, and marriage in urban America.* Philadelphia: University of Pennsylvania.

Wilcox, W. B., Doherty, W., Glenn, N., & Waite, L. (2005). *Why marriage matters: Twenty-six conclusions from the social sciences* (2nd ed.). New York: Institute for American Values.

Wilcox, W. B., & Hernández, E. I. (2007). Bendito Amor: Religion and relationships among married and unmarried Latinos in urban America. (unpublished paper).

Wilson, W. J. (1996). *When work disappears: The world of the new urban Poor.* New York: Knopf.

Increased Family Involvement in School Predicts Improved Child–Teacher Relationships and Feelings About School for Low-Income Children

Eric Dearing
Holly Kreider
Heather B. Weiss

ABSTRACT. Family involvement in school, children's relationships with their teachers, and children's feelings about school were examined longitudinally from kindergarten through fifth grade for an ethnically diverse, low-income sample (N = 329). Within-families analyses indicated that changes in family involvement in school were directly associated with changes in children's relationships with their teachers and indirectly associated with changes in children's feelings about school, with student–teacher relationships mediating this latter association. Increases in family involvement in school predicted improvements in student–teacher relationships, and, in turn, these improvements in student–teacher relationships predicted improvements in children's

Eric Dearing, PhD, is affiliated with the Lynch School of Education, Boston College, MA; Holly Kreider, EdD, is a Senior Research Associate at Sociometrics, Sunnyvale, CA; and Heather Weiss, EdD, is affiliated with Harvard University, Cambridge, MA.

perceptions of competency in literacy and mathematics as well as improvements in children's attitudes toward school, more generally. These results are consistent with systems theories of child development and help answer why family educational involvement matters for low-income children. This research was supported by a grant to the authors from the National Institute of Child Health and Human Development (5R03HD052858-02). Principal investigators of the School Transitions Study were Deborah Stipek, Heather Weiss, Penny Hauser-Cram, Walter Secada, and Jennifer Greene, who were supported in part by grants from the John D. and Catherine T. MacArthur Foundation, The Foundation for Child Development, and the William T. Grant Foundation.

INTRODUCTION

Family involvement in their children's education is a central component of national policy aimed at improving the academic performance of low-income children, with policymakers citing "overwhelming" empirical support for family involvement as a means of bolstering children's achievement (U.S. Department of Education, 2003, p. 16). Indeed, recent meta-analyses have further clarified the empirical consensus that achievement is higher for children of more involved families than for children of less involved families (Fan & Chen, 2001; Jeynes, 2003, 2005). Further, longitudinal work focused on low-income families indicates that early involvement in schooling predicts later achievement outcomes and increased involvement predicts improved achievement outcomes (Dearing, Kreider, Simpkins, & Weiss, 2006; Englund, Luckner, Whaley, & Egeland, 2004; Grolnick, Kurowski, & Gurland, 1999; Izzo, Weissberg, Kasprow, & Fendrich, 1999). Why involvement matters for low-income children remains less clear, however.

As Hoover-Dempsey and Sandler (1995) noted, one of the most important questions for family involvement research is to determine the mechanisms by which involvement influences children. That is, we must move beyond knowing that involvement matters to understanding why it matters, in part because the answers to this question can help interventions target the processes most likely to benefit children. Yet, much work in this area remains theoretical with few empirical studies aimed at documenting mechanisms. With this in mind, we examine children's relationships with teachers in the present study as a potential mechanism linking family involvement in school and low-income children's feelings about school. To do so, we integrate past work on family involvement with theory and research on the importance of child–teacher relationships for shaping children's perceptions of school.

Family Involvement in School

Family involvement in children's education takes place in a variety contexts, including in the home (e.g., help with homework), in the community (e.g., parent-to-parent communication), and in the school (e.g., attending open houses) as well as through means that cut across multiple contexts (e.g., home–school communication). Each of these provides unique, albeit complementary, opportunities to promote children's academic success. Family involvement in the school context, for example, often provides face-to-face interactions between parents and teachers as well as one of the few opportunities for children, parents, and teachers to interact together as a triad. Because of this, family involvement in school may be uniquely suited, compared with other types of educational involvement, to influence children's relationships with their teachers, which in turn may have consequences for children's feelings about school.

Children's Relationships With Teachers and Feelings About School

In addition to the importance of instructional practices, children's likelihood of success in school may be determined by their social–emotional relationships with teachers. Following attachment theory, theory on social–emotional relationships between children and their teachers suggests that emotional closeness and support from teachers likely promote positive representations of self, teachers, and the more general schooling context (e.g., Baker, 2006; Howes & Hamilton, 1992; Howes & Matheson, 1992). Thus children who experience positive relationships with their teachers may develop more positive attitudes toward learning and school, thereby increasing academic engagement, motivation, and, in turn, achievement (Birch & Ladd,

1997; Eccles, 1993; Pianta & Steinberg, 1992; Valeski & Stipek, 2001). Children who report more positive relationships with their teachers are, in fact, more likely to be engaged and motivated in the classroom and more likely to demonstrate higher levels of academic achievement compared with children who report less positive relationships with their teachers (Crosnoe, Johnson, & Elder, 2004; Furrer & Skinner, 2003; Roeser, Eccles, & Sameroff, 2000), and the benefits of positive relationships with teachers may be exceptionally high for children of low socioeconomic status and others at risk for educational failure (Hamre & Pianta, 2005).

Baker (1999), for example, found that positive relationships with teachers predicted greater satisfaction with school for low-income children during elementary school. Similarly, in a sample of low-income kindergartners and first-graders, Valeski and Stipek (2001) found that positive relationships with teachers were associated with better attitudes toward school and greater perceived competency in literacy and mathematics. Importantly, these authors also found that children's feelings about school and perceived competencies were associated with literacy and mathematics performance such that children who had positive feelings and believed they were competent performed better than their peers who had negative feelings and believed they were incompetent.

Given these potential benefits of high-quality child–teacher relationships, some researchers have sought to determine what types of factors promote emotional closeness and support from teachers within the classroom. Much of this research has been focused on characteristics of children and characteristics of schools that may promote or inhibit positive student–teacher relationships (Crosnoe et al., 2004; Ladd, Birch, & Buhs, 1999; Murray & Murray, 2004; Murray & Greenberg, 2000, 2001; O'Connor & McCartney, 2006). Children who have positive relationships with their parents, for example, are more likely than other children to have positive relationships with their teachers (e.g., O'Connor & McCartney, 2006). Further, children in schools with a positive overall social–emotional climate are more likely than other children to have positive relationships with their teachers (e.g., Crosnoe et al., 2004). Although the implications of family educational involvement for child–teacher relationships have received less attention empirically, ecological systems and family systems perspectives on child development (e.g., Bornstein & Sawyer, 2006; Bronfenbrenner & Morris, 1998) indicate that processes such as involvement should have direct and indirect influences on the child–teacher relationship, beyond what children and schools contribute to these relationships.

Family Involvement and Children's Relationships With Teachers

Relationships that connect home and school contexts have been emphasized as an important influence on child development, with the general assertion that relationships between children, parents, and teachers are interrelated components of a dynamic system in which each member contributes to and is influenced by dyadic and more complex interactions that occur within the system (Bornstein & Sawyer, 2006; Bronfenbrenner & Morris, 1998; Pianta & Rimm-Kaufman, 2006; Sameroff, 1994). Thus by connecting home and school components of this dynamic system, family involvement in school has the potential to influence child–teacher relationships. If, for example, parents develop relationships with teachers through involvement in school, then one benefit of this involvement may be that parents model for children the importance of relationships with teachers. In fact, as Hoover-Dempscy and Sandler (1995) argued, modeling is one of the primary processes by which involvement may affect children's academic experiences. Beyond modeling, school involvement provides teachers with a more nuanced understanding of individual children's developmental needs by allowing parents an opportunity to share knowledge about their children (Connors & Epstein, 1995; Henderson & Mapp, 2002; Hoover-Dempsey & Sadler, 1995; Lawrence-Lightfoot, 2003).

In addition, involvement in school may benefit child–teacher relationships to the extent that this involvement promotes positive interactions between families and teachers. There is, in fact, evidence that parents who are more involved in their children's schools have better relationships with their children's teachers than parents who are less involved (Izzo et al., 1999). These positive parent–teacher relationships may in turn increase the probability of positive child–teacher relationships via processes proposed by family systems theorists such as spillover effects, whereby emotional closeness and warmth in parent–teacher relationships may bolster teachers' abilities to be warm, supportive, and responsive in child–teacher relationships (Cox, Paley, & Harter, 2001; Katz & Gottman, 1996; Margolin, Oliver, & Medina, 2001).[1] Spillover from parent involvement in the school into child–teacher relationships may also occur if such involvement communicates to teachers that families are invested in their children's academic success and, thereby, promotes teachers positive attitudes toward children.

Present Study

Following ecological and family systems perspectives on why involvement should matter in children's lives, we examined associations between family involvement in school and low-income children's relationships with teachers. In addition, we examined children's relationships with teachers as a potential mechanism linking family involvement in school and children's feelings about school. To do so, we used statistical methods for analyzing longitudinal data that allowed us to estimate associations between *changes* in family involvement, *changes* in children's relationships with teachers, and *changes* in children's feelings about school. It is important to note two strengths to using this approach.

First, by studying change we were able to address whether increases in involvement predicted improvements in relationships with teachers and, in turn, improvements in feelings about school. Thus our methodological approach was intended to move beyond analyses of whether low levels of involvement are bad and begin to inform policy and practice on the value of increasing involvement among low-income families. Second, by using within-families estimates (e.g., when a family is highly involved in school, does the child within that family have a better relationship with his or her teacher compared with times when the family displays lower levels of involvement?), we were able to rule out between-families heterogeneity as a potential source of omitted-variable bias (Duncan, Magnuson, & Ludwig, 2004).

Because most studies of family involvement use nonexperimental data, estimated associations are potentially biased by unmeasured characteristics of children, their families, or their environments that may be causally related to involvement. Although within-families estimates are not a panacea for potential sources of bias in nonexperimental studies (e.g., like other nonexperimental analyses, within-families estimates of change can be biased by reciprocal causation), they are a useful means of dealing with bias due to potentially omitted variables that are fixed over time (Duncan et al., 2004). If, for example, changes within families in school involvement predict changes in children's relationships with teachers, then characteristics of children, their families, and their environments that do not change over time (i.e., characteristics that are stable over time) may be ruled out as potential sources of bias.

FIGURE 1. Hypothesized Indirect Association Linking Family Involvement in School, Child–Teacher Relationships, and Children's Feelings About School.

With this conceptual background and methodological approach in mind, we addressed the following three study questions:

1. Do changes in family involvement in school predict changes in children's relationships with teachers such that increased involvement predicts improved relationships?
2. Do changes in family involvement in school predict changes in children's feelings of competency (in literacy and mathematics) and attitudes toward school such that increased involvement predicts improved feelings of competency and attitudes toward school?
3. Are changes in family involvement in school indirectly associated with feelings of competency and attitudes toward school via children's relationships with teachers (see Figure 1)? That is, is there a pathway of mediation by which changes in family involvement in school predict changes in children's relationships with teachers and, in turn, changes in children's relationships with teachers predict changes in children's feelings of competency and attitudes toward school?

METHODS

Participants

The present study draws on child and family data that were collected as part of two interrelated projects: (1) an experimental impact evaluation of the Comprehensive Child Development Program (CCDP) and (2) the follow-up School Transition Study (STS). The CCDP was a federally funded early intervention program for low-income children and their families at 21 sites across the United States (for further description of the CCDP, see St. Pierre, Layzer, Goodson, & Bernstein, 1999). From childbirth until entry into kindergarten, the intervention included services aimed at children (e.g., high-quality preschool) and their families (e.g., education and job training) with the goals of enhancing child development and family economic self-sufficiency. For the impact evaluation, approximately half of children were randomly assigned to receive these intervention services and the other half were included in a control group.

In the fall of 1995, when many of the CCDP children were entering kindergarten, children and families from three of the CCDP sites began participating in the STS (for further description of the STS, see Harvard Family Research Project, 2006; Weiss et al., 2005). A primary aim of the STS was to examine the developmental implications of family and school contexts for low-income children during elementary school. The three CCDP study sites that were included in the STS were selected to provide a diverse sample with regard to geographic region and ethnicity, including a Northeastern city with a primarily African-American population, a rural New England town with an almost entirely European-American population, and a Western city with a primarily Latino population.

The present study is focused on the 329 children and their families from these three sites who were followed from kindergarten through the fifth grade in the STS. For these children and families, our analyses capitalize on data drawn from both the CCDP and the STS. Data were collected in English or Spanish depending on child and family language preference.

Measures

Child, Family, and School Covariates

Demographic data on children and families were collected during recruitment into the CCDP and at kindergarten as part of the STS, including child ethnicity, gender, birth weight (i.e., low birth weight vs. other), and birth order (i.e., first born vs. later); maternal age at childbirth (i.e., teenager vs. other), education level when the study child was in kindergarten, partner status when the study child was in kindergarten, and primary language (i.e., English vs. other); and family income when the child was in kindergarten, CCDP status (i.e., control group vs. experimental group), and study site (i.e., two dummy codes for which study site 1 was the rural New England site and study site 2 was the Northeastern city).

TABLE 1. Sample Descriptive Statistics

	Means (SD)/%
African-American ethnicity	34.3%
Latino-American ethnicity	22.8%
Male gender	49.2%
Low birth weight	15.2%
Birth order was first born	35.3%
Teenage childbirth	28.9%
Mother had resident partner	55.0%
Primary language was English	79.9%
Mother was employed	13.8%
Maternal education[a]	4.15 (1.43)
CCDP experimental group	49.8%
Total family income[b]	4.72 (2.20)
Study site 1	35.9%
Study site 2	25.9%
Principal perceptions of school quality	.26 (.25)

[a]Maternal education was assessed on an eight-point scale ranging from 1 (no formal education) to 8 (graduate school). The average level of education (4.23) was slightly greater than high school completion, which was indicated by a value of 4.

[b]Family income was assessed on a 10-point scale for which the mean score of 4.72 indicated that the sample average was more than $15,000 in annual income but less than $20,000.

SD, standard deviation.

In addition, as part of the STS, school principals reported on a wide variety of characteristics of their schools. Factor analyses of the individual question items from these reports indicated that three factors explained over 30% of the variance in principals' perceptions of their schools: (1) child and family strengths (e.g., the percentage of students at or above grade level for reading and math as well as the proportion of parents in the school who participate in school activities), (2) supports and services (e.g., level of specialized learning services available in the school), and (3) staff and community investment (e.g., staff commitment to high standards and level of community support for school). Principal reports in these three areas were correlated (i.e., r ranging from .52 to .59) such that schools with high ratings in one area were also likely to have high ratings in the other two areas. To compute a single summary indicator of school quality, we averaged questionnaire item scores across these three areas such that higher scores indicated higher average quality.

Descriptive statistics for this school indicator and all child and family demographic indicators are presented in Table 1.

Family Involvement in School

Mothers reported on family involvement in children's schools at kindergarten, at third grade, and at fifth grade. Specifically, eight dichotomous (yes/no) items were used to assess involvement at school during the year (i.e., "Did you attend parent–teacher conferences?," "Did you visit your child's classroom?," "Did you attend any school performances?," "Did you attend any social events at your child's school?," "Did you attend any field trips?," "Did you attend meetings, like PTO or PTA?," "Did you attend classroom open houses?," and "Did you volunteer in the classroom?"). These eight items were averaged at the three time points so that scores ranged from 0 to 1 with higher scores indicating higher levels of involvement (e.g., a score of .5 indicated that families were involved in four of eight activities). At each grade, the inter-item reliability of involvement scores was moderate to good (i.e., α ranged from .65 to .73).

Children's Feelings About School

At kindergarten, third grade, and fifth grade, children completed the self-report Feelings About School (FAS) measure (Valeski & Stipek, 2001; for the primary sources from which the measure was adapted, also see Eccles, Wigfield, Harold, & Blumenfeld, 1993; Wigfield et al., 1997), which was used to assess four domains of children's feelings about school: (1) *relationships with teachers* (e.g., "How do you feel about your teacher?"), (2) *perceived competencies in literacy* (e.g., "How good are you at reading?"), (3) *perceived competencies in math* (e.g., "How good are you at learning something new in math?"), and (4) *general attitudes toward school* (e.g., "How do you feel when you are at school?"). On the FAS measure, children answered questions in each of these four domains using five-point, Likert-type items on which higher scores indicated relatively more positive feelings and higher perceived competencies.

Children's ratings of their relationships with teachers on the FAS measure have been validated using teacher reports of these relationships (Valeski & Stipek, 2001). Children's ratings of their competencies and general attitudes toward school on the FAS measure have been validated via assessments of academic skills and teachers' ratings (Valeski

& Stipek, 2001). In the present study, the inter-item reliability of children's ratings in the four domains was, in general, moderate to good (i.e., α ranged from .59 to .79), although there were two exceptions for which reliability scores were lower: At kindergarten, the inter-item reliability for general attitudes toward school was .51, and at fifth grade, the inter-item reliability for relationships with teachers was .41.

Analysis Plan

Multilevel models (Raudenbush & Bryk, 2002; Singer & Willett, 2003) were used to examine stability and change in family involvement and children's feelings about school as well as direct and indirect associations among these constructs. Analyses were conducted in three steps. First, we estimated unconditional growth models to examine the average kindergarten status and rate of change between kindergarten and fifth grade for family involvement and each of the four domains of children's feelings about school. Second, we estimated two-level models that included family involvement in school as a time-varying predictor of children's feelings about school to determine if increases and decreases over time in family involvement predicted improvements or declines in the quality of children's relationships with their teachers, their perceived competencies, and their general attitudes toward school.

As part of this second step, we examined the potential mediating role of children's relationships with teachers. More specifically, we examined whether children's relationships with teachers provided an indirect link between family involvement and children's perceived competencies and general attitudes toward school with the expectation that increased family involvement in school would predict improved relationships with teachers that, in turn, would predict improved perceived competencies and attitudes toward school. To examine these indirect associations (i.e., mediator effects), we followed Krull and MacKinnon (1999, 2001) for testing mediation hypotheses in multilevel models. Specifically, we computed the product of the indirect effects and the corresponding standard errors using estimates of unbiased variance (Goodman, 1960; Sobel, 1982).[2]

Third, we estimated alternative direct and indirect associations between family involvement in school and children's feelings about school, using the same methods outlined for our second analytic step but with alternative orderings of the variables that were specified as predictor variables, mediator variables, and outcome variables. We

FIGURE 2. Pathways of Associations That Provide Potential Alternatives to the Hypothesized Pathway of Association Depicted in Figure 1.

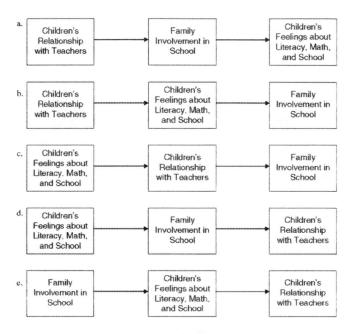

took this third step primarily because changes in family involvement in school may be related to changes in children's feelings about school in ways other than the direction of relations that are depicted in Figure 1.

Consider, for example, the five alternative conceptual models depicted in Figure 2. By estimating alternative model specifications as our third analytic step, we were able to determine whether our results were more consistent with the theoretical model displayed in Figure 1 or one of the alternative models displayed in Figure 2.

In the multilevel models that we estimated for our second and third analytic steps (i.e., time-varying predictors), time-varying predictors such as family involvement were centered *within* families (this strategy is alternatively referred to as "group-mean" centering; Raudenbush & Bryk, 2002; Singer & Willett, 2003). By using this centering strategy, our models provided estimates of associations between *changes* in the predictors and *changes* in the outcomes within families. For example, we examined whether increased family involvement within families predicted improved child relationships with teachers.

Missing Data

Given the longitudinal nature of the present study, there was missing data on most indicators other than the demographic data collected in the CCDP. On the family involvement indicator, for example, 49.8% of sample children had no missing data, 26.1% were missing one observation, 15.2% were missing two observations, and 8.8% were missing all three observations. Methodologists (e.g., Schafer & Graham, 2002) recommend using multiple imputation to replace missing data over other options (e.g., list-wise deletion or mean replacement) for most studies in which attrition occurs. Multiple imputation replaces missing data with values computed from multivariate analyses of participants' nonmissing data on other variables plus random variation (Schafer & Graham, 2002). For the present study, we used multiple imputation by chained equations (i.e., MICE, Royston, 2004) to generate five complete data sets that combined observed and imputed values. We then used the multiple imputation option in HLM6 (Raudenbush & Bryk, 2002) to estimate our multilevel models from these five complete data sets and combine estimates.

RESULTS

Unconditional Growth Models

As a first step in our analyses, we estimated unconditional growth models for family involvement in school and children's relationships with teachers, feelings about literacy, feelings about math, and attitudes toward school. From these unconditional models, the sample averages for kindergarten status and linear rate of change from kindergarten through fifth grade are presented in Table 2. Consider, for example, that families participated, on average, in about 58% of the school involvement activities (i.e., a little more than four of eight school involvement activities) at kindergarten, as indicated by the coefficient of .58.

Also note, however, that there were statistically significant ($\chi^2 = 582.44$, $p < .001$) differences in involvement across families at kindergarten status such that families one standard deviation above the mean participated in about 75% of the involvement activities (i.e., six of eight) and families one standard deviation below the mean

TABLE 2. Family Involvement in School and Children's Feelings About School: Kindergarten Status and Rate of Change to Fifth Grade

	Fixed Effects Coefficient (SE)	Random Effects	
		SD	χ^2
Family involvement in school			
Kindergarten	.58*** (.02)	.17	582.44***
Rate of change from K to fifth grade	.00 (.01)	.03	409.21**
Relationship with teacher			
Kindergarten	4.34*** (.07)	.77	631.71***
Rate of change from K to fifth grade	.03 (.02)	.24	714.29***
Feelings about literacy			
Kindergarten	3.72*** (.06)	.72	710.80***
Rate of change from K to fifth grade	.07*** (.02)	.18	597.35***
Feelings about math			
Kindergarten	4.00*** (.09)	.85	828.05***
Rate of change from K to fifth grade	.00 (.02)	.21	657.92***
Attitudes toward school			
Kindergarten	4.38*** (.06)	.60	601.13***
Rate of change from K to fifth grade	.06*** (.01)	.15	527.30***

Note. Fixed effects are the estimated sample averages for kindergarten status and rate of change from kindergarten through fifth grade. Standard errors for fixed effects are provided in parentheses below the estimates. Random effects are the estimated variations around the sample averages. K, kindergarten; SD, standard deviation; SE standard error.

*p < .05; **p < .01; ***p < .001.

participated in approximately 41% of the involvement activities (i.e., three of eight). In addition, although school involvement was, on average, stable between kindergarten and fifth grade (as indicated by the coefficient of .00), there were statistically significant ($\chi^2 = 409.21$, $p = .002$) differences such that families one standard deviation above the mean increased their involvement in school by 15% and families one standard deviation below the mean decreased their involvement in school by 15% across the study period.

For children's feelings about school at kindergarten, average scores ranged from 3.72 for feelings about literacy to 4.38 for general attitudes toward school. For all four of these indicators, there were statistically significant differences across children at kindergarten (standard deviations ranged from .60 for general attitudes toward school to .85 for feelings about math). In addition, although general attitudes toward school were, on average, decreasing over time and feelings about literacy were, on average, increasing over time, there were significant differences across children such that some children were increasing over time and others were decreasing over time on each of these four scales.

Change in Family Involvement to Changes in Children's Feelings About School: Direct and Indirect Effects

As a second step in our analyses, we examined time-varying associations between family involvement in school and children's feeling about school to determine if increased involvement predicted improved feelings. As part of this second step, we were interested in the potential mediating role of children's relationships with their teachers. That is, we examined whether there was an indirect association between involvement and feelings about school such that increased involvement predicted improved relationships with teachers and whether improved relationships with teachers, in turn, predicted increased perceptions of competency in literacy and math as well as improved general attitudes toward school.

Because we examined the potential mediating role of relationships with teachers, we conducted this second step using two model specifications. First, in what we refer to as model 1, we estimated family involvement in school as a time-varying (within-family centered) predictor of the four feelings about school variables: relationships with teachers, feelings about literacy, feelings about math, and attitudes toward school. Second, in what we refer to as model 2, we simultaneously estimated family involvement in school *and* children's relationships with their teachers as time-varying predictors of feelings about literacy, feelings about math, and attitudes toward school. Finally, following the estimation of these two models, we calculated and tested the product of the coefficients comprising the hypothesized mediation effect.[2]

In addition, to control for characteristics of children, families, and schools, the following covariates were included at level-2 of model 1 and model 2: child gender, ethnicity, birth order, and birth weight; maternal age at childbirth (adolescent vs. older), partner status, level of education, and primary language (English vs. other); family CCDP group (experimental vs. control), income, and study site; and school affordances. Specifically, these covariates were specified as level-2 predictors of kindergarten status and rate of change in children's feelings about school, thereby controlling for differences in children's

TABLE 3. Direct and Indirect Effects From Change in Family Involvement to Changes in Children's Feelings About School

	Relationship With Teacher	Feelings About Literacy	Feelings About Math	Attitudes Toward School
Model 1				
Family involvement in school	.50*** (.18)	.11 (.19)	.19 (.18)	.33 (.20)
Model 2				
Family involvement in school		.05 (.19)	.13 (.18)	.23 (.18)
Relationship with teacher		.16*** (.04)	.16** (.04)	.24** (.07)
Indirect effect				
Involvement → relationship		.08* (.03)	.08* (.04)	.12* (.04)

Note. The standard errors and corresponding test statistics for the indirect effects were computed using estimates of unbiased variance (Goodman, 1960) as Krull and MacKinnon (1999, 2001) recommend for indirect effects in the first level of multilevel models with the present study's sample size. Nonetheless, the indirect effects were statistically significant across all commonly used methods for computing the standard error of $\alpha\beta$, including first-order Taylor series expansion (Sobel, 1982) and second-order Taylor series expansion (Goodman, 1960).

*p < .05; **p < .01; ***p < .001.

feelings that were correlated with these child, family, and school characteristics.

In Table 3, we present a summary of the results from the second analytic step. In the top row we present associations that were estimated in model 1 between family involvement in school and children's feelings about school. As predicted, changes in family involvement in school were positively associated with changes in children's relationships with their teachers (coefficient = .50). Specifically, increased involvement in school by families predicted improvements in children's perceptions of relationships with their teachers. Conversely, decreased involvement predicted declines in children's perceptions of relationships with their teachers.

Beyond statistical significance, the size of this association also appeared to be of practical significance. If, for example, families engaged in an additional two involvement activities during the year, the estimated change in children's relationships with their teachers was .13 points. This amount was nearly half of a standard deviation more the sample mean for yearly change in relationships with teachers (i.e., one standard deviation above the sample mean was an increase of .27 points per year). In addition, the effect size for this association, a partial correlation of .15, was the largest effect size in the model, indicating that family involvement in school was more strongly predictive of children's relationships with teachers compared with the wide range of child, family, and school characteristics that were included as covariates (e.g., the second largest effect size in the model, a partial correlation of .12, was for the association between CCDP program status and children's relationships with teachers at kindergarten; children enrolled in the CCDP program had more positive relationships with their teachers at kindergarten than did children in the control group).

On the other hand, family involvement in school was not a significant predictor of children's feelings about literacy, feelings about math, or attitudes toward school. Nonetheless, we examined the possibility that family involvement in school was indirectly related to these constructs. As methodologists have noted (for a review of this work, see Dearing & Hamilton, 2006), there are instances in which an association between a relatively distal predictor variable and an outcome variable may be evident *only* when accounting for a more proximal mediating process that links the predictor and outcome, and this may be especially likely to occur in longitudinal analyses such as ours (Shrout & Bolger, 2002). In other words, even though family involvement was not significantly associated with feelings about literacy, feelings about math, and attitudes toward school in model 1, the indirect path from family involvement to these constructs (via relationships with teachers) may still have been significant, as predicted, if relationships with teachers provided a proximal link between family involvement and children's feelings about school.

In the bottom half of Table 3, we displayed the coefficients from model 2 as well as the product of the coefficients from models 1 and 2 that were used to estimate the mediating effects of children's relationships with teachers. There are two important patterns of results worth noting. First, changes in children's relationships with their teachers were positively and significantly associated changes in children's feelings about literacy, feelings about math, and attitudes about school (i.e., .16, .16, and .24, respectively). Thus when children's relationships with their teachers improved, their feelings about literacy and math as well as their more general attitudes toward school also improved. And, conversely, when children's relationships with their teachers worsened, their feelings about literacy and math as well as their attitudes toward school also worsened.

Second, the estimated indirect effects from changes in family involvement in school to changes in children's relationships with their teachers (i.e., .08, .08., and .12, respectively) were statistically significant. In other words, changes in family involvement in school were related to changes in children's feelings about literacy, math, and school, because changes in involvement were associated with changes in children's relationships with their teachers and, in turn, these relationships were associated with children's feelings about literacy, math, and school. Specifically, increased family involvement in school predicted improved relationships with teachers and thereby predicted improved feelings about literacy, math, and school, more generally. And, conversely, decreased family involvement in school predicted worsening relationships with teachers and thereby worsening feelings about literacy, math, and school, more generally.

Estimates of Alternative Direct and Indirect Effects

Although we found evidence of a direct association between changes in family involvement in school and changes in children's relationships with their teachers as well as evidence of indirect associations between changes in family involvement and changes in children's feelings about school, demonstrating causality was not possible given the nonexperimental nature of our data. It is possible, for example, that changes in children's relationships with their teachers influence changes in family involvement such that improvements in child–teacher relationships lead to increased family involvement in school rather than vice versa. Given this potential for alternative explanations, we examined alternative direct and indirect associations between family involvement and children's feelings about school. These alternative model specifications are presented conceptually in Figure 2.

In summary, there was very little empirical support for the conceptual models displayed in Figure 2. Consider, for example, that changes in children's relationships with their teachers did not significantly predict changes in family involvement in school (this relation is crucial to the conceptual models displayed in Figure 2, a and c). Further, changes in children's feelings about literacy, math, and school were not directly related to changes in family involvement in school, regardless of which was specified as the predictor (these relations are crucial to the conceptual models displayed in Figure 2, b, d, and e). Finally, none of the mediation effects displayed in Figure 2 was statistically significant. Thus, although we cannot make causal inferences from these data, our results were most consistent with the hypothesis that changes in family involvement in school lead to changes in children's relationships with their teachers and, in turn, changes in these relationships lead to changes in children's feelings about literacy, math, and school.

DISCUSSION

In the present study, we investigated within-family associations between family involvement in school, children's relationships with teachers, and children's feelings about school for a sample of low-income children. In our analyses of longitudinal data from kindergarten through fifth grade, there were two primary findings. First, changes in family involvement in school predicted changes in children's perceptions of their relationships with teachers such that increased involvement was associated with improved relationships and decreased involvement was associated with worsened relationships. Second, changes in family involvement were indirectly associated with changes in feelings about literacy, math, and school such that changes in children's relationships with teachers mediated these associations. The results of this study provide some of the first evidence that increased family involvement in the school pays dividends for low-income students relationships with their teachers and, in turn, their perceptions of competency and feelings about school, more generally.

Family Involvement and Children's Relationships With Teachers: Within-Families Associations

Despite considerable evidence on the importance of both family educational involvement and child–teacher relationships for children's academic success, there has been little empirical work, to date, investigating interdependent links between these two processes. Following theories of why involvement may matter for children's achievement (Connors & Epstein, 1995; Henderson & Mapp, 2002; Hoover-Dempsey & Sadler, 1995) and dynamic systems theories of child development (Bornstein & Sawyer, 2006; Bronfenbrenner &

Morris, 1998; Sameroff, 1994), we examined associations between family involvement in school and child–teacher relationships with the expectation that increases in family involvement in children's schools has the potential to improve child–teacher relationships for low-income students. Consistent with this hypothesis, changes in involvement within families significantly predicted changes in children's perceptions of their relationships with teachers. More specifically, when parents increased their participation in school involvement activities, children reported improved relationships with their teachers. Conversely, when parents decreased their participation in school involvement activities, children reported worsened relationships with their teachers.

Beyond statistical significance, the size of the association between family involvement in school and children's relationships with their teachers appeared to be of practical importance. Based on our model estimates, an additional two involvement activities per year were associated with improvements in student–teacher relationships that were nearly half of a standard deviation larger than the sample mean for yearly change in student–teacher relationships. In addition, because a useful way of examining practical importance is to consider relative effect sizes within statistical models (McCartney & Rosenthal, 2000), we compared the effect size for family involvement in school with the child, family, and school covariates in our models. The effect size for family involvement was larger than all of the effect sizes for covariates.

Family Involvement in School and Children's Feelings About School: Indirect Effects

In our initial analyses of associations between family involvement in school and children's feelings about school, changes in involvement did not significantly predict changes in children's perception of competency in literacy or math, nor did changes in involvement significantly predict changes in children's general attitudes toward school. Yet, when we followed up on these initial analyses by examining indirect associations, there was evidence that involvement and feelings about school were related via the mediating effect of children's relationships with their teachers. More specifically, our results indicated that increases in family involvement in school were indirectly associated with improvements in children's perceptions of competency in literacy and mathematics as well as improvements in their general attitudes toward school, because increased involvement predicted improved student–teacher relationships and these improved relationships in turn predicted improved feelings of competency and attitudes toward school.

Thus relationships with teachers appear to be one mechanism by which family involvement in school influences low-income children's experiences in school. That is, improved child–teacher relationships may provide at least part of the answer as to *why* involvement has the potential to benefit low-income children. These results are, in fact, consistent with theory suggesting that involvement is a means of modeling the importance of relationships with teachers as well as theoretical and empirical work indicating that family involvement allows parents to share knowledge about their child and thereby provides teachers with a more nuanced understanding of children's developmental needs (Connors & Epstein, 1995; Henderson & Mapp, 2002; Hoover-Dempsey & Sadler, 1995; Lawrence-Lightfoot, 2003). Indeed, family involvement in the school offers one of the few opportunities for children, families, and teachers to interact together, perhaps providing direct modeling experiences for children.

Our results are also consistent with the theoretical perspective that family involvement in school functions as part of dynamic social system in children's lives. Spillover effects, whereby one dyadic relationship (e.g., parent–parent relationship) influences other dyadic relationships (e.g., parent–child relationships) in children's social systems, have been well-documented *within* families (Cox et al., 2001; Katz & Gottman, 1996; Margolin et al., 2001). Theorists have suggested that similar processes are at work in relationship systems that connect home and school contexts (Bornstein & Sawyer, 2006; Bronfenbrenner & Morris, 1998). We argue that spillover effects from parent–teacher to child–teacher relationships offer one plausible explanation for the results of the present study.

Teachers working with low-income students value the involvement of families in the schools and report the desire to increase this involvement (Lawrence-Lightfoot, 2003). Not surprisingly, therefore, involvement appears to promote positive relations between low-income parents and teachers (Izzo et al., 1999). We suspect that these positive relationship qualities then spillover into the child–teacher relationships. Future studies that examine family involvement, the parent–teacher relationship, and teacher behaviors with children such as emotional support and responsiveness could provide further detail on such processes.

Strengths, Limitations, and Implications of the Present Study

Methodologically, two strengths are worth noting for our results. First, the predictive utility of changes in family involvement in school was evident when controlling for both variations in child–teacher relationships that were associated with child grade (i.e., linear time trends in child–teacher relationships between kindergarten and fifth grade) and several child, family, and school characteristics. With regard to the former, we controlled for individual differences in the linear rate of change in child–teacher relationships between kindergarten and fifth grade. In other words, although relationships with teachers were improving for some children as they got older and worsening for other children as they got older (and for some children remaining relatively stable across years), our estimated effects of family involvement in school were evident even after controlling for these age-related changes (or stability). Second, because we estimated within-families associations between involvement and child–teacher relationships, differences across children, families, and schools that were stable over time can be ruled out as potential sources of bias and cannot be offered as alternative explanations for our results. For example, although some families may display higher motivation to be involved than other families across their child's educational experiences, these between-family differences cannot bias our results if they are stable over time, because we did not compare more versus less involved families; we investigated the effects of high versus low involvement within families.

It is also important to note that we tested multiple alternative model specifications, and in the end our results supported only the expected mediation effect (i.e., involvement predicted child–teacher relationships and, in turn, children's feelings about school). We found no evidence that changes in student–teacher relationships or changes in children's feelings about school should be specified as predictors of changes in family involvement, and we found no evidence of any alternative pathways of mediation. Thus, although we cannot make causal inferences from these nonexperimental data, our results were most consistent with a pathway of influence whereby changes in family involvement in school led to changes in child–teacher relationships and, in turn, these changes in relationships led to changes in children's feelings about literacy, math, and school, more generally. Nonetheless, in the present study we cannot rule out sources of bias potentially caused by omitted time-varying variables such as time-varying family, classroom, or school factors (e.g., year-to-year changes in teacher personality).

Because we focused solely on family involvement in school, future work that considers the developmental impact of changes in other forms of educational involvement (e.g., increased involvement in the home) would further advance the field. Yet, given the current policy and practice focus on family educational involvement as a potential means of promoting the life chances of low-income children and much evidence that involvement in school is highly responsive to teacher and school outreach (Henderson & Mapp, 2002), our results are encouraging. Indeed, considering our results in the context of past empirical work suggests that family involvement in the school is a promising target for intervention, it can be changed for the better and, in turn, can produce change for the better.

There are practical aspects to increasing involvement in school among low-income families, however, that extend beyond the control of educators. Low-income parents, for example, are often employed in jobs that provide little flexibility to take time off for involvement activities during school hours; in particular, full-time employment poses a barrier to school involvement for low-income parents, limiting the usefulness of classroom- and school-level processes such as teacher outreach (Weiss et al., 2003). Addressing this issue may require policies that provide employers the incentives to give employees time off for investing in their children's education.

Recommendations for Future Research

In addition to the importance of examining changes in areas of family educational involvement other than school involvement (e.g., what are the implications of increased involvement in the home for low-income children?), we have two recommendations for future research. These recommendations are intended primarily to build on the present study, with the potential for further clarifying the mechanisms by which involvement influences children and the resulting developmental effects of involvement. First, one missing link in the indirect chain of relations we examined was the quality of parent–teacher relationships.

Although we speculate that one reason children's relationships with teachers improved along with increased involvement was that parent–teacher relationships improved, a direct examination of the associations between changes in involvement and changes in parent–teacher relationships as well as the ramifications of changes in these relationships for child–teacher relationships is critical for helping determine the mechanisms by which involvement may improve children's attitudes toward school.

Second, an important next step in this line of inquiry will be determining the conditions under which increased family involvement is most likely to impact child–teacher relationships for the better and, more specifically, low-income children's lives for the better. Indeed, a fundamental proposition of ecological models of human development is that the affect of any one process on development is determined by characteristics of both the child and the context in which the process of interest occurs (e.g., Bronfenbrenner & Morris, 1998). Consistent with this theory, the quality of parent–child relationships can alter the value of family educational involvement such that children with higher quality parent–child relationships experience greater benefits of involvement than children with poorer quality parent–child relationships (Simpkins, Weiss, Kreider, McCartney, & Dearing, 2006). Teacher, classroom, and school characteristics may similarly moderate the impact of increased involvement on child–teacher relationships and, in turn, children's attitudes toward school. A better understanding of these variations could help target intervention efforts to maximize the benefits of increased involvement.

CONCLUSION

Meta-analyses have documented the empirical consensus that achievement is higher for children of more involved families than for children of less involved families (Fan & Chen, 2001; Jeynes, 2003, 2005). In addition, research on low-income families has demonstrated that increased involvement within families during the elementary school years predicts improved achievement outcomes for children (Dearing et al., 2006; Izzo et al., 1999). Adding to this knowledge base, the present study provides evidence on why changes in family involvement in school may matter for low-income children, a question that theorists argue is one of the most important issues deserving attention in this field of study (Hoover-Dempsey & Sandler, 1995).

Using within-families analyses of longitudinal data from kindergarten through fifth grade for an ethnically diverse sample of low-income children, we found that changes in children's relationships with their teachers mediated associations between changes in family involvement in school and changes in children's feelings about school. Specifically, increased involvement within families predicted improved child–teacher relationships, and these improved relationships predicted improved perceptions of competency in literacy and math as well as improved attitudes toward school, more generally. These findings provide further evidence that increased family involvement in school is likely an effective means of promoting the life chances of low-income children. Although it is clear that teacher outreach and an inviting school context are crucial for increasing this form of involvement, policies that address families' abilities to take advantage of these invitations without risking employment opportunities and financial well-being are likely necessary as well.

NOTES

1. Most theory and research on spillover effects has been centered on links between parent–parent relationships and parent–child relationships (e.g., does interparental conflict result in spillover effects for the parent–child relationship?). Nonetheless, given the more general emphasis in family systems and ecological systems theories on relationship connections between home and school contexts, we argue that processes such as spillover effects are likely at work in relationship systems involving children, parents, and teachers.

2. To calculate the product of coefficients for mediation effects (i.e., indirect effects) the association between the predictor variable and the mediator variable is multiplied by the association between the mediator variable and the outcome variable (when the latter is estimated while controlling for the association between the predictor variable and the outcome variable). For example, for the hypothesized mediation effect from family involvement in school to children's relationships with teachers and, in turn, to children's feelings about literacy, the coefficient for family involvement in school from the model for which children's relationships with teachers is the outcome variable (i.e., coefficient .50 from Model 1 in Table 3) is multiplied by the coefficient for children's relationships with teachers from the model for which children's attitudes towards school is the outcome variable (i.e., coefficient .24 from Model 2 in Table 3). The corresponding test statistic is then calculated by dividing this product (i.e., $(.50)(.24) = .12$) by its standard error (for a complete discussion of the standard error appropriate for the product of coefficients estimated in multilevel models, see Krull & MacKinnon, 1999; 2001).

REFERENCES

Baker, J. A. (1999). Teacher-student interaction in urban at–risk classrooms: Differential behavior, relationship quality, and student satisfaction with school. *The Elementary School Journal, 100*, 57–70.

Baker, J. A. (2006). Contributions of teacher–child relationships to positive school adjustment during elementary school. *Journal of School Psychology, 44*, 211–229.

Birch, S. H., & Ladd, G. W. (1997). The teacher–child relationship and children's early school adjustment. *Journal of School Psychology, 35*, 67–79.

Bornstein, M. H., & Sawyer, J. (2006). Family systems. In K. McCartney & D. Phillips (Eds.), *Blackwell handbook of early childhood development* (pp. 381–398). Malden, MA: Blackwell Publishing.

Bronfenbrenner, U., & Morris, P. A. (1998). The ecology of developmental processes. In W. Damon & R. M. Lerner (Eds.), *Handbook of child psychology: Vol. 1. Theoretical modes of human development* (5th ed., pp. 993–1028). New York: Wiley.

Connors, L. J., & Epstein, J. L. (1995). Parents and school partnerships. In M. H. Bornstein (Ed.), *Handbook of parenting, Vol. 4: Applied and practical parenting* (pp. 437–458). Hillsdale, NJ: Lawrence Erlbaum.

Cox, M. J., Paley, B., & Harter, K. (2001). Interparental conflict and parent-child relationships. In J. H. Grych & F. D. Fincham (Eds.), *Interparental conflict and child development: Theory, research, and applications* (pp. 249–272). New York: Cambridge University Press.

Crosnoe, R., Johnson, M. K., & Elder, G. H. (2004). Intergenerational bonding in school: The behavioral and contextual correlates of student–teacher relationships. *Sociology of Education, 77*, 60–81.

Dearing, E., & Hamilton, L. C. (2006). Contemporary approaches and classic advice for analyzing mediating and moderating variables. *Monographs for the Society of Research in Child Development, 71*, 88–104.

Dearing, E., Kreider, H., Simpkins, S., & Weiss, H. B. (2006). Family involvement in school and low-income children's literacy performance: Longitudinal associations between and within families. *Journal of Educational Psychology, 98*, 653–664.

Duncan, G. J., Magnuson, K. A., & Ludwig, J. (2004). The endogeneity problem in developmental studies. *Research in Human Development, 1*, 59–80.

Eccles, J. (1993). School and family effects on the ontogeny of children's interests, self- perceptions, and activity choice. In J. Jacobs (Ed.), *Nebraska symposium on motivation, 1992: Developmental perspectives on motivation* (pp. 145–208). Lincoln, NE: University of Nebraska Press.

Eccles, J., Wigfield, A., Harold, R. D., & Blumenfeld, P. (1993). Age and gender differences in children's self- and task perceptions during elementary school. *Child Development, 64*, 830–847.

Englund, M. M., Luckner, A. E., Whaley, G. J. L., & Egeland, B. (2004). Children's achievement in early elementary school: Longitudinal effects of parental involvement, expectations, and quality of assistance. *Journal of Educational Psychology, 96*, 723–730.

Fan, X., & Chen, M. (2001). Parental involvement and students' academic achievement: A meta-analysis. *Educational Psychology Review, 13*, 1–22.

Furrer, C., & Skinner, E. (2003). Sense of relatedness as a factor in children's academic engagement and performance. *Journal of Educational Psychology, 95*, 148–162.

Goodman, L. A. (1960). On the exact variance of products. *Journal of the American Statistical Association, 55*, 708–713.

Grolnick, W. S., Kurowski, C. O., & Gurland, S. T. (1999). Family processes and the development of children's self-regulation. *Educational Psychologist, 34*, 3–14.

Hamre, B. K., & Pianta, R. C. (2005). Can instructional and emotional support in the first-grade classroom make a difference for children at risk of school failure? *Child Development, 76*, 949–967.

Harvard Family Research Project. (2006). *School Transition Study: Project description.* Retrieved January 8, 2007 from http://www.gse.harvard.edu/hfrp/projects/sts.html

Henderson, A. T., & Mapp, K. L. (2002). *A new wave of evidence: The impact of school, family, and community connections on student achievement.* Austin, TX: National Center for Family and Community Connections with Schools.

Hoover-Dempsey, K. V., & Sandler, H. M. (1995). Parental involvement in children's education: Why does it make a difference? *Teachers College Record, 97*, 310–332.

Howes, C., & Hamilton, C. E. (1992). Child relationships with child care teachers: Stability and concordance with parental attachments. *Child Development, 63*, 859–866.

Howes, C., & Matheson, C. C. (1992). Contextual constraints on the concordance of mother–child and teacher–child relationships. In R. C. Pianta (Ed.), *Beyond the parent: The role of other adults in children's lives: New directions for child development* (pp. 25–40). San Francisco: Jossey-Bass.

Izzo, C. V., Weissberg, R. P., Kasprow, W. J., & Fendrich, M. (1999). A longitudinal assessment of teacher perceptions of parent involvement in children's education and school performance. *American Journal of Community Psychology, 27*, 817–839.

Jeynes, W. H. (2003). A meta-analysis: The effects of parental involvement on minority children's academic achievement. *Education and Urban Society, 35*, 202–218.

Jeynes, W. H. (2005). A meta-analysis of the relation of parental involvement to urban elementary school student academic achievement. *Urban Education, 40*, 237–269.

Katz, L. F., & Gottman, J. M. (1996). Spillover effects of marital conflict: In search of parenting and coparenting mechanisms. Special Issue: Understanding how family-level dynamics affect children's development: Studies of two-parent families. *New Directions for Child Development, 74*, 57–76.

Krull, J. L., & MacKinnon, D. P. (1999). Multilevel mediation modeling in group-based intervention studies. *Evaluation Review, 23*, 418–444.

Krull, J. L., & MacKinnon, D. P. (2001). Multilevel modeling of individual and group level mediated effects. *Multivariate Behavioral Research, 36*, 249–277.

Ladd, G. W., Birch, S. H., & Buhs, E. S. (1999). Children's social and scholastic lives in kindergarten: Related spheres of influence? *Child Development, 70,* 1373–1400.

Lawrence-Lightfoot, S. (2003). *The essential conversation: What parents and teachers can learn from each other.* Random House Publishing.

Margolin, G., Oliver, P. H., & Medina, A. M. (2001). Conceptual issues in understanding the relation between interparental conflict and child adjustment: Integrating developmental psychopathology and risk/resilience perspectives. In J. H. Grych & F. D. Fincham (Eds.), *Interparental conflict and child development: Theory, research, and applications* (pp. 9–38). New York: Cambridge University Press.

McCartney, K., & Rosenthal, R. (2000). Effect size, practical importance, and social policy for children. *Child Development, 71,* 173–180.

Murray, C., & Greenberg, M. T. (2000). Children's relationship with teachers and bonds with school: An investigation of patterns and correlates in middle childhood. *Journal of School Psychology, 38,* 423–445.

Murray, C., & Greenberg, M. T. (2001). Relationships with teachers and bonds with school: Social emotional adjustment correlates for children with and without disabilities. *Psychology in the Schools, 38,* 25–41.

Murray, C., & Murray, K. M. (2004). Child level correlates of teacher-student relationships: An examination of demographic characteristics, academic orientations, and behavioral orientations. *Psychology in the Schools, 41,* 751–762.

O'Connor, E., & McCartney, K. (2006). Testing associations between young children's relationships with mothers and teachers. *Journal of Educational Psychology, 98,* 87–98.

Pianta, R. C., & Rimm-Kaufman, S. (2006). The social ecology of the transition to school: Classrooms, families, and children. In K. McCartney & D. Phillips (Eds.), *Blackwell handbook of early childhood development* (pp. 490–507). Malden, MA: Blackwell Publishing.

Pianta, R. C., & Steinberg, M. S. (1992). Teacher-child relationships and the process of adjusting to school. *New Directions for Child Development, 57,* 61–80.

Raudenbush, S. W., & Bryk, A. S. (2002). *Hierarchical linear models: Applications and data analysis methods. Advanced quantitative techniques in the social sciences: Vol. 1* (2nd ed.). Newbury Park, CA: Sage Publications.

Roeser, R. W., Eccles, J. S., & Sameroff, A. J. (2000). School as a context of early adolescents' academic and social–emotional development: A summary of research findings. *Elementary School Journal, 100,* 443–471.

Royston, P. (2004). Multiple imputation of missing values. *The Stata Journal, 4,* 227–241.

Sameroff, A. (1994). Developmental systems and family functioning. In R. D. Parke & S. G. Sheppard (Eds.), *Exploring family relationships with other social contexts. Family research consortium: Advances in family research* (pp. 199–214). Hillsdale, NJ: Lawrence Erlbaum.

Schafer, J. L., & Graham, J. W. (2002). Missing data: Our view of the state of the art. *Psychological Methods, 7,* 147–177.

Shrout, P. E., & Bolger, N. (2002). Mediation in experimental and non-experimental studies: New procedures and recommendations. *Psychological Methods, 7,* 422–445.

Simpkins, S., Weiss, H. B., Kreider, H., McCartney, K., & Dearing, E. (2006). The moderating effect of parent-child relationship qualities on the relations between parent educational involvement and child achievement. *Parenting: Science and Practice, 6,* 49–57.

Singer, J. D., & Willett, J. T. (2003). *Applied longitudinal data analysis: Modeling change and event occurrence.* New York: Oxford University Press.

Sobel, M. E. (1982). Asymptotic confidence intervals for indirect effects in structural equation models. In S. Leinhardt (Ed.), *Sociological methodology* (pp. 290–312). Washington, DC: American Sociological Association.

St. Pierre, R. G., Layzer, J. I., Goodson, B. D., & Bernstein, L. S. (1999). The effectiveness of comprehensive, case management interventions: Evidence from the national evaluation of the Comprehensive Child Development Program. *American Journal of Evaluation, 20,* 15–34.

U.S. Department of Education (2003). *No Child Left Behind: A parent's guide.* Retrieved January 8, 2007 from http://www.ed.gov/parents/academic/involve/nclbguide/parentsguide.pdf

Valeski, T. N., & Stipek, D. J. (2001). Young children's feelings about school. *Child Development, 72,* 1198–1213.

Weiss, H. B., Dearing, E., McCartney, K., Kreider, H., Mayer, E., & Simpkins, S. (2005). Family educational involvement: Who can afford it and what does it afford? In C. R. Cooper, C. Garcia Coll, T. Bartko, H. Davis, & C. Chatman (Eds.), *Developmental pathways through middle childhood: Rethinking context and diversity as resources* (pp. 17–39). Hillsdale, NJ: Lawrence Erlbaum.

Weiss, H. B., Mayer, E., Vaughan, P., Kreider, H., Dearing, E., Hencke, R., & Pinto, K. (2003). Making it work: Low-income working mothers' involvement in their children's education. *American Educational Research Journal, 40,* 879–901.

Wigfield, A., Eccles, J. S., Yoon, K. S., Harold, R. D., Arbreton, A. J. A., Freedman-Doan, C., & Blumenfeld, P. (1997). Change in children's competence beliefs and subjective task values across the elementary school years: A 3-year study. *Journal of Educational Psychology, 89,* 451–469.

Effects of Parental Involvement on Experiences of Discrimination and Bullying

William H. Jeynes

ABSTRACT. This study investigated the relationship between parental involvement and their children being picked on or bullied and being discriminated against based on their race during their elementary and secondary school years. The influence of parental involvement on academic achievement during that period was also examined. Specific aspects of parental involvement and an overall parental involvement variable were examined. Two different samples were examined. The first sample was made up of 139 college students, and the second sample consisted of 102 seventh to 12th grade students. Analysis of variance and logistic regression analysis were used. The results indicated that higher levels of parental involvement were associated with higher academic achievement among their children. However, the remainder of the analyses showed mixed results with the effects of parental involvement emerging as more robust with the college sample than for the 7th to 12th grade sample. Overall, it does appear that parental involvement is somewhat related to a lower incidence of children being picked on and discriminated against. The significance of these results is discussed.

William H. Jeynes, PhD, is Professor in the Department of Education, California State University at Long Beach, CA.

INTRODUCTION

Over the last two decades, researchers have sought to quantify the influence of parental involvement on a variety of outcomes (Spera, 2005; Wallace & Walberg, 1993). Most of this research has focused on the influence of parental involvement on the academic outcomes of school children (Griffith, 1996, 1997; Hampton, Mumford, & Bond, 1998; Jeynes, 2003, 2005, 2007; Marcon, 1999; Peressini, 1998). Moreover, educators have increasingly identified parental involvement as the primary vehicle by which to elevate academic achievement from current levels (Hara, 1998). The body of research has developed to a point in which increasingly social scientists not only realize that parental support aids in student school outcomes, but they have a much better idea about which components of parental involvement help the most (Jeynes, 2003, 2005). Although a considerable degree of knowledge exists about parental involvement's impact on academic variables, little is known about its influence on other youth experiences such as bullying, discrimination, and being mugged.

The current interest expressed by sociologists and educators on the influence of parental involvement is not surprising, particularly because the body of research indicates that family factors are considerably more influential than school factors on grades and scores (Coleman, Hoffer, & Kilgore, 1982; Hoffer, Greeley, & Coleman, 1987). In reality, such factors as the parental family structure, family education level, and family communication and engagement are better predictors of student achievement than are a conglomeration of school factors (Coleman et al., 1982; Hoffer et al., 1987; Jeynes, 2002). When one contemplates the amount of time children spend at home versus school, this finding really is not surprising.

Increasingly, parental involvement has become one of the hottest topics in the social sciences. It is not that the idea of parental involvement in school is new. It has been an emphasis in American schooling since the early 1600s (Chamberlin, 1961; Gangel & Benson, 1983). Nevertheless, within the last 20 years social scientists have resurrected the concept, and moreover they contend that it may concurrently represent the most underutilized and vitally important component of education (Epstein, 2001; Hoover-Dempsey, Walker, & Jones, 2002).

In recent years, three developments in parental involvement research have energized those interested in studying parental roles and functions. First, social scientists have propounded more sophisticated theories and models regarding the interaction of parents, schools, and communities and attempted to apply those models to foster positive academic outcomes (Epstein & Sanders, 2006; Sanders & Epstein, 2000). Second, recent meta-analyses have given the research community insight in the particular facets of parental involvement that are the most salient and the extent to which the effects of parental engagement hold across race and gender (Jeynes, 2003, 2005, 2007). These meta-analyses indicate that even if one examines only parental involvement programs, in which schools invite parents to become engaged in their children's education who in some cases otherwise would not, the effects of parental involvement are noteworthy (Jeynes, 2003, 2005, 2007). Third, social scientists have gained a greater understanding of the actions that teachers can take to foster parental support and the community agencies, such as churches and other houses of worship, that are available to expedite the formation of stronger ties between parents and schools (Green & Hoover-Dempsey, 2007; Hoover-Dempsey & Sandler, 1997).

At a symposium sponsored by the Harvard Family Research Project in 2005, four prominent researchers on parental involvement called for a broadening of the parental involvement research agenda to include the full gamut of social science disciplines (Redding, 2005). One of the objectives in this broadening was to examine parental involvement as it affects children's lives across a wider range of educational, psychological, and sociological dimensions (Redding, 2005). With this exhortation in mind, it is important for family scientists to realize that it is conceivable that parental involvement may affect other aspects of children's school and neighborhood experiences as well. Although it is no doubt important that parents help children succeed academically, if parental support can reduce the incidence of other deleterious experiences such as bullying and discrimination, this is important to note as well. Discrimination and bullying are frequent topics of academic articles (Gibbons, Gerrard, Cleveland, Wills, & Brody, 2004; Schafer, Carter, & Katz-Bannister, 2004). Nevertheless, there is very little research examining whether parental involvement is associated with a reduction in these experiences in the lives of children.

The question, therefore, emerges: Can parental involvement really improve the quality of life for children in terms of the experience of discrimination and bullying? This study surveys the elementary and secondary school experiences of students at a major university in California and a school in a major metropolitan area in California to address the following questions. First, to what degree is parental involvement associated with lower levels of discrimination experienced by these students in their K–12 experiences? Second, to what degree is parental involvement associated with lower levels of bullying experienced by these students in their K–12 experiences? Third, to what degree is parental involvement associated with higher levels of academic achievement? This study is particularly important because, in accordance with the Harvard Family Research Project recommendation, it expands the research base and academic discussion of parental involvement into relatively new and salient territory.

Consistent with the results of three recent meta-analyses on parental involvement, this study examines parental involvement generally and addresses the effects of specific components of parental involvement, such as parental expectations and parent-child communications, that studies have shown to be some of the most salient aspects of parental involvement (Afifi & Olson, 2005; Englund, Luckner, Whaley, & Egeland, 2004; Jeynes, 2003, 2005, 2007; Zhan, 2006). By parental expectations this does not mean standards established in an authoritarian way (Zellman & Waterman, 1998). In fact, if parental standards are too rigidly applied, this may backfire and cause resistance in the child (Zellman & Waterman, 1998). Rather, high parental expectations as defined in these meta-analyses refers more to an unspoken acknowledgment that the parents anticipate that the child will achieve at a certain level and that the child will go to college (Jeynes, 2005, 2007). Parent–child communication refers primarily to communication about school but can refer to other manifestations of communication as well.

METHODS AND DATA SOURCES

In this project surveys were administered to two groups of individuals: a group made up of college students from California and a group of 7th to 12th grade students attending a school in a major metropolitan area in California. A survey was developed that addressed various school experiences, including parental involvement, discrimination, bullying, academic achievement, and other experiences. The college survey included 25 questions made up of 23 multiple-choice questions and 2 open-ended questions. We randomly selected 139 (69.5%) college students from a sample of 200 students from a major California university. The 7th to 12th grade survey consisted of the same questions, with the exception of the questions on discrimination. This was because a set of pilot study interviews indicated that many of the students were not sufficiently able to recognize, understand, and describe the experience of discrimination. Permission was obtained from the school principal and teachers to conduct the study in the school. In the case of the secondary school student sample, we randomly selected 102 (69.4%) students from a sample of 147 students. We then analyzed the results using analysis of variance and logistic regression analysis.

Both the college and secondary school students were asked to respond to these questions, based on their experiences as elementary and secondary school students. On the questionnaires, students identified themselves by race, gender, and income level for the period being examined. They also indicated the degree to which their parents were involved in their education along various dimensions of parental involvement: (1) parents' involvement in helping their child in school, (2) parent–child communication about school, and (3) parental expectations. Multiple-choice questions on discrimination and bullying asked the students whether they had experienced a given type of discrimination or bullying "never," "very rarely," "sometimes," "frequently," or "very frequently." Questions on discrimination were specific in terms of the source; on various individual questions, the students were asked the extent to which they had been discriminated against by teachers, neighbors, and so forth. Each type of response was assigned a number (0–4, where 0 = "never"). To determine the overall level of discrimination, the responses for the individual discrimination questions were added together. For questions regarding bullying, the students were asked not only the frequency of the bullying, but also the primary reason(s) why they were bullied (e.g., whether they were overweight, nerds, gay, and so forth). Students were also asked to report their school grade point average. Open-ended questions were also coded to give further insight into the quantitative results.

RESULTS

Table 1 lists the results for the effects of the three components of parental involvement combined (parental involvement in helping their child in school [i.e., the specific component of parental involvement], parent–child communication about school, and parental expectations) and separately the specific component of parental involvement as they relate to academic achievement, being picked on or bullied and experiencing discrimination. The results indicate that among the college students the overall parental involvement measure yielded statistically significant results for all three of the dependent variables. Statistically significant results emerged for the combined measure of parental involvement for academic achievement (F (1, 138) = 7.87, $p < .01$), being picked on or bullied (F (1, 138) = 7.94, $p < .01$), and experiencing discrimination (F (1, 137) = 7.29, $p < .01$). Analyses were then conducted controlling for race, gender, and family income and yielded the following statistically significant

TABLE 1. Effects of Parental Involvement (Combined and Specific Parental Involvement Variable)

	Combined Parental Involvement Measure for College Sample (N = 138)	Combined Parental Involvement Measure for School Sample (N = 102)	Parental Involvement Measure for College Sample (N = 138)	Parental Involvement Measure for School Sample (N = 102)
Never been picked on	11.55**	10.12	3.81**	3.44
Remainder of sample	9.32**	9.89	2.99**	3.42
GPA of 3.5 or higher	11.52**	11.47***	3.77**	3.43**
GPA of 3.5 or lower	9.47**	8.17***	3.03**	2.74**
Low incidence of being discriminated against	11.50**	NA	3.94**	NA
High incidence of being discriminated against	9.32**	NA	2.99**	NA

**$p < .01$; ***$p < .001$; NA = not available.

results for academic achievement (F (1, 138) = 7.68, $p < .01$), being picked on or bullied (F (1, 138) = 7.84, $p < .01$), and experiencing discrimination (F (1, 137) = 7.45, $p < .01$).

The results for the specific component of parental involvement indicated that the college group demonstrated statistically significant effects for all three variables, although the extent of the effects sometimes did not reach a level of statistical significance as for the combined measure of parental involvement for academic achievement. Effects were found for the specific component of parental involvement (F (1, 138) = 7.77, $p < .01$), for being picked on or bullied (F (1, 138) = 7.50, $p < .01$), and for experiencing discrimination (F (1, 138) = 8.07, $p < .01$). When race, gender, and family income were controlled for the following results materialized for academic achievement (F (1, 138) = 7.64, $p < .01$), being picked on or bullied (F (1, 138) = 7.54, $p < .01$), and experiencing discrimination (F (1, 137) = 8.00, $p < .01$).

The findings for the examination of 7th to 12th grade students indicated similar results to the college group for scholastic outcomes but a different pattern for being picked on or bullied. For the combined measure of parental involvement statistically significant results emerged for academic achievement (F (1, 101) = 8.49, $p < .01$) both for when race, gender, and family income were controlled for and when they were not. But this variable did not yield statistically significant results for being picked on or bullied. Similarly, for the specific parental involvement variable a statistically significant result emerged for academic achievement (F (1, 101) = 7.85, $p < .01$) both for when race, gender, and family income were controlled for and when they were not. However, a statistically significant result but did not arise for being picked on or bullied.

Table 2 shows the results for the other two components of parental involvement, parent expectations and parent–child communications, with similar patterns to the results listed in Table 1. For the college sample the parental expectations variable yielded statistically significant results for academic achievement (F (1, 138) = 7.61, $p < .01$), being picked on (F (1, 137) = 7.48, $p < .01$), and being discriminated against (F (1, 138) = 7.83, $p < .01$). When race, gender, and family income were controlled for, the results were different for academic achievement (F (1, 138) = 7.45, $p < .01$), for being picked on or bullied (F (1, 138) = 7.58, $p < .01$), and for being discriminated against (F (1, 137) = 7.55, $p < .01$). Parent–child communication was not

TABLE 2. Effects of Two Components of Parental Involvement: Parental Expectations and Parent–child Communication (Combined and Specific Parental Involvement Variable)

	Parental Expectations Measure for College Sample (N = 138)	Parental Expectations Measure for School Sample (N = 102)	Parent–Child Communication Measure for College Sample (N = 138)	Parent–Child Communication Measure for School Sample (N = 102)
Never been picked on	4.05**	3.52	3.72*	3.42
Remainder of sample	3.16**	3.38	3.29*	3.52
GPA of 3.5 or higher	3.84**	3.15	3.51	3.38**
GPA of 3.5 or lower	3.15**	3.32	3.35	2.78**
Low incidence of being discriminated against	4.00**	NA	3.71*	NA
High incidence of being discriminated against	3.27**	NA	3.34*	NA

$^*p < .05; ^{**}p < .01; ^{***}p < .001$; NA = not available.

quite as strongly associated with the dependent variables as were the other independent variables. Nevertheless, statistically significant results arose for being picked on or bullied ($F (1, 137) = 5.09$, $p < .05$) and for being discriminated against ($F (1, 137) = 4.82$, $p < .05$). When race, gender, and family income were controlled for the results were different for being picked on or bullied ($F (1, 137) = 4.90$, $p < .05$) and for being discriminated against, being picked on or bullied ($F (1, 137) = 4.87, p < .01$).

The results for the 7th to 12th grade parental expectations did not yield statistically significant results for academic achievement or for being picked on or bullied. As in the case of the college sample, the levels of statistical significance were somewhat less dynamic for parent child communication. Effects were found for when race, gender, and family income were controlled for ($F (1, 136) = 5.88$, $p < .05$) and when they were not ($F (1, 136) = 5.93, p < .05$). The results were statistically insignificant for being picked on or bullied. Further analyses also indicated no statistically significant differences between

TABLE 3. Results of Secondary Analyses by Family Structure and Race: Differences in College Sample According to Family Structure, Race, and Using Logistic Regression Analysis (N = 138)

	Average Grade Point Average	Extent Picked on or Bullied as a Child	Total Reported Discrimination From All Sources Combined	Intense Discrimination (i.e., being physically attacked by a person from another race)
By family structure				
Child from intact family	3.51**	1.35*	11.42*	1.15
Child from nonintact family	2.88**	1.87*	12.86*	1.20
By race				
White	3.63**,a	1.51a	11.77*,a	1.42*,a
Asian-American	3.57*,a	1.57a	12.20a	1.46*,a
African-American	2.87**,a	1.92a	16.09*,a	0.50a
Latino	3.05*,a	1.98*,a	12.87a	0.72a

aStatistical significance determined on this basis of mean number for this race when compared with all other races combined.
*p < .05; **p < .01.

children with parents who were highly involved or had high expectations versus those who did not in terms of the likelihood that they were mugged.

Secondary analyses of the college sample also indicated that students from intact families obtained higher grades and were less likely to be bullied or discriminated against than those youth who lived in nonintact families (Table 3). In addition, African-Americans were the most likely to report that they had been discriminated against on all measures combined. However, Whites and Asian-Americans were the most likely to report the most intense discrimination measured, being physically beaten by a person of another race.

Additional secondary analysis indicated that students of all races were more likely to identify discrimination as coming from strangers than from people who were neighbors or who were otherwise familiar with the student. The most and least likely reasons for which students were bullied included (1) being perceived as too nice to fight back,

(2) being overweight, (3) being unpopular with the availability of few friends to help, (4) racial issues, and (5) being a nerd. The least likely reason for being bullied was being gay.

DISCUSSION

The results affirm the relationship between parental involvement and academic achievement, but more importantly for the purpose of this study they suggest that parental involvement is related to the two other student experiences, namely being picked on or bullied and being discriminated against. In this study the association between parental involvement and school outcomes was more ostensible than that between parental involvement and the two more sociologically based outcomes just mentioned. For the college sample the relationship between the combined measure of parental involvement and being picked on or bullied and being discriminated against was patent and consistent. In the case of 7th to 12th grade students their experience of discrimination was not examined for reasons previously addressed in the Methods section. However, the experience of being picked on or bullied was addressed. Unlike the findings that emerged for the college sample, no statistically significant result emerged for the combined parental involvement variable and being picked on or bullied.

The pattern of the results raises the possibility that parental involvement may have more of an influence on scholastic outcomes than it does on the experience of being picked on or bullied or being discriminated against. However, beyond this the question emerges as to why strong statistically significant effects emerged for the college sample for this variable but did not materialize for the secondary school sample. One possibility is that the secondary school sample is more reliable because the memory of those new to college has faded, and they either no longer remember the degree to which their parents were involved in their schooling or they do not recall to the degree to which other children bullied them. On the other hand, one can argue that the college sample is more reliable. After all, one can posit that college students on average have a more mature and accurate perspective than do secondary school students. For example, adolescents can become blind to the multifarious ways that their parents sacrifice for them and become involved in their lives.

What makes this issue difficult to resolve is that both perspectives appear somewhat intuitive. It may well be that the college sample is somewhat more reliable because they likely possess a more mature perspective. Moreover, given that this sample consists overwhelmingly of young adults, it is unlikely that the college sample's memory of youthful experiences faded to a considerable degree.

Although it seems reasonable to conclude that the responses of the college sample are more reliable than those of the secondary school sample, one cannot definitively reach this conclusion. Therefore social scientists need to conduct further research to determine the extent to which concurrent ratings of parental involvement and school experiences by secondary school students or ratings of recent parental involvement by young adults (i.e., college students) are more accurate. Nevertheless, whatever findings emerge from this recommended research, it is likely that the association between parental involvement and academic outcomes is more powerful.

This study supports the notion that parental involvement and parental expectations are associated with positive outcomes, beyond the realm of academic achievement. Specially, college students who reported that their parents were highly involved in their education indicated that, on average, they were less likely to be discriminated against and they were less likely to be picked on when they were children. In addition, these college students also reported that when their parents had high expectations of them, on average, they were less likely to be discriminated against and they were less likely to be picked on when they were children. This trend held not only for the overall measure of discrimination, but for the different components of discrimination as well.

The findings of this study are very important because they support the notion that parental involvement likely has an impact on more than just educational components of children's experiences. If family scientists, sociologists, educators, and psychologists are aware of these facts, they can instruct parents accordingly. Equally important is the fact that this study reinforces the validity of the call for broader parental involvement research by the researchers of the American Educational Research Association symposium sponsored by the Harvard Family Research Project in 2005. The results of this study suggest that simply examining the influence of parental involvement on academic achievement is too narrow an approach. It could well be that, consistent with the beliefs of Americans dating back to the

Puritans, parental support influences virtually every dimension of a child's life and that the present research agenda in the social sciences should reflect this fact.

Future research should build on the findings of this study and seek to examine the full gamut of potential effects that increased parental involvement might have. If the researchers who presented at the Harvard University symposium are correct, social scientists have thus far only scratched the surface in their cognizance of the wide-ranging impact of parental engagement. Therefore there is a patent need for academics and practitioners to place themselves in a position in which they can divulge more about the influence parental involvement. Additional studies should also be undertaken to investigate the pattern of results regarding parental involvement differing for secondary and postsecondary students. Studies such as those described will both enhance and broaden the body of knowledge regarding parental engagement in the lives of youth.

REFERENCES

Afifi, T. D., & Olson, L. (2005). The chilling effect in families and the pressure to conceal secrets. *Communication Monographs, 72,* 192–216.

Chamberlin, J. G. (1961). *Parents and religion: A preface to Christian education.* Philadelphia: Westminster Press.

Coleman, J., Hoffer, T., & Kilgore, S. (1982). *High school achievement: Public, catholic, and private schools compared.* New York: Basic Books.

Englund, M. M., Luckner, A. E., Whaley, G. J. L., & Egeland, B. (2004). Children's achievement in early elementary school: Longitudinal effects of parental involvement, expectations, and quality of assessment. *Journal of Educational Psychology, 96,* 723–730.

Epstein, J. (2001). *School, family, and community partnerships.* Boulder, CO: Westview Press.

Epstein, J. L., & Sanders, M. G. (2006). Prospects for change: Preparing educators for school, family, and community partnerships. *Peabody Journal of Education, 81,* 1–120.

Gangel, K. O., & Benson, W. S. (1983). *Christian education: Its history and philosophy.* Chicago: Moody.

Gibbons, F. X., Gerrard, M., Cleveland, M. J., Wills, T. A., & Brody, G. (2004). Perceived discrimination and substance abuse. *Journal of Personality and Social Psychology, 86,* 517–529.

Green, C. L., & Hoover-Dempsey, K. V. (2007). Why do parents homeschool? *Education & Urban Society, 39,* 264–285.

Griffith, J. (1996). Relation of parental involvement, empowerment, and school traits to student academic performance. *Journal of Educational Research, 90,* 33–41.

Griffith, J. (1997). Linkages to school structure and socio-environmental characteristics to parental satisfaction with public education and student achievement. *Journal of Applied Social Psychology, 27,* 156–186.

Hampton, F. M., Mumford, D. A., & Bond, L. (1998). Parental involvement in inner city schools: The project FAST extended family approach to success. *Urban Education, 33,* 410–427.

Hara, S. R. (1998). Parent involvement: The key to improved student achievement. *School Community Journal, 8,* 9–19.

Hoffer, T., Greeley, A. M., & Coleman, J. S. (1987). Catholic high school effects on achievement growth. In E. H. Haertel, T. James, & H. Levin (Eds.), *Comparing public and private schools* (pp. 67–88). New York: Falmer Press.

Hoover-Dempsey, K. V., & Sandler, H. M. (1997). Why do parents become involved in their children's education? *Review of Educational Research, 67,* 3–42.

Hoover-Dempsey, K. V., Walker, J. M., & Jones, K. P. (2002). Teachers involving parents (TIP): Results from an in-service teacher education program for enhancing parental involvement. *Teacher and Teacher Education, 18,* 843–867.

Jeynes, W. (2002). *Divorce, family structure, and the academic success of children.* Binghamton, NY: Haworth Press.

Jeynes, W. (2003). A meta-analysis: The effects of parental involvement on minority children's academic achievement. *Education & Urban Society, 35,* 202–218.

Jeynes, W. (2005). A Meta-analysis of the relation of parental involvement to urban elementary school student academic achievement. *Urban Education, 40,* 237–269.

Jeynes, W. (2007). The relationship between parental involvement and urban secondary school student academic achievement: A meta-analysis. *Urban Education, 42,* 82–110.

Marcon, R. A. (1999, March). Impact of parental involvement on children's development and academic performance: A three cohort study. Paper presented at the meeting of the Southeastern Psychological Association in Savannah, Georgia.

Peressini, D. D. (1998). The portrayal of parents in the school mathematics reform literature: Locating the context for parental involvement. *Journal for Research in Mathematics Education, 29,* 555–582.

Redding, S. (2005). Rallying the troops. *School Community Journal, 15,* 7–14.

Sanders, M. G., & Epstein, J. L. (2000). The National Network of Partnership Schools. *Education for Students Placed at Risk, 5,* 61.

Schafer, J. A., Carter, D. L., & Katz-Bannister, A. (2004). Studying traffic stop encounters. *Journal of Criminal Justice, 32,* 169–170.

Spera, C. (2005). A review of the relationship between parental involvement and student motivation. *Educational Psychology Review, 17,* 125–146.

Wallace, T., & Walberg, H. (1993). Parent programs for learning: A research synthesis. In F. Smit, W. van Esch, & H. Walberg (Eds.), *Parental involvement in education* (pp. 151–155). Nimegen, The Netherlands: ITS.

Zellman, G. L., & Waterman, J. M. (1998). Understanding the impact of parent school. involvement on children's educational outcomes. *Journal of Educational Research, 91*, 146–156.

Zhan, M. (2006). Assets, parental expectations and involvement, and children's educational performance. *Children & Youth Services Review, 28*, 961–975.

How Parents and Teachers View Their School Communities

Sam Redding

ABSTRACT. This study examines the perceptions of more than 11,000 parents and 1,500 teachers about their schools, themselves, and their relationships with each other within their school communities. It provides insights into the health of our public schools, their reservoirs of social capital, and the context they provide for student learning. The nature and strength of relationships within school communities is assayed through examination of parents' and teachers' perceptions about their roles, the roles of students, school–home communication, the common experience and climate of the school, and their face-to-face association with one another. Teachers' perceptions are compared with those of parents, and the perceptions of White, non-Hispanic, Black, non-Hispanic, and Hispanic parents are compared with each other.

Sam Redding, EdD, is Executive Director of the Academic Development Institute, Lincoln, IL.

INTRODUCTION

Families, Schools, and School Communities

Schools' curricula, instructional practices, organizational configurations, and operational procedures are closely scrutinized, analyzed, and explicated these days. The same can be said for families—their socioeconomic status, ethnicities, language preferences, structures, and habits. Holding side-by-side these two channels of inquiry—our probes of schools and our investigations of families—we hope to better understand the contextual contributors to a child's learning. To some extent, this dualistic approach has borne fruit, and we make incremental gains in understanding the component parts of these systems, both families and schools.

A shortcoming in our method of analysis, studying families and schools separately, is that we overlook a third line of inquiry that could prove fecund in bolstering the capacities of both families and schools to advance children's learning. That third line of inquiry begins by lumping the people who inhabit families and schools—parents, children, teachers, staff, volunteers—into one vital stew and then examining the relationships among them. This approach views the school as a community unto itself, one in which families are not external to the school but a core constituency. The relationships between parents and their children and the connections between parents and teachers are important, but so also are the interactions among various families, among various teachers, between students and students, and between students and teachers.

What is the nature of relationships between parents and teachers today? Between parents and other parents? Teachers and other teachers? How do parents and teachers view their roles within their school communities? What do parents and teachers think of their schools, themselves, and of each other? In some ways, these questions are reminiscent of those that should have been asked following the Coleman report (1966) and the scholarly work it spawned, including the effective schools research that challenged its conclusions. Instead, research has primarily focused on schools (their practices and climates) and families (their status and makeup) separately and not specifically in their relationship to one another.

Although Congress wanted The Equality of Educational Opportunity Study (Coleman, 1966) to provide a formula for investing in high-leverage school resources that would boost the educational attainment of poor and minority students, the study's investigators, after examining data from 4,000 schools and 600,000 students, reported that resources were less predictive of school success than family background and the socioeconomic mix of the school's student population. Later studies confirmed these conclusions but also pointed to school practices as something apart from school resources. James Coleman himself, in comparative studies of parochial schools and public schools (see Coleman & Hoffer, 1987), asserted that what the school *does* matters and that a school culture could provide an escalator to success that ameliorated the negative weight of the contextual community. To do so, however, the school culture must incorporate the families of its students into a community of its own, a community with high expectations, mutually accepted responsibilities and obligations, and a central regard for the dignity and promise of the individual child. In other words, the context of family and community are critical to a child's school learning, but the school is not impotent in affecting the beliefs and behaviors of adults outside the school who influence the child's learning and development. In fact, the school and the families it serves can define their own community, with its sense of purpose, patterns of relationship, and expectations of all its members according to their roles.

Families, Schools, and Student Learning

Learning standards provide one metric for a school community's expectations and its progress in fulfilling its purpose. In meeting those expectations, both the family and the school have a role, and the practices of each matter, as does the relationship between the two. A 1993 meta-analysis of the factors that affect performance (Wang, Haertel, & Walberg, 1993) ordered the magnitude of effect of each of 28 factors. The most powerful factor, the study concluded, was the teacher's classroom management, followed by the student's own meta-cognitive and cognitive abilities, followed closely by the student's home environment. The teacher, the student, the parents—this remains the magic triangle of relationships and competencies that determine the student's trajectory to school success. Standards give us an answer to the question of what is to be taught and learned.

Where the education-relevant resources, background, knowledge, skills, and time of a family are limited, as in many high-poverty communities, children are placed at a disadvantage, and the school community's ability to build and supplement these influences is all the more critical (Jeynes, 2002; Weiss et al., 2003).

Henderson and Mapp (2002) draw convincing conclusions about schools where parental involvement is measurably high, in specific programs that demonstrate effects on learning outcomes, and in schools that exhibit high levels of achievement. In these schools' relationships with parents, there exists a foundation of trust and respect, a connection between parent-engagement strategies and learning objectives, and an ability to reach out to engage parents beyond the school. These conclusions echo those of Swap (1993), who found that effective parent engagement must be comprehensive in nature, with the school consistently interfacing with parents at many points, in many venues, over the course of the school years.

Jeynes (2005) further substantiated the importance of comprehensive parental involvement practices that reflect a school culture that includes parents in systematic ways rather than through activity-based parental involvement strategies that make isolated overtures to parents. In a meta-analysis of studies of parental involvement programs, Jeynes found significant effect sizes (around three-quarters of a standard deviation) in relation to elementary school student academic achievement. He concluded (p. 262) that "it was not particular actions such as attending school functions, establishing household rules, and checking student homework that yielded the statistically significant effect sizes. Rather, variables that reflected a general atmosphere of involvement produced the strongest results." Studies of the relationship between such routine parent involvement activities as checking homework and attending school events fail to yield significance in their association with student achievement, perhaps because they are such universally practiced parental activities that they fail to distinguish among parents or schools. This conclusion does not diminish the importance of routine parent practices but accentuates the necessity of a pervasive ethos within a school community that evokes an expectation of school success, an expectation that is communicated to students by teachers and parents in a manner that is genuine and constant, and relationships among the constituents of a school community that nurtures their understanding of their roles and of each other.

Families and Schools as Partners

"Partnership" is the term in common coinage that describes intentional school actions that strengthen the cooperative ties between parents and school personnel on behalf of students. The notion of family–school partnerships takes us half-way to a consideration of the relational qualities that might characterize a school community, but its image is one of two hands reaching out to clasp from separate bodies. The family is critical to a child's cognitive, social, and emotional development, and for school-age children, so is the school. Therefore the links between the home and school are important to the child's healthy development (Bronfenbrenner, 1979; Epstein, 2001; Reynolds, Temple, Robertson, & Mann, 2001). A constructive school–family partnership is multidimensional and "differs from the fragmented offering of isolated parent involvement activities in that it reflects a relationship between home and school rather than occasional interface of the two institutions" (Patrikakou, Weissberg, Redding, & Walberg, 2005, p. 3). The belief system (values, expectations, aspirations) of a family has significant effect on children's academic performance (Fan & Chen, 1999; Hoover-Dempsey & Sandler, 1995), and a family's belief system can be influenced by the prevailing values of the school community to which the family belongs.

Purpose in the School Community

Academic learning is the central purpose of a school, but it is artificial to separate academic learning from social and emotional learning. Not surprisingly, positive behavior at school correlates with positive learning outcomes (Haynes, Ben-Avie, & Ensign, 2003). Social and emotional learning go hand in hand with academic learning (Zins Weissberg, Wang, & Walberg, 2004). Parents, as much as teachers, place a high value on children's character development (respect and responsibility), sense of personal worth, and social competence. In a healthy school community, responsibility for social and emotional learning is shared by the school and the home. That being the case, whether chosen or assigned, the school must function as a community and attend to the connections and desires of its constituents.

METHODS

The school's efficacy resting, in part, on the quality of relationships among its constituents, educators will benefit from a clearer understanding of how parents and teachers view their connection to their school and to each other. This study examines parents' and teachers' perceptions about their school community, particularly in regards to the school community's purpose: academic, social, and emotional learning. A school community is defined as the collection of people intimately attached to a school—students and their families, teachers and other school personnel, volunteers—who, through their communication and association with one another, articulate common understandings of their school's purpose and arrive at expectations placed on and obligations assumed by members according to their roles. The central questions asked in this study are as follows:

1. What aspects of school community do parents and teachers view as generally strong?
2. What aspects of school community do parents and teachers view as generally weak?
3. In what aspects of school community do parents and teachers have divergent opinions?
4. To what extent do parents' perceptions of school community vary among White, Black, and Hispanic parents?
5. How do parents' and teachers' perceptions about their school communities point to promising paths for improving schools and better educating children?

Subjects

The School Community Survey was administered between 2003 and 2006 in 63 elementary and middle schools in five states. Forty schools were in urban settings and 23 schools in rural areas or small towns. The surveys were completed by 1,571 teachers and 12,364 parents in the schools. Respondents represented 87.2% of all teachers in the schools and the parents of 58.9% of all students enrolled in the schools. The mean poverty rate (percent of students receiving free or reduced lunch) in the schools was 64.2%. Of the parents completing the survey, 83% were females and 17% were males. The parent

TABLE 1. Schools Participating in the Study

State	Number of Schools	Total Enrollment	Total Faculty	Mean Poverty (%)
Illinois	44	18,142	1,091	69.1
Pennsylvania	7	4,160	326	44.6
Delaware	7	4,090	203	54.9
Virginia	3	1,400	111	71.1
Wisconsin	2	565	69	47.4
Total	63	28,357	1,800	64.2

respondents were 44% White, non-Hispanic; 30% Hispanic; 24% Black, non-Hispanic; 1% Asian; and 1% American Indian/Aleutian Islands. Of the parent respondents, 61% were married, 21% had never been married, 11% were divorced, 6% were separated, and 1% was widowed. The children reported on by the parents were 51% female and 49% male. The analysis provided here includes the 11,502 parents who indicated their ethnicity as White, non-Hispanic, Black, non-Hispanic, or Hispanic to examine similarities and differences in the perceptions of the three largest ethnic groups in these schools. Table 1 provides a demographic summary of the participating schools.

In 41 of the 63 schools (65%), the student enrollment of one of the three ethnic groups included in this study constituted 70% or more of the student body. In 18 schools (29%), White students made up 70% or more of the student body; in 10 schools (16%), Hispanic students made up 70% or more of the student body; and in 13 schools (21%), Black students made up 70% or more of the student body. In the remaining 22 schools (35%), no single ethnic group constituted 70% or more of the student enrollment.

It is important to reiterate that the parents in this study each responded to survey questions about their child's school, and the teachers each responded to survey questions about the school in which they taught. There were 63 schools in the study. Differences in respondent perceptions, then, reflect both the individual experiences of the respondents and the nature of the particular school about which they are recording their impressions.

The Instrument

The School Community Survey consists of a Perceptions Section completed by teachers and parents, a Parent Involvement Section completed only by parents, and a Curriculum of the Home Section completed only by parents. This study includes data only from the Perceptions Section. On the Perceptions Section of the School Community Survey, parents and teachers respond to 65 Likert-scale items. Fifty-nine of the items are identical for both parents and teachers. Six items are parallel but specific to the role of either parents or teachers. For example, an item for parents is "Parents are included in making important decisions in this school." The parallel item for teachers is "Teachers are included in making important decisions in this school."

The Likert scale includes five points: 1 = uncertain, 2 = strongly disagree, 3 = disagree, 4 = agree, and 5 = strongly agree. The responses are recoded to produce two categories: uncertain/strongly disagree/disagree and agree/strongly agree. The first category is scored as 0 and the second category as 1. The items are constructed to all have positive valence for a measure of school community. Agreement with the item, therefore, is considered a positive indication of the strength of the school community.

The Perceptions Section of the survey was completed by both parents and teachers, and the results of the survey were reported as a whole for parents and for teachers. Categories and scales within the Perceptions Section include aspects of the school community's purpose (academic development, studying/homework, reading, and character development) and elements of relationships among its constituents (role of parent/teacher, role of student, school-home communication, common experience/school climate, and association of school community members).

In the study the surveys were completed anonymously. Principals were asked to see that 90% of teachers completed the survey and that the parents of at least 40% of the students completed the survey. Parent surveys were typically sent home with the student, completed by the parent, and returned to the teacher. The School Community Survey was provided to parents in both English and Spanish versions.

On the Perceptions Section, parents and teachers were asked to respond to statements about the school or school community in general, not necessarily about their particular experience. For example, an item asked if in this school "parents feel welcome when they visit." The question dis not ask if the respondent feels welcome when he or she visits, although it is likely the respondent generalizes from his or her own experience. The items are worded to capture the respondent's general perceptions about the school community rather than confining them to experiences particular to themselves.

Validity

Face and content validity for the instrument and its scales were verified by a panel of experts including an educator, educational psychologist, social psychologist, and sociologist. All four experts held a doctorate in their field. The panel was asked to assess the relationship of the survey items and categories to the operational definition of a school community as "the collection of people intimately attached to a school—students and their families, teachers and other school personnel, volunteers—who, through their communication and association with one another, articulate common understandings of their school's purpose, and arrive at expectations placed on and obligations assumed by members according to their roles." The panel members independently reviewed the instrument and recorded their observations about validity of both individual items and the scale categories to which they were assigned. The panel then met for discussion, suggested revision, and arrived at consensus regarding the face and content validity of the final instrument, its items, and its categories.

Reliability

Internal reliability was checked for the respondents in this study using Cronbach's alpha. The alpha coefficient for the total Teacher Perceptions scale (65 items) was .9263; for the total Parent Perceptions scale the coefficient was .9214. Coefficients for the categorical scales ranged between .6392 and .7955 on the Teacher Perceptions, with the exception of the Reading subscale with a marginal reliability coefficient of .5443. The subscale coefficients on the Parent Perceptions ranged between .6909 and .8218.

RESULTS

Looking for commonly perceived strengths in school communities, a pattern emerges from the survey data in what both parents and teachers rate highly about their schools: the centrality of academic purpose and high expectations for students. Students are expected to complete homework on time (parents, 95%; teachers, 93%), teachers regularly assign homework (parents, 89%; teachers, 89%), and parents are expected to see that it is completed (parents, 94%; teachers, 81%). Students are expected to do their best work (parents, 91%; teachers, 95%). The importance of reading is stressed (parents, 89%; teachers, 94%), and teachers encourage children to read for pleasure (parents, 82%; teachers, 89%). Students are taught to behave respectfully and responsibly (parents, 88%; teachers, 84%), they are treated with respect (parents, 79%; teachers, 91%), they are expected to behave properly (parents, 95%; teachers, 91%), and their teachers are models of respectful and responsible behavior (parents, 81%; teachers, 91%). Teachers communicate with parents, by notes and e-mail (parents, 81%; teachers, 92%), and teachers listen and help when parents have a concern about a child (parents, 84%; teachers, 94%). To all of this, parents and teachers overwhelmingly agree (Table 2).

Even though academic purpose and high expectations for students rate high in parents' and teachers' estimation of their school communities, both groups reveal an uncertainty that students are well-prepared for the challenges that lie ahead of them (parents, 59%; teachers, 58%). Doubts about students' preparation for future academic challenges may stem from teachers' and parents' weak affirmation that the school's high expectations are accompanied by consistent teaching practices related to independent study. Although 88% of parents and 74% of teachers say that homework is important in their school, only 59% of parents and 55% of teachers believe students are taught how to study, and only 61% of parents and 43% of teachers agree that teachers' homework practices are fairly consistent. Similarly, although parents and teachers assert that students are taught to behave respectfully and responsibly (parents, 88%; teachers, 84%) and that they are treated with respect (parents, 79%; teachers, 91%), they are not confident that students generally treat each other with respect (parents, 60%; teachers, 53%) (Table 3).

Teachers and parents reveal weakness in the interrelationships among members of their school communities. Teachers do not visit the homes of students according to 82% of parents and 88% of teachers. Parents do not know most of the other parents in their children's classes in the opinion of 60% of parents and 69% of teachers. Students are not routinely used to tutor other students in the view of 48% of parents and 53% of teachers, and adult volunteers

TABLE 2. Items Teachers and Parents Rated Highest (Mean of Parents and Teachers 85% or Above)

Survey Item (N = 11,502 Parents and 1,571 Teachers)	Percent Parents Agree or Strongly Agree	Percent Teachers Agree or Strongly Agree	Mean of Parents and Teachers Percent Agree or Strongly Agree
In this school:			
Students are expected to complete their homework on time	95	93	94
Students are expected to behave properly	95	91	93
Students are encouraged to do their best work	91	95	93
The importance of reading is stressed	89	94	92
Teachers regularly assign homework	89	89	89
If a parent has a concern about a child, the teacher will listen and help	84	94	89
Parents are expected to see that their children complete their homework	94	81	88
Teachers communicate with parents by e-mail or written notes	81	92	87
Students are taught to behave respectfully and responsibly	88	84	86
Most teachers are models of respectful and responsible behavior	81	91	86
Teachers encourage children to read for pleasure	82	89	86
Students are treated with respect	79	91	85

are not routinely used to help students learn according to 42% of parents and 55% of teachers. Forty-nine percent of teachers do not believe teachers are included in making important decisions at the school, and 45% of parents report that parents are not included in making important decisions at the school.

About some items, teachers and parents disagreed sharply (Table 4). Teachers' perception of parents is much more negative than parents' perception of themselves, as shown in the responses to the following items:

- Parents are models of respectful and responsible behavior (parents, 66%; teachers, 41%),
- Parents encourage their children to read for pleasure (parents, 79%; teachers, 26%),

TABLE 3. Items Teachers and Parents Rated Lowest (Mean of Parents and Teachers 60% or Lower)

Survey Item (N = 11,502 Parents and 1,571 Teachers)	Percent Parents Agree or Strongly Agree	Percent Teachers Agree or Strongly Agree	Mean of Parents and Teachers Percent Agree or Strongly Agree
In this school:			
Students who graduate from this school are well prepared for the challenges that lie ahead of them	59	58	59
Students are taught how to study	59	55	57
Students generally treat each other with respect	60	53	57
Parents let teachers know when their children have benefited from their teaching	69	42	56
Most parents are models of respectful and responsible behavior	66	41	54
Parents/teachers are included in making important decisions at the school	55	51	53
Parents encourage their children to read for pleasure	79	26	53
Homework practices are fairly consistent from teacher to teacher	61	43	52
Adult volunteers are routinely used in the school to help students learn	58	45	52
Students are routinely used to tutor other students	52	47	50
Most parents know most of the other parents in their children's classes	40	31	36
Teachers visit the homes of students	18	12	15

- Parents let teachers know when their children have benefited from their teaching (parents, 69%; teachers, 42%),
- Parents listen and help when the teacher has a concern about their child (parents, 86%; teachers, 52%),
- Parents contact teachers to discuss their children's progress (parents, 77%; teachers, 51%).

Whereas neither parents nor teachers believe they are included in making important decisions at the school, parents are far more likely than teachers to say that their opinions really count at the school

TABLE 4. Items on Which the Difference Between Parents and Teachers Was 15 Percentage Points or More

Survey Item	Parents (N = 11,502) Percent Agree or Strongly Agree	Teachers (N = 1,571) Percent Agree or Strongly Agree	Difference
In this school:			
Parents encourage their children to read for pleasure	79	26	53
If a teacher has a concern about a student, the parents will listen and help	86	52	34
Teachers talk with parents on the telephone	67	94	27
Parents let teachers know when their children have benefited from their teaching	69	42	27
Parents contact teachers to discuss their children's academic progress	77	51	26
Most parents are models of respectful and responsible behavior	66	41	25
Teachers are generally supportive of each other	68	87	19
The opinions of parents/teachers really count	78	60	18
Homework practices are fairly consistent from teacher to teacher	61	43	18
Parents/teachers have ample opportunity to voice their opinion	77	60	17
The building is kept clean	88	73	15
The school building is in good repair and is well maintained	81	66	15
Students are encouraged to help one another learn	72	87	15

(parents, 78%; teachers, 60%) and that they have ample opportunity to voice their opinions (parents, 77%; teachers, 60%). Parents also are more likely than teachers to describe their schools as clean (parents, 88%; teachers, 73%) and well-maintained (parents, 81%; teachers, 66%). Likewise, 85% of parents say that parents feel welcome at the school, but only 74% of teachers agree.

Considering that in 65% of the schools in the study the student body included one ethnic group (White, non-Hispanic; Black, non-Hispanic; or Hispanic) that accounted for 70% or more of its

TABLE 5. Items on Which the Difference Between White and Black Parents Was 10 Percentage Points or More

Survey Item	White	Black	Difference
In this school:			
Teachers visit the homes of students	12	24	12
A wide range of activities is offered for students	68	57	11
Most parents are models of respectful and responsible behavior	61	71	10
Teachers seem to enjoy teaching at the school	81	71	10

students, we know that comparing the perceptions of parents of different ethnic groups means that, to a large extent, we are also comparing different sets of schools. Despite this de facto segregation of ethnic groups, due primarily to neighborhood residential patterns in elementary schools, the differences in parent perceptions between the groups was not dramatic.

White, non-Hispanic and Black, non-Hispanic parents differed markedly on very few items. On only four items was the difference 10 percentage points or more, and the greatest was 12 percentage points (Tables 5 and 6). goehBlack parents were twice as likely as White parents to report that teachers visit the homes of students, even though the percentage was low for both groups (12% for White parents and 24% for Black parents). White parents more than Black parents believe their schools provide a wide range of activities for students (White, non-Hispanic, 68%; Black, non-Hispanic, 57%) and that teachers seem to enjoy teaching at their school (White, non-Hispanic, 81%; Black, non-Hispanic, 71%). On the other hand, Black parents (71%) more than White parents (61%) believe most parents are models of respectful and responsible behavior.

Hispanic parents responded differently than either White, non-Hispanic parents or Black, non-Hispanic parents by a margin of 10 or more percentage points on 17 of the 65 items. On all but one item the percentage of Hispanic parents agreeing with a positive statement about their school community was higher than that of White and Black parents. The single exception was the item, "Teachers talk with parents on the telephone" (Hispanic, 55%; Black, non-Hispanic, 74%; White, non-Hispanic, 72%), where language differences may account for the difference.

Hispanic parents were considerably more sanguine than either White or Black parents that students are taught how to study (Hispanic, 79%; White, non-Hispanic, 48%; Black, non-Hispanic,

TABLE 6. Items on Which the Difference Between White and Hispanic Parents Was 10 Percentage Points or More

Survey Item	White	Hispanic	Difference
In this school:			
Students are taught how to study	48	79	31
Teachers talk with parents on the telephone	72	55	17
All students are sufficiently challenged to learn the most they can	71	87	16
All students are helped to learn the most they can	70	85	15
Students have an opportunity to learn more about topics of interest to them	61	76	15
Teachers teach students how to read to master material	67	82	15
The school has a homework policy	62	76	14
Students are routinely used to tutor other students	46	59	13
Teachers contact parents to discuss their children's academic progress	72	85	13
Discipline at the school is consistent and fair	65	78	13
Teachers visit the homes of students	12	23	11
Programs are provided for parents to assist them with thoir role in their children's education	68	79	11
Parents are included in making important decisions at the school	50	60	10

54%), are sufficiently challenged to learn the most they can (Hispanic, 87%; White, non-Hispanic, 71%; Black, non-Hispanic, 71%), are helped to learn the most they can (Hispanic, 85%; White, non-Hispanic, 71%; Black, non-Hispanic, 75%), and have an opportunity to learn more about topics of interest to them (Hispanic, 76%; White, non-Hispanic, 61%; Black, non-Hispanic, 63%). Hispanic parents, more than White or Black parents, believe teachers teach students how to read to master material (Hispanic, 82%; White, non-Hispanic, 67%; Black, non-Hispanic, 68%), that the school has a homework policy (Hispanic, 76%; White, non-Hispanic, 62%; Black, non-Hispanic, 66%), and that discipline at the school is consistent and fair (Hispanic, 78%; White, non-Hispanic, 65%; Black, non-Hispanic, 64%).

More than White or Black parents, Hispanic parents say that teachers contact parents to discuss their children's progress (Hispanic, 85%; White, non-Hispanic, 72%; Black, non-Hispanic, 76%) and that programs are provided for parents to assist them with their role in their children's education (Hispanic, 79%; White, non-Hispanic, 68%; Black, non-Hispanic, 72%). Hispanic parents more than White parents or Black parents say that students are routinely used to tutor other students (Hispanic, 59%; White, non-Hispanic, 46%; Black, non-Hispanic, 53%) or that teachers visit the homes of students (Hispanic, 23%; White, non-Hispanic, 12%; Black, non-Hispanic, 24%). More than Black parents or White parents, Hispanic parents believe their school offers a wide range of activities for students (Hispanic, 73%; White, non-Hispanic, 68%; Black, non-Hispanic, 57%) and that all students are encouraged to participate in activities (Hispanic, 76%; White, non-Hispanic, 70%; Black, non-Hispanic, 66%). Also more than Black or White parents, Hispanic parents report that parents are happy their children are enrolled at the school (Hispanic, 84%; White, non-Hispanic, 76%; Black, non-Hispanic, 69%), that students are treated with respect (Hispanic, 83%; White, non-Hispanic, 80%; Black, non-Hispanic, 73%), and that students are proud to be at the school (82%; White, non-Hispanic, 80%; Black, non-Hispanic, 72%).

The health of school communities in this sample of schools gets mixed reviews if we judge through the lens of a few key items. White parents (81%) and Hispanic parents (80%) sense that teachers enjoy teaching at their schools, even though agreement with that impression is somewhat lower for Black parents (71%) and the teachers themselves (72%). Also, 84% of Hispanic parents and 76% of White parents believe parents are happy their children are enrolled at their school, whereas Black parents (69%) and teachers (63%) are less positive about this. How well do the constituents of these elementary and middle school communities know each other? Seventy-three percent of teachers say that the teachers in their school know each other well, but only 40% of parents and 31% of teachers believe that most parents know most of the other parents in their children's classes. Most parents know their children's teachers according to 79% of parents, but only 66% of teachers think so. Sixty-five percent of teachers and 70% of parents think most teachers know their students' parents.

CONCLUSION

Parent and teacher perceptions about their school communities show that schools may successfully impress upon their constituents a high expectation for academic achievement but are less adept in nurturing the social capital, civic participation, character development, and mutual respect that provide a context most conducive to learning. Further, teachers' low regard for parents' example and support for children's academic and social learning is problematic. This is not to say that teachers' perceptions about parents are at odds with reality, but they do not align with parents' own perceptions about themselves.

Given that only 40% of parents and 31% of teachers believe that most parents know most of the other parents in their children's classes in a sample of elementary and middle schools, which tend to be neighborhood-based, James Coleman (1988) might warn of an absence of intergenerational closure (parents knowing and interacting with their children's friends' parents), depressing social capital that is necessary to children's well-being and the vitality of a school community. Coleman argued that social capital, the social resources embedded in social relationships and networks, was an asset of particular value to children, and both its quantity and quality were important. Parents who know and interact with one another are able to negotiate and enforce social norms for their children, share child-rearing experiences, reciprocally assist each other by assuming obligations and expectations in looking out for each others children, and contribute more effectively to the quality of their children's schools.

The common school, in the vision of its 19th-century advocates, held the promise of unifying local communities around collective values for educating children. In the rhetoric of that time, civic participation and moral virtue were prominent goals of public education, forming the common values around which community was shaped. With only 55% of parents and 51% of teachers believing they are included in making important decisions at their school, civic participation in American public schools leaves room for considerable improvement. As for moral virtue, with only 41% of teachers (and an anemic 66% of parents themselves) agreeing that most parents are models of respectful and responsible behavior, another desired aspect of common schooling appears wanting. Teachers (84%) and parents (88%) are in general agreement that the schools teach students to behave respectfully and responsibly, but only 53% of teachers and 60% of parents observe that students generally treat each other with respect. In fact, only 63% of teachers and 74% of parents believe that students generally treat teachers with respect. Apparently, students are not exhibiting the behavioral expressions of the virtues the school is teaching.

Most revealing of all may be one single item: Parents encourage their children to read for pleasure. Seventy-nine percent of parents think so, but only 26% of teachers agree. In short, teachers give themselves high marks (91% say most teachers are models of respectful and responsible behavior and that they treat students with respect, 89% believe that teachers encourage children to read for pleasure, 94% assert that teachers listen and help when a parent has a concern about their child), but they are not so positive about the contribution parents make. Although 86% of teachers report that teachers let parents know good things their children have done, only 42% agree that parents let them know when their child has benefited from the teachers' teaching.

It is possible that teachers, in contact with many parents, are in a better position to make an accurate assessment about parents than are parents themselves, especially if these parents are not in touch with each other. But must it be this way? Can the school do a better job of bringing parents together to know each other, of impressing upon parents the importance of reading at home, of dealing head on with the assumption that children's perceived disrespect and irresponsibility is a consequence of too many homes where parents are not models of desired behavior themselves? Is it likely that in knowing more parents better, teachers' own perceptions might change?

The somewhat rosier picture Hispanic parents paint of their school communities than do White, non-Hispanic and Black, non-Hispanic parents comports with the findings of the Pew Hispanic Center and Kaiser Family Foundation (2004) in their interview survey of 1,508 Latinos, 1,193 White, non-Latinos, and 610 African-American, non-Latinos. The Pew/Kaiser survey concluded that "In general, Latinos, especially the foreign-born, are more positive about public schools and more optimistic that schools are improving than either whites or African-Americans. Latinos are also upbeat about their dealings with teachers and school administrators" (p. 3). Which outlook will prevail over time—that of the most recent members of American school communities or that of groups with longer histories with our schools?

The school communities in this study are seen by parents and teachers as strong in academic purpose, but both groups are anxious about their children's and students' preparation for the challenges that lie ahead of them. That anxiety provides a focal point for regeneration of school communities, a concern around which parents and teachers can engage to better articulate how they want children to be prepared and what roles they, parents and teachers, play in getting the job done. Meaningful engagement of parents and teachers in this conversation means that both groups must ultimately perceive that they are involved in making important decisions about their school. If these decisions are not theirs, then who makes them? If these decisions are not theirs, then what stake do they have in the improvement of their schools? Learning standards give us one metric for gauging a school's progress. This study illustrates that children's social and emotional learning are of equal concern to parents and teachers and deserve their own metric. With these yardsticks for success in place, parents and teachers can more directly and collectively guide the betterment of their schools and strengthen their school communities through this common pursuit.

REFERENCES

Bronfenbrenner, U. (1979). *The ecology of human development*. Cambridge, MA: Harvard University Press.

Coleman, J. S. (1966). *Equality of educational opportunity*. Washington, DC: U.S. Department of Health, Education, and Welfare.

Coleman, J. S. (1988). Social capital in the creation of human capital. *American Journal of Sociology, 94*, S95–S120.

Coleman, J. S., & Hoffer, T. (1987). *Public and private high schools: The impact of communities*. New York: Basic Books.

Epstein, J. L. (2001). *School, family, and community partnerships: Preparing educators and improving schools*. Boulder, CO: Westview.

Fan, X., & Chen, M. (1999). Parental involvement and students' academic achievement: A meta-analysis. *Educational Psychology Review, 13*, 1–22.

Haynes, N. M., Ben-Avie, M., & Ensign, J. (Eds.). (2003). *How social and emotional development add up: Getting results in math and science education*. New York: Teachers College Press.

Henderson, A. T., & Mapp, K. L. (2002). *A new wave of evidence: The impact of school, family, and community connections on student achievement*. Austin, TX: Southwest Educational Development Laboratory.

Hoover-Dempsey, K. V., & Sandler, H. M. (1995). Parental involvement in children's education: Why does it make a difference? *Teachers College Record, 97*, 310–331.

Jeynes, W. H. (2002). A meta-analysis: The effects of parental involvement on minority children's academic achievement. *Education and Urban Society, 35*, 202–219.

Jeynes, W. H. (2005). A meta-analysis of the relation of parental involvement to urban elementary school student academic achievement. *Urban Education, 40*, 237–269.

Patrikakou, E. N., Weissberg, R. P., Redding, S., & Walberg, H. J. (2005). *School-family partnerships for children's success*. New York: Teachers College Press.

Pew Hispanic Center/Kaiser Family Foundation. (2004). *National survey of Latinos: Education*. Summary and chartpack. Retrieved May 18, 2007 from www. pewhispanic.org

Reynolds, A. J., Temple, J. A., Robertson, D. L., & Mann, E. A. (2001). Long-term effects of an early childhood intervention on educational achievement and juvenile arrest: A 15-year follow-up of low-income children in public schools. *Journal of the American Medical Association, 285*, 2339–2346.

Swap, S. (1993). *Developing home-school partnerships: From concepts to practice*. New York: Teachers College Press, Columbia University.

Wang, M. C., Haertel, G. D., & Walberg, H. J. (1993). Toward a knowledge base for school learning. *Review of Educational Research, 63*, 249–295.

Weiss, H. B., Mayer, E., Kreider, H., Vaughan, M., Dearing, E., Hencke, R., & Pinto, K. (2003). Making it work: Low-income working mothers' involvement in their children's education. *American Educational Research Journal, 40*, 879–901.

Zins, J. E., Weissberg, R. P., Wang, M. C., & Walberg, H. J. (Eds.). (2004). *Building school success on social and emotional learning: What does the research say?* New York: Teachers College Press.

Altering the Curriculum of the Home: Learning Environments for Korean and U.S. Students

Susan J. Paik

ABSTRACT. The family and home environment are considered the most significant influences on children's development and learning. These factors directly influence student ability, motivation, and interest in learning. This study focuses on alterable factors in the home environment (i.e., homework time, attitudes, expectations, reading). A multiple-factor model provides a framework to discuss the family influences that appear to explain achievement differences. To gain perspective from international comparative studies, statistical findings highlight family practices in Korea and the United States. The implications from this article discuss altering the curriculum of the home, providing supportive family conditions, early intervention, and family–school collaborations. Altering constructive factors in the home environment in any culture may strongly influence children's learning and development.

Susan J. Paik is Associate Professor at the School of Educational Studies at Claremont Graduate University, Claremont, CA.

INTRODUCTION

Policymakers and educators have long been concerned with the achievement of U.S. students in light of international comparisons. In the well-known report, "A Nation at Risk," the National Commission for Excellence in Education (1983) first called public attention to U.S. students' low rankings on international achievement tests. Studies, such as the Second and Third International Math and Science Studies (e.g., SIMSS, TIMSS, TIMSS-Repeat, etc.) confirm that U.S. students continue to lag behind, while Korea ranked on top. Achievement has remained largely stagnant for the United States as East Asian students continue to perform well (U.S. Department of Education, 1996).

Studies show that the U.S. students are equally competitive in first grade but fall increasingly behind at each grade level to their East Asian counterparts and rank near the bottom in their high school years. By the fifth grade, the worst Asian class exceeded the best American class (Stevenson, Lee, & Stigler, 1986; Walberg, Harnisch, & Tsai, 1984). Researchers have sought to understand the academic disparity between the United States and East Asia in the middle and high school years. Although numerous factors exist, studies continue to emphasize the importance of early academic experiences attributing the success of Asian students to practices in the home and school.

The National Commission (1983) reported that the achievement of Japanese, Taiwanese, and more recently Korean students appears attributable not only to study time in school but to extraordinary effort outside of school. Consequently, the Commission brought forth several recommendations including the importance of parents as partners and the investment of study time. Among other reforms, they identified parents as children's first and most influential teachers, emphasizing the home as a central place to fostering development and learning. In an age of technology and globalization, learning and achievement were described as critical components to economic success for individuals and countries.

Over two decades have now passed since the 1983 report, and despite similar reforms from the National Goals in 2000 and the No Child Left Behind (NCLB) Act in 2001, achievement gaps still persist nationally and internationally. Among other reforms, national attention continues to emphasize the importance of parents and families in education. Given the importance of parental involvement, the National Goals 2000 encouraged family–school partnerships in every school, and NCLB in 2001 emphasized and defined parental involvement as a critical ingredient to school success.

Research has long shown the beneficial effects of parental involvement and the home environment within and outside of school. Parents, like teachers, structure their home environment and develop a "curriculum of the home." Researchers have found that what students bring to school largely accounts for the differences in learning (Coleman et al., 1966; Walberg, 1984). The curriculum of the home is considered more powerful than socioeconomic status, accounting for three times more learning variance. Students from economically disadvantaged backgrounds can excel given supportive conditions, daily practices, and concentrated efforts. Studies show that parental stimulation in the home environment is highly correlated with motivation and achievement (Iverson & Walberg, 1982; Walberg, 1984). The International Association for the Evaluation of Educational Achievement (IEA) also confirmed that home factors were strongly related to achievement in 45 countries (IEA, 1996). High educational expectations, learning materials, and other resources in the home facilitate children's learning (IEA, 1996; Paik, 2001; Peng & Wright, 1994; Schneider & Lee, 1990).

In light of international comparisons, U.S. policymakers and researchers have seldom investigated Korean home environments and achievement (IEA, 1996; Paik, 2001; Sorenson, 1994). Having achieved world status in such a short time, researchers have sought to explain the educational success in Korea. In addition to high standards and a longer school year, studies report that the curriculum of the home may contribute to the success of Korean students (Educational Testing Service, 1992). These alterable factors influence the learning environments of Korean students (e.g., homework behavior, time spent watching television). Researchers have found that Korean students study more in school and out of school than most countries (Barrett, 1990; Sorenson, 1994).

Parents differ vastly in how they monitor and invest their time in their children. Such differences in a home environment may go a long way in their schooling experiences. Through the school years, parents nominally control roughly 88% of the student's waking time in the first 18 years of life. Not only is this by far the largest fraction, but it strongly influences the productivity of the remaining 12% of time spent in school (Paik, 2001; Walberg, 1984). Extensive evidence for both Korea and the United States suggests that the efficiency of the home has positive effects in fostering learning. The first 6 years of life and the curriculum of the home are undoubtedly powerful, alterable influences on academic achievement (IEA, 1996; National Commission, 1983; Walberg, 1984).

This article discusses the importance of alterable factors in the home environment. The curriculum of the home is similar to a school curriculum, where quality and quantity do matter. Parents, like teachers, can monitor time, talk with their children, provide necessary feedback and guidance, and encourage a supportive learning environment. The article provides a comparative look at home environments in Korea and the United States to understand the impact of alterable factors. Alterable factors in this study are practices associated within the home that can be constructively changed, such as study time, homework, attitudes, exposure to cultural activities, and reading more. Although there is no simple formula to success, conducive learning environments and an investment in time and efforts would undoubtedly be helpful to any student (Walberg, 1984).

Theoretical Framework: Defining the Curriculum of the Home

Many studies have found that achievement and learning depend on multiple factors, such as student aptitude, classroom instruction, and family and school environments (Coleman, 1988; Ibe, 1994; Paik, 2001, 2004; Walberg, 1984). Walberg's nine-factor productivity model[1] provides a framework for understanding learning (Walberg, 1984) and, moreover, when comparing another culture or educational system (Paik, 2001, 2004). The generalizable model includes the following: (1) *ability*, (2) *development*, and (3) *motivation*; (4) *quantity of instruction* and (5) *quality of instruction*; (6) *classroom climate*; (7) *peer groups*; (8) *home environment*; and (9) *time spent outside of school* (e.g., television viewing).

Walberg's productivity model serves as a general framework to understand family influences. The first five factors, *ability, motivation, development*, and *quantity and quality of instruction*, are only partly alterable by teachers (Walberg, 1984). Factors such as socioeconomic status, gender, ethnicity, and financial expenditures of schools are also less direct and alterable. The last four environmental factors, *classroom climate, peer groups, home environment*, and *time spent outside of school* (e.g., television viewing), directly influence the student. Factors such as *ability* and *motivation* are influenced directly by parents and the students, particularly in the home environment (Walberg, 1984). Parents can directly influence the student by altering the last two factors, *home environment* and *time spent outside of school* (e.g., monitoring television viewing or extracurricular activities).

Redding (2003) describes the curriculum of the home as "patterns of family life that contribute to a child's ability to learn in school" (p. 7). More specifically, the curriculum of the home can be classified as (1) *parent–child relationships* (e.g., conversation about everyday events, family discussion of books and television programs, family visits to libraries and museums, etc.), (2) *routine of family life* (e.g., study time at home, a daily routine that includes time to eat, sleep, play, work, study, and read, etc.), and (3) *family expectations and supervision* (e.g., priority given to school work, parental expectations, parental monitoring of television and other time usage, etc.). In summary, the curriculum of the home can involve anything from physical resources to family socioeconomic status and stability, parental guidance, discipline and effort, extra lessons, and other monitored time (Mordkowitz & Ginsburg, 1986; Peng & Wright, 1994; Redding, 2003).

This article focuses on the alterable factors directly related to the curriculum of the home. Based on Redding's definition and Walberg's nine-factor model, the curriculum of the home includes the last two factors from the productivity model: *home environment* and *time spent outside of school* (e.g., television viewing). These factors include characteristics of the home, such as family structure, parents' educational background and expectations, educational experiences and resources, and monitored and other time usage. To gain a purified measure of the *curriculum of the home*, the home environment and time indicators were analyzed in context of the model.

Research Questions

Studies have shown that Korea outperforms the United States in international achievement tests (IEA, 1996; Paik, 2001). This article highlights comparative findings on alterable factors that increase learning in Korea and the United States. Because it appears that learning depends on multiple factors, the productivity model was used to statistically control for all the other factors while asking the question, "How does the *curriculum of the home* predict achievement in Korea and the United States?"

METHODS

Sample

National random samples included seventh and eighth grade Korean and U.S. students from The Third International Mathematics and Science Study (TIMSS) in 1995. The Korean sample included 5,846 students from 150 schools. The U.S. sample included 10,975 students from 183 schools. Seventh and eighth grade students were selected because we know that the United States starts to lag behind by the fifth grade. Middle school students may also respond more accurately than younger students in terms of their own experiences.

Survey Instrument

TIMSS in 1995 conducted a comprehensive study involving over 41 ministries of education. They surveyed over 500,000 primary, middle, and high school students (IEA, 1997a, 1997b; U.S. Department of Education, 1996). This survey reflects cross-sectional data obtained at a single point in time, which does not offer the advantages of longitudinal data. However, the comprehensive data set and large sample from Korea and the United States provide generalizability in this study.

Developing Reliable Scales[2]

In developing reliable indicators, multiple factor analyses were conducted. The factor analyses were conducted using principal components (varimax rotation, eigenvalue of 1). Correlations and alpha reliabilities were used to measure the consistency in scales. Most of the reliable scales were above .60, consisting of several correlated items. Single items were also included as indicators, in which reliabilities and correlations were not applicable.

Independent Variables (Indicators) for Curriculum of the Home

Home Environment

This factor has eight indicators as shown in Table 1. To help the reader understand the indicators, there are four general categories: (1) family structure, (2) about parents, (3) educational experiences and resources, (4) books and reading.

TABLE 1. Item Analysis and T-Tests

Curriculum of the Home Indicators	Korea			United States				
	a	Mean	SD	a	Mean	SD	T-test	Significance
Family structure								
1. Lives with mother	NA	0.94	0.24	NA	0.92	0.26	3.87	**
2. Lives with father	NA	0.89	0.31	NA	0.68	0.47	32.16	**
About parents								
3. Parents' educational background	0.81	3.88	1.56	0.70	4.87	1.63	−34.27	**
a) Mother		3.61	1.60		4.85	1.80	−44.18	**
b) Father		4.15	1.82		4.71	1.94	−18.11	**
4. Parents' expectations	0.73	3.40	0.51	0.66	3.47	0.51	−9.78	**
a) My mom believes it is important for me to do well in math?		3.53	0.60		3.68	0.55	−16.16	**
b) … in English/Korean?		3.30	0.61		3.63	0.56	−35.49	**
c) … to be placed in classes with high achieving students?		3.39	0.69		3.15	0.84	18.51	**
Educational experiences and resources								
5. Cultural exposure	0.75	1.28	0.41	0.71	1.63	0.55	−45.68	**
a) How often do you go to a museum or art exhibit?		1.30	0.57		1.34	0.67	−3.24	**
b) …a concert?		1.19	0.49		1.44	0.75	−23.20	**
c) …movies?		1.46	0.65		2.33	0.84	−69.30	**
d) …theatre?		1.16	0.47		1.55	0.84	−32.19	**
6. Educational tools	0.98	0.37	0.48	0.88	0.56	0.46	−21.34	**
a) Do you have a computer at home?		0.38	0.48		0.56	0.50	−22.44	**
b) …a calculator, study desk, dictionary?		0.37	0.48		0.51	0.50	−18.11	**
Books and reading								
7. Books at home	NA	3.41	1.20	NA	3.44	1.29	−2.03	*
8. Reading	NA	2.79	0.99	NA	2.91	1.08	−7.11	**

(Continued)

TABLE 1. Continued

Curriculum of the Home Indicators	Korea			United States			T-test	Significance
	a	Mean	SD	a	Mean	SD		
Monitored and other time (outside of school)								
Study time								
1. Studying math	NA	2.21	0.75	NA	2.12	0.73	6.98	**
2. Extra math lessons	NA	2.07	1.27	NA	1.43	0.72	39.89	**
TV viewing								
3. Time spent watching TV	NA	2.84	1.07	NA	3.25	1.05	−25.43	**
4. Educational TV	0.54	2.30	0.68	0.51	1.98	0.72	26.91	**
5. Leisure TV	0.60	2.72	0.69	0.58	3.07	0.72	−30.31	**
Other time								
6. Playing	NA	2.04	0.91	NA	3.08	1.10	−61.87	**
7. Working	NA	1.07	0.41	NA	4.12	1.37	−173.00	**
8. Sports	NA	1.80	0.79	NA	3.41	1.23	−86.98	**

M, mean; SD, standard deviation; T-test = significant values ** $p < .01$, * $p < .05$ level; a = alpha reliability for scales; NA, not applicable.

Coding Scales:

For Items 1, 2, 6: yes = 1, no = 0.

For item 3: I don't know = 1, elementary school = 2, some high shcool = 3, high school = 4, some vocational/tech education = 5, some community college or university courses = 6, bachelor's degree at a college or university = 7.

For Item 4: strongly agree = 4, strongly disagree = 1.

For Items 5 and 8: every day = 4, once a week = 3, once a month = 2, rarely = 1.

For Item 7: 0–10 books = 1, 11–25 books = 2, 26–100 books = 3, 101–200 books = 4, 200+ books = 5.

For monitored and other time scales:

For Items 1–8: no time = 1, less than an 1 hour = 2, 1–2 hours = 3, 3–4 hours = 4, more than 4 hours = 5.

For Items 1, 3, 6, and 8 = on a normal school day.

For Items 2 and 7 = during the week.

The category, family structure, includes two indicators: (1) *lives with mother* and (2) *lives with father*. The category, about parents, consists of (3) *parents' educational background* and (4) *parents' expectations*. The educational experiences and resources category consists of (5) *cultural exposure* and (6) *educational tools in the home*. The books and reading category includes (7) *books at home* and (8) *reading*. As shown in Table 1, alpha reliabilities ranged from .66 to .98 for Korea and the United States. Single item indicators were not applicable.

Time Spent Outside of School

As shown in Table 1, this factor also has eight indicators that were classified into three general categories: (1) time spent studying, (2) television viewing, and (3) other time usage. The two indicators under the time spent studying category were (1) *studying math* and (2) *extra math lessons*. The category, television viewing, includes (3) *time spent watching television*, (4) *educational television*, and (5) *leisure television*. The other time usage category includes (6) *playing*, (7) *working*, and (8) *sports*. The alpha reliabilities are .51 to .64 for both Korea and the United States. The remaining items were not applicable because they were single items.

Dependent Variables

Math achievement scores were selected because Korean students outperform U.S. students (Korea: mean, 592; standard deviation, 108; United States: mean, 488; standard deviation, 91). Math is also considered the most "culture free" topic in comparing different countries. Little research also exists in terms of math comparisons for the two countries.

Statistical Analyses

Independent samples T-tests and multiple regression models were conducted for Korea and the United States.[3] The regression equations[4] included the independent variables (indicators of the factors), dependent variable (math scores), a Korean binary variable to control for country comparisons, and product terms.

RESULTS

Correlations for the Curriculum of the Home

Zero-order correlations were conducted on all the indicators and achievement scores. Based on the model, the findings show that the indicators for *curriculum of the home* (home environment and time spent outside of school) were highly correlated with achievement for both Korea and the United States (Table 1). Of the 10 most highly correlated indicators,[5] 6 indicators fall under the Korean curriculum of the home: *books at home* (.33), *extra math lessons* (.27), *parent's educational background* (.25), *parent's expectations* (.24), *reading* (.23), and *educational tools* (.20). Of the 10 most highly correlated indicators,[6] 7 indicators fall under the U.S. curriculum of the home: *books at home* (.31), *educational tools* (.25), *parent's educational background* (.23), *parents' expectations* (.16), *lives with father* (.15), and *reading* (.15); *cultural exposure* (−.24) was negatively correlated to achievement.

Curriculum of the Home Indicators: Home Environment and Time Factors

Independent Samples T-Tests

Table 1 shows that T-test values were all significant at the .05 or .01 alpha level for both Korea and the United States. The indicators, *lives with mother* and *lives with father*, were significantly higher for Korean students, especially when living with their natural father. All other indicators involving *parents' educational background, parents' expectations, cultural exposure* and *educational tools, books at home,* and *reading* were significantly higher for U.S. students. One of the items (e.g., to be placed in classes with high achieving students) in the parents' expectations category was significantly higher for Korean students. In general, both Korean and U.S. students were rarely exposed to cultural activities (e.g., going to the museum).

Table 1 also shows that *studying math* and *extra math lessons* indicators are significantly higher for Korean students. Both students spend a lot of *time watching television,* but U.S. students watched more *leisure television* and less *educational television* than Korean students. U.S students were significantly higher in *playing, working,* and *sports.*

Regression Analyses

Table 2 shows that almost all variables for the United States and Korea were significant at the .05 or .01 level. Separate regression analyses[7] show that the *curriculum of the home* factors are related to math achievement. Both standardized and unstandardized regression coefficients are presented in the findings.

The indicator, *lives with mother*, is significant for both Korea and the U.S. The *lives with father* indicator is insignificant for Korean students but appears to be significant for U.S. students. *Parents' educational background* and *parents' expectations* are significant influences on both countries. *Cultural exposure* (or lack of) has a negative impact on achievement for both countries. Students should be exposed more to educational experiences (e.g., museum, opera, concert, movies). *Educational tools* is significant for both students. The *books at home* (one of the strongest predictors) and *reading* indicators are significant influences to achievement for both countries.

Studying math was significant for both countries. In the United States, the indicator, *extra math lessons*, appears to be negatively significant, which may mean private tutoring or summer school for remedial work. Korean students often take extra tutoring or classes to get ahead, which may explain the highly significant predictor. The *time spent watching television* appears to be negative for U.S. students but appears to be positive for Korean students, perhaps because they watch more *educational television*. The indicators, *leisure television* and *playing*, have negative influences for both students. *Working* and *playing sports* influences U.S. students positively, but not Korean students.

Interaction Effects

Based on the interaction effects regression model,[8] the product terms are presented to show which indicators in the *curriculum of the home* enhance achievement more for Korean and U.S. students. In Table 2, there are no significant findings for the indicators *lives with mother*, *parent's educational background*, and *cultural exposure*. However, the *lives with father* and *educational tools* indicators have a bigger influence on U.S. students. *Parents' expectations*, *books at home*, and *reading* indicators have a bigger influence on Korean students.

TABLE 2. Multiple Regression Analyses

Curriculum of the Home Indicators	Korea				United States				Product Terms	
	r	B	Beta	t	r	B	Beta	t	Diff	t
Family structure										
1. Lives with mother	.10	10.69	.02	2.04*	.08	6.22	.02	2.20*	4.46	.77
2. Lives with father	.06	−5.77	−.02	−1.46	.15	9.20	.05	5.60**	−14.97	−3.67**
About parents										
3. Parents' educational background	.25	4.52	.06	5.42**	.23	5.99	.11	12.57**	−1.48	−1.62
4. Parents' expectations	.24	13.49	.06	4.75**	.16	16.54	.09	9.48**	−3.05	2.40c*
Educational experiences and resources										
5. Cultural exposure	−.12	−34.50	−.13	−11.58**	−.24	−28.97	−.17	−19.91**	−5.53	−1.73
6. Educational tools	.20	9.38	.04	3.71**	.25	22.48	.11	13.13**	−13.10	−4.49**
Books and reading										
7. Books at home	.33	13.96	.16	13.06**	.31	10.97	.15	17.02**	2.99	2.44**
8. Reading	.23	13.80	.13	11.38**	.15	8.24	.10	11.30**	5.56	4.10**
Monitored and other time (outside of school)										
Study time										
1. Studying math	.14	5.68	.04	3.38c**	.06	3.72	.03	3.12c*	1.96	2.10c*
2. Extra math lessons	.27	8.28	.10	8.42**	−.07	−7.89	−.06	−7.38**	16.17	11.19**
TV viewing										
3. Time spent watching TV	.00	8.01	.08	7.09**	−.12	−2.84	−.03	−3.79**	10.84	8.29**
4. Educational TV	.07	4.76	.03	2.62c**	−.01	−2.90	−.02	−2.66c**	7.36	2.20c*
5. Leisure TV	−.03	−4.08	−.03	−2.21c**	−.06	−3.40	−.03	−3.00c*	−.68	−.84
Other time usage										
6. Playing	−.10	−4.38	−.04	−3.29**	−.11	−3.60	−.04	−5.17**	−.78	−.54
7. Working	−.08	−8.03	−.03	−2.86**	.02	1.52	.02	2.78c**	−6.51	−3.29**
8. Sports	−.04	−6.49	−.05	−4.12**	.12	3.87	.05	6.43**	−10.36	−6.55**

B, unstandardized regression coefficients; *Beta*, standardized regression coefficients; c, collinear with one or more variables; r, correlation to achievement; t, tests linear relationship between achievement and indicators, **p < .01, *p < .05.

298

Leisure television and *playing* had no apparent influences for both students. However, *extra math lessons* and *studying math* significantly influences achievement more for Korean students. *Time spent watching television* and *educational television* also appeared to be more positive on Korean students. *Working* and *playing sports* appear to have a more positive influence on U.S. students.

DISCUSSION

The productivity model shows that multiple factors predict achievement, particularly the home environment and time factors. The *curriculum of the home* is strongly related to achievement and appears to be significant influences for both groups. The study shows that the *curriculum of the home* is important and alterable for both Korea and the United States. These factors include expectations, educational experiences and resources in the home, books and reading, and monitored and other time usage. The study shows that both Korean and U.S. parents expect their children to do well in school and their expectations do influence learning for both students. The findings confirm that educational experiences and resources, such as cultural exposure and educational tools in the home, also influence both groups positively (IEA, 1996; Sorenson, 1994). Reading more and the number of books are also correlated to achievement for all students. The study also confirms that time well spent on homework and other constructive activities help both students.

Family structure and relationships with parents can also make a difference to Korean and U.S. students. The study shows that student achievement was generally higher when living with their natural mother or father. Although both groups (92–94%) typically live with their natural mother, fewer U.S. students (<70%) live with their natural fathers in comparison with Korean students (~90%). Students in the United States who live with their mothers do well, but those who live with their natural fathers do even better. In contrast, Korean students who live with their father did not achieve as highly as did those who live with their mother. In Korea, it may be because the typical father does not get involved in household affairs, such as the child's education. The schooling process is typically left to the Korean mother, who strictly monitors their time and enrolls them in extra classes or private tutoring to get ahead (Ellinger & Carlson, 1990; Paik, 2004; Sorenson, 1994).

Although the study found that many of the factors did predict achievement for both students, it also found that U.S. parents were more educated, had higher expectations in general, provided more educational tools and books, and encouraged students to read more. U.S. parents also exposed their children to slightly more cultural activities, although both students generally lacked exposure to cultural activities. Korean parents appeared to be more concerned with the students' usage of time. Korean achievement was influenced by all the indicators but strongly influenced by time factors and family structure. Korean parents did have higher expectations for their children to be placed in high achieving classes, which encouraged them to monitor their time and activities after school, such as homework, extra classes, and television viewing.

The study found that studying more is obviously helpful to both students, but Korean students invest more time and energy in studying math and taking extra math classes. Time spent on extra math classes shows one of the highest correlations for Korean students. Studies have found that Asian students had more lessons outside of school than any other group (Peng & Wright, 1994), which is the norm for Korean students to attend "ha-gwuan" (extra classes to get ahead). However, extra classes in the United States typically mean summer school or private tutoring from performing poorly in a subject area. For Korean students, attending school after school is very common to prepare for national exams.

Studies have shown that homework produces positive cognitive, behavioral, and affective effects to learning. Homework is three times the learning variance than family socioeconomic status (Walberg, 1984). The findings in this study show that Korean students spend more time on their homework. Educational Testing Service (1992) also found that Korea tied with the former Soviet Union for averaging more than 4 hours of math homework per week in comparison with other countries. Compared with their Western counterparts, Schneider & Lee (1990) also found that East Asian students spend a great deal of time on their homework.

Television viewing is also considered a time-consuming activity for many students. Studies have found that Korean parents not only control after-school time but also the quantity and quality of television viewing (IEA, 1996; Mordkowitz & Ginsburg, 1986). Comparative studies show that on average U.S. high school students watch 30 hours of television per week (Walberg, Bole, & Waxman, 1980). Although the United States watches more television, the findings show that both U.S. and Korean students watch a lot of television. The findings show that U.S. students watch more leisure television, whereas Korean students watch more educational television. More educational viewing appears to be helpful to Korean students. Studies have found that many Korean teachers also assign educational shows as part of their homework assignment. For example, Thomson (1989) reported that roughly 44% of Korean middle school students watched 3 to 4 hours of television, of which 2 were educational and often assigned as homework.

Regarding television viewing in Korea, it is important to note that Korean broadcasting is nationally controlled and not available around the clock as it is in the United States. Because Korean broadcasting is controlled, there are more shows for Korean students on the weekends and television is used as a form of relaxation, because they rarely spend time in other social activities (Williams, 1985). Studies have also found that watching television together as a family occurs more often in Asia. Consequently, parents can monitor television viewing (Shanahan & Morgan, 1992).

Regarding other usage of time, playing with friends obviously does not influence achievement positively for both students. Korean students do not have time to play with their friends and are discouraged to work or play sports because they are too busy taking extra classes or doing their homework. U.S. students are more involved in sports and work more often than Korean students. Paid work and sports appear to influence learning positively for U.S students, perhaps because both provide skills and responsibilities for students. Working part-time during the week provides a form of discipline and responsibility for a young student. Sports are also often tied to team efforts and academic regulations, where students may feel more pressure to do well in their studies as well.

CONCLUSION

The *curriculum of the home* is strongly related to achievement and appears to significantly influence both groups. The alterable factors in this study suggest that constructive changes in the home environment and time usage can make a difference. Developing parent–child relationships, providing a routine for family life, and family expectations and supervision are critical to providing a supportive learning environment for any student. For example, family visits to libraries and museums, discussing books and television programs, study time at home and daily routine, parental expectations, and monitoring of television and other time usage are helpful to children.

Many studies indicated that learning depends on multiple factors regarding the individual, family, and school factors. This study demonstrated the importance of alterable practices that are associated within families and homes. One of the critical findings was the usage of time, for example, monitoring homework and television viewing. For decades, studies have reported that television watching correlates negatively with low achievement. Television takes away from important activities such as homework, reading, family time, and other quality time. More constructive activities, such as homework, do provide a longer school day for students. Research shows that homework is correlated to learning, which has a greater substantial effect than family socioeconomic status (Walberg, 1984).

This study shows that Korean students enroll in extra classes and spend hours on their homework. Why do Koreans study so hard? This study found that practices in the home are critical, but it is important to understand Korean culture, national organization, and schooling. Passing national examinations and pleasing their parents are also related to the motivational issues behind their hard work. In preparing for national exams that dictate life choices, students are encouraged to work hard, spend fewer hours on extracurricular activities, and attend extra classes to get ahead. Getting accepted to prestigious universities is an incentive that reinforces daily academic habits in the early years (Paik, 2001; Woessman, 2000). Further research should be conducted on the motivational factors behind school performance to shed light on alterable factors in the home and school.

Although family structure may not be so alterable, the study highlights the importance of parent–child relationships. The changing family demographic trends in the United States may provide more reason to try to understand the curriculum of the home. From 1860 to 1960 the divorce rate in the United States increased dramatically (Cherlin, 1983). At current rates, statistics show that more than one-third of all U.S. children will witness divorce and family separation. The National Center of Health Statistics (1991) also found that family structure and children's emotional well-being were related. Children from two-parent families had the lowest scores of behavioral problems and were the least likely to have seen a counselor. In comparison, children from single-parent families or from mothers who never married had twice as many problems in school, parent–teacher conferences, and school suspensions. These rates are very low in Korea as the findings indicate that most students live in nuclear families with two parents. Traditionally, Korea has always held the family as a sacred unit based on cultural and religious values, which may also explain the general findings in this study. Although family demographic trends are dramatically higher in the United States, this is changing for Korea as well. In addition to other factors, the comparative findings show that learning is related to family structure. This study provides perspective and highlights the need for further research regarding family dynamics and its relationship to children's well-being and learning.

In summary, education starts in the home, as we know that the first 6 years are critical in building a foundation. Early intervention is essential for students at home and in the early school years. Many homes lack a supportive learning environment, in which it is even more critical for parents and teachers to work together. In addition to altering factors to constructively change the curriculum of the home, other practical recommendations include building family–school partnerships to support learning at home and school, and constructive after-school or weekend programs for students.

NOTES

1. Empirically founded on roughly 3,000 studies, Walberg's productivity model is comprehensive in comparison with other models.

2. In utilizing the productivity model to understand family influences, the nine factors consisted of 35 total indicators. The focus of this article, however, is the curriculum of the home, which consists of the home environment (eight indicators) and time spent outside of school (eight indicators).

3. TIMSS house-weights were also included in the analysis.

4. Although the reliabilities showed that the scales were consistent, some results should be interpreted carefully as some items were collinear or may still be weak measures. Due to collinearity, some items were tested in new regression equations.

5. The categories, math attitude (.34), self academic expectations (.26), aspiration to attend college (.25), and class size (.18), were also highly correlated to Korean achievement. Most of

these items are part of the motivation factor, which is influenced directly by the curriculum of the home.

6. The categories, math attitude (.19), aspiration to attend college (.15), and absenteeism (−.15), were also highly correlated to U.S. achievement. Two of these items are part of the motivation factor, which is influenced directly by the curriculum of the home.

7. The overall model predicts achievement for Korea ($R^2 = .36$, $p < .01$) and the United States ($R^2 = .30$, $p < .01$).

8. Based on the interaction effects regression model, multiple factors still predict achievement (adjusted R^2 of .47).

REFERENCES

Barrett, M. (1990, November). The case for more school days. *The Atlantic Monthly.* Retrieved from www.theatlantic.com/politics/education/barr2f.

Cherlin, J. (1983). A changing family and household. In R. H. Turner & J. F. Short (Eds.). *Annual Review of Sociology: Volume 9.* Palo Alto, California: Annual Reviews.

Coleman, J. S. (1988). Social capital in the creation of human capital. *American Journal of Sociology, 94*, 94–120.

Coleman, J. S., Campbell, E. Q., Hobson, C. J., McPartland, J., Mood, A. M., Weinfeld, F. D., & York, R. L. (1966). *Equality of educational opportunity.* Washington, DC: U.S. Government Printing Office.

Educational Testing Service. (1992). *Learning mathematics: The international assessment of educational progress.* Princeton, NJ: Author.

Ellinger, T. R., & Carlson, D. L. (1990). Education in Korea: Doing well and feeling bad. *Foreign Service Journal, 67*, 16–18.

Ibe, R. E. (1994, April). *The enduring effects of productivity factors on eighth grade students' mathematical outcome.* Paper presented at the annual meeting of the American Educational Research Association, New Orleans.

International Association for the Evaluation of Educational Achievement (IEA). (1996). *Mathematics achievement in the middle school years: IEA's third international mathematics and science study (TIMSS).* (No. 96-71251). Boston: Center for the Study of Testing, Evaluation, and Educational Policy, Boston College.

International Association for the Evaluation of Educational Achievement (IEA). (1997a). In E. J. Gonzales & T. A. Smith (Eds.), *User guide for the TIMSS international database—Primary and middle school years 1995 assessment.* Boston: TIMSS International Study Center, Boston College.

International Association for the Evaluation of Educational Achievement (IEA). (1997b). *International version of the background questionnaires. Population 2— Supplement 2. User guide for the TIMSS international database—Primary and middle school years 1995 assessment.* Boston: TIMSS International Study Center, Boston College.

Iverson, B. K., & Walberg, H. J. (1982). Home environment and learning: A quantitative synthesis. *Journal of Experimental Education, 50*, 144–151.

Mordkowitz, E., & Ginsburg, H. (1986). *Early academic socialization of successful Asian-American college students.* Paper presented at the annual meeting of the American Educational Research Association, San Francisco, April 16–20.

National Center for Health Statistics. (1991). New from NCHS. *American Journal of Public Health, 81,* 1526–1528.

National Commission on Excellence in Education. (1983). *A nation at risk: The imperative for school reform.* Washington, DC: U.S. Government Printing Office.

Paik, S. J. (2001). Educational productivity in South Korea and the United States. Research monograph. *International Journal of Educational Research, 35,* 535–607.

Paik, S. J. (2004). Korean and U.S. families, schools, and learning. *International Journal of Educational Research, 41,* 71–90.

Peng, S., & Wright, D. (1994). Explanation of academic achievement of Asian American students. *Journal of Educational Research, 87,* 346–352.

Redding, S. (2003). *Parents and learning.* Educational Practices Series 2. Geneva, Switzerland: International Academy of Education.

Schneider, B., & Lee, Y. (1990). A model of academic success: The school and home environment of East Asian students. *Anthropology and Education Quarterly, 21,* 358–377.

Shanahan, J., & Morgan, M. (1992). Adolescents, families, and television in five countries: Implications for cross-cultural educational research. *Journal of Educational Television, 18,* 35–55.

Sorenson, C. (1994). Success and education in South Korea. *Comparative Education Review, 38,* 10–35.

Stevenson, H. W., Lee, S. Y., & Stigler, J. W. (1986) Mathematics achievement of Chinese, Japanese, and American children. *Science, 231,* 693–699.

Thomson, S. (1989). How much do Americans value schooling? *NASSP Bulletin, 73,* 51–67.

U.S. Department of Education. (1996). *Pursuing excellence,* NCES 97–198, by Lois Peak. National Center for Educational Statistics. Washington, DC: U.S. Government Printing Office.

Walberg, H. J. (1984). Improving the productivity of America's schools. *Educational Leadership, 41,* 19–27.

Walberg, H. J, Bole, R., & Waxman. H. (1980). School-based family socialization and achievement in the inner city. *Psychology of the Schools, 17,* 506–514.

Walberg, H. J., Harnisch, D., & Tsai, S. L. (1984). High school productivity in twelve countries. *Journal of Educational Research, 12,* 237–248.

Williams, T. M. (1985). Implications of a natural experiment in the developed world for research on televisions in the developing world. *Journal of Cross-cultural Psychology, 16,* 262–287.

Woessman, L. (2000, July). *Why human capital differs: International evidence.* Retrieved from http://www.iae.csic.es/publicaciones/summer/woessmann

Caregiver Engagement in Religious Urban Elementary Schools

Martin Scanlan

ABSTRACT. This article examines how school leaders in a religious school serving traditionally marginalized students improve their school communities through constructing space for caregiver engagement. This study suggests how counter-narratives of critical care can inform social justice leadership in schools. The results, from a case study of a Catholic urban elementary school that uses innovative and effective strategies to engage caregivers, show that educational leaders create spaces for engaging caregivers by developing relationships with them and systematically reducing barriers to their participation in the school community. Analyzing these results through the critical care theory lens illuminates how these spaces value diverse forms of social and cultural capital are strengthened by alliances with nontraditional support structures. This research contributes to our evolving understanding of caregiver engagement by presenting a textured analysis of a case study as viewed through a critical care conceptual framework.

Martin Scanlan, PhD, is Assistant Professor in the Department of Educational Policy and Leadership, School of Education, Marquette University, Milwaukee, WI.

INTRODUCTION

A core principle of social justice education is reciprocal community relationships (Carlisle, Jackson, & George, 2006). By this, Carlisle et al. (2006) refer to the school involving "families, local agencies, and community organizations in meeting its mission" (p. 59). This article explores reciprocal community relationships by examining the role of school leaders in facilitating the engagement of caregivers in schools serving traditionally marginalized students, specifically students of color and students in poverty. Analyzing data from a case study of a Catholic urban elementary school that uses innovative and effective strategies to engage caregivers, this study suggests how counter-narratives of critical care can inform social justice leadership in schools.

Significance of Problem

Educational researchers have a long-standing interest in caregiver involvement (Coleman, 1991; Epstein, 1990, 1997; Hanafin & Lynch, 2002; Henderson & Mapp, 2002; Mandara, 2006; Rodgers & Rose, 2001; Stolz et al., 2004; Ysseldyke & Algozzine, 2006), and increasingly school districts and state agencies are instituting mechanisms to hold schools accountable to actively engage caregivers, to monitor the effectiveness of their strategies, and to respond to these assessments to continually improve in these endeavors (Christie, 2005). Rodgers and Rose (2001) report that although especially important in nonintact families, "Regardless of family structure, higher parental support and monitoring [are] predictive of academic success" (p. 58). Evidence abounds indicating that strong caregiver engagement is related to effective schools (Charles A. Dana Center, 1999; Fan & Chen, 2001; Henderson & Mapp, 2002; Osterman, 2000). Key to this is the expectations of caregivers. As Hoge, Smit, and Crist (1997) show, caregivers' high expectations about their children's achievement "has more impact than having interest in their grades or classes, being involved in school events, or having open communication with the children" (p. 34). This implies that schools promote student achievement when they engage caregivers around specific expectations of student success. Schools that successfully engage caregivers (i.e., parents and guardians) are more likely to be successful educational settings for students (Berger, 2000; Dwyer & Hecht, 1992; Eccles & Harold, 1996; Jeynes, 2005a,b).

Schools that engage diverse families are characterized by collaborative cultures respectful of differences (Henderson & Mapp, 2002). Epstein (Epstein, 1986, 1990, 1993, 1997; Epstein & Salinas, 2004), who has written extensively about school involvement with families and communities, enumerates multiple types of this engagement. Schools can support families in parenting their children and in assisting their children's academic achievement through home supports. Schools are responsible for cultivating communication with families about the educational processes and outcomes. Schools facilitate family involvement in the schools through volunteering and decision-making mechanisms. Additionally, schools can help families access social service, educational, and enrichment resources in the community.

Yet all caregiver participation is not equal. As Perez Carreon, Drake, and Calabrese Barton state (2005), "[Caregiver] involvement is not a fixed event but a dynamic and everchanging practice that varies depending on the context in which it occurs, the resources parents and schools bring to their actions, and the students' particular needs" (p. 465). Jeynes (2005b) finds that "some of the more subtle aspects of parental support and involvement, such as communication and parental family structure, may impact children's educational outcomes more than some of the more overt typical aspects of parental involvement that are more often regarded as important" (p. 114). Distinguishing meaningful caregiver participation entails critically reflecting on issues of privilege and marginalization (Lareau & Shumar, 1996). Issues of power, authority, and control shape the involvement of caregivers in their children's education (Abrams & Gibbs, 2002; Fine, 1993), which can negatively impact caregivers who are marginalized by poverty (Hanafin & Lynch, 2002) and race (Lareau & Horvat, 1999). Thus, to effectively involve caregivers in their children's education, schools must use multiple strategies of communicating with caregivers, define caregiver participation broadly, and avoid deficit orientations (Gutman & McLoyd, 2000; Lopez, 2001; Lopez, Scribner, & Mahitivanichcha, 2001; Valencia, 1997).

Participation of caregivers in schooling can be critiqued as lacking authenticity. Anderson (1998) maintains that discourses of participation are at times wielded as tools of public relations or mechanisms to control dissent, as "sites for collusion among dominant groups" (p. 574). To Anderson, "authentic" participation incorporates the micropolitical considerations of the local conditions that impact who participates and in which spheres as well as the macropolitical considerations of coherence between the means and ends of participation. Anderson cautions that "politics and power are embedded in a school's culture, resulting in a form of cultural politics that makes successful implementation of participatory structures more complex than current research indicates" (p. 592).

In short, the literature shows that engaging caregivers is an important and complex role for schools. The research reported in this article builds on and departs from this literature in two ways. First, it examines caregiver engagement under a novel conceptual framework of critical care theory (described below). Second, it uses this conceptual framework to analyze a school community frequently ignored in extant literature: a private school serving traditionally marginalized students. The engagement of caregivers is particularly salient in these schools. By their private nature, they are compelled to attract caregiver support to maintain enrollment and thereby remain viable school settings. By serving traditionally marginalized students, they are compelled to broaden their support beyond the caregivers to reduce dependence on tuition and to expand their resource base.

The question that guides this research is as follows: How do educational leaders create spaces for engaging caregivers in a religious school that primarily serves traditionally marginalized students? Though parochial in setting, the implications of this research are relevant to educators in both public and private settings committed to improving their school communities by more authentically engaging caregivers. The unit of analysis, educational leaders in a private school primarily serving students marginalized by racism and poverty, is well suited to this exploration. The profile of typical private schools that cater primarily to middle- or upper-class, tuition-paying caregivers (Alt & Peter, 2002) does not fit this school, which serves students of low socioeconomic status and relies on diversified sources of funding. Moreover, the conceptual framework guiding this research recognizes race, racism, and White privilege as central factors. The participants in this research were predominantly White, middle-class women, whereas the students and families in their schools were people of color and of low socioeconomic status. The phenomenon of White educators effectively attracting support for private schools serving communities of color and communities of poverty speaks to how all school leaders can effectively facilitate caregiver and community participation across racial and class lines.

Conceptual Framework

I approached this inquiry into how school leaders create space for engaging caregivers in private schools serving traditionally marginalized students through a conceptual framework of critical care theory. Critical care theory is emerging out of care theory, which emphasizes the role of schools and school leaders to foster nurturing, collaborative communities (Beck, 1994; Noddings, 2005b). According to care theory, educators must build trusting, respectful relationships with students. These relationships facilitate the empathy of the educators for the experiences of their students. Another dimension of care theory emphasizes collaboration. In a study of an inclusive Catholic high school, Bauer and Brown (2001) illustrate that collaboration "is a style for direct interaction between at least two equal parties engaged in shared decision making and working toward a common goal" (p. 16) and that collaboration can lead to "support, sharing, and relationship building among teachers, parents, and students" (p. 16). Finally, Noddings (2005a) points out that "An ethic of care is . . . future-oriented. Its work begins where an ethic of justice often ends" (p. 147).

Care theory becomes critical by placing issues of inclusion and marginalization at the center of inquiry. In their studies of Latino students' experiences of schooling, Rolon-Dow (2005) and Valenzuela (1999) bridge care theory with critical theories to better analyze sociocultural and racialized contexts. Valenzuela's critical analysis of how schools fail to effectively engage students across chasms of race and ethnicity, language, and class suggests that care theory needs to include a critical analysis of power, privilege, and marginalization. Rolon-Dow (2005) articulates an essential premise of critical care praxis: "to care for students of color in the United States, we must seek to understand the role that race and ethnicity has played in shaping and defining the sociocultural and political conditions of their communities" (p. 104). Rolon-Dow found "deficit-based, racialized caring narratives were often articulated when teachers used their own experiences as well as the historical experiences of White immigrant groups as ideological foundations" (p. 104).

Beauboeuf-Lafontant (2002) contributes to articulating critical care theory in developing the notion of "womanism." According to

Beauboeuf-Lafontant, womanism is "the cultural, historical, and political positionality of African-American women, a group that has experienced slavery, segregation, sexism, and classism for most of its history in the United States" (p. 72). Womanism is supported by three central tenets. The first tenet is a concern with oppression, defined as "an interlocking system, providing all people with varying degrees of penalty and privilege" (p. 72). The second tenet is social transformation, which involves "individual empowerment combined with collective action" (p. 72). Third, womanists are not solely concerned with their own interests but with social justice more broadly and accordingly "seek the liberation of all" (p. 72). Beauboeuf-Lafontant characterizes womanists as demonstrating "political clarity" that allows them to "see racism and other systemic injustices as simultaneously social and educational problems. Consequently, they demonstrate a keen awareness of their power and responsibility as adults to contest the societal stereotypes imposed on children" (p. 77).

Beauboeuf-Lafontant (2002) draws from womanists the implication that "caring need not be regarded simply as an interpersonal, dyadic, and apolitical interaction" (p. 83) but rather is a key tool to "communal engagement and political activism" (p. 83). In this analysis I apply these notions of womanism to analyze the actions of White educators. Though rooted in black feminism, Beauboeuf-Lafontant notes that "not all womanists are African-American women. Because womanism is a politicized appropriation of some of the cultural values of black women, people choose whether or not to become womanists" (p. 85).

Thus my conceptual framework is best characterized as care theory with critical influences. Perez Carreon and colleagues (2005) argue that caregiver involvement "must be studied in connection to the spaces in which this involvement takes place, along with the physical, material, and organizational boundaries embedded in these spaces" (p. 468). My conceptual framework focuses attention on these "spaces" as sites where social and cultural capital are negotiated and ethics of care are established and practiced.

METHODS

This study of caregiver engagement draws from data collected in a broader study. Using a multicase study design (Stake, 1985, 1995; Yin, 2003), I conducted a study of five Catholic elementary schools serving students in poverty (i.e., qualify for free or reduced price lunches), linguistic minorities (i.e., live in homes where a language other than English is spoken), people of color, and/or students with disabilities (Scanlan, 2006). Qualitative methods provided an avenue to examine the ways these schools understood and pursued inclusion of traditionally marginalized students (Carspecken, 1996; Lincoln & Guba, 1985; Patton, 1990). During the 2004–2005 school year I collected data through interviewing, observing, and conducting archival research. My primary data were drawn from interviews with 75 research participants from administration, faculty, staff, and school boards. Seeking the perspectives of people who worked directly in the school or directly with the school, I conducted an initial semi-structured interview with each participant for 45 minutes to an hour. Through conducting a second interview with each of the administrators and written correspondences with select teachers, I gained additional data. I transcribed and coded these data, building a theoretical understanding of the way each school served the diversity of students (Maxwell, 1998; Strauss & Corbin, 1990).

In addition to these interviews, I gathered observations though detailed descriptions, digital photographs, and audio-visual recordings of school events, along with archival documents related to each school's policies, procedures, and practices. I made between three and five site visits to each school, each lasting approximately 2 days. During these visits I made these observations and recorded them through field notes, digital photographs, and brief video recordings. Archival documents related to each school's enrollment trends, mission, policies and procedures of recruitment and retention, and funding and governance structures provided further data. My understanding of the inclusive practices in the schools was enhanced by observations of school artifacts such as classrooms, bulletin boards, and exhibits. In a similar manner to my interview data, I coded archival documents and observations through an interactive process of categorizing the data, contextualizing the relationships among these categories, and building theory (Maxwell, 1998; Strauss & Corbin, 1990).

This article presents a reanalysis of select data gathered from this larger study, namely the strategies of caregiver engagement in one school, St. Josephine Academy (SJA) (all names are pseudonyms). SJA is a rich case for this analysis because the efforts to engage caregivers in this school were particularly well developed. For this article I reanalyzed data from SJA, including interviews of individuals in formal and informal leadership roles, observations, and archival documents, relating specifically to how this school community engaged caregivers.

RESULTS

The data suggest that the leaders in SJA recognize that the onus is on them to engage stakeholders into the space and that failure to attract and maintain the support of caregivers will be costly. The term "leaders" is understood broadly as all educators in the school with roles of formal and informal authority. I present these data by first providing snapshots of the school, illustrating how its student body is composed across various dimensions of diversity. I then describe in depth how the school leaders create space for engaging caregivers.

SJA: A Responsive, Caregiver-Oriented School

Although SJA serves many students who traditionally could be considered as marginalized, the school is strikingly homogenous: The student body is composed of 260 African-American students in preschool to eighth grade (94% live in poverty). No students are linguistic minorities. Thus the school was not characterized by diversity.

SJA, as a Catholic school, has persisted against the odds. Ms. Mayes, an alumnus of the school who now works as an aide, explains: "There used to be 10 Catholic schools in [this] area—now there are 3." In this Midwestern metropolitan neighborhood, over 30% of the people in the neighborhood live in poverty. Abandoned and dilapidated buildings line the streets, and criminal activity is frequent. The school has tight security measures in place, including secured doors and parking and video monitoring of entrances. During one of my site visits, a neighborhood resident was shot less than a block from the school. Moreover, SJA has grown isolated from other Church-based supports, losing both its local parish and a community of religious sisters in the past two decades.

The school has significant mismatches in race and ethnicity and socioeconomic status between the research participants and the students. Serving students of color and students in poverty, SJA is mostly staffed by White women who are not living in poverty. Though the school managed to attract and retain select teachers for significant periods, each year it relies heavily on an influx of new, young, and relatively inexperienced teachers. Safety concerns force the principal to forbid staff members from staying late to work in school. In addition, the school is located in an area that made it difficult to find, squirreled away off main thoroughfares, surrounded by one-way streets and avenues. From her 22 years teaching in the middle school, Ms. Abrams describes SJA as "the best kept secret [in the neighborhood]."

This context helps explain the paramount challenges at SJA: maintaining a steady student enrollment and ensuring financial viability. The monthly tuition expense ($260 for one child, $374 for two children) is the most significant barrier to attracting and retaining students in SJA. Many families receive tuition assistance in the form of tuition scholarships, provided through external fundraising efforts led by the school principal, Ms. Green. According to Ms. Wallace, secretary for 17 years, "Ms. Green does a very good job of keeping children here. A lot of people have stayed after talking to her and after her finding patrons and finding people to help with tuition—that keeps a lot of our families here." One teacher's comments reflect what many research participants expressed: "Usually, the reasons for [students] leaving will be financial."

In addition to serving many students who cannot afford to attend a school that charges tuition, SJA makes concerted efforts to serve students with disabilities. According to an audit by the Diocesan Office (the central organizing unit for Catholic schools, akin to a public school district), approximately 1 in 10 students in SJA has a disability. SJA does not label students with disabilities in the manner typical of public schools (such as with Individualized Educational Plans); the educators at SJA have "staffings" on students who are struggling. The principal, Ms. Green, reported that during the spring of 2004 the school was "selected as a site for inclusion by the diocese." The diocese assigned a "learning specialist [to] join [the staff] with a background in special ed. and speech." In addition, the staff at SJA has been focusing professional development on improving service delivery to all students. They have brought in a consultant from a local university to work with teachers 1 day a week on differentiating the curriculum and more effectively reaching students who are having challenges in class. Teachers rely on consultation with the principal, with peers, and with other professionals (i.e., school counselors) in the school when adapting to meet the needs of the students. One student in SJA has a significant mobility impairment. A retrofit of the building with an elevator and other accommodations has made the site accessible.

Finally, the mission of SJA advocates reaching out to children and families with an atmosphere of openness and welcome:

> The Mission of SJA is to nurture the body, mind, and spirit of each child entrusted to our care. Our goal is to forge a partnership with our families so together we foster the spiritual, social, intellectual, emotional and physical development of our young people. We aim to provide for our students a caring but disciplined environment, which encourages the pursuit of excellence, enthusiasm for learning, pride of accomplishment, self-discipline, and consideration for others.

Perhaps more importantly than the written version, the tacit mission in SJA emphasizes that all are welcome. In a response typical of her colleagues, Ms. Harris, who has taught at the school for two decades, described the goal of the school in these terms:

> I think that the purpose that the principal has tried to set here is that we serve every child, in spite of whatever their needs are, in spite of the troubles they might have had. We want to be able to work with any child—no matter how low their educational abilities might be. We want to be able to serve everyone—anyone and everyone—any child.

This snapshot of SJA sets the stage for understanding how the educational leaders at SJA articulated their role in creating a school community that is extraordinarily responsive to caregivers. The educators work to cultivate a space that fosters supportive relationships with caregivers and reduces barriers to their participation. An overview of this snapshot is provided in Figure 1.

Caregiver Engagement at SJA

These findings show that educational leaders in SJA create spaces for engaging caregivers by developing deep relationships with their students and students' families. Ms. Wallace, the school secretary for the past two decades, interacts with families more than anyone. She describes the supportive culture of the school as stemming from "the hospitality and the caring" and "the attention that is given to the

FIGURE 1. Overview of SJA.

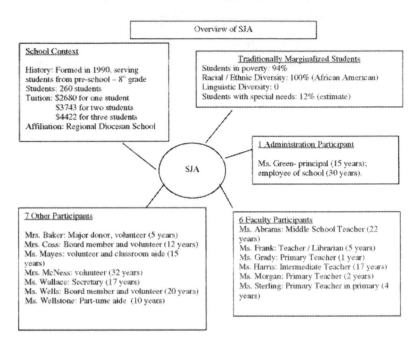

children." Elaborating, she connects this to how teachers forge deep relationships with the children and their families: "It's not just the kids, it's the family: getting involved with the family and the children." She explained:

> The teacher may have 20 some odd children in the classroom but it just seems like that personal attention is geared towards that one student as far as from the time they walk in that door 'til the time that they walk home.... The teachers and the staff here are always so concerned and they know what goes on throughout the whole day of the child. It's not like the child comes in to the classroom, does the work, and that's it.

These strong relationships are best exemplified by (1) the personal attention the principal models, (2) the strong teacher–family communication networks, and (3) the systems that reduce barriers to families.

Personal Attention From the Principal

A fundamental way SJA engages caregivers is through the personal attention of the principal. Ms. Green, the principal of SJA, lays the foundation for the strong school–caregiver relationship by conducting an entry interview with each new family.

Ms. Morgan, a teacher for the last 2 years in the primary grades, mentioned the importance of these entry interviews when describing how she would frequently consult with Ms. Green about concerns with particular students. She explained that in addition to paying attention to their grades by regularly reviewing student work, the principal brings a depth of knowledge about their families: "She knows their family history because she interviews every family—long interviews—15–20 minutes and learns their family history, their jobs, family background, relationships—and parents are just drawn to come in and talk to her . . . . She really tries to meet the needs of each family." A veteran teacher in the intermediate grades, Ms. Harris indicated that this entry interview process allows SJA to serve families whose children have struggled and failed in public schools:

> When [Ms. Green] starts the interviews with students who might have been put out of public schools she'll talk with them about how they plan on making changes in our school, so they'll know that it's a loving, caring, safe environment. And that she always makes sure that if there was a problem that she'll hook up counseling with the child right away—a lot of time the counselor will be in the room right away with the child.

The power of this connection between the principal and the families in the school is illustrated in an anecdote from Ms. Wells, a neighborhood resident who has volunteered at the school for over a decade and now serves on the school board. She sent her child, who is now in high school, through SJA. Her story captures the way Ms. Green in particular and this school community in general brings parents into a deeper relationship with the school. She went into Ms. Green's office one day to let her know that she would not be able to keep her daughter, who was in first grade at the time, in SJA. She was behind on payments and was not going to be able to sustain them. Instead of leaving the school with an unpaid bill, Ms. Wells went to settle her account. She recalls what happened:

> I came to transfer my little girl. I'd lost my job . . . and Ms. Green asked if I could volunteer for her a little. At first I was reluctant, and then I said why not? I've been here ever since! My daughter's now a sophomore in HS—she's doing good . . . . Ms. Green tries really hard. You come in that door, and you sit in her office, and financial reasons, which I've experienced myself—for some reason—I don't know why . . . but you can't leave here! I'll see what I can do to help, but you can't leave here. I walked in this door to transfer my child and pay a balance, and I've been captured in here ever since!

Thus a mother who was on the brink of leaving this school community wound up becoming a dedicated volunteer, who continues to assist the school even after her daughter has graduated.

Ms. Coss, a board member and parent of an SJA alumnus, provides another perspective on this: "Ms. Green is concerned about not only how the child is doing at school but at home as well." She noted, "If the parent needs to do something—like attend a parenting class or something like that—we have that also." Asking a family to withdraw their child happens rarely. The infrequency is largely due to the tone set by the principal: "Ms. Green is very tolerant, and she tries to help us be tolerant too." Ms. Harris, a veteran teacher of the intermediate grades, attributes this to making the expectations clear when a child is entering the school:

> It's kind of like making a commitment, especially when you're coming out of other schools where you've had a problem. It takes a commitment and taking responsibility for their part in whatever happened, and what is going to make a difference here—and they have to commit to making a difference when they come to our school. And that might mean pulling out a contract with the counselor or with Ms. Green.

The comments of Ms. Harris suggest asking uncooperative parents to leave is infrequently done precisely because the supportive relationships in the school are so strong. Successfully integrating students who come with a track record of having struggled at previous schools is tricky. Ms. Harris credits Ms. Green with setting the tone for this (tolerance) as well as the structure to facilitate it (e.g., getting family commitment, creating a contract with students).

Observations during site visits further supported these reports of research participants. Ms. Green spent considerable time with individual parents and families in both formal and informal meetings. She balanced this by making her presence ubiquitously felt among the student body, frequently interacting with students in the hall, speaking with them by name and discussing personal as well as academic matters. She is, in the words of Ms. Wallace, the secretary, "the glue to the school."

In summary, Ms. Green builds strong relationships with the students in the school and their families. As she put it, "You have to stay connected—the foundation of this school is to be connected." She intentionally brings parents into a deep relationship with the school from their initial encounter and maintains these relationships throughout. This personal attention from the principal is one way that educational leaders create spaces for engaging caregivers in SJA.

Proactive, Positive, Focused Communication From Teachers

A second way that educational leaders in SJA create spaces for engaging caregivers is by teachers developing strong bonds with the families. These bonds are built through initiating and sustaining contact that is both positive and focused on student growth and success.

The principal, Ms. Green, has worked hard to establish a culture of communication within the school. The teachers universally expressed this. Ms. Morgan, a new teacher, described this culture:

> We all communicate. It's just something we all do.... It sounds cliché but it really is like family here. I don't know many places that are like this.... [Other schools] are like apartment buildings—you go in your classroom and you're there. This really is like a house—you can't get away from people. You can't get away from help and you can't get away from support. And I think that really makes a world of difference.

Ms. Sterling, a primary teacher for the past 4 years, described frequently calling home to report both negative *and* positive behavior. When asked how often she called her students' families, she replied: "Half the class a week.... I guess it's easier for me to call them first. I'll just check in and say, '[W]ell, so and so is doing fine. Do you have any questions or concerns?'"

This communication is focused on student success. Ms. Morgan explained that this was non-negotiable: "Our parents would have our heads if they didn't have communication with us throughout a quarter before they got here for report cards! That's just what they're used to." Ms. Grady, working with the primary grades, emphasized that these relationships were connected to caring for the individual success of each child and recognizing them in the context of a family:

> I think that there's a special kind of care that happens here and there's a belief that every student can succeed. And in the relationships that we've built with the parents. It's only a couple months into school and I've spoken to every one of my parents several times. You just do it—it's an expectation. It's there and you need to. In addition to four positive phone calls a week, there are many negative phone calls: there are many times I say we're trying to correct behavior—we're trying to work with your student on such and such, academically, behaviorally, that all needs to be communicated to the parents.... And I think the parents appreciate that. We treat them like real people and people who are also involved with the execution. It's not just the teacher's efforts, it's not just the student's efforts—it's going to take all of us. And parent cooperation is crucial.

Strong, multifaceted communication and collaboration building relationships of mutual understanding and respect is an important dimension to the way the school creates a space of caregiver engagement. Along with requiring that all teachers make positive contacts to caregivers weekly, Ms. Green requires that they focus conferences with the parents primarily on academic, not behavioral, matters. Grade conferences are three-way (Freeman, 1975; McKenzie & Scheurich, 2004), involving teachers, students, and caregivers together.

Ms. Grady talked about how the frequent communication with parents about seemingly minor details was a way in which the school affirmed the dignity of all the members. She pointed out that although this was sometimes burdensome on the teachers, it was beneficial to them as well:

> I think [our Catholic identity] is shown in a more real way in the phone calls. How many teachers actually take the time ... to call

in the week and say, "I really like the way so and so wrote his name down on the paper"? That attention speaks volumes.

This is a practical example of how the school attempts to meet the goal mentioned in the school's mission "to forge a partnership with our families."

Ms. Morgan explained the strength of these relationships with families as a counterbalance to the weak formal supports for students with disabilities that the school is able to offer. "We're working on inclusion. We have a grant that is teaching the teachers how to be inclusive of all children," she explained, but when asked if the school was able to meet the needs of all the children, she candidly acknowledged the school's limitations: "To be honest, a lot of times they're not totally met here. But the difference with this school we have constant communication with the parents."

An additional effect of these strong relationships is the influence on teacher dispositions. Another teacher, Ms. Sterling, has taught in the school for 4 years. She reflects that her perspective toward caregivers has shifted over these years:

> I think parents play a more important role in my teaching now than they did my first year. I think that's gained through a little more respect—probably me respecting them more, and them respecting me more for being here.... Obviously there's [sic] always exceptions—there are always difficult parents and that's going to happen. But my relationship with the parents has been much different and even the past two years than my first year—I didn't see them as supportive. I didn't see them! If they came with concerns I almost saw it as them complaining. Now whenever I do get parents who are like, "Why did my kid get this mark?" or "How come they don't know that?" I always say immediately, "Please come in so we can talk about it!" Because they're concerned and they're not complaining. I guess it's that I see engaged and interested parents as ones who will come talk to you and will come ask questions, whereas I've realized that someone that doesn't say anything and is never around—well, that's not really doing any good for their kids.

The strong relationships between teachers and caregivers contribute to a caring culture in SJA. The culture of the school reflected this care for students in many ways, including artifacts of student work lining in hallways, the atmosphere of exuberance at student assemblies, and a controlled but lively tenor in the cafeteria at breakfast and lunch. These relationships are not left to the independent dispositions of individual teachers but rather are encouraged, fostered, and compelled from multiple directions. The culture of the school has created this expectation of proactive, positive, focused communication. This is a second significant way that SJA creates an engaging space for caregivers.

Systems to Reduce Barriers to Families

A final way SJA creates this space by fostering relationships with caregivers is through systematically reducing barriers to caregiver participation. SJA depends on attracting and retaining families in the school and thus has a strong incentive to make these connections. In a comment reflective of many participants, Ms. Grady describes this pressure to serve families well:

> There's a huge effort in the primary grades to have as many students as possible in the student body [whose] experience is positive [so that] by the time they get on to 6th and 7th grade we'll still have a good size graduating class. I feel a huge responsibility in light of that, because I think a lot of these students could easily turn to public schools or to another school, and they don't. Their families continue to come back.

One key barrier the school is constantly focused on reducing is the financial burden of the tuition. SJA offers to all families a tuition subsidy of $600 if they participate in the school's Stewardship Program. Participating families (and virtually all families in SJA participate) are required to regularly attend some church (regardless of the denomination) and participate in school-based enrichment or service projects. Some of these projects include personal enrichment sessions, such as reading instruction workshops and parenting support sessions.

SJA also offers scholarships to families who could not otherwise afford the school's tuition. All Our Children is a local, independent, not-for-profit organization whose mission is to "provide support to the Catholic schools in the neediest areas of inner city and serves to help raise scholarship funds for students attending Catholic schools in the inner city." The average amount of annual support for scholarships during the last 6 years from All Our Children was just over $40,000. The other funds they have provided have been primarily allocated to operating expenses or capital expenses. SJA also pursues tuition scholarships from other agencies and donors.

Also, SJA reduces the barrier of fear that caregivers have for their children's safety. Situated in a rough neighborhood, SJA strives to provide to caregivers a trusted haven for the children. Ms. Wells, a volunteer in the school for decades who sent her own children through the school, has a historical perspective on this: "It's a safe place here. A lot of children leave here . . . graduate, and go to high school—they come back [and] . . . bring their children here. They were safe—they felt safe." Ms. Mayes, an alumnus of the school who now works as an aide, spoke to this as well:

> The parents, our parents know this: they drop their kids off sometime 6:30 in the morning and when we see them again it's 6:00 at night. And they don't say [to their children], "Have you had a snack? Have you done this or that?" They say [to us], "Thank you."

In a community where violent acts are not uncommon, lack of safety is a significant barrier. The caregivers who send their children to SJA trust that their children are well cared for in a safe environment.

Finally, SJA attempts to mitigate many of the other barriers that many Catholic schools present by virtue of their private nature, such as excluding students with disabilities or learning problems or behavior problems. SJA systematically increases its capacity to serve students with diverse needs by drawing upon external agencies for support. For instance, the school collaborates with local nonprofit agencies to provide counseling services to students and families. Collegial relationships build a supportive culture in the school. Ms. Wellstone comes into SJA once a week to help teachers strategize methods for differentiating instruction within their classrooms. As a Black woman and a doctoral candidate in education at a local university, Ms. Wellstone brings an important perspective, racially and educationally. When considering what was working in this regard at SJA, she began with mentioning the leadership:

> The success of a school lies in the leadership. I think a lot of that goes back to leadership. There's very strong leadership here.

You have leadership that wants the best for the students and teachers and uses everything it does as a partnership. You don't find that at a lot of schools. You find a lot of schools with inhibitions or that rely on a lot of people within their school with inhibitions or with biases that they won't admit that they have. Therefore the attainment of their goal is not really met. On paper it looks good, but it's not really met. You don't have that here. You don't have people saying, "Oh those poor little black children, oh they don't know how to learn." No, you don't have that.

Ms. Wellstone then moved to capture the sense of strong expectations, openness to new ideas, and collaboration among the educators throughout SJA:

You have people [at SJA] that are like, "You can do this, you *will* do this." They might be struggling to find the best method to make it work, but then again they're not wed to just one method—they're committed to finding what is going to work. Bottom line is, what's going to work? The collaboration and the willingness to work with people in general... if someone has a gift, and they're willing to share it, then you're welcome.

Ms. Wellstone's reflections are representative of an array of participants who spoke to the ways that the educators sought to meet the diverse learning needs of all students in the school community.

Thus by systematically working to reduce barriers to families, SJA illustrates a school community that takes seriously its responsibility to be accessible. Access to students with exceptionalities is one example of this. Barriers of fear and tuition are two other impediments that the school has established clear structures to address.

The focus of this inquiry was on how educational leaders in a religious school that primarily serves traditionally marginalized students create spaces for engaging caregivers. These data show that three ways this is accomplished at SJA are through the personal attention of the principal, the strong relationships of the teachers, and the systems to reduce barriers to caregivers. Analyses of these data show that SJA creates space to negotiate social and cultural capital and practice ethics of care.

DISCUSSION

As described earlier, caregiver involvement is connected to the spaces in which it occurs (Perez Carreon et al., 2005). The critical care theory lens illuminates how these educational leaders create spaces for engaging caregivers and building community support. I present three dimensions to these spaces of engagement: These spaces (1) value diverse forms of social and cultural capital, (2) are strengthened by alliances with nontraditional supports, and (3) are limited. I conclude by suggesting that the caregiver engagement in SJA provides a counter-narrative to stock stories of how private schools serve traditionally marginalized students.

Spaces Valuing Diverse Forms of Social and Cultural Capital

Diverse forms of social and cultural capital are valued in the spaces created by the relationships and the reduction of barriers to the school. The findings suggest that the educators in SJA approach caregivers through an asset-oriented framework, working to build connections to them. The efforts of the educational leaders in SJA to create spaces that valued diverse forms of social and cultural capital can be interpreted as tactical and as value-laden. In a way, the schools were forced to create these spaces as a tactic to build their enrollments. The educators in these schools literally are beholden to the people of color in the communities to keep their schools open. Specific strategies to attract and maintain students included fostering interpersonal communications between faculty and caregivers, creating school-facilitated occasions for caregiver learning, and promoting various opportunities for community investment into the school.

Foremost among the barriers to attending SJA were the per-pupil costs of running the schools serving families with limited means for paying tuition and the limitations of the schools' capacities to address the diverse needs of the pluralistic community (e.g., differentiation in instruction for students with diverse learning needs). As a result, SJA undertook multifarious efforts to expand the base of financial support through private donors and foundations as well as the base of human resource support through volunteers. This may have an effect of compelling the (White, privileged) educators to paradoxically recognize their role as one of service and dependence. Delpit (1988) asks, "Will Black teachers and parents continue to be silenced by the very forces that claim to 'give voice' to our children?" (p. 296). The evidence in this study suggests that in certain schools, the answer is no. Some schools, even where the majority of the teachers are racially and economically privileged, make concerted efforts to listen to the voices of the caregivers and community members, most of whom have been traditionally marginalized.

In another way, these spaces can be understood as rooted in values, not tactics. If the enrollment pressures drive these schools to expand their communities from a resource perspective, the religious values of the schools compelled this expansion as well. In a sense, the enrollment pressure could be considered the stick, compelling the educators to expand their practices of caregiver engagement, whereas the religious values could be considered the carrot, luring the educators to make these changes. The religious discourse in SJA grounds these educators in values that are asset-oriented rather than deficit-orientated. This context allows the principal of SMS to refer to the children as "priceless gifts from God" and the mission at SJA to espouse "nurtur[ing] the body, mind, and spirit of each child entrusted to our care."

This emphasis on valuing diverse forms of social and cultural capital is supported by previous research in the area of caregiver engagement. For instance, as Henderson and Mapp (2002) report in their summary of research on caregiver and community engagement, successful initiative are welcoming, collaborative, and serve diverse parent and community needs by "recogniz[ing], respect[ing], and address[ing] cultural and class differences" (p. 48). Viewing the data in this study through the lens of critical care theory foregrounds certain race-based and class-based dimensions these values. Specifically, the case of SJA suggests ways certain educational leaders are approaching communities of color through more nuanced lenses. The school's dependence on increasing participation from communities of color to support the schools, along with their espoused values, may reduce tendencies toward racism. SJA has not formalized this yet indicated many culturally responsive and asset-oriented approaches toward caregivers.

The data here imply that religious overtones serve to drown racial undertones, but a thorough examination of this is beyond the scope of this study. As Lipsitz (1998) suggests, Whites can ameliorate the inequities perpetuated by White privilege by adopting and acting on equity-oriented dispositions: "We do not choose our color, but we do choose our commitments" (p. viii). Educators in SJA showed commitments to working across racial and ethnic lines. In summary, the spaces valuing diverse forms of social and cultural capital are rooted in both values and strategies of the school.

Alliances with Nontraditional Supports

In addition to creating spaces that value diverse forms of social and cultural capital, SJA educators consistently cultivated innovative supports, both in the immediate and in the broader community, to more effectively serve their increasingly diverse students. For example, as part of the Stewardship Program, families were rewarded for active participation in a faith community of their choosing. Families demonstrated their participation by attending worship services and personal enrichment programs at these faith communities. Though a Catholic school, SJA supported the social networking of caregivers by encouraging them to attend a faith community of their choosing.

In addition, the educators gained support by way of grants of financial and in-kind support from numerous organizations in the broader community. The principal at SJA placed concerted efforts into building networks of support. From capital improvement projects (e.g., building a new playground area, painting the school, replacing windows) to tuition scholarship funds, businesses and local foundations were vital to the stability of SJA. The principal was also successful in finding personnel at reduced rates, including a special education consultant (supported by a local university), counselors (provided at a reduced rate by a local social service agency), and subsidized teachers (supported by a local teaching service corps organization).

Rather than being isolated from one another, these support structures tended to overlap and interconnect. They were typically created through a combination of innovation and desperation and strengthened the schools' capacities to value diverse forms of social and cultural capital. For instance, some of the support personnel (special education consultant and counselors) raised the capacity of the educators to recognize of the assets that the caregivers brought to the school and the uniqueness of each individual. Their efforts helped SJA create a teaching and learning community more responsive to the whole child.

Certain features of womanism are evident here. Beauboeuf-Lafontant (2002) describes womanism as promoting "individual empowerment combined with collective action... [and] seek[ing] the liberation of all" (p. 72). Through this lens, caring is a tool of engaging the community in political activism. The risks that womanism entails to working for others are rooted in this connectivity (p. 81):

> [C]ommitments to working for social justice rest on a concept of self that is part of rather than apart from other people.... It is an intimacy with and not an aloofness from other people that motivates womanist educators to see personal fulfillment in working toward the common good.

By recognizing the ways that their students and families were marginalized and seeking to provide schooling that would be transformative and empowering to these individuals and families, educators in SJA show womanistic tendencies.

Limitations to Spaces

Although strong in many ways, these spaces of engagement are limited as well. The two limitations I discuss here are the lack of antiracism and the lack of creatively engaging caregivers outside the school setting.

One key limitation is the lack of an explicitly antiracist focus in the culture of the school. Despite the strengths of establishing strong personal relationships, educational leaders—who were primarily White women—failed to acknowledge the racial dynamics that are inherent in such a racially mismatched school setting. As illustrated in Table 1, those in positions of formal authority were predominantly White, whereas the majority of Black school personnel were not in leadership roles. Only one of the teacher research participants was Black. The secretary was Black and held considerable experiential authority, though more limited positional authority. Although two board members who were research participants were Black, these positions are of relatively limited authority, as the board serves solely as advisory. By contrast, virtually all the White research participants had strong roles in the school, at the administrative, teaching, or donor level.

The lack of explicitly acknowledging the dynamics of race indicated a level of "racial erasure" (McKenzie & Scheurich, 2004), implying that issues of race were nonexistent or not important. By

TABLE 1. Race of Research Participants at SJA

White	Black

Adminstrator:
  Ms. Green, principal (15 years, plus 15
    more as teacher)	

Teachers:
  Ms. Abrams: middle school teacher (22
    years)
  Ms. Frank: teacher and librarian (5 years)
  Ms. Grady: primary teacher (1 year)
  Ms. Morgan: primary teacher (2 years)
  Ms. Sterling: primary teacher in primary
    (4 years)
	Teacher:
	  Ms. Harris: intermediate teacher
	    (17 years)

Other participants:
  Mrs. Baker: major donor and volunteer for
    5 years
	Other participants:
	  Mrs. Coss: board member and
	    volunteer (12 years)
	  Ms. Mayes: volunteer and classroom
	    aide (15 years)
	  Mrs. McNess: volunteer (32 years)
	  Ms. Wallace: secretary (17 years)
	  Ms. Wells: board member and
	    volunteer (20 years)
	  Ms. Wellstone: part-time aide
	    (10 years)

contrast, making a commitment to acknowledging White privilege and working toward antiracism would have strengthened these spaces. Professional development support and training to facilitate antiracism in schools were available to SJA through the central office. However, at the time of this research, the principal had not chosen to make use of this support.

In addition to failing to explicitly apply antiracist commitments, these spaces were limited by the failure of SJA educators to imaginatively extend these spaces outside the school. For instance, though educators in SJA were focused in engaging caregivers in innovative ways, they were not encouraged to conduct home visits or to conduct conferences in nonschool locations, such as community centers. By more creatively looking to discover the funds of knowledge that can become evident by interacting with families in nonschool settings (ERIC Digest, 1994; Moll & Gonzalez, 2004), educators in SJA may have fostered stronger connections with caregivers. At the time of this research, no such efforts had been made.

In this discussion I argued that the educational leaders in SJA, beholden to the diverse student bodies for enrollment and grounded in a value system that espouses inclusion, created spaces that value diverse forms of social and cultural capital. However, these spaces have been limited in key ways. I now turn to the implications that emerge from this discussion.

CONCLUSION

Efforts to improve schools often focus on innovative approaches to caregiver and community engagement (Brooks, 2005; Christie, 2005; Haynes, 2005; Lopez, 2001; Lopez et al., 2001; Perez Carreon et al., 2005). Presenting a religious school that uses innovative and effective strategies to engage caregivers, this case study contributes to a deeper understanding of how critical care theory can build social justice practices in schools. This case indicates that educators may experience both a push and a pull toward engaging caregivers. This push and pull can occur at both the institutional and the individual level. At the school level, SJA was compelled to engage caregivers as a strategy of maintaining enrollment and was drawn to do so from its religious mission. At the individual level, the educators in the school were required to initiate consistent, focused, positive-oriented contacts with families, but they also expressed satisfaction in doing so.

The findings here indicate that many of the efforts to create spaces of engagement—from the personal attention of the principal and the strong relational networks of teachers with families—are more driven by dispositions and commitments more than by budgets. In other words, many of the significant features of SJA reported here did not depend on an influx of resources but rather on the attitudes of the educators. Further, this study suggests that the limitations of such efforts (for instance, the lack of an antiracist focus) are not necessarily due to the dearth of resources. Finally, the findings indicate ways in which nontraditional support structures can broaden the capacity of a school community to more effectively engage caregivers.

The case of SJA suggests that creating spaces valuing diverse forms of social and cultural capital is not inhibited by resources but by dispositions. The critical elements in this case—namely the intense personal relationship of the principal to caregivers, the proactive, positive, and focused attention from teachers, and the concerted efforts to reduce barriers to families—were all pursued without significant influxes of external resources. In particular, the systems to build these relationships, such as by the principal personally interviewing families, teachers initiating weekly positive contacts with families, and three-way conferencing.

The case of SJA can serve as a counter-narrative. Delgado (1989) explains that counter-narratives "open new windows into reality, showing us...possibilities for life other than the ones we live" (p. 2414). Counter-narratives accomplish this by presenting an alternative to the stock story, which, Delgado illustrates, "picks and chooses from among the available facts to present a picture of what happened: an account that justifies the world as it is" (p. 2421). The stories of critical care illustrated here are counter-narratives because they suggest alternatives to what Rolon-Dow (2005) described as "deficit-based, racialized caring narratives" (p. 104) that hamper many school communities. Counter-narratives are tools to highlight a key barrier toward equity, which Delgado (1989) refers to as "the prevailing *mindset* by means of which members of the dominant group justify the world as it is, that is, with whites on top and browns and blacks at the bottom" (p. 2413). By contrast, the educators in SJA showed a willingness to challenge the inequities of the "world as it is." The research participants repeatedly reflected deep commitments to the dignity of each individual child and a respect for the caregivers in their lives. This was evident in the interview responses and supported by observations of the community and artifacts within it, such as the school mission.

A central limitation to this research is the focus on the perspectives of the educational leaders. This study fails to capture the perceptions of families and other community members. Including these perspectives would strengthen this research. This study also focuses on how the school pursues caregiver engagement. Moving toward students as the unit of analysis would reveal important insights into the effects of this engagement on social, emotional, and academic success. Although a certain level of school success is implied by the fact that parents are choosing to enroll their children as students in SJA, at no small personal and financial cost, a more focused examination of the elements of student outcomes would be valuable in future research.

A key implication of this study for future research is that diverse school settings may contain important lessons regarding caregiver and community engagement. Educational researchers would benefit from seeking counter-narratives from diverse settings. Mixed methods of ethnographies combined with survey data would contribute to a richer understanding of these contexts. Additionally, future research should examine links between caregiver and community engagement and multiple student outcomes, including academic, social, and personal measures.

An implication for educational leadership programs is the value of attending to case studies of schools seeking to systematically value diverse forms of social and cultural capital. Caregiver engagement is related to how schools look outward to both serving and being served by their multiple constituencies. School leaders would learn from more practical examples and theoretical models to help them navigate these terrains, especially ones that explicitly address racial and class differences. Both preservice and practicing school leaders would benefit from critically analyzing such case studies that illustrate these complexities.

In conclusion, this research contributes to our evolving understanding of caregiver engagement by presenting a textured analysis of a case study as viewed through the critical care conceptual framework. The educational leaders in SJA create spaces for engaging caregivers and building community support through a combination of desperation and innovation, on one hand compelled by pressures to attract students to enroll and on the other hand drawn by espoused values affirming the dignity of all students. They forged innovative alliances that strengthen these spaces, and their stories are counter-narratives to both deficit-oriented care models and to caricatures of private schools as bastions of elitism. These leaders provide important lessons for all educators committed to the social justice values of authentically engaging caregivers.

REFERENCES

Abrams, L., & Gibbs, J. T. (2002). Disrupting the logic of home-school relations: Parent involvement strategies and practices of inclusion and exclusion. *Urban Education, 37,* 384–398.

Alt, M. N., & Peter, K. (2002). *Private schools: A brief portrait*. Washington, DC: National Center for Education Statistics.

Anderson, G. (1998). Toward authentic participation: Deconstructing the discourses of participatory reforms in education. *American Educational Research Journal, 35,* 571–603.

Bauer, A., & Brown, G. D. M. (2001). *Adolescents and inclusion: Transforming secondary schools.* Baltimore: Paul H. Brookes Publishing Co.

Beauboeuf-Lafontant, T. (2002). A womanist experience of caring: Understanding the pedagogy of exemplary black women teachers. *Urban Review, 34,* 71–86.

Beck, L. (1994). *Reclaiming educational administration as a caring profession.* New York: Teachers College Press.

Berger, E. H. (2000). *Parents as partners in education: Families and schools working together.* Upper Saddle River, NJ: Merill.

Brooks, S. (2005). *Increasing minority parent involvement by changing the parameters from teacher-centered to parent-centered models.* Paper presented at the National Conference of the University Council for Educational Administration, Nashville, Tennessee, November 10–13, 2005.

Carlisle, L. R., Jackson, B. W., & George, A. (2006). Principles of social justice education: The social justice education in schools project. *Equity and Excellence in Education, 39,* 55–64.

Carspecken, P. F. (1996). *Critical ethnography in educational research.* New York: Routledge.

Charles A. Dana Center. (1999). *Hope for urban education: A study of nine high-performing, high-poverty, urban elementary schools.* Washington, DC: U.S. Department of Education, Planning, and Evaluation Service.

Christie, K. (2005). Changing the nature of parent involvement. *Phi Delta Kappan, 86,* 645–646.

Coleman, J. (1991). A federal report on parental involvement in education. *The Education Digest, 57,* 3.

Delgado, R. (1989). Storytelling for oppositionists and others: A plea for narrative. *Michigan Law Review, 87,* 2411–2441.

Delpit, L. (1988). "The silenced dialogue: Power and pedagogy in educating other people's children". *Harvard Educational Review, 58,* 280–298.

Dwyer, D., & Hecht, J. (1992). Minimal parental involvement. *School Community Journal, 2,* 53–66.

Eccles, J. S., & Harold, R. D. (1996). Family involvement in children's and adolescents' schooling. In A. Booth & J. F. Dunn (Eds.), *Family school links: How do they affect educational outcomes?,* pp. 3–33. Mahwah, NJ: Lawrence Erlbaum.

Epstein, J. (1986). Parents' reactions to teacher practices of parent involvement. *The Elementary School Journal, 86,* 277–294.

Epstein, J. (1990). School and family connections: Theory, research, and implications for integrating sociologies of education and family. *Marriage & Family Review, 15,* 99–126.

Epstein, J. (1993). Power in partnership. *Teachers College Record, 94,* 710–717.

Epstein, J. (1997). Six types of school-family-community involvement. *Harvard Education Letter* (September/October). Retrieved May 2, 2008 from http://www.edletter.org/past/issues/1997-so/sixtypes.shtml.

Epstein, J., & Salinas, K. C. (2004). Partnering with families and communities. *Educational Leadership, 61,* 12–18.

ERIC Digest. (1994). Funds of knowledge: Learning from language minority households. *ERICRIE0,* 19940201.

Fan, X., & Chen, M. (2001). Parental involvement and students' academic achievement: A meta-analysis. *Educational Psychology Review, 13*, 1–22.

Fine, M. (1993). [Ap]parent involvement: Reflections on parents, power, and urban public schools. *Teachers College Record, 94*, 682–710.

Freeman, J. (1975). Three-way conferencing. *Teacher, 93*, 40–42.

Gutman, L. M., & McLoyd, V. (2000). Parents' management of their children's education within the home, at school, and in the community: An examination of African-American families living in poverty. *The Urban Review, 32*, 1–24.

Hanafin, J., & Lynch, A. (2002). Peripheral voices: Parental involvement, social class, and educational disadvantage. *British Journal of Sociology of Education, 23*, 35–49.

Haynes, K. (2005). *The alchemy of hardship: Transmuting Latino's parent capital.* Paper presented at the National Conference of the University Council for Educational Administration, Nashville, Tennessee.

Henderson, A., & Mapp, K. L. (2002). *A new wave of evidence: The impact of school, family, and community on student achievement.* Austin, TX: Southwest Educational Development Laboratory.

Hoge, D., Smit, E., & Crist, J. (1997). Four family process factors predicting academic achievement for sixth and seventh grade. *Educational Research Quarterly, 21*, 27–42.

Jeynes, W. (2005a). A meta-analysis of the relation of parental involvement to urban elementary school student academic achievement. *Urban Education, 40*, 237–269.

Jeynes, W. (2005b). Effects of parental involvement and family structure on the academic achievement of adolescents. *Marriage & Family Review, 37*, 99–116.

Lareau, A., & Horvat, E. M. (1999). Moments of social inclusion and exclusion: Race, class, and cultural capital in family-school relationships. *Sociology of Education, 72*, 37–53.

Lareau, A., & Shumar, W. (1996). The problem of individualism in family-school policies. *Sociology of Education, 69*, 24–39.

Lincoln, Y., & Guba, E. (1985). *Naturalistic inquiry.* Beverly Hills, CA: Sage Publications.

Lipsitz, G. (1998). *The possessive investment in whiteness: How white people profit from identity politics.* Philadelphia: Temple University Press.

Lopez, G. R. (2001). The value of hard work: Lessons on parent involvement from an (im)migrant household. *Harvard Educational Review, 71*, 416–437.

Lopez, G. R., Scribner, J. D., & Mahitivanichcha, K. (2001). Redefining parental involvement: Lessons from high-performing migrant-impacted schools. *American Educational Research Journal, 38*, 253–288.

Mandara, J. (2006). The impact of family functioning on African American males' academic achievement: A review and clarification of empirical literature. *Teachers College Record, 108*, 206–223.

Maxwell, J. (1998). Designing a qualitative study. In L. Bickman & D. Rog (Eds.), *Handbook of applied social research methods* (pp. 69–100). Thousand Oaks, CA: Sage Publications.

McKenzie, K. B., & Scheurich, J. J. (2004). Equity traps: A useful construct for preparing principals to lead schools that are successful with racially diverse students. *Educational Administration Quarterly, 40,* 601–631.

Moll, L., & Gonzalez, N. (2004). Engaging life: A funds-of-knowledge approach to multicultural education. In J. A. Banks & C. A. M. Banks (Eds.), *Handbook of research on multicultural education* (pp. 699–715). San Francisco: John Wiley & Sons.

Noddings, N. (2005a). Identifying and responding to needs in education. *Cambridge Journal of Education, 35,* 147–159.

Noddings, N. (2005b). *The challenge to care in schools: An alternative approach to education* (2nd ed.). New York: Teachers College Press.

Osterman, K. (2000). Students' need for belonging in the school community. *Review of Educational Research, 70,* 323–367.

Patton, M. Q. (1990). *Qualitative evaluation and research methods.* Newbury Park, CA: Sage Publications.

Perez Carreon, G., Drake, C., & Calabrese Barton, A. (2005). The importance of presence: Immigrant parents' school engagement experiences. *American Educational Research Journal, 42,* 465–498.

Rodgers, K. B., & Rose, H. (2001). Personal, family, and school factors related to adolescent academic performance: A comparison by family structure. *Marriage & Family Review, 33,* 47–52.

Rolon-Dow, R. (2005). Critical care: A color(full) analysis of care narratives in the schooling experiences of Puerto Rican girls. *American Educational Research Journal, 42,* 77–111.

Scanlan, M. (2006). Problematizing the pursuit of social justice education. *UCEA Review, XLX (3),* 6–8.

Stake, R. (1985). Case study. In J. Nisbet, J. Megarry, & S. Nisbet (Eds.), *World yearbook of education, 1985: Research, policy, and practice.* New York: Nichols Publishing Company.

Stake, R. (1995). *The art of case study research.* Thousand Oaks, CA: Sage Publications.

Stolz, H., Barber, B., Olsen, J., Erickson, L., Bradford, K., Maughan, S., & Ward, D. (2004). Family and school socialization and adolescent academic achievement: A cross-national dominance analysis of achievement predictors. *Marriage & Family Review, 36,* 7–33.

Strauss, A., & Corbin, J. (1990). *Basics of qualitative research: Grounded theory procedures and techniques.* Newbury Park, CA: Sage Publications.

Valencia, R. (Ed.). (1997). *The evolution of deficit thinking: Educational thought and practice.* Washington, DC: Falmer Press.

Valenzuela, A. (1999). *Subtractive schooling: U.S.-Mexican youth and the politics of caring.* Albany, NY: State University of New York Press.

Yin, R. (2003). *Case study research: Design and methods* (3rd ed.). Thousand Oaks, CA: Sage Publications.

Ysseldyke, J., & Algozzine, B. (2006). *Working with families and community agencies to support students with special needs.* Thousand Oaks, CA: Corwin Press.

High School Family Centers: Transformative Spaces Linking Schools and Families in Support of Student Learning

Karen L. Mapp
Vivian R. Johnson
Carol Sills Strickland
Catherine Meza

ABSTRACT. This study explores school, family, and community partnership at the high school level, using eight family centers as the entry point for the investigation. The purpose of the study was to identify ways that parents and school staff could collaborate to support high school students' achievement. The study findings led to the development of a model that represents three inputs that are crucial to the creation of a successful family center: (1) a supportive infrastructure, (2) the existence of skilled center staff, and (3) the presence of responsive programming. These three inputs led to the creation of a

Karen L. Mapp, EdD, is Lecturer on Education, Harvard University, Cambridge, MA; Vivian R. Johnson EdD, is Professor Emerita, Boston University, Boston, MA; Carol Sills Strickland, EdD, is Director of Research and Evaluation, DC Children & Youth Investment Trust Corporation, Washington, DC; and Catherine Meza, EdM, JD, was Assistant Director for the Institute for Responsive Education, and she is currently practicing law.

thriving center that acts as a transformative space, a "zone of community," that results in four outputs: (1) the creation of relational trust among adults, (2) shift in parents' role construction and efficacy, (3) the generation of student relational trust, and (4) the development of student efficacy. The data from this study suggest that the relational trust developed in these transformative spaces called family centers can have a positive effect on student efficacy. The study concludes with seven recommendations for schools and districts looking to establish family centers in high schools as a way to expand family engagement at the high school level.

INTRODUCTION

I don't believe that you can get student achievement done without your parents.... They must be part of the process.... They're not an add-on.... Having the Parent Center, I think, has made a real positive impact, both in atmosphere as well as the need to insure that parents have to be involved in their kids' lives.... The major function [in my opinion], of a parent center, is getting directly involved in the education of a child.... Because teenage kids need this type of support, ongoing.

High School Principal

These words from a veteran high school principal capture the value of family centers to involve families in their children's education at the secondary level. In this article we provide a detailed look at what happens in eight family centers based on data from the High School Family Center Research Project, a study conducted by the Institute for Responsive Education through a grant from the Charles Stewart Mott Foundation. Through stories and examples gathered from site visits and interviews, we describe the core elements that characterize the capability of these centers to welcome families and encourage their engagement. The data from this study suggest that the relational trust developed in these transformative spaces, called family centers, can have a positive effect on student efficacy.

Rationale and Description of Study

This study explores school, family, and community partnership at the high school level, using family centers as the entry point for our investigation. Our intent was to aid in the understanding of why and how some parents choose to be involved in their children's high schools despite the usual decline in family engagement at this level. Our hope was that the findings from this research would reveal ways that parents and school staff could collaborate to support high school students.

Research over four decades has established that partnership among school, family, and community plays a critical role in students' educational development (Cochran & Henderson, 1986; Eccles & Harold, 1996; Epstein, 1991, 1996; Henderson & Mapp, 2002). The benefits of various forms of family engagement such as encouragement, talking to children about homework, and engaging in two-way conversation with school staff about children's learning, include improved grades and standardized test scores (Epstein, Simon, & Salinas, 1997; Jeynes, 2005; Shaver & Walls, 1998; Westat, Rockville, & Policy Studies Associates, 2001), better school attendance (Clark, 1983; Epstein et al., 1997), increased expectations of postsecondary enrollment (Trusty, 1999), and more positive attitudes about school (Shumow & Lomax, 2001).

Real progress has been made in understanding the value of family support of children's education in the preschool, elementary, and middle school grades (Dauber & Epstein, 1993; Henderson & Mapp, 2003; Ho Sui-Chu & Willms, 1996; Hoover-Dempsey & Sandler, 1995). However, fewer efforts have been made to explore effective practices and strategies that have been used to engage families and community members in support of students' learning in high schools (Brian, 1994; Epstein & Connors, 1994; Simon, 2004). Unfortunately, the trend appears to be that as students move from elementary through middle and high school, family engagement in their education declines (Epstein & Connors, 1994; Dauber & Epstein, 1993). Many school reform models and the No Child Left Behind legislation include parent and community engagement as a key component; however, it is difficult to find evidence of implementation of successful parent engagement strategies at the high school level.

One strategy used by schools to foster partnership is the establishment of a parent or family center. A family center (or parent center) is a designated room or space in a school where activities take place that are meant to invite parents to be involved in their children's education. Managed or coordinated by a person (or persons) familiar with the needs of parents, students, and school staff, the family center is a place that welcomes not only parents, but also teachers, students, and community members. It can serve as an invitation to parents and family members to become involved in their children's education.

In the early 1990s, Vivian Johnson (1993, 1994) conducted the first studies of family centers in elementary and middle schools for Institute for Responsive Education and Boston University as part of the federally sponsored Center on Families, Communities, Schools and Children's Learning, a research and development project focused on family–school–community collaboration from birth through high school. Her work clarified the dimensions of functioning of family centers in 28 schools in 14 states and in four case studies examined the dynamics of school–family collaboration in the centers. This study continues and builds on Dr. Johnson's initial family center research.

Designed as an environmental scan of family centers in high schools, our objectives were to gain a better understanding of the following:

1. The various functions, activities, and roles of family centers at the high school level;
2. The influences of the centers on the educational development of high school students;
3. How and why parents, students, and school staff are involved in the centers; and
4. The most effective practices in high school family centers for enhancing partnerships and positive student outcomes.

The family centers in this study were located on-site, in the high schools. Some of the centers provided information, training, and services primarily for the parents at the school, whereas others offered a range of programmatic offerings intended for parents both at the school and within the district. The study focused on schools in five urban areas that serve economically distressed communities. We collected data from the staff working in the schools and the centers as well as from the parents and students being served by them. We also heard the perspectives of school staff (principals, teachers, and administrators) and community members on the usefulness and value of the centers to the school community.

Conceptual Framework

The conceptual framework for this study was developed using Bronfenbrenner's (1979) ecological systems theory, Epstein's (1991) concepts of overlapping spheres of influence and partnership, Mapp's (2003) research on practices that help partnerships flourish, and research on how and why families engage in their children's education (Hoover-Dempsey & Sandler, 1995; Mapp, 2003).

Bronfenbrenner's (1979) perspective challenged the tradition of studying the influence of family, school, and community as separate spheres in children's development. He conceptualized the ecological environment as "a set of nested structures, each inside the next, like a set of Russian dolls" (p. 3), with, for example, the individual at the innermost level, the home at the next level followed by the school and other organizations, and the larger society at the outermost level. The interconnections between persons within each level of the environment and the linkages between the different settings all have an effect on the individual's development.

Joyce Epstein (1987), basing her work on Bronfenbrenner's theoretical orientation, conceptualized a model of overlapping spheres of influence on children's learning: family, school, and community. These spheres can be pushed together or pulled apart by forces within each environment. When the spheres are brought together and operate in a collaborative manner to support children's learning, the result is the creation of a partnership among the adult stakeholders.

How are these partnerships between home and school developed and sustained? Mapp's (2003) study of parent engagement in an elementary school in Boston concluded that the school staff engaged in a "joining process" where they purposefully welcomed parents into the school, honored and validated families for any contribution they made to their children's education, and connected with families in ways that kept the children's educational development at the center of the partnership. This joining process resulted in the development of trusting and respectful relationships between school staff and families.

Family centers, therefore, operate within an ecological framework and may be viewed as spaces designed to bring together the stakeholders within the various spheres of a child's educational development. Research conducted by Kathleen Hoover-Dempsey and Howard Sandler (1995) provides an understanding of how and why parents are involved in their children's education. Hoover-Dempsey and Sandler identified three key concepts that influence the choices parents make about their engagement with the children's education:

1. Parents' "role construction." What parents believe about how they are supposed to be engaged in their children's education and what their peers, family, and community deem important and acceptable affects what parents decide to do. Cultural norms and values about a parent's role also affect their decisions.
2. Parents' sense of "efficacy." When parents believe they have the skills and knowledge needed to help their children and when they experience a positive relationship between school and home, this enhances their capacity to provide the type of home support that has a positive influence on student outcomes. Efficacy is the concept that Hoover-Dempsey and Sandler use to describe the confidence and capacity that parents experience as they become more involved in their children's education.
3. Parents' "sense of invitation." When parents receive clear invitations from both school staff and their children that their involvement is expected and welcomed, parents are motivated to be engaged.

Given the fact that family engagement decreases at the high school level, we wondered if the existence of a family center would impact parents' views about their role in their children's education and/or whether their confidence to be a positive influence on their teenager would be enhanced.

The concepts of overlapping spheres, school–family–community partnership, the joining process (welcoming, honoring, and connecting), and efficacy provided guidance for the study focus and assisted us in developing the research design. These conceptualizations also influenced the instruments that we used for data collection, including the background questionnaire, protocols for interviews, and decisions about what to include in the document review and field notes.

METHODS

Research Design

We used a qualitative research design to explore the dynamics of these family centers. We were keenly interested in collecting stories from the people working in the centers as well as the parents and students being served by the centers. We also wanted to gather the perspectives of principals, teachers, administrators, and community members on the usefulness and value of the centers. By understanding what went into making a family center work (inputs) and what participants got out of the family center (outputs), we hoped to understand whether and how a family center might influence positive outcomes for high school students. The study focused on schools in urban areas serving economically distressed communities, a priority area for the Institute for Responsive Education.

Choosing the Centers for the Study

To identify a sample of high school family centers for the study, we contacted central office staff at 57 urban public school districts who we thought would be aware of high school parental engagement initiatives. This was a tedious and often frustrating process, because many of the people we contacted either did not know whether there were family centers at any of the high schools or transferred us to other offices and departments that also lacked the information we were requesting. Some of the offices we were directed to (and through) included student support, guidance, high school development, public affairs and parent engagement, community relations, student, and family and community services.

After making contact with more than 57 school districts, we identified 26 high schools with family centers. We mailed introductory letters to the principals of those high schools describing our study and requesting their cooperation. Based on the framework of Johnson's 1994 study on parent/family centers, we designed a survey to gather descriptive background data such as how the center was initiated and funded, who provided the staffing, and the kinds of activities it sponsored.

In choosing the sites we sought geographic and ethnic diversity. Eight family centers were selected for the study: two in Boston, one in Memphis, two in Houston, one in San Diego, and two in Los Angeles (Table 1). All the high schools had seen moderate gains in

TABLE 1. High School Family Center Project Study Participants

School	District
Gompers High School/Harold J. Ballard Parent Center	San Diego Unified School District, San Diego City Schools
Belmont High School	Los Angeles Unified School District, District F
Lincoln High School Los Angeles, CA 90031	Los Angeles Unified School District, District F
Jeremiah E. Burke High School	Boston Public Schools
East Boston High School	Boston Public Schools
Frayser High School	Memphis City School
Sharpstown High School	Houston Independent School District
Furr High School	Houston Independent School District

the last 5 years in student outcomes such as achievement, attendance, and graduation rates.

At least two members of the research team visited each center for 2 full days. During each site visit, research team members were able to observe and participate in the daily activities of the family center and the school. The family center coordinator at each site arranged most of the formal interviews with parents, students, and members of the school staff such as the principal, guidance counselor, and teachers. We also conducted informal interviews with individuals as they "dropped in" to the center or arrived for workshops and classes. In total, we made field notes and tape-recorded interviews with over 100 people. We also collected informational and outreach materials, such as family center newsletters, brochures, flyers, parent handbooks, and other written matter about the school and family center. In addition, we downloaded information about the schools' demographic and academic information from district websites.

RESULTS

Our findings led to the development of a model that represents three inputs that are crucial to the creation of a successful family center: (1) a supportive infrastructure, (2) the existence of skilled center staff, and (3) the presence of responsive programming. These three inputs lead to the creation of a thriving center that acts as a transformative space, a "zone of community," that results in four outputs: (1) the creation of relational trust among adults, (2) shift in parents'

FIGURE 1. Core Elements of a High School Family Center.

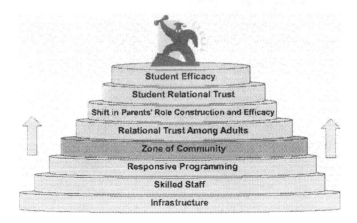

role construction and efficacy, (3) the generation of student relational trust, and (4) the development of student efficacy (Figure 1).

Input 1: Infrastructure

The first core element that we identified as essential to the functioning of a high school family center is a supportive infrastructure. We define infrastructure as the multifaceted foundation upon which the strategy for school–family–community partnership rests. Based on the centers we studied, we identified five key components of infrastructure: purpose and mission, administrative support, funding, space, and staffing.

Purpose and Mission

First and foremost, the family centers all had a purpose or mission that was "logically linked to learning" (Henderson & Mapp, 2003). Each center had a clear purpose driving its work: to help parents support their children's achievement in school. Members of the school staff appeared to know and embrace the mission of the center. For example, the principal at Frayser High School in Memphis stated, "The mission of the Frayser family center is to help families do anything that is necessary to prevent the students from being away from school." He also noted that the center at Frayser was "part of the school's overall effort to improve students' academic performance."

In most of the family centers, the mission statement was posted on the wall and served as a focusing vehicle for the work of the centers. Mission statements included the following language about the purpose of the center:

- To strengthen partnerships between home, school, and community
- To enable all children to reach their full potential by developing positive parenting skills of families
- To assist parents in supporting their children's academic, emotional, and social development
- To help families understand high school curriculum and how families can help support student achievement
- To help families to what is necessary to prevent the students from being away from school
- To help parents become effective partners in their children's education

The mission, goals, and purpose of the family centers were responsive—they were shaped to meet and respond to the needs of families and students served by the schools. Despite addressing a diversity of needs, a consistent goal of all the centers was to strengthen the link between students and their education.

Administrative Support

Family centers flourish in schools where they have the support of the principal and administration. The most dynamic centers were located in schools where the principal was an integral participant and advocate of the center. For these principals, the family center was a manifestation of their commitment to family engagement and a demonstration of their belief that home–school partnerships are key to whole school reform and to student success. One principal from Los Angeles stated, "My philosophy and my vision with all the staff is—we're here to welcome parents. This is their school, and we are always to be receptive to parents."

A former East Boston principal described his transformation from a "traditional principal who thought his parents should be kept at a distance" to, after seeing the benefits to the school climate and to students, an "ardent supporter" of family engagement at his high school:

> I don't believe you can get student achievement without your parents clearly in front of you, to push you. What [parents]

remind me of, as an educator, is what my job is all about . . . my job is to service kids. Every parent that pushes me and watches me makes absolutely sure that we are on track.

Administrative support for family centers also came in the form of encouragement, access to resources, and scheduling of professional development focused on family engagement. Principals who championed family centers set a tone of welcome in their schools. School staff, parents, and students all agreed that a family center could not exist in a school without administrative backing.

Support at the district level was also important. In Los Angeles the superintendent of the district encompassing Belmont High School was very supportive of parent engagement and intervened to allow parents to keep the room used as the family center despite overcrowding in the school. Project Reconnect in Houston was another example of how family centers thrive as part of a larger district initiative. This program, designed to cultivate family engagement and community participation in education, was spearheaded by Rod Paige in 1998. The fact that Project Reconnect was sustained even after Paige moved on to become U.S. Secretary of Education was due to "support at the top," according to Carrie McAfee, Houston Independent School District's Director of Parent Programs.

As these examples show, support from both the school leadership and the district is critical in constructing an efficient and sustainable foundation for a family center and its programming.

Funding

The sources of funding for the family centers varied. All the centers obtained at least a portion of their funding from federal grants such as Title One, Bilingual Education, or Healthy Start, but the funds allocated were inconsistent from year to year. Although some centers were funded through the district (Houston), most others obtained their resources through a variety of sources, including private foundations.

Family center budgets covered salaries for coordinators (ranging from $18,000 to $36,500) and also included expenses such as stipends for teachers of workshops or classes, food, supplies, and postage. In-kind contributions from the school, community, or business partners included space, telephone service, volunteers to conduct workshops, and reproduction costs for newsletters and flyers.

Dependence on soft dollars, according to the family coordinators and school administrators, always put the sustained existence of the centers at risk. Center staff were always looking for requests for proposals and other funding opportunities for the centers, and all commented about the need for the center to be included as a line item in the school's general operating budget. Only Houston had general operating money for their centers in the district budget ($1.4 million in 2001).

Space

Symbolically, the family centers sent a powerful welcoming message to families and students. The centers signaled a change in families' role from outsiders to insiders as they were encouraged to integrate into the school's daily life (Johnson 1993, pp. 1–2). By providing a space for families, schools indicated to them that were welcomed into the school any time.

Because the centers represent an unusual use of space in schools, they were vulnerable to the pressure of schools' usual needs for space. According to family center staff at some of the high schools, space for the centers was not easy to come by and was even harder to retain. At the Houston schools where overcrowding was also a problem, the family centers were located in "temporary buildings," prefabricated structures that, according to school staff, seem to have become "permanent." At one of the schools, teachers collaborated with the family center coordinator, allowing their classrooms to be used for parents' computer and English as a Second Language (ESL) classes.

At Frayser, the family center coordinator stressed the importance of having the center located in the school building. She stated, "Even if it was across the street at the church it would not function as well. It's right here and if they can get to it, they will come to it."

All the centers made an effort to create a space designed for comfort, although furnishings were often secondhand sofas or standard school chairs. Colorful posters on the walls and a warm welcome to everyone who crossed the threshold were commonly found. Most, though not all, centers also provided some form of nourishment, whether in the form of muffins and milk at the East Boston Center or snacks and juices sold for a nominal fee at the schools in Memphis. Food always seemed to be a planned component of family center activities. Another aspect of comfort was found in the corner play areas for children provided by some family centers.

Despite differences in size, location, and level of activity, each of the family centers we visited was a unique space, a comfort zone that brought a feeling of family into the school and helped make the school more welcoming to families.

Staffing

Every center had at least one person acting as a coordinator or manager of the center. Some center coordinators worked full-time and others were paid a part-time stipend, usually through Title I funds. Additional staff included paid part-time staff who were funded through other grants or special programs that served the school population.

The center coordinators usually reflected the ethnic/cultural background of the majority of students in each school. Their ties to the community helped them to make connections to families and resources, whereas their link to the school enabled them to act in a variety of roles that bridged many of the differences between the home and school. We identified the skills and competencies of these staff as the next core element of the high school family centers we studied.

Input 2: Skilled Staff

The next core element we identified as being crucial to the effective functioning of the family centers is the presence of skilled staff. What we observed and heard from not only the family center staff but from students, administrators, community members, and parents was that the staff played a pivotal role in making the centers a success. The family center staff act as the "glue" that holds the center together and ensures its success or failure. The staff brought and held together the three overlapping spheres—school, family, and community—that support student academic and social success. Although the staff who served in these positions displayed highly developed "people skills," many of them had also received specific training that helped them to be more effective in their various roles.

We discovered one role that served as the foundational competency for the job. Family center staff served as cultural brokers (Delgado-Gaitan, 2001), exhibiting an uncanny ability to bring various diverse groups of stakeholders together to support children's learning. In her book, *The Power of Community*, Concha Delgado-Gaitan (2001) provides a rich ethnographic description of a parent activist organization in Carpinteria, California, the Comite de Padres Latinos/Committee of Latino Parents. In her description of the various individuals who made up the organization, she highlights the role of the director of special projects in the Carpinteria School District. She describes his role as that of a "cultural broker," a person who is able to build bridges between immigrant families and schools. In explaining this role of cultural broker, Delgado-Gaitan states, "For children, as well as adults, learning a new language and culture often necessitates a mediator between the familiar and the new. Someone who knows the rough parts of the road for an immigrant and can facilitate the appropriate knowledge and means that will allow people to participate more fully in their new community" (p. 16).

Our research identified six key skills that the family center staff exhibited in their role as cultural brokers bringing together families, school staff, community members, and students:

- **Authentic connectors:** Family center staff shared an authentic cultural connection with the families and students they served.
- **Border crossers:** Staff crossed over and moved through traditional barriers that exist between school staff and stakeholders such as parents, activists, and students.
- **Bridge builders:** In addition to being accepted and trusted by diverse stakeholders, family center staff were able to build bridges among the groups, bringing them together to support student achievement.
- **Nurturers and caregivers:** Staff were friendly and welcoming to everyone who came into the family center, whether it was parent, student, teacher, other school staff, or a visitor. They knew how to listen and always seemed available to help.
- **Creative communicators:** Staff had to come up with creative ways to attract parents, students, teachers, and other school staff to the center. They learned about what people needed to know and could "translate" between languages, both literally (most often English and Spanish) and in terms of the norms or expectations that might differ between school and home. Staff also went the extra mile to connect with families and students.
- **Advocates/mediators:** Staff were adept at balancing the very tricky role of advocating for parents and students *while also* being employees of the schools and, in many cases, reporting to the principal.

What we heard and saw as we interviewed the families and students who frequented the family centers was that school can be an intimidating and foreign place for all families. Several parents stated that current school practices and policies were confusing to them and that their children's homework seemed foreign. Many families spoke of being intimidated by and disconnected from schools and their staff. Some parents spoke of how their own negative experiences when they were in school adversely affected their relations with their children's school staff. Given the asymmetrical power relationships between school personnel and families where families, especially those from economically distressed communities, feel disenfranchised by school, the role of family center staff as cultural broker is of tremendous importance. The family center staff were effective problem-solvers and mediators, persistent and patient, and, above all, caring and respectful of people regardless of differences in socio-economic class, color, ethnicity, or educational level. They also had the ability to work in collaboration with both teachers and community organizations.

Input 3: Responsive Programming

The third essential input for a high school family center is the level and type of programming emanating from the center. Nearly all the work of the family centers we studied was connected in some way to learning, even though programming focused on different themes and patterns in the different schools. No two centers we saw had exactly the same programs because each met the specific needs of its population; however, all seemed to allow positive relationships to grow and flourish. Whether programming focused on parents or students, a primary purpose was to help students do better in school.

Programming for Parents

The family center programming for families was designed to enhance parents' sense of efficacy and to have a positive effect on teens' educational outcomes. The centers in this study encouraged parents to come to schools not simply to help out in the office or raise funds through bake sales, but to improve their skills and support their children's learning. The three primary types of programming for parents focused on relationship building, social capital development and self-improvement, and understanding the educational process.

Building Relationships Between Home and School

In all the centers, building nurturing relationships between families and the schools drove many of the practices and activities. For example, the Family Center Coordinator at East Boston High School enlisted the help of the school's ROTC cadets to greet parents at the first open house and direct them to a sign-in sheet, which was then used to create a database of families' names and addresses. Cadets were also instructed to ask parents how they heard about the open house—whether by newsletter, phone call, newspaper, or from their student—so that the coordinator could keep track of how parents received information.

In several centers, this intentionality around relationship building meant having snacks and coffee available at all times for families or sponsoring a multicultural potluck dinner for the school. It also meant providing information, guidance, and a listening ear to parents, especially those who were coming to the school for the first time. Making a connection with parents also entailed making referrals and connections to community resources (such as food banks, clothing, counseling), sponsoring raffles or food giveaways at school functions, or using surveys and need assessments to find out how the school might help parents help their children.

Programming for Social Capital Development and Self-Improvement

Family centers offered formal and informal services and opportunities that enhanced parents' self-efficacy. Courses, workshops, and training sessions allowed parents to improve their skills and knowledge, see themselves as learners, provide models for their children, and enhance their social capital. For example, parents learning English at the centers in Houston and San Diego identified themselves as "learners" and spoke of how they were better able to relate to their children's school work and described how they enjoyed "doing homework together" with their children. Parents spoke of being more confident to communicate with teachers and other school staff after learning about school practices and policies from workshops at the centers. Such activities and programs increased parents' social capital by introducing them to other parents and resources and by enhancing their own ability to be helpful to their children.

Parents of high school students often need a boost in their skills and confidence in dealing with the social, academic, and emotional needs of their teen-aged children. Family centers provided opportunities for learning about teen development issues. A Los Angeles parent stated the following:

> Five of my children have graduated from this school. So I've been here since the parent center opened. I've had problems with my kids, and I go to the family center and they've helped me. I feel very welcomed, and they have provided me with a lot if support. They've accompanied me places in the school I'm not familiar with. If I have a question, I can call them from home. And the coordinator tells me what I have to do.

Parents' descriptions of the benefits of their engagement at the centers focused on issues of empowerment. They indicated that participation in center programs offered them the opportunity to gain skills and knowledge that helped them serve as more effective educational advocates for their children. One San Diego parent expressed her experience as follows:

> I think the parent center is very important. Not only for us personally, but for our children. The parent center is where one has the opportunity to attend workshops to help us as parents, and by benefiting us, these things benefit our children. They train us how to talk to our children and interact with them. They motivate us to motivate our children.

Expanding Knowledge About Academics and Schooling

Family centers provided workshops, classes, and activities that gave parents information about high school policies and procedures, information on the various tests and standards students were expected to meet, and about high school curriculum. Parents stated that this programming helped them make sense of complex high school curriculum and the criteria their students would have to meet to be eligible for postsecondary opportunities. For example, East Boston High School parents wanted to know more about the high stakes state tests that all students must pass to graduate. In response, the family center staff took parents to training about how the

Massachusetts Comprehensive Assessment Test (MCAS) is scored. Parents stated that they became more knowledgeable about what students needed to know to pass the test. Parents who took part in the training then facilitated workshops on MCAS for other parents at the school.

Bridge-Building Support for School Staff

Because family centers were usually the first checkpoint in the school for many parents, they were seen as essential and pragmatic support for staff, guidance counselors, and administrators. Center coordinators helped to schedule parent–teacher conferences or provided a listening ear for parents to vent their frustrations before meeting with school staff.

The general atmosphere of the centers was characterized by notions of inclusion, connection, and collaboration with school staff. The welcoming space of the family center provided an equitable and safe environment where people could interact despite differences in role, racial/ethnic/economic background, or language. Several teachers and administrators indicated that they couldn't "reach out" to parents as effectively if the family center did not exist at their school.

Supportive Programming for Students

Although not all family centers intentionally provided programming for students, the warm and welcoming atmosphere offered a "comfort zone" where adults could provide an informal kind of support and encouragement for students. We found that a few of the centers also involved students in programs that were more formally linked to learning, both academically and socially.

An Informal, Safe-Haven for Students

Although most of the centers originated as places for parents to become involved in their children's school, students often found their way to these havens. Once in the family center, students found adults who were willing to listen to them and help them in ways that teachers and counselors might not always have the time to do. One East Boston student stated the following:

> To go with our problems to a teacher, it's really not the same thing. Most teachers don't have the time to help. They're always busy doing something else, so we know that we can go to the parent center.

For example, the center coordinator in one Los Angeles school acted as an advocate for students, supporting their fundraising efforts and arranging for them to attend a special event for immigrants at the state capitol. In other centers, students found a place where they could snack on "little munchies" if they hadn't had breakfast or where they could discuss problems with a caring adult.

One administrator made it clear that the family center "was not designed for students to just drop in," but he admitted that "some kids just migrate" to the center. This "migration" was explained by students who commented about the stark difference in the relationships they had with family center staff compared with other adults in the school. Students valued the open-door policy of the centers, the availability of the staff, and the ability of the staff to relate to their issues. Students who we met in the various centers talked about how much they appreciated having a place to go in the school where they could find an adult who was available to listen and who could be counted on to be understanding and caring. Students were willing to hear reminders about improving their behavior from family center staff. A Memphis student described how the family center staff kept her from making bad decisions about her behavior:

> Many students avoid suspension by coming up here and talking about it first. I know people that will be ready to fight, and they come up here before, they talk and get common sense in their heads. Last year I was into fighting. And before I fought, I came up here and talked about my problems. And they told me, "You'll be a senior next year. You don't have time for that!" And I left it alone. Because it was childish, you know.

Center staff encouraged students to do their schoolwork and helped with the college application process. Although not explicitly created for students, the family centers served an important and unique function for many students. In the words of one student, "They're there serving as my parents away from home."

Formal Programming for Students

Although nearly all the family centers we visited served as a "comfort zone" in the school that students were drawn to informally, a few of the family centers involved students more directly. The Memphis center viewed its programs for students as supporting families to keep children in school. Their efforts included a summer academic enrichment program, opportunities for community service, and social support systems for young women and teen parents. The summer math and science camp that took place for 2 weeks in June was designed to encourage entering seventh grade students to be better prepared in math and science and also helped to ease the transition from elementary to the high school. In their "Teens for Peace" program, students worked to promote less violence by participating in projects to improve both the school and the community. The "Sister-to-Sister" program, described by one of the student participants as "talking about girlie things," brought over 100 young women together to improve their self-esteem, self-control, communications, and connections.

Several other family centers provided students with opportunities to participate in work and community service projects where they made connections with other students, parents, and adults. For example, in Houston students volunteered to teach parents in family center–sponsored classes in computer basics and ESL. Another center sponsored a Mexican folkloric dance group that gave performances for the parents who had completed the ESL class. Students reported that their participation in these activities had a positive influence on the way they felt about and engaged in school.

Inputs Summary

Our study indicates that the three input components of a solid infrastructure at both the school and district level, skilled staff to run the center, and programming that is responsive to the needs of all stakeholders—especially the families and students—are the levers needed to implement and sustain a successful family center.

The fourth ring in our diagram represents the family center as a functioning entity in the school. Becuase participants described family centers as communal places in schools where everyone is welcome, we refer to this unique space in the school as a "zone of community."

A Transformative Space: Zone of Community

We arrived at the conclusion that these family centers were zones of community after our data analysis revealed that parents, teachers, principals, students, and community members frequently described the centers as special places where they all felt welcomed, respected, comfortable, encouraged, and safe. They mentioned that their individual needs were met and that the positive environment of the centers promoted mutual respect. One teacher stated the following:

> The center is actually like a small community center in which you get help for everything. Not only do the teachers get the help, but also the parents. They go to workshops to improve, to help their kids. I see it as a community center where everybody comes. They state what's going on or what their needs are, and their needs are met.

During the analysis phase of our study, Karen Mapp saw a documentary about haloclines. A halocline is an ecosystem where freshwater and saltwater meet and where the needs of certain freshwater and saltwater species are met. The idea of a place that accommodates differences and provides the nutrients to meet the needs of the different components sharing the space served as a powerful analogy for our findings.

Other spaces in schools, such as classrooms and offices, have more traditional functions where parents, teachers, and students have traditional expectations about what is supposed to occur. The spaces outside the school—the homes and communities where families spend much of their time—may be perceived as having different expectations for how people interact. Family centers in schools do not have a "traditional" function but a clearly defined purpose to promote family–school–community partnership. Thus these centers are like the halocline, the space where "freshwater" and "saltwater" denizens can meet in new ways and try different types of relationships that cultivate mutual respect. Family centers are spaces where hierarchy is flattened, new activities can happen, and transformations can occur.

Our study identified the following characteristics that, taken together, formed these zones of community:

- **Mutual respect for all:** In the family centers, all stakeholders were encouraged to treat each other with mutual respect. One parent stated, "Both young and old can talk while having mutual respect for one another."
- **Family-like comfort:** Family centers were often described as comfortable places that resembled one's home, with food, furniture, and surroundings that created less "office-like" and more "home-like" environments.

- **Everyone is welcomed and supportive:** The belief that all stake-holders are important to elevate students achievement was prevalent in the centers, and therefore all were welcomed into the centers. A parent stated, "We're open to helping anyone, in the same way that we've been helped."
- **Individuals are recognized and acknowledged:** Stakeholders described the family centers as being places where their ideas and views were recognized and supported. A teacher noted that family centers are "the means by which parents are allowed to voice their needs, their concerns, and just to be part of our system; our school."
- **Stakeholders communicate and hear each other's perspectives:** The environment in the family center fosters a reciprocal respect that people respond to positively. One teacher stated, "If we take the parent to the main office or to the classroom, it's not a nice place. So we have the parent conference in the parent center, and we have all the persons listening and participating in the conference." The kind of dialogue that tends to be practiced in a family center can facilitate communication between parents and teachers and students because it is an environment that is conducive to collaborative, friendly communication.

Our findings indicate that the existence of a high school family center that serves this transformative function leads to four important outcomes that ultimately enhance students' ability to successful negotiate the academic and social challenges of high school.

Output Element 1: Relational Trust Among Adults

Respondents stated that the enthusiastic welcome to the entire school community, the support for individual needs, the encouragement of mutual respect, and the improved communications in these zones of community promoted a transformation in the attitudes, climate, and culture at the schools. The schools became places where the engagement of parents was seen as a crucial aspect of whole school reform. Center staff stated that the family centers were a signal to everyone—including students—that the families were expected and would receive support to be engaged in their children's education. A principal described this transition, noting that it was both slow and challenging:

> We went through a process of negativity at first. Why are these parents here? Are they here to look? What are they overseeing?

How can they really help me? It was an attitude issue.... But what has happened here, there has been a cultural shift within the building. The major function to me of a parent center is getting [people] directly involved in the education of the child. I don't want to lose sight that that's truly what we're supposed to evolve into; a partnership, a real and true partnership.

As adults in the school—the parents and school professionals—experienced the more inclusive, safe, and comfortable culture and climate in the centers, they developed more trusting relationships with each other. Through the increased opportunity to talk and listen to one another in the family center and during center sponsored activities, the adults shed old and negative perceptions and began the process of building relational trust (Bryk & Schneider, 2002), and families spoke of feeling more welcomed into the school.

Output Element 2: Shift in Parents' Role Construction and Efficacy

Shifts in Parents' Role Construction

Our study findings reveal that as a result of the support and encouragement of family center staff, the new positive relationships with school staff, and the knowledge and skills acquired from the various workshops and activities, parents experienced a shift in the concept of their role in their teenagers' education. Parents learned that their engagement was as important—if not more so—at the high school level than at any other time in their children's academic experience. The messages from the center pushed against strong cultural cues that family engagement at this level is unnecessary and viewed as excessive. One East Boston parent had this to say:

I believe that it is very important to have parent centers in high school, middle school, and elementary. Why? Because any individual who is given the opportunity to learn and improve themselves is going to be able to help their children. Yesterday I was talking to a woman whose son is in high school. She is going through the difficulty that her son does not want her to be involved in the school. We all understand why—he's at an age where he can say, "Well, Mom, I'm older and I don't need you to take care of me." But as parents, and through our experience, we know that parents should always be involved in their children's lives because, unfortunately, there are too many wrong paths that a child may be led to follow. And who better than a parent to be close to their children?

Shifts in Parents' Efficacy

Several parents revealed that, as a result of their engagement with the family center, they felt more confident that they could have a positive impact on their children's educational and social development. Many parents stated that the support they received from center staff and the skills acquired from workshops and classes helped them become better advocates for their children and to know what to do to help their child. One parent described the support she received from family center staff and the impact it had on her ability to help her daughter:

> Well, I mean, I had problems with my daughter . . . she was having problems with math. They got me all the right connections, even talked to the teachers themselves. I got a lot of input fast that I wouldn't have gotten if I did it all on my own and I didn't come here and learn about it. And they just helped me a lot. They're really, just really very helpful. I mean, I really, if it wasn't for them . . . I was ready to go crazy with my daughter. And they just helped me, they helped me to relax and to do things differently. I just felt better when I came out of there.

Parents' exposure to workshops and classes, such as working through teenage emotional issues, navigating the high school curriculum offerings, preparing for college, and self-help classes such as GED, ESL, and computer courses, all boosted their confidence to be engaged in their children's education. Given what we know from the research of Hoover-Dempsey and Sandler about the influence of parental role construction and efficacy on parents' choices about engagement in their children's education, our finding that family centers create the conditions to shift this role construction and increase efficacy is significant.

Output Element 3: Students' Relational Trust With Adults

Findings from our study revealed that students who were informally or formally involved with the family centers developed trusting relationships with family center staff. Students described the dynamics of these trusting relationships:

- *Students felt cared for and comfortable.* During our interviews, students often noted the importance of feeling comfortable in school, the difficulties they encounter in this regard, and the role of the family center in meeting their needs. Students frequently spoke about feelings of greater care, attention, support, and comfort in their relationship to the family center, which positively influenced their overall attitudes about and behavior in school.
- *Family center staff acted as "second parents."* One outstanding feature of the interviews with students was their feeling that family center staff acted like caring parents or, as they put it, "second moms and dads." For example, when asked what qualities he would expect in a family center coordinator, one student responded: "Kind of like a mother. Most kids need it. Most kids try to act like they don't need a mom or their daddy; but we really do—a lot of times in high school. No matter how much you try to hide it, you need it—you can't live without it."
- *Students valued the advocacy role of family center staff.* Students commented that family center staff often lobbied for them when they needed adult support. For example, one family center coordinator pushed for students to go to the state capital to lobby for school reform because she believed that students should be included in such trips. She stated, "Nobody ever advocates for students [to participate]. Parents and everybody else could go and nobody asked students, I'm the only one. I said, do you think you guys might let some students come with you?"
- *Students responded favorably to the "academic press" provided by family center staff.* Academic press is defined as the extent to which school members, including students and teachers, experience a strong emphasis on academic success and conformity to specific standards of achievement (McDill, Natriello, & Pallas, 1986). To succeed in schools that press them hard to learn, students need strong social support (Lee & Smith, 1999).

Our findings indicated that family center staff often played a critical role in students' lives by being a consistent source of academic press. Using the words of students, this academic press came in the form of a "hug and a push." The hug is symbolic of the way that center staff hold students close by demonstrating that they care. Students are affirmed by the "hug" and therefore respond to the academic "push" that the staff provide when students need it. One student commented about the pressure he received from one of the family center staff when he appeared to be distracted from his school work:

> She's tough like that. I like that, though. I mean, there's not too many teachers that are on our backs. We'd just be slacking through the whole school year. I rather that she'll be on my back ... I was beginning to slack and stuff.

Family center staff reported visits by students who returned to thank them and tell them they appreciated their efforts. The following story illustrates a student's willingness to publicly express his appreciation for a caring adult in front of his friends. A family center coordinator said that while shopping at the mall, she heard her name called and turned to find a former student:

> He had two of his friends with him. He's a young man now. And he said: "Yo—you see her? She used to be my teacher." ... It felt like the whole mall was looking at me, because he was loud and his friends were there. He said: "She used to come to my house and beg me to get out of bed and come to school." He went on. He was telling his friends. I said: "Shh. You know, could you keep it down." So, he said: "But I want to tell you, if it wasn't for her, I wouldn't have made it. I'm an electrician now." ... And he hugged me, and I hugged him.

This powerful expression of a student's appreciation illustrates his recognition of the interaction between adult support and academic press that he received from the family center staff.

Output Element 4: Student Efficacy

The final output that we identified from our study of high school family centers was of increased student efficacy. As parents became more knowledgeable of how to support children's academic development and as students developed increased levels of relational trust with adults, students' experienced elevated levels of confidence and resistance to setbacks, an understanding of why academics were important, a renewed desire to stay in school, and increased feelings of achievement and accomplishment. The following framework describes these four elements of student efficacy. We offer the following framework to describe these four elements of student efficacy.

I Can (Self-Confidence and Resiliency)

Increases in students' self-confidence and resilience were evident in their statements about their interactions with center staff. One student who had failed the ninth grade and dropped out of school returned after her parents and the family center staff encouraged her to do so. She described being "on track" and confident that she could do her school work, despite the fact that she had to catch up.

Another example of the development of resilience was that of a teen mother trying to graduate from high school while also caring for her young son. She noted how she profited from the support and reinforcement of the combined efforts of her parents and center staff:

> Ms. S. has been my parent away from home. She's kept me in line. If I wanted to slip away, if I was stressed—if I felt I just can't go on; I can't deal with William's crying at night, I can't deal with my homework at 11 o'clock because I have to make sure he's okay first—anytime I had problems like that, she was my shoulder. I went to her; and she would tell me, "You cannot give up. You have too much potential. Go on, I know you can do it!" And hearing that from her at school every time I had this problem, then hearing it from my Mom and Dad when I was home with them—it just kept me going. I mean, anytime they weren't there, she was.

That year, this young woman ended up graduating as the valedictorian of her class.

I Am Present (Improved Attendance)

Students in our study connected improvements in their attendance with the support they received from family center staff. For example, one student remarked, "Talking to Miss D. for 4 years has helped me come back to school and get the education that I need to succeed in life."

I Know (an Increased Knowledge of the Value of Education and of Adult Support)

Students described an increased awareness of what was required to do well in school and in life as a result of their exposure to programs in the center and the academic press of the adults. Students valued what they learned from supportive adults and connected it to their future success.

I Did it and I Received Recognition (Graduation, Awards, Accolades)

Receipt of scholarships, awards, and accolades from schools, families, and communities was further evidence of students' efficacy. As students joined us for interviews at one school, family center staff pointed out their accomplishments as scholarship winners at several colleges, including University of Massachusetts, Morris Brown in Atlanta, and Boston University. One student from East Boston was so proud that he said he was going to walk around with his college admissions letters in his pocket while he waited for responses from other colleges to which he applied. In his discussion with our interview team and the family center staff, this student demonstrated his self-confidence, knowledge about options and choices, as well as his achievement in receiving college admissions.

Although the schools in this study reported rising graduation rates and test scores, a direct correlation cannot be attributed to the presence of a family center. However, study participants gave overwhelmingly consistent responses that the existence of the family center and its role in connecting home and school was a key factor in the promotion of positive student outcomes. Students described various outcomes that they directly attributed to the presence of the family center and its staff such as greater self-confidence, pride in themselves and their school, improved attendance, better understanding of what is expected of them, and keeping "on track" with their school work. Students said that because these adults were demonstrating care for them in a variety of ways, they wanted to please and not disappoint them. Feeling affirmed by the fact that trusted adults "go out of their way" for them, students lose their sense of anonymity and alienation. They feel accountable to these adults who believe in them and are there for them if and when they need support.

CONCLUSION

Our findings from this study of eight high school family centers reveal that family engagement at the high school level is viewed as critical by various stakeholders: teachers, school administrators, district leaders, parents, and students. However, as we continue to work with educators from around the country, we hear of the challenges to engage families at the high school level. According to our findings, family centers, by serving as "zones of community," create the conditions for the cultivation and sustenance of partnerships between home and school. Both youth and adults told us why they are attracted to the centers, what is special about them, and what they offer that is not available elsewhere in schools.

Based on our findings, we offer seven recommendations for schools and districts looking to establish family centers in high schools as a way to expand family engagement at this level:

1. Family center initiatives require the support of school and district leadership. School leaders must promote the work of the center among all staff and encourage its use.
2. Family centers should have a clear mission that connects their purpose to student learning and development.
3. Funding for family centers must come from general operating funds to ensure the sustainability of the center.
4. Skilled staff must be hired to operate the centers and coordinate the center programming. Hire staff who can act as "cultural brokers" to diverse families and students. If possible, include parents on the hiring committee for the coordinator of the center.
5. Develop programming that is responsive to parents' needs and that is linked to student learning.
6. Seek partnerships with businesses, colleges and universities, and community organizations to support programming at the center.
7. Locate the center in a space easily accessible to parents. Make the space physically comfortable and welcoming to all families.

Our study yielded evidence about the role of the family center for participants as "a support place," as noted by Johnson (1993) in discussing the role and dimensions of functioning of these centers in her baseline study. The fact that students as well as adults described the types of support they received in these zones of community illustrates the criticality of these family center spaces in shaping positive attitudes and behaviors that support student success.

REFERENCES

Brian, D. J. G. (1994). *Parental involvement in high schools.* Paper presented at the Annual Meeting of the American Educational Research Association, New Orleans, April, 4–8.

Bronfenbrenner, U. (1979). *The ecology of human development: Experiments by nature and design.* Cambridge, MA: Harvard University Press.

Bryk, A. S., & Schneider, B. (2002). *Trust in schools: A core resource for improvement.* New York: Russell Sage Foundation.

Clark, R. (1983). *Family life and school achievement: Why poor black children succeed or fail.* Chicago: University of Chicago Press.

Cochran, M., & Henderson, C. R., Jr. (1986). *Family matters: Evaluation of the parental empowerment program.* Ithaca, NY: Cornell University Press.

Dauber, S. L., & Epstein, J. L. (1993). Parents' attitudes and practices of involvement in inner-city elementary and middle schools. In N. F. Chavkin (Ed.), *Families and schools in a pluralistic society* (pp. 53–71). Albany, NY: State University of New York Press.

Delgado-Gaitan, C. (2001). *The power of community: Mobilizing for family and schooling. Immigration and the transnational experience.* Blue Ridge Summit, PA: Rowman & Littlefield.

Eccles, J. S., & Harold, R. D. (1996). Family involvement in children's and adolescents' schooling. In A. Booth & J. F. Dunn (Eds.), *Family school links: How do they affect educational outcomes* (pp. 3–34). Mahwah, NJ: Lawrence Erlbaum.

Epstein, J. L. (1987). Toward a theory of family-school connections: Teacher practices and parent involvement. In K. Hurrelmann, F. Kaufmann, & F. Losel, (Eds.), *Social intervention: Potential and constraints* (pp. 121–136). New York: DeGruyter.

Epstein, J. L. (1991). Effects on student achievement of teachers' practices of parental involvement. *Advances in reading/language research, Vol. 5* (pp. 261–276). Greenwich, CT: JAI Press.

Epstein, J. L. (1996). Perspectives and previews on research and policy for school, family, and community partnerships. In A. Booth & J. F. Dunn (Eds.), *Family-school links: How do they affect educational outcomes* (pp. 209–246). Mahwah, NJ: Lawrence Erlbaum.

Epstein, J. L., & Connors, L. J. (1994). *Trust fund: School, family, and community partnerships in high school* (Report No. 24). Washington, DC: Center on Families, Communities, Schools, and Children's Learning.

Epstein, J. L., Simon, B. S., & Salinas, K. C. (1997). *Involving parents in homework in the middle grades* (PDK Research Bulletin No. 18). Bloomington, IN: Phi Delta Kappan International.

Henderson, A., & Mapp, K. (2002). *A new wave of evidence: The impact of school, family, and community connections on student achievement.* Austin, TX: Southwest Educational Development Laboratory/National Center for Family and Community Connections in Schools.

Ho Sui-Chu, E., & Willms, J. D. (1996). Effects of parental involvement on eighth-grade achievement. *Sociology of Education, 69,* 126–141.

Hoover-Dempsey, K., & Sandler, H. M. (1995). Parental involvement in education: Why does it make a difference? *Teachers College Record, 9,* 310–331.

Jeynes, W. H. (2005). A meta-analysis of the relation of parental involvement to urban elementary school student academic achievement. *Urban Education, 40,* 237–269.

Johnson, V. R. (1993). *Parent/family centers: Dimensions of functioning in 28 schools in 14 states* (Report No. 20). Baltimore, MD: Center on Families, Communities, Schools & Children's Learning.

Johnson, V. R. (1994). *Parent centers in urban school: Four case studies* (Report No. 23). Boston: Center on Families, Communities, Schools, & Children's Learning.

Lee, V. E., & Smith, J. B. (1999). Social support and achievement for young adolescents in Chicago: The role of school academic press. *American Educational Research Journal, 36,* 907–945.

Mapp, K. L. (2003). Having their say: Parents describe why and how they are engaged in their children's learning. *School Community Journal, 13,* 35–64.

McDill, E. L., Natriello, G., & Pallas, A. (1986). A population at risk: Potential consequences of tougher school standards for student dropouts. *American Journal of Education, 94,* 135–181.

Shaver, A. V., & Walls, R. T. (1998). Effect of title I parent involvement on student reading and mathematics achievement. *Journal of Research and Development in Education, 31*(2), 90.

Shumow, L., & Lomax, R. (2001). *Parental efficacy: Predictor of parenting behavior and adolescent outcomes.* Paper presented at the Annual Meeting of the American Educational Research Association, Seattle.

Simon, B. S. (2004). High school outreach and family involvement. *Social Psychology of Education, 7,* 185–209.

Trusty, J. (1999). Effects of eighth-grade parental involvement on late adolescents' educational experiences. *Journal of Research and Development in Education, 32,* 224–233.

Westat & Policy Studies Associates. (2001). *The longitudinal evaluation of school change and performance (LESCP) in title I schools. Final report. Volume 2: Technical report.* Washington, DC: US Department of Education.

Families Home Schooling in a Virtual Charter School System

Carol Klein

Mary Poplin

ABSTRACT. Contemporary educational options have increased in recent years as families have sought alternatives to traditional choices. Three of these, home schooling, charter schools, and virtual schools, provide the foundation for a new institution called the virtual charter school. This new alternative provides curriculum to home learners through advanced technologies within the charter school setting, allowing for innovation, freedom from traditional structure, and tuition-free education for students. The California Virtual Academies, a network of virtual charter schools, provided the opportunity to explore the phenomenon from the families' perspectives. The following questions were posed: What are the characteristics of families that are currently involved in home schooling through this innovative model? Why do families pursue this means of education? What are their experiences? How does it look in daily practice?

Carol Klein, Ph.D., is a Teacher on Special Assignment at Magnolia Elementary School District in Anaheim, California, and Mary Poplin, Ph.D., is Professor of Education at the School of Education Studies at Claremont Graduate University, Claremont, CA.

INTRODUCTION

Families of all socioeconomic levels are seeking alternatives to public schools. Many parents, after considering the lackluster results of traditional schools, have sought alternate forms of education that could meet their own standards of excellence (Hetzel, Long, & Jackson, 2001). Three powerful innovations—home schooling, charter schools, and, most recently, virtual or cyber-schools—are each having an impact on our society's contemporary ways of educating its young. Although these are providing new choices to parents, teachers, and students, they have also, perhaps unknowingly, changed the face of a once monolithic public school system.

Adding to the list of reform-oriented alternatives is a new pioneering effort that appears to have successfully merged all three of the aforementioned innovations—the virtual charter school. This innovation uses advanced technologies to deliver curriculum, and the recipients of this curriculum are home learners, including those of the home schooling population. This institution also functions within the charter school setting, which allows for innovation, freedom from traditional structure, and tuition-free education for all its students. We posed the following questions: What are the characteristics of families that are currently involved in home schooling through a popular network of virtual charters? Why do families pursue such an arrangement in the first place? What are their experiences? How does it look in practice during a typical day? First, we briefly present the most recent research on each of the three alternatives before focusing on virtual charters for home schooling.

Home Schooling

Home schooling, the oldest and largest of the three reforms, continues to be an increasingly popular alternative to traditional schooling (Belfield & Levin, 2005). It is now recognized as more mainstream, given the diversity and numbers involved in the movement (Collom, 2005). Ray (2006) states that the population is quickly growing among minorities (15% is now non-White/non-Hispanic) and has had an annual growth rate for several years of between 7% and 12% in the United States, making it one of the fastest growing forms of education today. Estimates on the number of students involved are between 1.9 and 2.4 million for the 2005–2006 school year. Home schooling has been defined by Russell (1994) as "75% or more of what the family considers to be schooling is provided by or conducted under the supervision of the parent(s)" (p. 2). Lines (1991) viewed it as instruction and learning that take place primarily at home in a family setting with a parent acting as teacher or facilitator of activities. Activities may be planned or not, but learning involves pupils who are family members doing grade K–12 work.

According to Ray (2002), this home-school movement grew out of an alternative school movement in the 1960s and 1970s and was also reinforced in the 1980s and 1990s by a public perception that government schools were on a downward spiral (Hetzel, 1998), through reports such as "A Nation at Risk," the decline of Standardized Achievement Test (SAT) scores, international comparisons, and safety concerns. Hetzel et al. (2001) found that the 332 parents who responded to their survey believed that their children receive "better instruction in morals, values, and academics, in a safer environment if they are home schooled."

Mayberry, Knowles, Ray, and Marlow (1995) found certain trends to be identifiable in the home schooling sample they studied. First, they found it to generally be a "white, middle-class movement, chosen primarily by relatively young parents living in traditional nuclear families" (p. 43). These parents also tended to be well educated, with the fathers often employed in jobs with flexible hours. For many of these parent educators, religious and spiritual convictions were found to be a prominent feature of their daily lives that directly affected their decision to home school. Third, this group was found to be politically conservative. Finally, these parents have had "little confidence in a wide spectrum of social institutions, including those commonly perceived to be conservative in nature" (p. 43). In spite of these trends, Mayberry et al. did stress that the movement is by no means homogeneous.

Though a variety of structures may be used, studies reveal that students in these environments are thriving (Medlin, 2000; Rudner, 1999; Taylor, 1986). Academic achievement scores of home-schooled youngsters have been found to range from above average (Van Galen & Pitman, 1991; Witt, 1999) to exceptionally high (Rudner, 1999). Two large studies exemplify these findings. The first, released in 1992 by the National Center for Home Education, was composed of a nationwide sample of over 10,000 K–12th-grade home-educated children. Data revealed that the average percentile rank scores ranged from 65 to 82 on the complete battery of subtests, whereas the national average was 50 (Medlin, 1994). The second study, a 1998 study completed by Rudner (1999) of 20,760 students using the Iowa Tests of Basic Skills (grades K–8) or the Tests of Achievement and Proficiency (grades 9–12), found home-schooled students were typically in the 70th to 80th percentile. Interestingly, Rudner concluded that these findings represent a 1-year lead for younger students and a 4-year advantage for children in eighth grade, compared with traditionally schooled children. Ray (2006) states that home-schooled children continue to typically achieve 15% to 30% higher scores on standardized tests.

Though research is limited, parental motivation for this choice is another common research theme or at least serves as a beginning point for further inquiries into this phenomenon. The research of Montes (2006) found top motivators for home schooling to be religious convictions (41.31%), better education provided at home (47.12%), and poor learning environment at school (23.47%). Collom (2005) identified four motivations of home schoolers in a charter in Southern California to be 1) academic and pedagogic issues, 2) dissatisfaction with public schools, 3) religious values, and 4) issues related to family life. Collom concluded that differing motivations do not translate neatly into distinct groups of home educators, that the population is heterogeneous with varying and overlapping motivations, and that parents who are home schooling have higher levels of education. He also suggested that religious reasons had subsided some since earlier studies.

Charter Schools

Though home-schooling parents have withdrawn from the system to deal with their concerns, another wave of reformers has opted to address challenges from within the system. Public charter schools have emerged in the last 10 to 12 years to pursue alternative ways of meeting the high academic standards that are essential for today's students. They are the most widely used form of school choice in the United States today (Fowler, 2003). Their appearance, which had its beginnings in the early 1990s in Minnesota (Marshall, Gibbs, Greene, Nelson, & Schofield, 2001; Morse, 2001), has spawned great controversy, with reactions ranging from a sense of great hope and promise by advocates to sincere alarm and vigorous opposition from differing voices.

Though no silver bullet, school choice, which is the impetus behind the charter school movement, appears to be here to stay (Fowler, 2003), perhaps because our society has long since become accustomed to the need for multiple choices in everything. By 2002, 39 states had charter school legislation (Kennedy, 2002) with more than 600,000 students attending 3,000 charter schools nationwide (Schemo, 2004). According to Stuart Wells, Slayton, and Scott (2002), this success is attributed in part to the uniting of multiple reform groups (e.g., Black separatists, civil rights leaders, progressive or free school educators, and conservative free-market economists), thus affording broad-based popularity and bipartisan support.

Manno, Finn, and Vanourek (2000) define public charter schools as "an independent public school of choice, freed from rules but accountable for results" (p. 736). The charter school must meet accountability standards in return for funding and autonomy. Its goal is to close the achievement gap and curtail bureaucratic excesses. Specific legislation is in place to monitor and review charter school practices usually every 3 to 5 years. Charters can be revoked if the set standards or guidelines on management and curriculum have not been met (National Center for Education Statistics, 2003).

Even though the charter schools provide an alternative to the traditional educational setting, they must be open to all students. In theory, anyone (e.g., private business, interested parents, and/or community members) can apply for a charter and form a public school if their plan is valuable, workable, and accepted by local governing authorities. State boards of education have been receptive to different philosophies with innovative pedagogical approaches for their conception (Marshall et al., 2001).

The Center for Education Reform has provided up-to-date information on charter schools. According to their report, the charter school movement is still unfolding and in its adolescent phase. In the fall of 2005–2006 the number of operating charters in the United States stood at 3,617 and was spread across 40 states plus the District of Columbia with over a million students enrolled (Allen & Heffernan, 2006). This is an increase from the previous year of 217 charters (Georgiou, 2005), attesting to the rapid increase in interest. The Center for Education Reform reported that states with multiple charting authorities have four and a half times more charter schools than those who only allow school board approval. Also noted was a rise in the number of universities/colleges who are becoming sponsors. Though many might still believe that charters take only the best students, 75% of students actually fall into the category of "at risk." Georgiou found that charter school students are more likely to be proficient in reading and math than students in neighboring conventional schools. She also stated that housing developers and community-based organizations are now assisting charter schools by renovating, building, or leasing new facilities. Some developments in city centers may help to reduce middle-class flight.

LaFevre (2005) reports several studies that suggested charter schools are especially beneficial to low-income and minority students while serving diverse populations of students. It was found that fewer charter students repeated grades or dropped out compared with their traditional counterparts. According to the same analysis, California (the state in this study) has an above average ranking for charter school law and by April 2005 had authorized 533 charters that serve 181,928 students. At that time, student ethnic composition for these charter schools was White, 54.4%; Hispanic, 26.6%; Black, 10.8%; Asian/Pacific Islander, 4.4%; and Native American, 2.5%.

Finally, Manno (in Peterson, 2006) offers evidence that although charters may cause trouble for some school districts, they often wind up saving money for the state. Charters may cost less to operate per student than traditional schools. For example, charters in Ohio received $2,300 less per pupil than local school districts in 1999–2000. It was estimated that seven of the largest districts in Ohio would have each received $20–60 million dollars less in state funds had they operated under the charter school funding formula. Manno cautioned that some charter schools have attracted greedy operators; thus it is crucial to have a system of review and monitoring firmly in place to hold all participants accountable to state expectations.

Virtual Charter Schools

Fundamental changes in society have driven, at least in part, the new demands for virtual charter education (Davis and Roblyer, 2005). Anytime, anywhere access to information is now common-place, and learners are coming to expect such experiences to be a part of their educational opportunities. This kind of schooling is offered by virtual charter models, which have recently been defined as "a hybrid of public, charter, and home schooling, with ample dashes of tutoring and independent study thrown in, all turbocharged by Internet technology" (Greenway and Vanourek, 2006, p. 4).

Growth of these new schools continues to soar. Currently, there are 147 online-only (virtual) charter schools in 18 states serving 65,354, which is 4% of the public charter population (Rotherham, 2006). The benefits of virtual charters include the ability to serve a wide range of students, public financing, innovative curriculum and its delivery, and the ability to retain students who may otherwise drop out of public education (Rapp, Eckes, & Plucker, 2006).

New questions are beginning to arise as new policies, programs, and roles require greater definition. Judicious responses will help pave the way for greater efficacy as foundations are laid in these areas. Huerta, Gonzalez, and d'Entremnont (2006) state, "As non-classroom-based charters expand to other states, policymakers will need to identify the teaching and learning, organization and governance models employed by non-classroom based charters, and address how they fit within the existing definitions of what is permissible under both charter legislation and general state education statutes" (p. 3).

Addressing these issues will not only provide clarity for charter contract fulfillment, but will strengthen accountability measures as well. Huerta et al. found the following emerging issues to be salient: (1) determining per-pupil funding for non–classroom-based charter schools, (2) establishing accountability measures of student performance and program quality, (3) defining enrollment boundaries and funding responsibilities, and (4) monitoring the influx of traditional home schoolers who are new to public education.

Another area that will need attention as virtual schools increase is teacher preparation. Although good communication and organization skills are always endemic to teacher success, a good classroom teacher is not necessarily a good online teacher. Those who succeed in online learning need to possess a certain set of skills to enable them to thrive in cyberspace (Davis & Roblyer, 2005). Necessary will be a paradigm shift in perceptions of instructional time and space, ways of engaging students through virtual communications, and virtual management techniques, just to name a few. The role of the teacher is sure to evolve in these new environments. Davis and Roblyer see these roles as counselor, assistant, teacher, and designer. The new demands on the teacher will require preservice programs to become well versed in these emerging competencies.

METHODS

This study sought to describe the demographics of parents participating in six virtual charter schools in California, their reasons for
participating and their experiences, their children's achievement,
and their daily routines. The study included all six of the California
Virtual Academies (CAVA),[1] the first of which was established in
2002. The six virtual charters were diverse in terms of location, urban
to rural, and size. (For extensive detail of the academies and their
operation, as well as California charter laws, see Klein [2006].) The
CAVA network is part of a larger national network of virtual
charters that operate in 12 states and partners with the for-profit
educational company "K12." The Virginia-based K12 Company
was created in 1999 by a team of educational experts, including the
board of directors' chairperson, William Bennett, former Secretary
of Education. The mission of the company, according to Ron Pack-
ard, K12's first CEO, was to provide "a world class curriculum that
every child could have access to." K12 provides CAVA with curriculum as well as administrative staff, computer systems, infrastructure,
and systems to fully manage the schools. The K12 curriculum covers
six subjects: math, language arts, science, history, art, and music. It
provides more than 600 lessons per grade level. Part of its foundation
is the Core Knowledge Sequence of E. D. Hirsch (1999), who asserts
the importance of cultural literacy and intellectual capital.

At the time of the study (2004–2005 school year) CAVA student
enrollment was 2,051, serving a total of 1,422 families. The number
had approximately doubled each of the 3 years that CAVA has been
in existence. The six sites ranged in enrollment from 99 to 1,059
students. Class sizes range from 30 to 35 students (currently 25),
and teachers are expected to be in touch with families regularly
through e-mail and phone. Face-to-face meetings with families are
scheduled every 45 days. Teachers monitor attendance and academic
progress of the students, support families with instructional and
learning needs, and complete report cards.

Data Collection

The head of schools at CAVA provided an administrative contact
person for the study who permitted the parent survey invitation to be
electronically mailed to all 1,422 families in CAVA through their

teachers. This contact person also provided a list of parents to approach for the 10 interviews. The survey was developed based on the literature review and expert examination and gathered background and demographic information as well as parental perceptions using both forced-choice questions and open-ended prompts. The survey was piloted before posting online through Zoomerang, which provided survey software. State test results were also obtained from three of the six sites—an urban, suburban, and rural site (largest, mid-size, and next to the smallest site). In phone interviews parents were asked to describe their experiences with the virtual home school charter, the benefits and/or positive outcomes from the partnership, and any areas they would like to see improved. Finally, four parents offered to journal a typical day in their lives.

RESULTS

Characteristics of Parents in this Virtual Home School Charter

Of the 1,422 surveys that were sent by the Internet teacher, 146 parents voluntarily completed the survey, 143 mothers and 3 fathers. Detailed results are presented in Table 1. Slightly over 90% of the parents are married. Approximately 30% of the respondents were parents of color, and 70% were white. There was a wide range in parent ages and family income. The educational level attained by the mothers who predominantly responded was high, with only 5.6% having either not completed high school or only completed high school. Over 60% of the families have more than two children with grade levels spanning K–7 (the highest grade available in CAVA at that time), and over 60% have been home schooling for 2 or more years. Ninety-seven percent of the children work on school for 3 or more hours per day.

Most parents who returned the survey claimed religious affiliation: Protestant (41%), Catholic (17%), Jewish (1%), other (33%), and no religion (7%). Future work should request clarification from those who mark "other"; it could be members of nondenominational Christian churches, Muslims, or other faiths. Our intuition from this and other data is that these are largely members of the newer nondenominational Protestant churches who either do not overtly know and/or express their affiliation to Protestantism. If this is true, as

TABLE 1. Demographic Information ($N = 146$)

Characteristic	n	%
Age[a]		
20–29 years	7	4.9
30–39 years	59	41.0
40–49 years	70	48.6
50–59 years	8	5.6
Gender		
Female	143	97.9
Male	3	2.1
Ethnicity		
Asian	5	3.4
Black/African	8	5.5
Hispanic or Latin American	17	11.6
Native American/Alaskan Native	2	1.4
White	102	69.9
Other	12	8.2
Educational level[a]		
No high school diploma	4	2.8
High school graduate	4	2.8
Some college/university	54	37.5
College/university graduate	48	33.3
Postgraduate	34	23.6
Religion[a]		
Catholic	25	17.4
Jewish	2	1.4
Protestant	59	41.0
None	10	6.9
Other	48	33.3
Annual family/household income[a]		
Under $15,000	2	1.4
$ 15,000–29,999	10	7.0
$ 30,000–49,999	34	23.8
$ 50,000–69,999	26	18.2
$ 70,000–99,999	33	23.1
$100,000–149,999	24	16.8
$150,000–199,999	11	7.7
$200,000 and over	3	2.1
Marital status[a]		
Unmarried	14	9.7
Married	130	90.3
Number of children[a]		
1	19	13.1
2	42	29.0
3	40	27.6
4 or more	44	30.3

(Continued)

TABLE 1. Continued

Characteristic	n	%
Number of years in home schooling[a]		
0–1	50	34.5
2–5	75	51.7
6–9	11	7.6
10 or more	9	6.2
Grade levels of children enrolled[b]		
K	28	19.2
1	28	19.2
2	32	21.9
3	25	17.1
4	27	18.5
5	29	19.9
6	18	12.3
7	33	22.6
Number of hours school work per day[a]		
1–2	4	2.9
3–4	80	57.6
5 or more	55	39.6

[a]Contained missing data.
[b]More than one response was possible.

much as 90% of the respondents may have been Christian. Administrators at CAVA had the same intuitions.

Like previous studies, we find the population to be very diverse demographically. However, it would appear that the parent-teacher tends to more educated, more religious, and more likely to be married than the general population.

Achievement Results

The CAVA schools must submit annual standardized testing data from their students to the state as a requirement of their public school status. Testing sites are arranged each year in the spring, and students assemble to complete mandatory portions of the California Standardized Testing and Reporting (STAR) program. In 2004 the California Achievement Test (CAT/6) and the California Standards Test (CST) were required in grades 2 through 8. Also required that year was a written assessment in grades 4 and 7 and a physical education assessment in grades 5 and 7. The state expects 95% participation in each assessment to avoid the risk of receiving a serious penalty (in accord with the No Child Left Behind Act).

Because of the newness of some of the CAVA schools and the fact that California test results for 2005 were not available at the time of the study, the results of 2004 testing were available from only three sites. School averages for grades 2 through 7 were compared with state averages for both the CST and CAT/6 portions of the STAR program. CAVA schools scored above the state averages in 15 of 18 grade categories on the CST English Language Arts. All but one grade category was above the state average in reading on the CAT/6 and all but two on the CAT/6 English. Two sites performed above the state average at all grade levels. Math performance in CAVA was weaker, however, with only 2 of 18 on par with state averages for the CST and 6 of 18 for the CAT/6. An improvement plan is in place to rectify this problem with proficiency goals to increase by 5% each year for 3 subsequent years when 75% of all students are expected to achieve at the proficient or advanced level.

The Academic Performance Index uses STAR results to measure school performance while monitoring growth over time by setting growth targets. CAVA was able to meet its Adequate Yearly Progress requirements and Academic Performance Index growth targets in two of its schools. The third school experienced a drop in Academic Performance Index due to increased enrollment. Plans for improvement and expansion were underway at the time of the study.[2]

Quantitative Survey Results

The parent survey was administered online and collected demographic data on the participants as well as 37 forced choice (Likert scale) inquiries that sought parent perceptions on reasons for choosing to home school and the virtual charter, as well as their experiences (Table 2). In addition, four open-ended questions sought parent reasons for choosing to home school in the virtual charter as well as the quality of their experiences and any suggestions for improvement. Overall, results showed that these respondents were extremely positive toward this particular virtual charter home-school approach.

A total score for the 15 Likert scale items that measured respondents' evaluation of their experience with the virtual charter school

TABLE 2. Respondents' Survey (*N* = 146)

Reason	M	SD
Reasons for choosing home school		
To provide increased academic opportunities for my child(ren)	4.54	0.74
To embrace high expectations of excellence in learning	4.52	0.73
To ensure a safe environment for learning	4.50	0.83
To increase the opportunity for instilling moral values	4.48	0.87
To meet the unique learning needs of my child(ren)	4.41	0.87
To strengthen family bonds	4.34	0.87
For greater flexibility in scheduling studies	4.15	1.05
To become an effective role model for my child(ren)	4.09	0.94
Because of disapproval of some formal school practices	3.91	1.11
To express religious freedom	3.64	1.29
Reasons for choosing virtual charter		
To have tuition-free access to learning tools, materials, and resources	4.55	0.87
To provide instruction at home where I can have greater control over my child(ren)'s education	4.42	0.82
To benefit from the individualized program pacing (self-paced progression)	4.41	0.84
To increase my direct involvement with my child(ren)'s education	4.37	0.68
To gain a higher level of education than is available elsewhere	4.27	0.84
To enjoy the convenience of technologies that support learning	4.21	0.81
To take advantage of the built-in system of assessment that provides timely feedback on learning progress	4.17	0.91
To have the flexibility to plan learning activities around the family schedule	4.16	1.00
To utilize a more comprehensive instructional program than was formerly used	4.09	0.94
To belong to a reputable community of learners	3.83	0.99
To obtain professional support for instructional challenges if they arise	3.79	1.12
To receive customized support for special student needs (e.g., learning disabilities)	3.10	1.09
Evaluation of experience with virtual charter		
The curricular resources provided have saved me the time of gathering them on my own.	4.79	0.44
I appreciate having access to the high-quality learning materials.	4.79	0.43
If the possibility for this educational opportunity was repeated, I would take it again.	4.68	0.56
My child(ren)'s academic needs have been met.	4.65	0.60
Overall, the reasons that motivated me to home school have been sustained through this arrangement.	4.51	0.68
My family has enjoyed learning through the technologies provided in this educational program.	4.50	0.64
I value the accountability for learning that this school provides.	4.33	0.87

(Continued)

TABLE 2. Continued

Reason	M	SD
This arrangement has accommodated my family's needs for flexibility in scheduling.	4.30	0.90
When technology challenges have occurred, support has been readily available.	4.14	0.87
My child(ren) has/have become more self-motivated to learn through this educational approach.	4.04	0.96
This approach was selected because it reduced educational costs for my family.	4.02	1.22
This relationship has helped solve instructional challenges by providing ongoing professional support.	3.84	0.92
My child(ren)'s social needs have been met.	3.70	1.06
My family has valued the opportunities to network with other families through this program.	3.64	0.96
This choice has been limiting to my style of home schooling.	2.19	1.14

The scale was as follows: strongly disagree = 1, disagree = 2, no opinion = 3, agree = 4, strongly agree = 5.

was calculated. Higher scores indicate a more favorable experience. Scores ranged from 45 to 75 (out of a possible 15–75) with a mean of 64.17 (standard deviation, 6.16). This indicates that generally respondents had very favorable experiences with the virtual charter school. Cronbach's alpha was used to determine the internal consistency of the scale. The alpha was .79.

Independent samples t tests were used to determine any differences in experience with virtual charter school by age (20–39 years vs. 40–59 years), ethnicity (White vs. non-White), and marital status. There was no significant difference in the evaluation of their experience between the groups by age ($t = 0.93$, $df = 129$, $p = .354$), ethnicity ($t = 1.35$, $df = 131$, $p = .178$), or marital status ($t = 0.98$, $df = 25.01$, $p = .337$).

Analyses of variance were used to determine differences in experience with virtual charter school by educational level, annual family/household income, number of children, and number of years home schooling. Once again, there was no significant difference in experience between the groups by educational level ($F = 1.27$, $df = 4$, $p = .287$), income ($F = 1.35$, $df = 5$, $p = .937$), number of children ($F = 0.98$, $df = 3$, $p = .423$), or number of years home schooling ($F = 0.63$, $df = 3$, $p = .594$).

DISCUSSION

Open-Ended Parent Survey Questions

Parents also were asked to respond to four open-ended items in the survey: (1) Why did you become involved with a virtual charter school? (2) What motivated you and what has sustained your involvement? (3) What is the best part of your participation with the virtual charter school? (4) How could it be better?

Why Did You Become Involved and What Motivates and Sustains Your Involvement?

When asked why they became involved and what motivated and sustained their involvement, five top themes emerged in the 137 open-ended responses from parents:

1. *Quality of the curriculum:* The quality of the curriculum was most frequently mentioned (61% of respondents) as the reason for selecting and remaining in this virtual charter school. Parents described the curriculum as "high quality," "rigorous," "thorough," "comprehensive," "engaging," and "easily accessible." It was also mentioned that the curriculum "takes advantage of the internet/computer" and is not in conflict with their values. Interestingly, the values issue was expressed in two very different ways: "respectful to our Christian beliefs" and "not too faith based." Many just said they liked it or even loved the curriculum and had found it to be better than other home-schooling or public schools' curricula, whereas others were pleased that is was sound, traditional, and/or classic. Parents also indicated that they themselves enjoyed learning from the curriculum.
2. *Various structures of the program:* The various structures of the program offered by the virtual school ranked second in importance to parents (50% of respondents). Many were pleased that the planning and gathering of lesson materials had already been done for them so that more time could be spent on actual teaching and learning. Structural features, such as the online school, organization of the curriculum, the extensive and diverse lessons, and flexibility with time, were all mentioned. The opportunity to have someone holding them accountable and to have regular

assessments of their children's progress was also strong structural features that parents appreciated. The supports provided by the teachers were often mentioned as a valued part of the structure. Uniformly, parents were impressed with the quality and immediate responsiveness of the teachers.

3. *Negative experiences in public schools:* Negative experiences in the public schools was the third theme (47%) that led parents to join the virtual charter school. Several responses revealed disappoint- ment with the current public school system, and some responses involved children with special needs. Parents were dissatisfied with the quality and the content of instruction, pacing, lack of safety, conflicting values and morals, and the negative peer influence. Other negative experiences included overcrowding, too few teachers, and too little time with individual children.

4. *Program is free:* The fact that the program is free was the fourth theme repeated throughout the parent responses (18%). CAVA is tuition free, and many participants would not have been able to take advantage of this resource had it been otherwise. This clearly aids the diversity of the school population at CAVA.

5. *Family and religious values:* The final theme motivating parents to home school at this virtual charter were family and religious values (16%). One could easily argue that all reasons to embrace this educational choice are a matter of family values. However, some respondents specifically articulated how family and religion encouraged and sustained their participation in the virtual charter home school. Regarding religious values, one parent comments, "I wanted my child to learn at her own pace and keep Christ's word hidden in her heart." Another parent sums up many of the family values mentioned by respondents:

> Improved quality of family life and freedom from being a slave to the school calendar and homework schedules after so many years was another plus. We feel we "reclaimed" the raising of our children in many ways; 30+ hours per week in the company of strangers not of our choosing was not always best for our children. What has sus- tained my involvement through good days and bad is the thrill of seeing my children "get it" in various ways, the pleasure I have from being with them each day and having their time when they're at their best (not tired from a long day at school, with homework ahead), and not least, the amount of material I am "re-learning"

or learning for the first time. It has been intellectually stimulating. I have also met a nice community of like-minded mothers locally.

Best Part About Participation

There were 132 responses to this question, and six themes surfaced in the analysis of the texts. Again, with this open-ended question the quality of the curriculum came up as number one among the top six. Similar themes emerged in these open-ended responses primarily centered around the curriculum (36%), flexibility (20%), teacher support (14%), self-pacing (12%), ready to use (12%), and the features of testing and accountability (12%):

1. *Quality of curriculum:* The hallmark of CAVA appears to be the quality of the K12 curriculum. Parents repeatedly point to this as the best part of the CAVA experience:

   The curriculum is phenomenal. My son has really been able to excel in certain areas due to his ability to work at his own pace. The best thing, however, is being provided with such high quality materials at no charge to my family.

2. *Flexibility:* "The flexibility that allows me to meet my child's needs; I can slow down if I need to, or pause a subject for a time if she's hitting a wall," was the way one parent expressed the value of flexibility. Parents value the freedom afforded with this type of education to set their own schedules and make certain curricular choices that customize learning to the individual learner.
3. *Teacher support:* The advantage of teacher support in the virtual charter, which many independent home schoolers may not have, allows parents to receive prompt answers to curricular questions and advice for individual instructional or learning needs. Professional support motivates some who would otherwise not accept the challenge of this unique model of learning. One parent describes the teacher support in the context of the quality curriculum:

   The best part of this experience is the system itself. The high expectations of the curriculum backed with repetitive, consistent lessons leading them into new ideas and subjects is amazing to watch as it works. The teacher support is wonderful. I feel I can talk to my son's teacher about anything I need for my son's success. I feel the whole system is a wonderful well-planned curriculum that makes it easy for kids to learn and succeed.

4. *Pacing:* Families who choose this means of education are often willing to sacrificially provide for the individual needs of their children. This means that if their child excels, they want a program that can accommodate the needs of their quick learner. But if their child requires repeated exposure to new concepts and increased practice with certain academic skills, parents expect support for these needs as well. Parents note that the system allows for either of these needs to be accommodated so that students are able to progress at their own rate with the support and guidance of professional educators. One parent notes, "I am able to tailor my son's learning experience to his needs, move along at his pace, build on his strengths and focus on any areas of weakness."

5. *Ready to use:* Parents appreciated the fact that lessons are already planned and materials already gathered and delivered. In fact, the curriculum is ready to use. This aspect seems to be especially appreciated by home schoolers who have had to do these tasks for themselves in the past. The new freedom can then be translated into more time spent with children in learning activities. One parent explains "that the planning and research has been done for me, and it leaves me more time to spend with my children."

6. *Assessment and accountability:* The regular assessment of progress, state testing, and other methods of accountability form the final dominant theme in parents' responses to best parts of the virtual charter. Parents appreciate being able to know how their children are performing on skills and how they perform relative to other children of their grade in the state as well as appreciate the various ways the program holds them accountable for time and progress. Parents appreciate the immediate feedback on their children's progress. Two parents' comments are instructive here: "I am able to see my child's strengths and weaknesses" and "I have the opportunity to see where my son's educational level is. . . . I am able to work with him one on one and see where he struggles and see where he is strong." One parent who monitors her child's progress from work explains as follows:

> The interface provided gives me the information that I need to help guide my child through the program. I monitor daily

progress from my work, and then I review the lessons with my child in the evenings and on weekends. Depending on the demonstrated level of mastery and the intuitive comfort level displayed by my child, I choose to either further review specific concepts or explore other concepts in greater depth utilizing other resources.

Two other parents note the advantage to the immediate feedback: "The accountability keeps me on track" and "Grading is done daily, which eliminates backlog."

What Could Be Better?

This question brought forth 123 responses from the parents. Analysis of these responses revealed one major theme: a need for increased social interaction, which 20% of the parents reported. Twenty percent of the parents said they could not think of a way to make it better, and the next most frequent comment, occurring only 7%, was a desire for more curriculum choice.

These data are interesting because they reveal great satisfaction with the CAVA program overall in that 20% of the respondents could find nothing to criticize. Two of the criticisms, increased social interaction and more choice in the curriculum, may be endemic to this educational model. For instance, some degree of isolation is to be expected when most of the learning occurs in the home away from other groups of learners. State curricular requirements for public institutions as well as online programs limit curriculum flexibility to some degree. Below are two rather typical responses that are related to the desire for increased socialization:

There is insufficient local community of practice interaction with virtually no social interaction available in the local areas covered by each of the teachers. Other home school programs utilize local facilities to provide enrichment and social opportunities for the children. While the chat areas created on Yahoo are great, they do not provide for parent meetings where curriculum or other items can be demonstrated or displayed. Such interactions should not be dependent on parent organized clubs and trips. One excursion and one teacher meeting a quarter do not supply the necessary face-to-face interaction need for children. Also, due to time conflicts evening and weekend activities are needed.

Another parent reveals the need from a different perspective:

> Because we home school and only have one source of income, extra activities are out of the question. Some examples would be music lessons, dance, language and sports. I wish that my children would be able to participate in these activities at the local school. Some parents have tried to include this as part of the home school experience by putting in their own time and money, but this has not been very successful.

Parent Interviews

Ten parents were interviewed; two of these parents were also board members of CAVA. All parents interviewed were women, even though at one household the father was the home-schooling parent. Two of interviewees had only one child, one had two, three had three, two families had four, one had six, and one had nine children. They were all asked one major question: "Describe your experience with CAVA and the virtual home school and what have been some of the benefits and positive outcomes and then think if there are any things you would like to see improved." The interviewer then probed for additional benefits and suggestions for improvement when participants hesitated. The themes that emerged confirmed the themes found with the open-ended survey questions and therefore they are not elaborated upon here. This was a good indication for use of data saturation, that themes emerging in the survey data were comprehensive. Briefly, these interview themes included how they had come to join the K12 virtual charter; the satisfaction with the curriculum, assessments, scheduling, and teachers; the importance of socialization, family values, and religious faith; and few diverse suggestions for improvement. All 10 parents had found CAVA and/or K12 from friends or family, although 2 parents mentioned specifically they had also come to know about K12 from either an interview or advertisement on Christian radio. They all reported in one way or another that home schooling was challenging and demanded sacrifices of income, time, and career opportunities, especially as they became one-income families.

In terms of their experiences, universally parents praised the curriculum with expressions such as "rigorous," "comprehensive," and "higher than the public schools." Several again mentioned the placement and achievement testing as a distinct advantage. Most importantly, each one believed it made their own efforts to home school their children much better in that not only was the curriculum of high quality in all areas but it provided a structure and multiple opportunities to support learning. Two mentioned the fact that it was free, and all mentioned the advantage of being given all the materials they needed to do the program, including the computer and printer. Initially, four parents were concerned that K12 would have their students on the computer too much but were pleasantly surprised that this was actually not the case. Most of the parents had previous experience with either private schools or other home-schooling programs before CAVA.

A second issue that emerged in the interview data was the advantage of flexible scheduling. Some extended the school days into the summer and vacations, took time off during the week, and worked on Saturdays to keep up. The majority mentioned the issue of documenting their attendance as apparently required by state law as challenging. Some believed the curriculum was so complete and rigorous they felt pushed, whereas others had a peace about skipping certain things based on their children's achievement and interest. Parents of large families mentioned the challenge of motivating their children equally. They noted that some of their children were self-motivated and some needed to be constantly monitored, whereas some needed more help than others in particular subjects.

Uniformly, the parents mentioned the teachers as being helpful, making meetings convenient, and offering special sessions for parents (such as for Algebra). Only one parent mentioned any concern and that was when one teacher was unable to explain an algebra problem.

Each parent addressed socialization and supplementary activities in which their children engaged: sports, opera, and church. Although some recognized that others were concerned about their children getting enough socialization, none of those interviewed believed it was a problem for them. The only exception was one parent with one son who wanted to play varsity sports; subsequently, he went back into the public schools to join a team. CAVA itself has some social activities periodically with field trips, and most parents were connected to other parents. One CAVA group has a chat room where parents provide help and schedule time together.

All but one of the parents (the board member) mentioned their faith, though this was not asked in the interview. This ranged from comments about Sunday school, Christian radio, using the Bible as curriculum, Wednesday Bible study day, to simply talking about God's plans for their families. One mother said she was "immersed in church." These church activities appeared to provide for some socialization as well. Again, it appears these parents are largely Protestant Christians.

None of the parents had significant concerns or recommendations for change. One parent who was a board member talked about different concerns such as assessments, attendance, record keeping, and meeting state demands that had arisen during the year. Interestingly, given that math scores are the lowest in the virtual charters, 5 of the 10 parents mentioned the difficulty of teaching math.

A Day in the Life of Virtual Home Schooling

Four of the 10 parents who were interviewed agreed to sketch out a typical day in their lives as virtual home schoolers, though they all commented that days were very diverse and "typical" might be a misnomer. The online questionnaire used to obtain these data was divided into the following sections: morning, afternoon, and evening scheduled activities, plus additional comments. Respondents were asked to write about their routines during these three daily time blocks. The three most revealing findings in reading these journal entries are (1) the richness and depth of family life, (2) the almost seamless integration of school and family life, and the (3) ways in which this form of schooling helps parents know and guide their children toward larger life goals.

Parents described routines they had developed that added to the depth and richness of family life. One parent described that after she gets up early and walks the dog, she also gets each of her three children up at different times so that she can have some "one-on-one time" with each one at the beginning of the day. She gets her older children started on their work first so that she can be more available to guide her first graders work. They work until about 2 or 3 p.m. and then the children (and parents) begin other activities (i.e., music, ballet, science group, scout activities, and various church activities in the evenings). After commenting on the "wild schedule" they keep, the mother remarks, "It takes a great deal of organization to home school three and it is very exhausting. I am thankful to be with my kids and generally I find them to be kinder to each other."

A second parent integrates cooking lessons into the school day, starting with the children making pancakes from scratch and the children cooking dinner for the entire family once a month. She describes what she calls an ideal day revealing how family life and school allow her and her husband the much needed interaction to help their children move toward to college and career goals:

> The children are taught that they are part of the family team and help with everything. They are learning to cook, clean, sew, organize, grocery shop, and do laundry. By learning these important life lessons they will be better prepared to organize and balance their college and professional lives. As parents, we can better understand who they are and help them choose career goals that match up with their strengths.

The importance of seeing their children learn in terms of knowing them better and being better able to guide them is a theme that emerges strongly in the journals.

A third parent details how the day begins for her two children with breakfast, a chore, 20-minute Bible study and prayer, and the pledge of allegiance. They alternate history and science in the afternoons, work on music and art in late afternoon, and schedule library and park days. Before bedtime she and her husband read to the children from optional lessons. Interspersed are all kind of family activities and chores. Her journal also reflects the blurring of interconnections between family and school and again praises the ability to know their children better: "The rewards are knowing what was taught and seeing it applied...in real life. Knowledge is one thing, but application is a blessing."

The fourth parent has children from kindergarten through 10th grade. They begin the morning with breakfast and cleaning the house in teams that switch assignments each week. They start the day by correcting any assignments from the day before, and she checks new schoolwork during lunch and readjusts the day if necessary. After lunch, the house is picked up again and the younger three take naps. They work again from 1 to 3 or 4 p.m. and then have free time, sports, physical education, and video and/or games. Her husband does any shopping during the weekdays. In the evenings she may help one who is struggling individually.

These brief overviews of four typical days give an extensive picture of the collaboration of family members with one another and the seamless, though complex, integration of (1) family interactions and values (chores, Bible reading), (2) the curriculum, (3) daily activities (meals, getting ready for the day, shopping, cooking), and (4) planning toward life and career goals. The juggling of children at various levels, organization and timing of different activities, independent and directed work, and integration of faith activities and other outside activities reveal a highly complex, delicately balanced day that requires extensive coordination and direction by parents.

CONCLUSION

The home schoolers in this virtual charter are similar to those in other studies. They have chosen home schooling for a variety of reasons, which include the curriculum, lack of confidence in the public schools in terms of teaching and learning, safety, and values. About 90% appear to be religious, and the desire to educate their children in ways consistent with the religious values plays a role in their decision and in the way they structure activities during the day. Perhaps the most revealing parts of the study are (1) the seamless way families have integrated work in the home, values such as religious instruction, and sibling cooperation with the work of schooling and (2) the importance of the assessment and accountability measures that are built into this particular system. Parents appear to use this information as ways to know their children better and to guide them toward future adult goals. This actually harkens back to preindustrial revolution education when families, their work, values, and religious beliefs, and their education were more unified (Jeynes, 2007). Could it be that our technological culture, born of the industrial revolution, has come full circle and offers again the opportunity to renew this integration of family, work, values, and schooling that was initially torn apart by the industrial revolution?

NOTES

1. The six California Virtual Academies are as follows: CAVA at Jamestown, Jamestown School District in Tuolomne County; CAVA at Kern, Maricopa Unified School District in

Kern County; CAVA at Kings, Armona Union Elementary School District in Kings County; CAVA at San Diego, Spencer Valley School District in San Diego County; CAVA at San Mateo, Burlingame Elementary School District in San Mateo County; and CAVA at Sonoma, Liberty Elementary School District in Sonoma County.

2. Update on CAVA since the study. This last year closed with six CAVA schools in operation with school enrollments now totaling approximately 3,500 students. CAVA has sustained a rate of growth that has doubled each year. A charter application for an additional school has been granted by the state and is scheduled to open on July 1, 2006 with an estimated enrollment of 150 students. Two more applications were processed recently, and CAVA increased to eight independent schools by the beginning of the 2006–2007 school year, generating a projected enrollment of between 5,000 and 6,000 students.

Additionally, since the study first took place the teaching staff has more than doubled to 177 credentialed, highly qualified employees. Yet this amount is still not enough to meet the demands of next year's enrollment projections. This fact, coupled with CAVA's commitment to smaller class size (25:1), requires the hiring of additional teachers. Already CAVA has received 550 applications for these positions and, of them, 100 will be hired for the next school year, bringing the total teaching staff to 277.

CAVA continues to extend its range of grade levels each year. Last year grades K–9 were offered; next fall (2006) 10th grade will be added and so on until it encompasses all elementary and secondary levels, K–12. Synchronous online classes are now provided (via Illuminate) where more direct instruction and teacher-student interaction are possible. Socialization opportunities have increased so that optional activities/outings are available weekly if desired.

CAVA students have excelled on standardized tests in the areas of reading and language arts, but they still struggle in the area of math. The K12, inc. curriculum that is used appears not to be in sync with the California sequence of teaching math standards. Lessons for grades K–2 were rewritten and were available in the fall of 2006. It is intended that other grade level adjustments will be made as well. Curriculum support has also increased for CAVA teachers in hopes of alleviating this problem.

Another change has come in the area of clientele. Initially, the attraction to CAVA was predominantly from preexisting home school families. Today, however, these families comprise less than 20% of the schools' populations. The majority of families (70%) are now coming out of public and private schools. Last year 75% of the families returned, and this year retention has increased to between 79% and 80%.

REFERENCES

Allen, J., & Heffernan, D. (Eds.). (2006). *Charter schools today: Changing the face of American education. Part 1: Annual survey of America's charter schools: 2005 data.* The Center for Education Reform. Retrieved from http://www.edreform.com

Belfield, C., & Levin, H. (2005). *Privatizing educational choice: Consequences for parents, schools, and public policy.* Boulder, CO: Paradigm Publishers.

Collom, E. (2005). The ins and outs of homeschooling: The determinants of parental motivations and student achievement. *Education and Urban Society, 37,* 307–335.

Davis, N., & Roblyer, M. (2005). Preparing teachers for the "schools that technology built": Evaluation of a program to train teachers for virtual schooling". *Journal of Research on Technology in Education, 37,* 399–409.

Fowler, F. (2003). School choice: Silver bullet, social threat, or sound policy? *Educational Researcher, 32,* 33–39.

Georgiou, D. (2005). *Charter schools and urban development* (Brief Analysis No. 531). Dallas, TX: National Center for Policy Analysis.

Greenway, R., & Vanourek, G. (2006). *The virtual revolution.* The Hoover Institution. Retrieved June 25, 2006 from http://www.educationnext.org/20062/34.html

Hetzel, J. (1998). *Factors that influence parents to homeschool.* Doctoral dissertation, The Claremont Graduate University, Claremont, CA.

Hetzel, J., Long, M., & Jackson, M. (2001). Factors that influence parents to homeschool in Southern California. *Home School Researcher, 14,* 1–11.

Hirsch, E. D. (1999). *The schools we need and why we don't have them.* New York: Anchor Books.

Huerta, L., Gonzalez, M., & d'Entremnont, C. (2006). Cyber and home school charter schools: Adopting policy to new forms of public schooling. *Peabody Journal of Education, 81,* 103–139.

Jeynes, W. (2007). *History of education: School, society and the common good.* Thousand Oaks, CA: Sage Press.

Kennedy, M. (2002). Charter schools: Threat or boon to public schools? *American School & University, 75,* 18–22, 24, 26.

Klein, C. (2006). *Virtual charter schools and home schooling.* Youngstown, NY: Cambria Press.

LaFevre, A. (2005). *Report card on American education: A state-by-state analysis, 1983–1984 to 2003–2004.* Retrieved June 22, 2006 from www.ALEC.org

Lines, P. (1991). Home instruction: The size and growth of the movement. In J. Van Galen & M. A. Pitman (Eds.), *Home schooling: Political, historical, and pedagogical perspectives* (pp. 9–41). Norwood, NJ: Ablex.

Manno, B., Finn, Jr., C., & Vanourek, G. (2000). Beyond the schoolhouse door: How charter schools are transforming U.S. public education. *Phi Delta Kappan, 82,* 736–744.

Marshall, P., Gibbs, D., Greene, T., Nelson, W., & Schofield, J. (2001). Teachers reflect on charter schools. *Kappa Delta Pi Record, 37,* 129–132.

Mayberry, M., Knowles, G., Ray, B., & Marlow, S. (1995). *Home schooling: Parents as educators.* Thousand Oaks, CA: Corwin Press.

Medlin, R. (1994). Predictors of academic achievement in home educated children: Aptitude, self-concept, and pedagogical practices. *Home School Researcher, 10,* 1–7.

Medlin, R. (2000). Home schooling and the question of socialization. *Peabody Journal of Education, 75,* 107–123.

Montes, G. (2006). Do parental reasons to home school vary by grade? Evidence from the National Household Education Survey, 2001. *Home School Researcher, 16,* 11–17.

Morse, J. (2001). Do charter schools pass the test? *Time, 157,* 60–62.

National Center for Education Statistics. (2003). *Fast facts. Charter schools.* Retrieved October 16, 2003 from http://nces.ed.gov/fastfacts/display.asp?id=30

Peterson, P. (2006). *Choice and competition in American education.* Lanham, MD: Rowman & Littlefield.

Rapp, K., Eckes, S., & Plucker, J. (2006, Winter). Cyber charter schools in Indiana: Policy implications of the current statutory language. *Education Policy Brief, 4,* 1.

Ray, B. (2002). *Worldwide guide to homeschooling.* Nashville, TN: Broadman & Holman.

Ray, B. (2006). *Research facts on homeschooling.* Retrieved October 17, 2006 from http://www.nheri.org/content/view/199/

Rotherham, A. (2006, April 7). *Virtual schools, real innovation.* nytimes.com. Retrieved June 22, 2006 from http://select.nytimes.com/search/

Rudner, L. (1999). Scholastic achievement and demographic characteristics of home school students in 1998. *Education Policy Analysis Archives (EPAA), 7*(8).

Russell, T. (1994). Cross-validation of multivariate path analysis of predictors of home school student academic achievement. *Home School Researcher, 10,* 1–13.

Schemo, D. (2004). *Nation's charter schools lagging behind, U.S. test scores reveal.* The New York Times.com. Retrieved October 13, 2004 from http://www. nytimes.com

Stuart Wells, A., Slayton, J., & Scott, J. (2002). Defining democracy in the neoliberal age: Charter school reform and educational consumption. *American Educational Research Journal, 39,* 337–361.

Taylor, J. (1986). Self-concept in home-schooling children. *Home School Researcher, 2,* 1–3.

Van Galen, J., & Pitman, M. (Eds.). (1991). *Home schooling: Political, historical, and pedagogical perspectives.* Norwood, NJ: Ablex.

Witt, V. (1999). A descriptive study and needs assessment of the typical Washington homeschool family. *Home School Researcher, 13,* 7–16.

Index

abortion 217, 221
access to resources 110, 120-8,
  134, 268-70, 295, 296-300, 302
advocacy and mediation 349, 350,
  354, 360
affection 17-18, 27
African-Americans *see also*
  ethnicity
  authoritarianism 26
  caregiver engagement in
    religious schools 310-11, 313,
    323-6, 328-9
  mothers 18, 21-2
  parenting styles 18, 21-2
  perceptions of parents and
    teachers 273, 279-82, 284
  psychological control 18
  teachers 323-6, 328-9
  womanism, notion of 310-11,
    328
authoritarianism 13, 14-17, 25-6
authoritative style 14-17, 21

barriers, removal of 322-6, 331, 349
behavioural control 14-17, 27
belief systems of families 28, 271
biological and resident fathers 73,
  79-82

Black persons *see* African-
  Americans; ethnicity
books and educational tools at
  home 295, 296-300, 302
born-again Christians 208-10,
  212-13, 220-1
boys, self-esteem of 19
bridge builders 349, 353
bullying and discrimination,
  effects of parental involvement
  on 6-7, 253-66
  communications between parent
    and child 256, 259-60
  ethnicity 258-62
  gender 258-60
  parental expectations 256
  socio-economic status 258-60
bureaucratization of schools 49-52

California Virtual Academies
  (CAVA) 374-86
caregiver engagement in religious
  urban elementary schools 8,
  306-35
  African-Americans 310-11, 313,
    323-6, 328-9
  authentic participation 308-9,
    332

barriers to families, systems to remove 322-6, 331
Black teachers 323-6, 328-9
communications 308, 309, 316-22
critical care theory 309-11, 325, 330, 332
disabled students 314, 321, 323
ethnicity 310-11, 313-14, 323-32
expectations of caregivers 307-8
external agencies, relationships with 323-4
limitations to spaces 328-30
linguistic minorities 312
marginalized students 309-14, 325-6
non-traditional supports, alliances with 327-8
personal attention of principal 317-19, 331
politics 309, 311
private schools 309-35
proactive, positive and focused communications from teachers 319-22
reciprocal community relationships 307, 325, 331-2
relationships, building 310, 316-24, 330-1
safety 323
school leaders, role of 8, 306-35
social and cultural capital, valuing diverse forms of 325-7, 330-2
socio-economic status 308-14, 332
structure of families 307-8

tuition assistance 314, 322-6
White women educators 309-14, 328-9
womanism, notion of 310-11, 328
charter schools 54-6 *see* home schooling in virtual charter school system
child labor 42, 44-5, 56
Chinese and Chinese-Americans 23, 25-6, 28
class *see* socio-economic status
classroom management 260-70
Coleman Report 1-2, 50-1
colonial America 40, 41-4, 56
communications
 bullying and discrimination, effects of parental involvement on 256, 259-60
 caregiver engagement in religious schools 308, 309, 316-22
 creative communications 349
 high school family centres 349, 357
 perceptions of parents and teachers 278-82
compulsory education 44-6
creationism, teaching of 218-19, 221
critical care theory 309-11, 325, 330, 332
culture
 acquisition of common culture 43
 brokers 348-9, 350
 caregiver engagement in religious urban elementary schools 325-7, 330-2

capital 325-7, 330-2
ecocultural theory 109-10
ethnicity 25-7
high school family centres 341,
  348-9, 350
Korean students and US
  students, comparison between
  296, 297-300, 302
parental involvement 4
parenting styles 23
public schools 38-41, 57-8
schools, perceptions of 269
curriculum of the home 289-91,
  293-4, 296-303

death penalty, views on 216-17
demographics 110-11, 120-2,
  133-4, 374, 376-7*see also*
  ethnicity; gender
denominational affiliation in
  England and Wales 5-6, 183-202
  census 185
  encasement 186-7
  Protestants 188-9
  religion and paranormal, views
    on 192, 195-9
  religious nominalism 185, 195
  sex, views on 193, 196, 198-9
  social concerns, views on 191,
    194-5, 197
  substances, views on 193,
    196-7, 198
desegregation 51-2, 53, 55-6
development/ecological theory
  66, 70
differentiation of self 20-1
disabled students 41, 51-2, 314,
  321, 323

discrimination *see* bullying and
  discrimination, effects of parental
  involvement on
divorce 1, 7, 215, 302-3

early learning 19, 51 *see also*
  father involvement, early learning
  and
ecocultural theory 109-10
ecological systems theory 340-1
economic influences on education
  38-9, 44-5, 56, 58
educational background of parents
  see parental educational
  background
England *see* denominational
  affiliation in England and Wales
equality 42-3, 50-3, 55-6
ethnicity *see also* African-
  Americans; Hispanic and Latino
  students
  achievement gap 2-3
  authoritarianism 25-6
  bullying and discrimination,
    effects of parental involvement
    on 258-62
  caregiver engagement in
    religious schools 310-11,
    313-14, 323-32
  charter schools 55, 372, 375,
    380
  Chinese and Chinese-Americans
    23, 25-6, 28
  culture 25-7
  desegregation 51-2, 53, 55-6
  equality 51-2, 53, 55-6
  father involvement, early
    learning and 75, 79-81, 89-94

gender 5, 25-6, 28, 137-60
high school family centres
　342-3, 348-50
home schooling 53, 368-9, 372,
　375, 380
Korean students and US
　students, comparison between
　7, 287-305
parental involvement 2-3
parenting styles 12, 18, 21-7,
　28, 30-1
peer group formation 25
perceptions of parents and
　teachers 273, 279-82, 284
psychological distress 26
public schools 42-4, 50-3, 55-6
Puerto Rican female high-
　achievers 5, 137-60
virtual charter school system,
　home schooling in 372, 375,
　380
White women educators 309-14,
　328-9
expectations *see* parent
　expectations
external agencies, schools'
　relationships with 323-4
extra tuition 297, 299-302
extracurricular activities 140-1,
　148-50, 155, 157, 290-1,
　295-302

family centres *see* high school
　family centres
father involvement, early learning
　and 4, 64-105
　absence-presence dichotomy 69,
　　83

academic and social outcomes
　85-90
biological and resident fathers
　73, 79-82
development/ecological theory
　66, 70
diversity of families 79, 92
ethnicity 75, 79-81, 89-94
historical context 68-70
language abilities 88, 89
non biological and non resident
　fathers 79-82
non profit and federal initiatives
　68
school readiness 65-7, 71, 83,
　87-90
social and emotional
　development 88
socio-economic status 65, 67,
　75, 79-81, 89-94
stereotyping 81
fathers
　early learning 4, 64-105
　educational background 23
　Korean students and US
　　students, comparison between
　　296, 297-9
　parenting styles 23, 24, 28
　perceptions 24, 28
feelings about school, students'
　226-7, 233-4, 236-45
funding
　high school family centres
　　346-7, 364
　public schools 47, 50
　religious urban elementary
　　schools 314, 322-6
　socio-economic status 51

tuition assistance 314,
322-6
virtual charter school system,
home schooling in 382

gender *see also* fathers; mothers
adolescents 19
belief systems 28
boys, self-esteem of 19
bullying and discrimination,
effects of parental involvement
on 258-60
differentiation of self, parents'
20-1
early parenting 19
egalitarian marital roles 18-19
equality 215-16
ethnicity 25-6, 28
girls 5, 18-20, 22, 137-60
grandmothers, role of 142
Hispanic and Latino students 5,
137-60, 215-16
homework 19-20
Korean students and US
students, comparison between
290-1
mathematics 19, 20, 27
ordination of women 215
parenting styles 12, 18-22, 24,
27, 28
psychological distress 26
Puerto Rican female high-
achievers 5, 137-60
science 20, 27
self-esteem 19
traditional stereotypes 20, 27, 148
White women educators 309-14,
328-9

womanism, notion of 310-11,
328
girls
mathematics 22
mothers' employment 22
Puerto Rican female high-
achievers 5, 137-60
self-esteem 19
stereotyping 20
graduation, awards and accolades,
achieving 363
grandmothers, role of 142

high school family centres
academic press, students
response to 360-1
administrative support 345-6
advocates and mediators, staff
as 349, 350, 354, 360
appreciation, expressions of 361
attendance, improving 362
authentic connectors 349
barriers, removal of 349
bridge builders, staff as 349, 353
cared for and comfortable,
students feeling 360
comfort zones, as 347-8, 353-5,
356
communications 349, 357
community partnerships 8,
336-66
community service and work,
opportunities for 355
coordinators or managers 348
creative communicators, staff as
349
cultural brokers, staff as 348-9,
350

cultural norms 341
district level, support at the 346
ecological systems theory 340-1
efficacy, development of student 344, 361-2, 363
efficacy, parents' sense of 341, 350, 358
ethnicity 342-3, 348-50
food 347, 351, 356
formal programming for students 354-5
functions of family centres 339
funding 346-7, 364
graduation, awards and accolades, receiving 363
home and school, building relationships between 351, 363
infrastructure 344-8
interconnections 340-1, 356
invitation, parents' sense of 341, 346-7, 350-1, 353, 356-7
key skills 349-50
knowledge about academics and schooling, expanding 352-3
location 339-40, 345-8
mission statements 344-5
nurturers and caregivers, staff as 349
overcrowding 347
parental involvement 8, 336-66
programming 350-5, 364
programming for parents 350
purpose and mission 344-5
recognition and acknowledgement of individuals 357, 361-2
relational trust, development of 337, 340, 344, 357-62

respect, encouraging 356, 357
responsive programming 350-5, 364
role construction 341, 358-9
safe-haven for students 353-4
second parents, staff as 360
self-confidence and resiliency, building 361-2, 363
self-improvement, programming for 351-2
skilled staff 348-50, 353-4, 360, 364
social capital development, programming for 351-2
staffing 348-50, 353-4, 360, 364
socio-economic status 339-40, 350
space 347-8
successful centres, models of 341-57
supportive programming for students 353
value of education and adult support, increased knowledge of 363
zones of community 341-2, 355-7, 364-5
Hispanic and Latino students 6, 161-82
abortion 217, 221
age 179
agreement on expectations 164, 168, 172-3, 177
availability of resources 110, 120-8, 134
born-again Christians 208-10, 212-13, 220-1

broadcasting, watching of
  religious 218-19
Catholics 208-15, 219-21
church attendance 127
church-state views 217-19
commitment to religion, level of
  210, 213-14, 221-2
community influences 108-11,
  123-5
creationism, teaching of 218-19,
  221
death penalty 216-17
divorce 215
ecocultural theory 109-10
Euro-American value system,
  influence of 215-16
family influences 108-11,
  128-32, 134
gender equality 215-16
high quality relationships 204-5,
  221-2
homework, hours spent on
  176
homosexual practices, attitudes
  to 216
language 4, 106-36, 170
libraries, access to 125-6
literacy 4-5, 106-36
marriage 204-5, 213-22
mathematics 166-8, 170, 175-6
parental educational background
  211-13
parental expectations 161-5,
  168, 170-9
parental involvement 2-3
perceptions of parental
  expectations 163-4, 168, 172
perceptions of parents and

teachers 273, 279-82, 284
Protestants 209-15, 219-20
reading 166-7
religion 6, 203-23
school vouchers 218
schools providing materials for
  home use 126-7
siblings, number of 176
social integration 107
social views 205, 214-21
sociodemographics 110-11,
  120-2, 133-4
socio-economic status 217, 221
stereotypes 219-20
unmarried parents 205
women, ordination of 215
historical role of parental control
  in education 40-2, 56
home learning environments,
  Korean and US students and 7,
  287-305
  ability 290-1
  achievement gaps between East
    Asian and US students 288-92
  alterable factors 290-1, 296-303
  books and educational tools at
    home 295, 296-300, 302
  cultural exposure 296, 297-300,
    302
  curriculum of the home 289-91,
    293-4, 296-303
    definition 290-1
    indicators 293-4, 296-300
    mathematics 296, 297
  demographic changes 302-3
  divorce rate 302-3
  environmental factors 290-1
  ethnicity 290-1

extra tuition 297, 299-302
family expectations and
    supervisions 291, 296-9, 302
fathers, living with 296, 297-9
gender 290-1
homework 300, 302
lone parents 302-3
mathematics 295, 296, 297, 300
mothers, living with 296,
    297-300
motivation 290-1, 302
parental-child relationships 291,
    301-2
parental control 289-90
parental educational background
    296, 297-300
parental involvement 288-91
partnerships 288, 303
playing 295, 296, 297-9, 301
quantity and quality of
    instruction 290-1
socioeconomic status 289,
    290-1, 300, 302
sports 295, 296, 297-8, 301
structure of family 292, 294,
    296, 298-9, 302-3
television, watching 295, 296,
    297-302
time spent outside of school
    290-1, 295-302
Walberg's nine-factor
    productivity model 290-9
home schooling *see also* home
  schooling in virtual charter
  school system
    achievement scores 369-70
    definition 369
    desegregation 53

ethnicity 53, 368-9
parental involvement 54
popularity 368
public schools 53
religion 369, 370
statistics 368-70
home schooling in virtual charter
  school system 8, 367-93
    Academic Performance Index
      378
    accountability 371, 373, 381-5,
      390
    achievement results 377-8
    assessments 377-8, 384, 388,
      390
    California Virtual Academies
      (CAVA) 374-86
    characteristics of parents 375-7
    class sizes 374
    curriculum 374, 381, 383-7,
      390
    day in the life 388-90
    definition of charter systems
      371, 372-3
    demographics 374, 376-7
    development 370
    ethnicity 372, 375, 380
    face-to-face meetings 374
    family values 382-3, 386
    flexibility 383, 387
    free, fact that program is 382
    increase in use 371-2
    K12 Company 374, 387
    motivation 381-2
    pacing 383, 384
    public schools, negative
      experiences in 382
    quality of curriculum 381, 387

ready to use, curriculum is 384
religion 375-7, 381, 382, 386, 388
satisfaction 385-6
savings 372
socialization and supplementary activities 387-90
socio-economic status 372, 375
statistics 371-2, 374-7
structures of the program, 381-2
teachers
 preparation 373
 responsiveness 382, 383-4, 387
homework
 gender 19-20
 Hispanic and Latino students 176
 Korean students and US students, comparison between 300, 302
 socio-economic status 300, 302
homosexuality 193, 196, 199, 216

identity, affirmation and maintenance of Puerto Rican 151-2, 156, 157
indifferent or neglectful styles of parenting 15-17
indulgent style of parenting 15, 17
industrial centers, growth of 46
information technology 58
intergenerational closure 141, 150, 155, 283
Internet 58
invitation, parents' sense of 341, 346-7, 350-1, 353, 356-7

involvement of parents *see* parental involvement

K12 Company 374, 387
Korean students *see* home learning environments, Korean and US students and

language
 father involvement, early learning and 88, 89
 Hispanic and Latino students 4, 106-36, 170
 linguistic minorities 4, 106-36, 312
 literacy 4, 106-36
 public schools 57
 Puerto Rican female high-achievers 140
 socio-economic status 227, 236-44
Latino students *see* Hispanic and Latino students
learning environment *see* home learning environments, Korean and US students and
learning standards 269-72, 275-7, 282-5
literacy 4-5, 106-36, 227, 236-44
lone parents 302-3
low-income children, family involvement and relationships with teachers 224-52
 feelings about school, children's 226-7, 233-4, 236-45
 literacy 227, 236-44
 mathematics 227, 236-44

motivation 226-7
quality of relationships 246-7
school, involvement in the 226,
    233, 234-48
School Transition Study (STS)
    230-3

marginalized students 51, 151,
    156, 309-14, 325-6 *see also*
ethnicity*;*
        socio-economic status
marriage 1, 7, 18-19, 204-5,
    213-22, 302-3
mathematics
    gender 19, 20, 27
    Hispanic and Latino students
        166-8, 170, 175-6
    Korean students and US
        students, comparison between
        295, 296, 297, 300
    mothers' employment 22, 27
    parental educational background
        22
    socio-economic status 227,
        236-44
mothers
    African-Americans 18, 21-2
    early learning 20
    employment 22, 27
    gender 18-21
    girls 22, 139-40, 142, 152-4,
        156
    Korean students and US
        students, comparison between
        296, 297-300
    mathematics 22, 27
    National Congress of Mothers
        (NCM) 49

parental educational background
    23
parenting styles 18, 21-2, 24,
    27-8
perceptions 24, 28
psychological control 18
Puerto Rican female high-
    achievers 139-40, 142, 152-4,
    156
motivation 140, 151, 156, 226-7,
    290-1, 302, 381-2

non biological and non resident
    fathers 79-82
non-traditional supports, alliances
    with 327-8
nurturers and caregivers, staff as
    349

paranormal, students' views on
    192, 195-9
parental control
    bureaucratization 49
    historical role of parental
        control in education 40-2, 56
    Korean students and US
        students, comparison between
        289-90
    parenting styles 12, 13-18, 27
    professionalization 49
    psychological control 14, 17-18,
        27
parental educational background
    12, 21-3, 27, 145-7, 296-300
    fathers 23
    Korean students and US
        students, comparison between
        296, 297-300

mathematics 22
mothers 23
parenting styles 12, 21-3, 27
Puerto Rican female high-
    achievers 145-7
parental expectations
    agreements 164, 168, 172-3,
        177
    bullying and discrimination,
        effects of parental involvement
        on 256
    caregiver engagement in
        religious urban elementary
        schools 307-8
    Hispanic and Latino students
        161-5, 168, 170-9
    Korean students and US
        students, comparison between
        291, 296-9, 302
    perceptions 163-4, 168, 172
parental involvement 2-7, 37-8, 44,
    50-9
    authentic participation 308-9,
        332
    bullying 6-7, 253-66
    caregiver engagement in
        religious urban elementary
        schools 8, 306-35
    culture 4
    discrimination 6-7, 253-66
    early learning 4, 20, 64-105
    engagement strategy 8, 270-,
        271, 306-35
    ethnicity 2-3, 288-91
    father involvement, early
        learning and 4, 64-105
    high school family centres 8,
        336-66

Hispanic and Latino students
    2-3
homeschooling 54
invitation, parents' sense of
    341, 346-7, 350-1, 353,
    356-7
Korean students and US
    students, comparison between
    288-91
low-income students 6
partnerships 7
perceptions of parents and
    teachers 270, 271, 273-4,
    278-9, 283
professional support for 52-3
religion 8, 306-35
restructuring of schools 54
school vouchers and charter
    schools 54-6
social structure of families 4
socio-economic status 224-52
teachers, relationship with 4, 6,
    224-52
parental styles 3-4, 11-35
    affection 17-18, 27
    African-American mothers 18,
        21-2
    age range 15
    authoritarian style 13, 14-17
    authoritative style 14-17, 27
    autonomy, development of 16
    behavioural control 14-17, 27
    belief systems 28
    Chinese and Chinese-American
        students 23, 25, 28
    counselling, implications for
        28-9
    culture 23

ethnicity and diversity 12, 18,
21-3, 24-7, 28, 30-1
fathers
educational background 23
perceptions of 24, 28
gender 12, 18-21, 22, 24, 27, 28
independence 23, 28-9
indifferent or neglectful styles
15-17
indulgent styles 15, 17
mothers
educational background 23
employment 22, 27
perceptions of 24, 28
parental control 12, 13-18, 27
parental education 12, 21-3, 27
perceptual differences between
parents and children 12-13,
23-4, 28
permissive style 13, 14-17
psychological control 14, 17-18,
27
role models 31
self-esteem, self-efficacy and
motivation 13, 30
parents *see also* fathers; mothers;
parental expectations; parental
involvement; parental styles
control 12-18, 27, 40-2, 49, 56,
289-90
differentiation of self 20-1
educational background 12,
21-3, 27, 145-7, 296-300
efficacy 341, 350, 358
parent teacher associations
(PTAs), development of 49-50
perceptions 267-86
virtual charter school system,

home schooling in 375-7
working hours of parents 57-8
partnerships 7-8, 271, 288, 303,
336-66
peer group formation 25
perceptions of parents and teachers
7, 267-86
academic learning 269-72,
275-7, 282-5
African-Americans 273, 279-82,
284
belief systems of families 271
classroom management
269-70
communication 278-82
culture of school 269
definition of a school
community 272, 275
ethnicity 163-4, 168, 172, 273,
279-82, 284
fathers 24, 28
Hispanic and Latino students
163-4, 168, 172, 273, 279-82,
284
intergenerational closure 283
interrelationships, weaknesses
in 276-7, 282-5
learning standards 269-72,
275-7, 282-5
mothers 24, 28
negative perceptions of parents
277-8, 283
parent engagement strategies
270, 271
parental expectations 163-4,
168, 172
parental involvement 270, 271,
273-4, 278-9, 283

parenting styles 12-13, 23-4, 28
partnerships 271
purpose of school 271-2, 275-7,
  282-5
quality of relationships 272
reading for pleasure,
  encouraging 277, 284
resources of schools 268-70
respect, teaching 276-7, 283
social and emotional learning
  271-2, 276, 283-5
socio-economic status 270
permissive style 13, 14-17
playing 295, 296, 297-9, 301
poor *see* socio-economic status
population growth 46
private schools 309-35
professionalization 46-9
programming 51, 350-5, 364
psychological control 14, 17-18,
  27
psychological distress 26
public schools, families and
  36-63
  bureaucratization of
    schools
  challenges to 49-52
  court challenges 50-2
  development of 46-9
  parent-teacher associations,
    development of 49-50
  change in influence of family in
    their children's education 41
  charter schools 54-6
  child labor 42, 44-5, 56
  choice 41, 55-6
  Coleman Study 50-1
  colonial America 40, 41-4, 56

compulsory education 44-6
culture 38-41, 43, 57-8
disabled children 51-2
disadvantaged children,
  financial support for 51
diversity amongst types of
  family 57
duration of school day 45
early childhood programs 51
economic influences 38-9, 44-5,
  56, 58
emergence of public education
  41-4
equality 42-3, 50-3, 55-6
ethnicity 43-4, 50-1, 53
farm labor 42, 44-5
financial support 47, 50-1
graded curriculum, utilization of
  a 46
Head Start programs 51
historical role of parental
  control in education 40-2, 56
homeschooling 53
home, choice of 37
immigration 57
industrial centers, growth of 46
information technology 58
Internet 58
language 57
legislation 51
licensing of teachers 48
National Congress of Mothers
  (NCM) 49
parent teacher associations
  (PTAs), development of
  49-50
parental control 40-1, 45, 49,
  56

parental involvement 37-8, 44, 50-9

political pressures 38-9, 45, 58-9

population growth 46

private education 43-4

professionalization 46-9

religion 40, 42

restructuring 54

school vouchers and charter schools 54-6

scientific management techniques 46-7

social class 40, 42-4, 48, 50-1

social forces 57-8

social structure of families 38-9

standardization and systemization 47

state matter, education as a 40, 41-4

superintendent's position, formation of 46-7

truancy laws 45

universal education 42-3

urbanization 46, 57

vagrant children 45-6

working hours of parents 57-8

Puerto Rican female high-achievers 5, 137-60

extracurricular activities 140-1, 148-50, 155, 157

gender roles 148

grandmothers, role of 142

identity, affirmation and maintenance of Puerto Rican 151-2, 156, 157

intergenerational closure 141, 150, 155

language 140

marginalization 151, 156

mothers, role of 139-40, 142, 152-4, 156

motivation 140, 151, 156

networks 148-9, 155, 157

parental education 145-7

religion 5, 141, 148-50, 155-6, 157

role identity theory 140

school kid identity 140-1, 156

socio-economic status 140, 143

stereotypes 138-40, 148, 151-2, 156, 158

teachers, influence of 154-5, 156

race *see* ethnicity

reading 166-7, 277, 284

recognition and acknowledgement of individuals 357, 361-2

reduced parental engagement 2

relationships, building

caregiver engagement in religious urban elementary schools 310, 316-24, 330-1

high school family centres 351, 353

perceptions of parents and teachers 272

quality of relationships 246-7, 272

socio-economic status 246-7

weaknesses in interrelationships 276-7, 282-5

religion

born-again Christians 208-10, 212-13, 220-1

broadcasting 218-19
caregiver engagement in
  religious urban elementary
  schools 8, 306-35
church-state views 217-19
commitment, level of 210,
  213-14, 221-2
creationism, teaching of 218-19,
  221
denominational affiliation in
  England and Wales 5-6,
  183-202
Hispanic and Latino students 6,
  127, 203-23
home schooling 369, 370
homosexual practices 216
literacy 127
nominalism 185, 195
parental involvement 8
public schools 40, 42
Puerto Rican female high-
  achievers 5, 141, 148-50,
  155-7
religious practices 212-13
virtual charter school system,
  home schooling in 375-7, 381,
  382, 386, 388
women, ordination of 215
resident fathers 73, 79-82
respect, encouraging 276-7, 283,
  356, 357
responsive programming 350-5,
  364
restructuring of schools 54
role construction 341, 358-9
role identity theory 140
role models 31

school kid identity 140-1, 156
school readiness 65-7, 71, 83,
  87-90
school vouchers 54-6, 218
science 20, 27
scientific management techniques
  46-7
self-confidence and resiliency,
  building 361-2, 363
self-esteem 13, 19, 30
self-improvement, programming
  for 351-2
sex, students' views on 193, 196,
  198-9
siblings, number of 176
social and cultural capital 325-7,
  330-2, 351-2
social and emotional development
  88, 271-2, 276, 283-5
social concerns, students' views on
  191, 194-5, 197
socialization and supplementary
  activities for students at virtual
  schools 387-90
socio-economic status
  bullying and discrimination,
    effects of parental involvement
    on 258-60
  caregiver engagement in
    religious urban elementary
    schools 325-7, 330-2
  family involvement 224-52
  father involvement, early
    learning and 65, 67, 75, 79-81,
    89-94
  funding 51
  high school family centres
    339-40, 350

Hispanic and Latino students
217, 221
homework 300, 302
Korean students and US
students, comparison between
289, 290-1, 300, 302
parental involvement 6
perceptions of parents and
teachers 270
public schools 40, 42-4,
48-50-1
teachers, relationship with 42,
48, 224-52
virtual charter school system,
home schooling in 372, 375
social integration 107
sociodemographics 110-11, 120-2,
133-4
South Korean students *see* home
learning environments, Korean
and US students and
sports 285, 296, 297-8, 301
standardization and systemization
of education 47
state matter, education as a 40,
41-4
stereotyping
father involvement, early
learning and 81
gender 20, 27, 138-40, 148,
151-2, 156, 158
Hispanic and Latino students
219-20
Puerto Rican female high-
achievers 138-40, 151-2, 156,
158
structure of families
attitudes, changing 7-8

biological and resident fathers
73, 79-82
caregiver engagement in
religious urban elementary
schools 307-8
father involvement, early
learning and 79, 92
Korean students and US
students, comparison between
292, 294, 296, 298-9,
302-3
non-traditional family structures
1, 7
public schools 57
social structure 38-9
styles of parenting *see* parenting
styles
substances, students' views on 193,
196-7, 198
supportive programming for
students 353

teachers
Black teachers 323-6, 328-9
licensing 48
parental involvement 4, 6
perceptions 267-86
Puerto Rican female high-
achievers 154-5, 156
relationships with teachers
224-52
socio-economic status 42, 224-52
virtual charter school system,
home schooling in 382, 383-4,
387
White teachers 309-14, 328-9
television, watching 295, 296,
297-302

time spent outside of school 290-1, 295-301
truancy laws 45
tuition assistance 314, 322-6

United States students *see* home learning environments, Korean and US students and
universal education 42-3
urbanization 46, 57

vagrant children 45-6

virtual schools *see* home schooling in virtual charter school system
vouchers 54-6, 218

Walberg's nine-factor productivity model 290-9
Wales *see* denominational affiliation in England and Wales
working hours of parents 57-8

zones of community 341-2, 355-7, 364-5